Automotive Heating, Ventilation, and Air Conditioning Systems

First Edition

D0144424

**By Chek-Chart Publications,
a Division of
H.M. Gousha**

Kevin Voss-Roberts, *Editor*
Gordon Clark, *Contributing Editor*
Victoria Easterday, *Contributing Editor*

HarperCollins*Publishers*

Acknowledgments

In producing this series of textbooks for automobile technicians, Chek-Chart has drawn extensively on the technical and editorial knowledge of the nation's carmakers and suppliers. Automotive design is a technical, fast-changing field, and we gratefully acknowledge the help of the following companies and organizations in allowing us to present the most up-to-date information and illustrations possible. These companies and organizations are not responsible for any errors or omissions in the instructions or illustrations, or for changes in procedures or specifications made by the carmakers or suppliers, contained in this book or in any other Chek-Chart product:

Bugformance, San Jose
Chrysler Motors Corporation
    AMC/Jeep
    Mopar Parts Division
CIMAT
Diesel Kiki Company, Ltd.
DK Engineering, Inc.
Everco
Falcone and Snyder Company, Inc., San Jose
Ford Motor Company
Gem Products
General Motors Corporation
    AC-Delco Division
    Buick Motor Division
    Cadillac Motor Division
    Chevrolet Motor Division
    Harrison Radiator Division
    Oldsmobile Division
    Pontiac Motor Division
Honda Motor Company, Ltd.
Hudson-Essex-Terraplane Club, Inc.
MAC Tools, Inc.
Mazda Motor Corporation
Murray Corporation
Nissan Motor Corporation
O. C. McDonald Co., Inc., San Jose

Omni Motors, San Jose
Prestone, Union Carbide Corporation
Snap-On Tools Corporation
SP^x Corporation
    Kent-Moore Tool Group
    Robinaire Automotive Division
Volkswagen of America
White Industries

The authors have made every effort to ensure that the material in this book is as accurate and up-to-date as possible. However, neither Chek-Chart nor Harper & Row nor any related companies can be held responsible for mistakes or omissions, or for changes in procedures or specifications made by the carmakers or suppliers.

The comments, suggestions, and assistance of the following reviewers were invaluable:

    Don Nilson, Chabot College, Hayward CA
    Ken Layne, Los Altos, CA
    Daniel L. Doornbos, Chek-Chart
        Publications

At Chek-Chart, Raymond C. Lyons managed the production of this book. Original art and photographs were produced by Dave Douglass, Carl M. Yoshihara, F. J. Zienty, Gerald A. McEwan, Catherine M. Godwin, and Richard K. DuPuy. The project is under the direction of Roger L. Fennema.

AUTOMOTIVE HEATING, VENTILATION, AND AIR CONDITIONING SYSTEMS, First Edition, Classroom Manual and Shop Manual Copyright © 1990 by Chek-Chart, H.M. Gousha, a Division of Simon & Schuster Inc.

All rights reserved. Printed in the United States of America. No part of this publication may be reproduced, stored in a retrieval system, or duplicated in any manner without the prior written consent of Chek-Chart, H.M. Gousha, a Division of Simon & Schuster Inc., P.O. Box 49006, San Jose, CA 95161-9006

Library of Congress Cataloging-in-Publication Data

Automotive heating, ventilation, and air conditioning systems/by Chek-Chart Publications of a division of H.M. Gousha: Kevin Voss-Roberts, editor...[et al.].
—1st ed.
      p. cm.
    Includes index.
    ISBN 0-06-454020-0 (set)
    1. Automobiles—Heating and ventilation.
2. Automobiles—Air conditioning. 3. Automobiles—Heating and ventilation—Maintenance and repair.
4. Automobiles—Air conditioning—Maintenance and repair. I. Voss-Roberts, Kevin.
TL271.A87   1990
629.27'7—dc20
                              90-24400
                                 CIP

Contents

On the Cover:
Front — A refrigerant recycling system is used to discharge air conditioning systems and clean the refrigerant for re-use. Courtesy of Everco.
Rear — A basic manifold gauge set or a more elaborate self-contained portable charging station are essential tools for automotive air conditioning service. Courtesy of White Industries.

Introduction to Automotive Heating, Ventilation, and Air Conditioning

Automotive Heating, Ventilation, and Air Conditioning is part of the Harper & Row/Chek-Chart Automotive Series. The package for each course has two volumes, a *Classroom Manual* and a *Shop Manual*.
Other titles in this series include:

- Automatic Transmissions and Transaxles
- Automotive Brake Systems
- Automotive Engine Repair and Rebuilding
- Engine Performance, Diagnosis, and Tune-Up
- Fuel Systems and Emission Controls
- Automotive Electrical and Electronic Systems
- Automotive Steering, Suspension, and Wheel Alignment (due 1992).

Each book is written to help the instructor teach students to become competent and knowledgeable professional automotive technicians. The two-manual texts are the core of a complete learning system that leads a student from basic theories to actual hands-on experience.

The entire series is job-oriented, especially designed for students who intend to work in the car service profession. A student will be able to use the knowledge gained from these books and from the instructor to get and keep a job in automotive repair or maintenance. Learning the material and techniques in these volumes is a giant leap toward a satisfying, rewarding career.

The books are divided into *Classroom Manuals* and *Shop Manuals* for an improved presentation of the descriptive information and study lessons, along with representative testing, repair, and overhaul procedures. The manuals are to be used together: the descriptive material in the *Classroom Manual* corresponds to the application material in the *Shop Manual*.

Each book is divided into several parts, and each book is complete by itself. Instructors will find the chapters to be complete, readable, and well thought-out. Students will benefit from the many learning aids included, as well as from the thoroughness of the presentation.

The series was researched and written by the editorial staff of Chek-Chart, and was produced by Harper & Row Publishers. For over 60 years, Chek-Chart has provided car and equipment manufacturers' service specifications to the automotive service field. Chek-Chart's complete up-to-date automotive data bank was used extensively to prepare this textbook series.

Because of the comprehensive material, the hundreds of high-quality illustrations, and the inclusion of the latest automotive technology, instructors and students alike will find that these books will keep their value over the years. In fact, they will form the core of the master mechanic's professional library.

How To Use This Book

Why Are There Two Manuals?

Unless you are familiar with the other books in this series, *Automotive Heating, Ventilation, and Air Conditioning* will not be like any other textbook you've ever used before. It is actually two books, the *Classroom Manual* and the *Shop Manual*. They have different purposes, and should be used together.

The *Classroom Manual* teaches you what you need to know about automotive HVAC systems: how they are designed, how they work, and what the different kinds are. The *Classroom Manual* will be valuable in class and at home, for study and for reference. You can use the text and illustrations for years to refresh your memory — not only about the basics of automotive heating, ventilation, and air conditioning systems, but also about related topics in automotive history, physics, and technology.

In the *Shop Manual*, you learn test procedures, troubleshooting, and how to overhaul the systems and parts you read about in the *Classroom Manual*. The *Shop Manual* provides the practical hands-on information you need to work on automotive HVAC systems. Use the two manuals together to fully understand how HVAC systems work, and how to fix them when they don't work.

What's In These Manuals?

These key features of the *Classroom Manual* make it easier for you to learn, and to remember what you learn:

• Each chapter is divided into self-contained sections for easier understanding and review. The organization shows you clearly which parts make up which systems, and how various parts or systems that perform the same task differ or are the same.
• Most parts and processes are fully illustrated with drawings or photographs. Important topics appear in several different ways, to make sure you can see other aspects of them.
• Important words in the *Classroom Manual* text are printed in **boldface type** and are defined on the same page and in a glossary at the end of the manual. Use these words to build the vocabulary you need to understand the text.
• Review questions are included for each chapter. Use them to test your knowledge.
• Every chapter has a brief summary at the end to help you to review for exams.
• Every few pages you will find sidebars — short blocks of ''nice to know'' information — in addition to the main text.

• There is a sample test at the back of the *Classroom Manual*, similar to those given for Automotive Service Excellence (ASE) certification. Use it to help you study and prepare yourself when you are ready to be certified as an expert in one of several areas of automobile technology.

The *Shop Manual* has detailed instructions on overhaul, test, and service procedures for modern components and current HVAC systems. These are easy to understand, and often have step-by-step explanations to guide you through the procedures. The *Shop Manual* contains:

• Helpful information that tells you how to use and maintain shop tools and test equipment
• A thorough coverage of the metric system units needed to work on modern HVAC systems
• Safety precautions
• System diagrams to help you locate trouble spots while you learn to read diagrams
• Test procedures and troubleshooting hints will help you work better and faster
• Tips the professionals use that are presented clearly and accurately

Where Should I Begin?

If you already know something about automotive heating, ventilation, and air conditioning systems, and know how to repair them, you will find that this book is a helpful review. If you are just starting in car repair, then the book will give you a solid foundation on which to develop professional-level skills.

Your instructor will design a course to take advantage of what you already know, and what facilities and equipment are available to work with. You may be asked to read certain chapters of these manuals out of order. That's fine. The important thing is to really understand each subject before you move on to the next.

Study the vocabulary words in boldface type. Use the review questions to help you understand the material. When you read the *Classroom Manual*, be sure to refer to your *Shop Manual* to relate the descriptive text to the service procedures. And when you are working on actual car systems and components, look back to the *Classroom Manual* to keep the basic information fresh in your mind. Working on such a complicated piece of equipment as a modern car isn't always easy. Use the information in the *Classroom Manual*, the procedures in the *Shop Manual*, and the knowledge of your instructor to help you.

The *Shop Manual* is a good book for work, not just a good workbook. Keep it on hand while you're working on equipment. It folds flat on the workbench and under the car, and can stand quite a bit of rough handling.

When you perform test procedures and overhaul equipment, you will need a complete and accurate source of manufacturers' specifications, and the techniques for pulling computer trouble codes. Most auto shops have either the carmaker's annual shop service manuals, which lists these specifications, or an independent guide, such as the Chek-Chart **Car Care Guide**. This unique book, with ten-year coverage, is updated each year to give you service instructions, capacities, and troubleshooting tips that you need to work on specific cars.

PART ONE

Basic Theory

Chapter One

History and Purposes of Heating, Ventilation, and Air Conditioning

The earliest automobiles were little more than horse-drawn carriages without the horse. Weather protection consisted mostly of heavy raincoats and goggles, figure 1-1. This was acceptable as long as the horseless carriages were limited to the low speeds and leisurely trips people associated with horse-drawn vehicles. Speed soon surpassed that of the typical buggy, however, and people began to expect more from their automobiles than they had from the family horse, especially regarding trips in poor weather. To accommodate their customers, manufacturers designed closed cars with fixed roofs and sliding glass windows, permitting drivers and passengers to make longer trips in weather conditions that used to keep them — or their horses — at home. At first, most closed cars were expensive luxury vehicles, but lower-priced closed-body cars were soon available to the general public. Henry Ford offered a few closed versions of the Model T as early as 1909, and by the 1920s an economical closed passenger compartment was an option available to almost anyone who could afford a car.

But driving in a closed car brought on a new set of problems. In cold weather, moisture that the passengers exhaled would condense on metal surfaces and window glass, making the passenger compartment damp and obscuring visibility. In an unheated car in very cold weather the condensation would freeze. Hot weather was no more comfortable. Except in the cities, early roads were unpaved. A driver of a closed car had to decide between enduring road dust and wind, or sweltering inside with the windows closed.

There was obviously a need for improvement, and automobile manufacturers and hardware suppliers soon began to provide systems and accessories designed to make travel a little more comfortable.

A BRIEF HISTORY

Automobile passenger compartments were first heated, ventilated, and cooled by the obvious and primitive solutions. Ventilation was fairly simple to arrange by opening the windows. However, the entering air was as hot, cold, or dusty as was the air outside, and so under very poor conditions they were often kept closed.

Clay bricks were easy to warm up on top of a cast iron stove, and could then be placed in a box on the floorboards to provide heat for as long as they remained warm. A more sophisticated approach was to purchase a small heater that burned coal or charcoal to warm the pas-

MANY PEOPLE

Patented in U. S. Nov. 15, '04
Patented in Canada Nov. 8, '04

are troubled with bronchial and throat afflictions during the cold weather, and remain indoors the greater part of the winter.
¶ If a Scott Muffler is worn when going out, those susceptible to zero weather will find that the Scott Muffler

MAKES ZERO WEATHER PLEASANT.

¶ They are neat and attractive, and really add to one's appearance.
¶ They can be taken off—not over the head—unfastened at the back—and put in the pocket, when not required for use.
¶ Our illustrated booklet tells all about them—prices, too. It will be sent as soon as you send for it.

The Scott Muffler Co., 175 Main St., Portsmouth, Ohio.

Figure 1-1. The original temperature control system: goggles and mufflers.

senger compartment continuously, a four-dollar accessory in 1910.

When the weather turned hot, most drivers simply put up with the discomfort, but more innovative travelers sometimes attempted to cool the passenger compartment by bringing along a block of ice. Neither solution was especially effective or convenient, and manufacturers soon discovered that improved weather protection could provide a marketing edge over their competition, figure 1-2.

Early Ventilation

The first system for ventilating closed cars consisted of simply opening windows, side curtains, or rotating a horizontal section of the upper or lower windshield. This uncontrolled air was not especially convenient, and did not exclude rain. Before long, accessory companies began marketing kits consisting of small trap doors or louvered panels to be installed over a hole cut in the sheetmetal, usually in the kick panel area between the side of the engine

cover and the leading edge of the front door. These could be opened or closed by the driver to admit fresh air into the passenger compartment.

Ventilation systems using a hinged or pivoting windshield were used for many years. In the first versions, the driver simply rotated the upper section of a horizontally-split two-piece windshield, holding the glass in place with locking screws or friction attachments. Locking the glass in a vertical position blocked the wind, while tilting it at various angles admitted more or less air, to suit the driver. Later versions were more weather-proof, and remained standard on commercial vehicles into the 1940s. These sealed the entire edge of the windshield frame into the car body with rubber weatherstripping. The windshield and frame pivoted to permit the driver to swing the glass slightly forward and away from the base and the windshield pillars.

Later and more sophisticated ventilation systems used cowl air intakes installed at the base

Figure 1-2. The importance of weather protection was recognized early in automobile history.

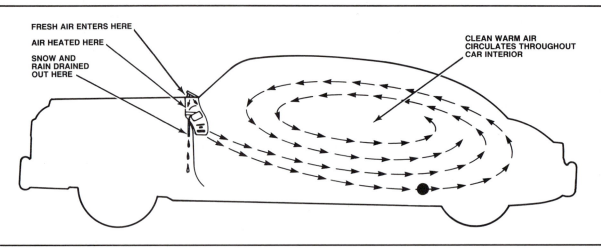

Figure 1-3. The 1950 Hudson used a hand-operated cowl intake system to supply forced-air ventilation through the heater unit to the passenger compartment and windshield defroster ducts.

of the windshield. These resembled a low air scoop or snorkel. Some versions were fixed in position, while others could be raised and lowered with a lever under the dashboard. An internal drain channeled rainwater out of the vent. Because there is a high-pressure region above the base of the windshield when the car is moving, an intake in this area is ideal for providing a strong flow of air into the passenger compartment, figure 1-3. Cars with factory-installed heaters often used the cowl air intake to supply the heating and window demisting system with fresh air, in which case the blower motor could draw fresh air into the passenger compartment even with the car stopped. Typically, no exhaust grilles were provided for the

Figure 1-4. The Allstate aftermarket automotive heater was completely self-contained, with an open bottom air vent, and separate doors for the driver's and passenger's sides. The remote switch attached under the dashboard.

outgoing air, so the driver and passengers opened rear door or quarter windows slightly to provide flow-through ventilation.

Early Heaters

Systems that recycled heat from the engine to warm the passenger compartment were fairly simple to design and install, but did not become standard equipment on medium and lower-priced cars and trucks until after the Second World War, when government standards finally required a means of keeping mist and ice off windows. Unless they bought a luxury vehicle, drivers paid their local mechanic to install the heater, or they did the work themselves.

Very early heaters used a heat exchanger mounted to the engine exhaust manifold. Some units designed for the Ford Model A were quite advanced, and consisted of a new casting in which the exhaust manifold and the heat exchanger were combined. The engine cooling fan was used to blow air into the mouth of the heat exchanger, where it was warmed by the hot cast iron. The warmed air then passed through a lever-operated on-off valve and was directed into the passenger compartment.

■ "Quicker Heat — Hotter Heat — More Heat"

In 1934, the Ford Motor Co. brought out a new, aftermarket heater to "air condition your V-8" — cars that up to this point had no heater. Ford called it "an entirely new principle in car heater design." It was a simple and straightforward design.

Once installed, the heater becomes a part of the exhaust system. Hot exhaust gases from the engine pass through flues in a small boiler-like compartment, before exiting through the exhaust pipe. Much of the heat from the exhaust is absorbed through the flue walls. The engine fan acts as a blower to force fresh air into an intake pipe and past the flue walls. Here it picks up the heat and delivers it through tubes to the front and back seat areas of the passenger compartment.

"There's no electric motor to consume current, no water connections, no changing of thermostats," said Ford.

All that, and it was only $14.00, installed while you wait.

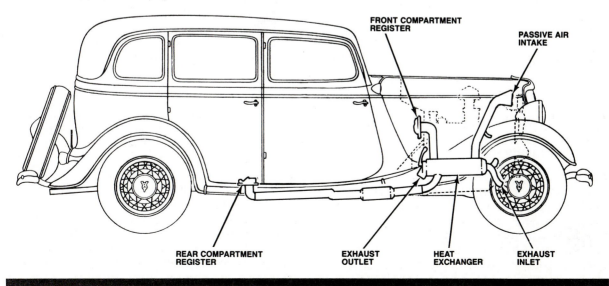

Figure 1-5. The 1950s Kool-Aire was a deluxe evaporative air conditioner, with an electric motor to keep the air moving when the car was stopped. It mounted to the top edge of a passenger door.

During the 1930s small gasoline burners were available that mounted under the dashboard and provided heat from a shielded flame. This system was used more recently in the air-cooled Chevrolet Corvair and still appears in the factory-installed optional heater in Volkswagen vans. 1931 was the first year for the "modern" automotive heater. Lincolns were available that year with a heater housing containing finned tubes through which hot engine coolant was circulated. An electric fan blew air over the fins, and volume and direction were controlled with flaps.

Aftermarket auto heaters continued to be sold in auto parts stores, department stores, and service stations until the 1950s. The commonest types were self-contained metal boxes designed to bolt to the firewall under the dash, figure 1-4. They contained a small heater core to be connected to the engine cooling system, an electric fan, and a system of flaps, ducts, and doors to direct the airflow. Fancier versions came with outlets that could be connected to windshield defroster ducts.

Early Air Conditioning

Like heaters, the earliest air conditioning systems were often aftermarket installations. Evaporative coolers were popular for many years, consisting of a lightweight metal canister that could be bolted or clipped to the outside of the passenger window, figure 1-5. Whenever the car was moving, air was funneled into the canister, through a water-soaked wire mesh and excelsior cone that cooled it, and into the passenger compartment through a vent on the side of the canister that protruded into the window. When water was added to a reservoir through a fill plug, it partially submerged the cone, which soaked up the water. As the air was forced into the canister, through the cone, and into the passenger compartment, it was cooled by the evaporating water. When the cone dried, the driver could restore cooling operation by pulling on a short string, spinning the cone in the water and re-wetting its entire surface. Cooling efficiency could be increased by dropping ice or "dry

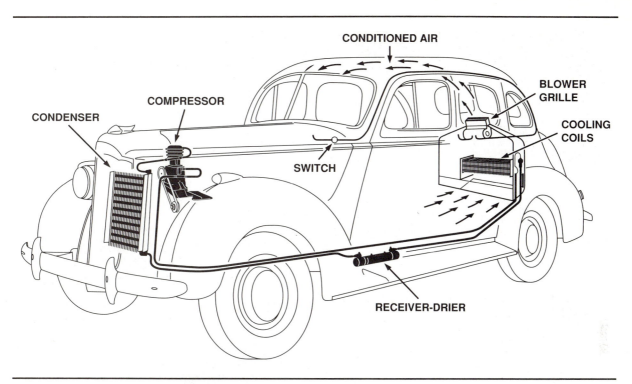

Figure 1-6. Packard's 1939 air conditioning system was controlled only by the blower switch. During the winter, owners removed the belt to turn the compressor off.

ice'' (frozen carbon dioxide) into the reservoir along with the water. More expensive versions contained a small electric motor plugged into the cigarette lighter to force air through the canister even when the car was stopped.While these devices could cool incoming air, they had several drawbacks. They were ineffective if the humidity was high, because they depended on water evaporation to cool the air. When they did work, they delivered air that was saturated with water vapor, raising the humidity inside the car. And when the car was moving, the airstream they provided was so powerful that drivers installed them on rear windows to keep the noise and air blast (and the cooled air) as far away as they could.

The first true mechanical air conditioning system was marketed by Packard for 1939, figure 1-6. A compressor was mounted to the engine, and a huge evaporator unit was installed into the trunk, incorporating a blower grille above the top of the back seat. Refrigerant was piped under the floorboards from the condenser in the front of the car all the way to the rear. The belt-driven compressor was engaged whenever the engine was running, and cooling could be controlled only by turning the blower on and off. Cadillac introduced a similar air conditioning system of its own as an option for 1941. Like Packard, it did not incor-

porate a clutched compressor. Both systems were very expensive, available in limited quantities, and filled half the trunk.

■ Refrigerant Recovery Coming Soon

Until recently, no one in the refrigeration business thought much about the refrigerant that is constantly being released into the atmosphere. Air conditioning systems were purged, components were vented, and refrigerant canisters were discarded without much concern about where the stuff ends up.

Times have changed. As private citizens become more concerned about the adverse affects of refrigerant in the air, automotive engineers (and government regulators) are also beginning to act. In the near future, recovery systems will undoubtedly become mandatory equipment for even the smallest shop.

Many tool makers and equipment suppliers now offer recovery systems. These generally range in price from about $2700 to more than $7000. The high-end systems are designed to accept refrigerant other than the familiar R-12, as newer and less damaging compounds become available.

For a small shop, the price tag may seem steep. However, when the cost is spread over all service jobs, this will become just another tool indicating a responsible, well-run business.

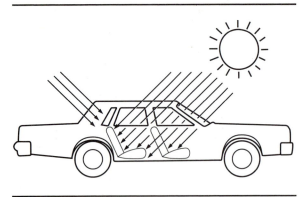

Figure 1-7. The temperature inside a car parked in sunlight will quickly rise as energy enters but cannot escape.

Air conditioning for the mass market was first introduced by Nash-Kelvinator in 1954. Nash had offered the "Weather Eye Conditioned Air" option from 1938 through the postwar years, but it was actually a fan-boosted, filtered ventilation system, not true air conditioning. For 1954, the Nash Weather Eye was a true refrigerated air conditioner, with all components installed under the hood or in the cowl area. This modern air conditioner was compact, easily serviced, and relatively inexpensive.

Heating, ventilation, and air conditioning of the passenger compartment in modern cars is provided by a single, integrated system. This **HVAC** (heating, ventilation, and air conditioning) system has the dual purpose of making the car more comfortable to drive or ride in, and safer and less distracting for the driver to operate. Modern refrigeration designs combine reliability and convenience with efficiency. Current air conditioning systems are so efficient that at normal highway speeds, a car with a running air conditioner uses less fuel than it would driving with the windows open.

COMFORT AND SAFETY

Today's typical drivers spend much more time in their cars than did drivers in the past. Commuting in a personal automobile has replaced mass transit systems for many millions of people, and the design of many modern cities requires automobile trips for errands or tasks that in the past might have been accomplished on foot.

Because the automobile has become such an important part of their daily routines, consumers demand a car with personal comfort as well as reliability and fuel efficiency. In the 1950's, air conditioning was still extremely rare. In 1968, 38% of domestic production was

delivered with the optional air conditioner, and the figure had increased to 82% by 1978. In the 1988 model year, over 90% of domestic cars and over 58% of all imports into the United States were supplied with air conditioning. Expensive cars now come with elaborate air conditioning systems as standard equipment.

The HVAC system plays a direct part in making auto travel safer. The driver and passengers in an unventilated passenger compartment increase the humidity inside as they exhale moisture. In cold weather (when the windows are also likelier to be closed), this moisture rapidly condenses on the inner surface of the windows. Even in warmer weather, condensation eventually forms on the windows when the humidity inside becomes high enough. Condensation on the windows obscures the driver's vision, and in very cold weather freezes on the glass into a layer of opaque frost. Even the most basic HVAC systems provide some means of preventing or removing condensation and frost from the windshield. Advanced models use the air conditioning system to dry the air before rewarming it and directing it at the windshield, making defrosting even more efficient.

In addition to helping maintain clear visibility, the HVAC system indirectly increases auto safety by helping to reduce driver fatigue. Long-haul truck drivers spend most of their workday in a cab that is specifically designed to be as comfortable and non-distracting as possible, and an effective HVAC system is a major component of that environment. Non-professional drivers benefit from the HVAC systems in their own cars in similar fashion.

SOURCES OF HEAT AND COLD

Most of the heat or cold the HVAC system must moderate is directly due to the air temperature around the car. Other environmental effects, however, play major roles under certain conditions. Solar radiation will heat an automobile interior no matter what the outside air temperature might be. Other factors include waste heat originating in the running engine and passenger body heat.

Solar Radiation

The interior temperature of an automobile in direct sunlight rapidly rises to a temperature much hotter than the air around it, figure 1-7. Dashboard temperatures of cars in the sun can reach 150°F (65°C) or more.

This heating is caused by solar radiation. Radiation in the form of ultraviolet light easily

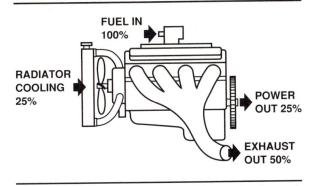

Figure 1-8. In a naturally aspirated (non-turbocharged) engine, much of the heat energy in the fuel goes out the exhaust system.

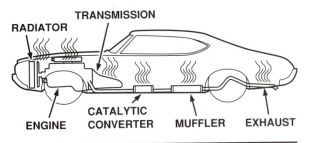

Figure 1-9. Even normal operation of an automobile will heat the passenger compartment.

penetrates the glass windows of an automobile and is absorbed into the surface of the dashboard and upholstery, raising their temperatures. The hot surfaces re-radiate the energy into the passenger compartment as infrared radiation, or heat. Unlike ultraviolet radiation, infrared cannot penetrate the window glass to leave the passenger compartment and is trapped inside, raising the air temperature. Because this is the same principle used to warm a greenhouse, we can call it the **greenhouse effect**. Automobile designers recognize this problem, and in fact, ''greenhouse'' is an industry term referring to passenger compartments with a great deal of window glass, such as the cargo area of a station wagon.

If the passenger compartment is air conditioned or properly ventilated, the hot air can be cooled or circulated to the outside as fast as it is warmed, and the air temperature inside the vehicle remains moderate. Circulating fresh or cooled air over the upholstery and dashboard also help to cool their surfaces.

Weather

In the United States, air temperatures can vary from –60°F (–51°C) in Alaska to 132°F (55°C) in Death Valley, California. These are extremes, of course, but they illustrate the range of air temperatures modern drivers expect their HVAC systems to cope with.

Aside from direct weather effects, another source of passenger compartment heat is that radiating from a hot road surface. On hot summer days the temperature of an asphalt road easily reaches 130°F (54°C) or more. The floorpan of a car parked or being driven over such a hot surface absorbs heat from it. This adds to the heat the air conditioning system must remove to cool the car.

In winter, ice and snow caked to the underside of a vehicle increase the heat needed to

warm the vehicle interior. The HVAC system also prevents interior and exterior condensation on the windows, and helps remove freezing rain and snow.

Engine Heat

A major source of passenger compartment heat comes from the engine. Of all the energy that is put into a car's engine, only a quarter to a third is actually converted into motion of the automobile, figure 1-8. The rest of this energy is removed as heat from the engine, transmission, and exhaust system, and is given off into the airstream outside the passenger compartment, figure 1-9. Some of the heat is transferred to the passenger compartment instead of escaping. The engine and transmission, and mufflers and catalytic converters under the floorpan warm the passenger compartment in spite of various types of heat shielding, figure 1-10.

This heat is essential to the effective operation of a modern heater in cold weather, as most HVAC systems use heat from the engine to warm the passenger compartment. The amount of heat the HVAC can draw from the engine is significant. On a hot day an automobile on the edge of overheating can be kept from doing so by turning the heater to a high setting.

The Passengers

Another source of passenger compartment heat are the passengers. The normal human body temperature is 98.6°F (37°C), and this

HVAC: An acronym for heating-ventilation-air conditioning systems.

Greenhouse Effect: In our usage, the warming of an enclosed space by trapped heat, resulting from sunlight entering through windows.

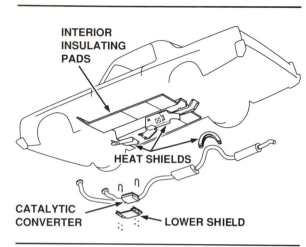

Figure 1-10. Many catalytic converters require heat shielding.

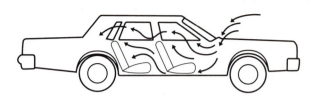

Figure 1-11. Air currents inside an automobile mix the air and even out temperature differences.

heat is constantly being transferred to the air from the skin and from exhaling air warmed in the lungs. When several passengers occupy the same vehicle, ventilation or air conditioning may be needed to keep the interior temperature comfortable.

Another purpose of the HVAC is to replace the air inside the vehicle rapidly enough to prevent passenger or cargo odors from accumulating within the car. Ventilation systems are designed to completely change the air in the passenger compartment once or twice per minute, expelling air contaminated with odors or tobacco smoke. Fresh air is drawn in from outside and is heated or cooled to the selected temperature.

Humidity also rises inside a closed passenger compartment as the passengers exhale air moistened in their lungs. This is most obvious on rainy or cold days when the moisture condenses to a mist on interior glass. The HVAC can remove excess humidity indirectly, by flushing out moisture-laden air and replacing it with dryer exterior air, or directly by air conditioning. Air conditioners condense water vapor from the air that passes over the surface of the evaporator, and channel it through a drain to the outside. The air that is discharged through the blower grille of a running air conditioner is dryer than air merely blown through the ventilation ducts. Even in cold weather, modern HVAC systems channel the air through the air conditioner evaporator to dry it before rewarming it and directing it at the windshield.

The same ventilating system that removes stale air from the passenger compartment also improves heater and air conditioner performance by maintaining air currents inside the

compartment, ensuring that all parts of the auto interior receive heated, cooled, or fresh air, figure 1-11.

THE PURPOSE OF AUTOMOTIVE HVAC SYSTEMS

There are three major features and functions of the heating, cooling, and ventilation system of the automobile:

- Regulating temperature — The HVAC system warms or cools the passenger compartment as needed by adding or removing heat as required.
- Controlling humidity — Preventing humidity from rising inside the passenger compartment prevents moisture from condensing on the windows, and keeps the air inside the car dryer and more comfortable.
- Circulating the air — The HVAC system circulates and replaces the air while maintaining a constant interior temperature.

SUMMARY

Early automobiles, like the wagons and carriages they replaced, were built without heating or cooling systems, and had no need for additional ventilation. As these open vehicles were replaced by others with closed passenger compartments, manufacturers designed and supplied heating, ventilation, and air conditioning systems. Modern automobiles are built with a combination system, which at the minimum contains heating and ventilation, and in a true HVAC system also includes air conditioning.

The HVAC system is also a vehicle safety feature that prevents condensation and icing on the windshield, and indirectly improves safety by reducing driver fatigue.

The HVAC system removes heat from the passenger compartment coming from solar radiation, from the engine, and the passengers.

The purpose of the vehicle's HVAC system is to cool, warm, dehumidify, and circulate the interior air.

Review Questions
Choose the single most correct answer.
Compare your answers with the correct answers on page 229.

1. Early automobile heaters included:
   a. Small gas burners
   b. Plumbing from the exhaust system
   c. Plumbing from the cooling system
   d. All of the above

2. Air conditioning is now installed in what percentage of new cars?
   a. 50%
   b. 75%
   c. Over 90%
   d. 100%

3. The dashboard temperature of a car in the sun can easily exceed:
   a. 75°F
   b. 100°F
   c. 150°F
   d. 200°F

4. The greenhouse effect is a result of which type of heat energy?
   a. Convection
   b. Radiation
   c. Conduction
   d. Weather

5. How much of the engine's energy output is used to drive the car?
   a. Less than a quarter
   b. A quarter to a third
   c. A third to two thirds
   d. More than two thirds

6. Each of the following is a purpose of a modern HVAC system EXCEPT:
   a. Dehumidifying the air
   b. Circulating the air
   c. Pressurizing the air
   d. Purifying the air

7. The early window-mounted air conditioners used the principle of _____ to provide chilled air.
   a. Condensation
   b. Dehumidification
   c. Vaporization
   d. Evaporation

2

Fundamentals of Heat, Temperature, and Pressure

Automotive technicians should have a clear understanding of the theory and technology that underlie the systems that they maintain. It is often possible to repair a heating, ventilation, or air conditioning (HVAC) assembly or component without understanding it. However, a technician who understands how the system works will identify and diagnose problems much faster, and will not waste time performing unnecessary tests or repairs.

Vehicles are much more complex than in the past, and this complexity is reflected in the design and construction of the HVAC system. The complexity, however, is usually related more to tailoring an HVAC system to a particular vehicle than it is to its operation. Underlying operating principles remain the same whether the vehicle is an economy subcompact or a luxury limousine.

BASIC PHYSICS

Automotive HVAC systems use chemical compounds (engine coolant and air conditioning refrigerant) to transfer energy between components, and warm or cool the passenger compartment interior by heat flow and phase changes (changes of state) in the refrigerant. To explain how the HVAC system operates, we must first define these terms and review some basic concepts of physics.

Elements

''Matter'' is a term given to any substance in the universe that has mass (for our purposes, mass is the same as weight) and occupies space. All matter in the universe is made up of basic chemical building blocks called **elements**. An element is a particular type of matter that cannot be reduced to anything simpler by chemical means. Iron is an element, as are hydrogen, aluminum, tungsten, and silicon. Physicists have isolated 105 elements, although not all of them occur naturally. The smallest part of an element that can be theoretically isolated and still have all the characteristics of that element is called an **atom**.

As small as it is, the atom is made of several other, much smaller units: the **proton**, the **electron**, and the **neutron**. The protons and neutrons make up the **nucleus**, in different numbers and combinations for each of the different elements. The electrons orbit the nucleus, so fast that their particular position at any time can be predicted only statistically, and their orbits are therefore referred to as electron clouds.

The internal structure of each type of atom differs, and is what distinguishes atoms of one

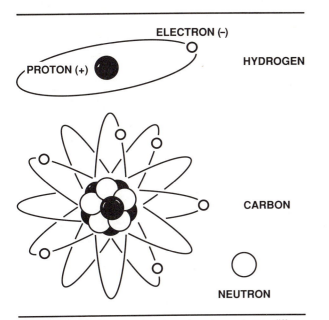

Figure 2-1. Hydrogen atoms and carbon atoms differ in the numbers of protons, neutrons, and electrons they contain.

element from atoms of another, figure 2-1. A hydrogen atom has one proton and one electron. A carbon atom has six protons, six neutrons, and six electrons. In normal chemical reactions with other atoms the numbers of protons and neutrons stay the same, but electrons can be added, lost, or shared.

When one atom combines chemically with one or more other atoms, a **molecule** is formed. A molecule can be made of atoms of

Element: One of 105 particular and unique chemical building blocks, that cannot be reduced to anything simpler by chemical means.

Atom: The smallest part of an element that still has all the characteristics of that element.

Proton: A positively charged particle within an atom.

Electron: A negatively charged particle within an atom.

Neutron: A particle in an atom that has no charge and is electrically neutral.

Nucleus: The center core of an atom that contains the protons and neutrons.

Molecule: Two or more atoms chemically bonded together.

Chemical Compound: A chemically pure substance composed of molecules containing atoms of different elements.

the same element, or of different elements. For example, the oxygen gas you breathe is made up of simple molecules consisting of two oxygen atoms each. If two or more of the atoms forming a molecule come from different elements, the molecule that results is called a **chemical compound**. Water is a chemical compound in which each molecule is composed of one oxygen atom and two hydrogen atoms. Attaching two chlorine and two fluorine atoms to one atom of carbon, figure 2-2, forms the chemical compound dichlorodifluoromethane: **Refrigerant 12** (or R-12), which is the substance used in most automotive refrigeration systems.

■ R-12 And The Ozone Layer

When refrigerant was first developed for air conditioning systems, it seemed the ideal material. It was odorless, nonflammable, nontoxic, and noncorrosive. It had a high stability and a low boiling point, and best of all, it was able to absorb great quantities of heat. For years, the standard statement was "R-12 is not harmful as a vapor."

Today, we know that was wrong.

The various refrigerants (R-11, R-12, and R-22) consist of a class of molecules called chlorofluorocarbons (CFCs), which are also used in industrial solvents, insulating foam and plastics, and as propellants in spray cans. Scientists are now discovering that these CFC molecules may not deteriorate for as much as 100 years and do not combine with any other molecules. The molecules tend to drift into the upper atmosphere, where they destroy the ozone layer surrounding the earth.

The ozone layer is a very thin region where atmospheric ozone (O_3) is concentrated. It forms a natural shield against the dangerous ultraviolet light from the sun. At least five types of gases are attacking the ozone and depleting it in some areas. Some of the gases occur naturally, or as byproducts of burning fossil fuels. The fifth gas is the family of CFCs, and is entirely man-made. We are now witnessing the gradual destruction of the ozone layer by these chemicals, and are losing the protection it gives us against dangerous ultraviolet light.

The most immediate danger from depleting the ozone layer will be the increase in skin cancer among light-skinned people, and injury to their immune system. The long-term effects on our environment remain to be seen.

In 1978, CFCs as aerosol propellants were banned in the U.S. and some other countries. By 1987, more than 37 countries had agreed to begin lowering the production of CFCs to half their 1986 levels. To date, an effective replacement for CFC as refrigerants has not been found. However, in the near future technicians can expect to see regulations prohibiting the open discharge of refrigerants into the atmosphere.

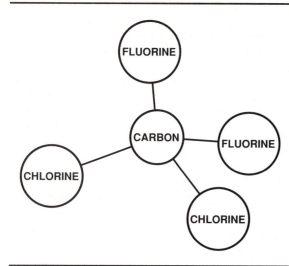

Figure 2-2. An R-12 molecule contains a carbon atom, and two atoms each of chlorine and fluorine.

Figure 2-3. Water is a substance that can be found naturally in solid, liquid, and gaseous states.

States of Matter

Matter on the earth is normally found in one of three different phases or states: solid, liquid, or gas. The state depends upon the nature of the material, the temperature, and the pressure or force exerted on it. Water occurs naturally in all three states: solid ice, liquid water, and gaseous water vapor, depending upon the temperature and pressure of the location, figure 2-3.

Solids
A **solid** is a material showing incompressibility and strong resistance to flow. The molecules of a solid attract each other strongly, resisting changes in volume and shape.

Materials are solid at any temperature below their melting point. A melting point is a characteristic of a material, and is essentially independent of pressure. For water, the melting point is 32°F (0°C), which means that we can observe changes between liquid water and ice under normal weather conditions. Iron, however, has a melting point near 2795°F (1535°C), which means that under normal conditions at the earth's surface it remains solid. Note that melting points and freezing points are the same temperature. The distinction is merely whether heat is being added or taken away.

Liquids
A **liquid** is also a material showing incompressibility, but much less resistance to flow than a solid. Since a liquid will flow, it is said to be fluid, but not all fluids are liquids. (Gases are fluids, too). This means that a substance in a liquid state has a fixed volume, but no definite shape. A given volume of liquid water, for example, takes on the shape of any container into which you put it. The water molecules attract each other strongly enough to maintain a constant volume, but not so tightly that the material cannot flow.

Materials are liquid at any temperature between their melting and boiling points. The boiling point for water at normal sea level conditions is 212°F (100°C). The boiling point for iron is approximately 5432°F (3000°C), a temperature not normally found at the earth's surface.

Gases
A **gas** is a material that can be easily compressed, has no resistance to flow, and no fixed volume. Because a gas will flow, it is considered a fluid just like liquids are. The molecules of a gas do not attract each other, and gases therefore expand (by becoming less dense) to fill a container of any size or shape into which they are contained.

Materials become gaseous if the temperature rises above their boiling point, and condense to liquid if the temperature falls below it. Like melting and freezing, boiling point and condensation point are the same temperature. Again, the difference is simply whether heat is being added or taken away. Boiling point and condensation point temperatures are not fixed, but vary with pressure, and will be discussed further in this section.

Even at temperatures below the **boiling** point, some molecules leave the surface of a body of liquid spontaneously and enter the gas phase. This process is called **evaporation**. Boiling specifically refers to the very rapid and energetic change from liquid to gas that occurs when the temperature of a liquid reaches the boiling point throughout its volume.

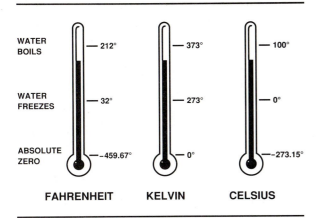

Figure 2-4. Different temperature scales will use different numbers to indicate the same temperature.

Heat and Temperature

Molecules in a substance tend to vibrate rapidly in all directions, and this disorganized energy is what we call **heat**. The intensity of vibration depends on how much **kinetic energy**, or energy of motion, the atom or molecule contains. We measure the level of this energy as **temperature**.

Heat

Because heat corresponds to molecular motion, it follows that removing all heat from a substance causes all molecular motion to cease. **Absolute zero** (–459.4°F; –273°C) is the temperature at which all movement of the molecules stops because all of the heat energy has been removed. Theoretically, there can be no temperature lower than absolute zero, because there is no way to lower the temperature of a substance that contains no heat.

Heat and temperature are not the same, in the same way that motion and speed are not the same. Heat is vibrational energy, and temperature is how we measure its intensity. To illustrate this distinction, suppose you heated a large barrel of steel ball bearings red-hot, and then dropped just one of them into a tub full of cold water. The overall temperature of the water in the tub probably wouldn't change very much at all. But if you then poured the entire barrel of red-hot ball bearings into the bathtub, you would heat up the water quite dramatically. That single ball bearing was at the same *temperature* as every other ball bearing in the barrel, but an entire barrel full of red-hot ball bearings obviously contains much more total *heat* than just one.

To keep this distinction clear, remember that heat is measured in **calories (c)**. The calorie is a metric unit expressing the quantity of heat necessary to raise the temperature of one gram

of water one degree Celsius. For example, 100 calories of heat can raise the temperature of one gram of water 100 degrees Celsius, or two grams of water 50 degrees Celsius, or 100 grams of water 1 degree Celsius, and so on. Older technical manuals refer to **British thermal units (Btu)**, instead of calories. One Btu is the heat required to raise the temperature of one pound of water 1 degree Fahrenheit at sea level. One Btu equals 252 calories.

Temperature is measured in degrees, and because different auto manufacturers use different measuring systems with different scales,

Refrigerant 12: A chemical compound used as the medium of heat transfer in a refrigeration system. It picks up heat by evaporating and gives up heat by condensing.

Solid: A state of matter of definite shape and volume.

Liquid: A state of matter of no definite shape, high incompressibility, and a tendency to flow and disperse.

Gas: A state of matter of no definite shape or volume, easily compressed, with a high tendency to disperse.

Boiling: The very rapid change of state of a liquid to a gas (vapor caused by rapidly adding heat or rapidly decreasing the pressure).

Evaporation: The slow change of state of a liquid to a gas (vapor) caused by slowly adding heat or slowly decreasing the pressure.

Heat: The disorganized energy in any substance caused by the rapid vibration of the atoms and molecules making it up.

Kinetic Energy: The energy associated with motion. The kinetic energy in vibrating atoms and molecules results in what we call heat.

Temperature: Heat intensity, measured by a thermometer.

Absolute Zero: The total absence of heat, when molecular motion ceases. Approximately –460°F (–273°C).

calorie (c): The amount of heat necessary to raise one gram of water one degree Celsius. One thousand calories are abbreviated "C."

British Thermal Units (Btu): The amount of heat necessary to raise one pound of water one degree Fahrenheit. One Btu corresponds to 252 calories.

you will need to understand their differences and how to convert between them. There are three common systems in use, figure 2-4:

- Fahrenheit
- Celsius
- Kelvin.

Fahrenheit

The most common system used in the United States is the Fahrenheit scale. Fahrenheit temperatures are identified by a capital letter "F" following the number. This scale was named after Gabriel Fahrenheit (1686-1736), the German physicist who proposed it in 1714. Fahrenheit originally defined his temperature scale so that the coldest temperature he could achieve with a freezing mixture of ice and salt defined zero, and normal human body temperature defined 96°F; a convenient range of eight dozen degrees. After his death, his standard temperatures were altered to the more convenient (and repeatable) freezing and boiling points of water. On the modern Fahrenheit scale, water freezes at 32°F, and boils at 212°F at sea level. Normal human body temperature is 98.6°F, and absolute zero is at −459.4°F.

Celsius

The most common system used in the world today is the metric Celsius scale. Older technical specifications might refer to this scale as Centigrade. Celsius temperatures are identified by a capital letter "C". Anders Celsius (1701-1744), a Swedish astronomer, proposed this system in 1742, based on the freezing and boiling points of water. The temperature at which water freezes defines 0°C, and the temperature at sea level at which it boils defines 100°C. Normal human body temperature is 37°C, and absolute zero is −273°C.

Kelvin

The Kelvin scale is universally used in physics and chemistry. Kelvin temperatures are identified by a capital letter "K" following the number. William Thomson Kelvin (1824-1907), an English physicist and aristocrat, devised the scale in 1848, based on that of Celsius. The Kelvin scale is an absolute scale of temperature, with 0°K defined as absolute zero, and without negative temperatures. The degrees used are the same magnitude as in the Celsius scale, so water freezes and boils 100 degrees apart, at 273°K and 373°K, respectively. Normal human body temperature is 310°K.

Converting temperatures

The Fahrenheit, Celsius, and Kelvin temperature scales measure the same phenomenon, the level of vibrational energy, or heat, present in a substance. The differences between scales are in the magnitudes of the degrees, and in the different numbers that correspond to the temperature of absolute zero.

The United States is presently the only industrialized country that uses the Fahrenheit scale. Celsius temperatures are used worldwide in meteorology and industry, and Kelvin temperatures in the sciences. Service literature and technical specifications for automobiles sold in the United States might give temperatures in Fahrenheit or Celsius, and technicians must be able to convert between these scales.

To convert Fahrenheit temperatures to Celsius:

$$0.556 \times (°F - 32) = \text{Degrees Celsius (°C)}$$

To convert Celsius temperatures to Fahrenheit:

$$(1.8 \times °C) + 32 = \text{Degrees Fahrenheit (°F)}$$

Specific heat

Different substances absorb different quantities of heat to cause the same increase in temperature, even if the weights of the materials being heated are the same. This relationship is expressed as a characteristic **specific heat**. The specific heat of a substance is the number of calories required to raise the temperature of one gram of the substance one degree Celsius. The higher the specific heat, the greater the heat transfer capacity. A substance with a low specific heat requires only a small amount of heat to warm it a certain number of degrees, and gives off a small amount of heat as it cools.

Water has a specific heat of 1, because it takes 1 calorie of heat to raise the temperature of 1 gram of water 1 degree Celsius. When water cools, each gram of water also gives off 1 calorie of heat for each degree of temperature drop.

The specific heat of copper is 0.093, less than one-tenth that of water. Raising the temperature of a piece of copper a certain number of degrees requires only about one-tenth as much heat as does the same mass of water. The specific heat of liquid Refrigerant 12 is 0.24 at about 80°F (27°C). This is not as high as that of water, but high enough to absorb and give off substantial heat as it changes temperature.

Sensible heat

The heat added to or given up by a material that causes a temperature change is called **sensible heat**. When you heat a solid without melting it, or a liquid without boiling it, the solid and the liquid are both absorbing sensible heat. For example, heating a container of water on a stove raises the temperature of the water because the water absorbs sensible heat

1 GRAM WATER + 540 CALORIES = 1 GRAM VAPOR
1 POUND WATER + 970 BTUs = 1 POUND VAPOR

Figure 2-5. The extra heat required to change a standard amount of water at its boiling point to a gas is called latent heat of vaporization.

from the burner. When solids or liquids cool, they give off sensible heat. You measure sensible heat in calories, and it causes a temperature change you can measure in degrees.

Latent heat

Latent heat is best explained by imagining a solid or a liquid being heated on a stove. At the point when the solid reaches its melting point, or the liquid reaches its boiling point, their temperatures stop rising. The solid begins to melt instead, and the liquid begins to boil, without any change in temperature, even though heat is still being poured in from the burner. The water in the container on the stove boils at a temperature of 212°F (100°C) at sea level, for as long as any liquid water remains. As you continue to add heat with the burner, it will all be absorbed in changing the state of the liquid to a gas.

This extra amount of energy necessary to change the state of a material is called **latent heat**. Every material has a characteristic latent heat needed to transform a standard amount of it from one state to another. To melt one gram of ice at 0°C to water at 0°C requires 79.7 calories, the **latent heat of fusion** of ice. To change one gram of water already at its boiling point to water vapor at the same temperature requires the addition of 540 calories, the **latent heat of vaporization** of water, figure 2-5. In the older English system of measurement, latent heats were expressed in Btu per pound, and degrees Fahrenheit. In that system, it takes 144 Btu to melt one pound of ice at 32°F to one pound of water at 32°F. To change one pound of water already at 212°F to water vapor at the same temperature requires 970 Btu.

Even though latent heat can be absorbed without causing a temperature rise in the sub-

Specific Heat: The number of calories needed to raise the temperature of one gram of a substance by one degree Celsius.

Sensible Heat: Heat that causes a change in the temperature of a material when absorbed or given off, that is not involved in a change of state of the material.

Latent Heat: Heat that is absorbed or given off during a change of state of a material without changing its temperature.

Latent Heat of Fusion: A characteristic amount of heat that is absorbed or given off while a standard amount of a material changes state between solid and liquid, without changing the temperature.

Latent Heat of Vaporization: A characteristic amount of heat that is absorbed or given off while a standard amount of a material changes state between liquid and vapor, without changing the temperature.

■ "The Greenhouse Effect"

When you leave your car parked in the sunlight, the temperature inside rises rapidly. We can call this mechanism the "Greenhouse Effect" when we talk about automotive temperature control, but the term was first used to describe temperature increases on a much greater scale, that of the entire earth.

Solar energy that penetrates the earth's atmosphere contains a high percentage of ultraviolet light. This energy warms the continents and the oceans, just like the sunlight that passes through a car's windows warms the upholstery inside. The earth then radiates this heat back into the sky as infrared radiation. Unlike ultraviolet radiation, however, infrared cannot penetrate the atmosphere (or the window glass of your car), and is trapped inside. This effect has kept the earth's temperature moderate for many millions of years.

The Industrial Revolution may have caused all this to change. Burning fossil fuels adds carbon dioxide to the atmosphere, and this carbon dioxide increases the amount of heat the atmosphere retains. Although scientists still argue about details, a gradual warming of the earth's atmosphere may already have begun.

This global warming would increase the size and numbers of deserts, and cause more frequent droughts in inland areas. At worst, it could even flood low-lying coastal areas with meltwater from the Antarctic icecap. On the other hand, temperate regions like Canada and Argentina would enjoy milder winters and longer growing seasons. Tropical regions wouldn't really be much warmer than today, but the mild tropical weather would extend further north and south than it does now.

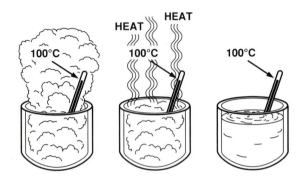

1 GRAM VAPOR - 540 CALORIES = 1 GRAM WATER
1 POUND VAPOR - 970 BTUs = 1 POUND WATER

Figure 2-6. The latent heat of vaporization that water vapor stores as a gas is all given off when the gas condenses to a liquid. The temperature stays the same.

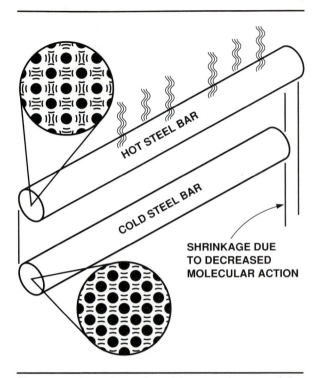

SHRINKAGE DUE TO DECREASED MOLECULAR ACTION

Figure 2-7. As a piece of steel (or any other material) cools, its molecules vibrate less and less, and the object's size decreases.

stance that absorbs it, it is not lost. When a vapor condenses to liquid, it gives off the latent heat of vaporization it held as a gas, figure 2-6. A liquid freezing into a solid gives up the latent heat of fusion it held as a liquid. In both cases, this heat may raise the temperature of other objects in the vicinity. For example, in a hand-cranked ice cream maker, liquid cream freezes into a solid (ice cream) inside a metal can. As this change of state occurs, latent heat of fusion is given off from the freezing cream and is absorbed by the ice in the bucket surrounding the can. The heat being given off from the cream is what causes the ice to melt as the ice cream solidifies.

Latent heat is important in air conditioning system operation because the cooling effect is derived from changing the state of liquid Refrigerant 12 to a gas. The refrigerant absorbs latent heat of vaporization, cooling the air blown into the passenger compartment.

Temperature and volume — Solids and liquids
When we add heat to a material, we increase the kinetic energy of the molecules that compose it. The intensity of the molecular vibration increases, and the temperature that registers on a thermometer rises. When heat is given off by a material, the kinetic energy decreases, the molecules vibrate with less intensity, and the temperature of the material decreases.

One consequence of changing the kinetic energy of the molecules in a solid or liquid is that the volume increases or decreases. Increasing the vibrational energy of the molecules forces

each molecule slightly apart from its neighbors. Decreasing the vibrational energy permits the molecules to pack closer together, figure 2-7. This expansion and contraction of solids and liquids with increased or decreased temperature is slight, but can be significant, especially in large objects. Long highway bridges, for example, have expansion joints built into their road surface to accommodate up to several feet of heat-induced expansion on hot, sunny days. Pistons, bearings, and valves in an automobile engine are designed with small but specific clearances to accommodate metal expansion as the engine warms up, without scuffing or seizing.

Different materials expand or contract at different rates with changes in temperature. For instance, some types of plastic show almost no change at all with temperature. Other materials may change by a considerable amount over the same temperature range. The value of the **coefficient of expansion** of a material is characteristic of it, and expresses how much a particular substance expands or contracts for a given temperature change. For example, aluminum has a greater coefficient of expansion than steel. An aluminum compressor piston would expand more than would a steel compressor piston the same size and shape, when both are warmed up to the same temperature.

Temperature and pressure — Gases

Unlike a solid or a liquid, a gas has no fixed volume. Increasing the temperature of a gas (while holding the volume fixed) increases the pressure, as the vibrating gas molecules collide more and more energetically with the walls of the container. Decreasing the temperature decreases the pressure. This relationship between temperature and pressure in gases is why a can of nonflammable Refrigerant 12 can explode when heated by a flame.

Increasing the pressure by compressing a gas increases the temperature, and decreasing the pressure by permitting the gas to expand decreases the temperature. This is the reason a bicycle pump becomes hot as you use it. When you compress the air into a smaller volume at higher pressure, you raise its temperature. Scuba divers also know that the valve at the top of the air tank becomes cold to the touch if they open it completely to empty the tank. In this case, the compressed air expands as it leaves the tank, and its temperature decreases. This happens because changing the volume of a quantity of gas does not change the total amount of heat it contains. When the gas is spread out into a larger volume, the heat (vibrational energy) it contains is spread out too, so that the temperature of the entire quantity is lowered.

Pressure-Temperature Relationships

There are two aspects of the relationship between pressure and temperature that are important to understanding the operation of an HVAC system:

• The temperature at which a liquid boils (and a gas condenses) rises and falls with the pressure.
• Pressure in a sealed system that contains both liquid and gas rises and falls with the temperature.

These two concepts are really two aspects of the same thing, as you will see in the next sections.

Boiling point temperatures

The boiling point of water is 212°F (100°C), at normal sea level atmospheric pressure. At any pressure less than atmospheric, the actual boiling point is lower. As pressure decreases, the temperature at which any liquid boils also decreases.

To illustrate, imagine a container of water at sea level. At this elevation, water boils into a gas when it reaches 212°F (100°C). In Denver, Colorado, the elevation is about 5300 feet (1600 m) and a container of water boils at about 206°F (97°C). In fact, if you could de-

crease the atmospheric pressure to zero, you could make water boil at just above its freezing point. This is one reason why radiator boilover in open, unpressurized cooling systems is more common in mountain driving. A neglected cooling system that provides marginal protection against boilover at sea level will not prevent boilover at higher elevations, where the system is under less absolute atmospheric pressure. Even a pressurized cooling system, which is sealed with a pressure cap at the radiator, provides less protection against boilover at high elevations where the atmospheric pressure is lower.

Automotive technicians remove water from air conditioning systems during service by evacuating the components and hoses with a vacuum pump that lowers the pressure inside the system. Any water that is contaminating the system eventually vaporizes at the lower pressure and is easily removed by pumping the air out.

As you would expect, this relationship also works in the same way in the other direction. As pressure is increased on any liquid, the temperature at which it boils becomes higher. If you tried to boil water under pressure equal to that found at a depth of about 7500 ft (3500 m) in the ocean, the water would not boil until the temperature reached about 705°F (374°C).

Automobile cooling systems are pressurized to keep the coolant liquid at high temperatures. An ordinary 50 percent antifreeze-water mixture boils at 226°F (103°C) at normal air pressure. When pressurized to 15 psi (103 kPa) above atmospheric pressure, it does not boil until the temperature reaches 268°F (131°C). Pressurizing coolant greatly increases the amount of heat the radiator can remove without the system overloading and boiling.

The relationship between pressure and boiling point for any material is unique to that material, and physicists determine it experimentally. The relationship between pressure and boiling point for Refrigerant 12 is also fixed, figure 2-8. Like any other liquid, the boiling point of R-12 increases as pressure increases. If the pressure is released suddenly, R-12 evaporates or boils very quickly. An air

---

Coefficient of Expansion: The characteristic rate of expansion of a substance resulting from increased molecular vibration as the temperature increases, or of shrinkage from decreased vibration as the temperature falls.

TEMPERATURE		R-12 PRESSURE		
°F	°C	psi	kPa	
−35	−37	8.3	57.2	
−30	−34	5.4	37.2	
−28	−33	4.2	29.0	VACUUM
−26	−32	2.9	20.0	
−24	−31	1.6	11.0	
−22	−30	0.2	1.4	
−20	−29	0.6	4.1	
−18	−28	1.3	9.0	
−16	−27	2.1	14.5	
−14	−26	2.9	20.0	
−12	−24	3.7	25.5	
−10	−23	4.5	31.0	
−8	−22	5.4	37.2	
−6	−21	6.3	43.4	
−4	−20	7.2	49.6	
−2	−19	8.2	56.5	
0	−18	9.2	63.4	
2	−17	10.2	70.3	
4	−16	11.3	77.9	
6	−14	12.4	85.5	
8	−13	13.5	93.1	
10	−12	14.7	101.4	
12	−11	15.9	109.6	
14	−10	17.1	117.9	
16	−9	18.4	126.9	
18	−8	19.7	135.8	
20	−7	21.1	145.5	
22	−6	22.5	155.1	PRESSURE
24	−4	23.9	164.8	
26	−3	25.4	175.1	
28	−2	26.9	185.5	
30	−1	28.5	196.5	
32	0	30.1	207.5	
34	1	31.8	219.3	
36	2	33.5	231.0	
38	3	35.2	242.7	
40	4	37.0	255.1	
45	7	41.7	287.5	
50	10	46.8	322.7	
55	13	52.1	359.2	
60	16	57.8	398.5	
65	18	63.9	440.6	
70	21	70.3	484.7	
80	27	84.3	581.2	
85	30	91.9	633.7	
90	32	100.0	689.5	
95	35	108.4	747.4	
100	38	117.4	809.5	
105	41	126.8	874.3	
110	43	136.7	942.5	
115	46	147.1	1,014.3	
120	49	158.0	1,089.4	
125	52	169.5	1,168.7	
130	54	181.5	1,251.4	
135	57	194.1	1,338.3	
140	60	207.2	1,428.6	
145	63	221.0	1,523.8	
150	66	235.4	1,623.1	
155	68	250.4	1,726.5	
160	71	266.1	1,834.8	

Figure 2-8. As long as there is any liquid R-12 in the system, the pressure and the temperature of the boiling R-12 always follow this relationship.

conditioning evaporator uses this principle to evaporate the R-12 after it passes through an expansion device. You will learn more about this process and how it is regulated in Chapters 6 and 7.

Pressures in a sealed system

If you were to partially fill a container with water, pump out all the air, and then seal the container, the water would begin to boil immediately. As explained in the previous section, decreasing the pressure automatically lowers the boiling point, and the vacuum above the liquid water would instantly begin to fill with gaseous water vapor.

After a short time, however, the space above the liquid water would become saturated with water vapor, and the liquid would stop boiling. The gas pressure above the liquid water would have risen so high that no more water vapor could force its way in. Another way to look at this is to say that the rising pressure has gradually raised the boiling point, until it finally reaches the actual water temperature, and boiling slows and stops.

At this point, a very useful relationship comes into effect. If you increase the temperature of the liquid and gaseous water in the container, the pressure inside it will rise. If you decrease the temperature, the pressure inside will fall. This relationship between the temperature and the saturated vapor pressure inside the sealed system is regular and predictable for any given substance. Once the system stabilizes, you can measure either temperature or pressure, and then look that value up in a table or perform a calculation to find the other.

Inside a sealed air conditioning system, liquid R-12 boils until the gas pressure exactly balances the tendency to boil, at that particular temperature. If the temperature then is increased, the pressure inside the system rises, too. If the temperature is decreased, the pressure inside it falls.

Technicians use this relationship to diagnose air conditioning problems, and HVAC system designers use it to construct automatic controls to regulate the system's operation. This pressure-temperature relationship is exactly the same as the pressure-boiling point relationship, figure 2-8. As we said earlier, pressure and boiling point, and temperature and pressure inside a sealed system are two aspects of the same thing. You can use the same chart to work with either.

Pressure and vacuum

The atmosphere we live in and breathe is many thousands of feet thick, and the weight of the air above us causes what is called air pressure, figure 2-9. Air is a fluid, so the pressure it exerts is spread evenly over any surface it contacts, just as in liquids. Normal **atmospheric pressure** at sea level is about 14.7 pounds per square inch (760 mm-Hg).

Atmospheric pressure is less than 14.7 psi (760 mm-Hg) at high altitudes because there is less overlying weight of air to support, figure 2-10. In valleys below sea level, air pressure is higher than normal atmospheric pressure. Changes in atmospheric pressure also accompany changes in local weather, with low pres-

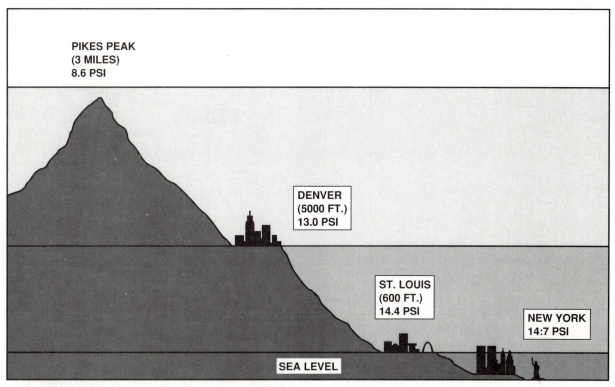

PIKES PEAK
(3 MILES)
8.6 PSI

DENVER
(5000 FT.)
13.0 PSI

ST. LOUIS
(600 FT.)
14.4 PSI

NEW YORK
14:7 PSI

SEA LEVEL

Figure 2-9. The blanket of air surrounding the earth extends upward for many miles. The weight of the air pushing on any surface is called air pressure.

sure systems often bringing storms, and high pressure systems bringing clear weather.

If a sealed container is emptied of the air it contained, the resulting empty volume is called a **vacuum**, and exerts no pressure on the walls of its container. A complete vacuum is extremely difficult to achieve, so the term usually refers to any pressure less than atmospheric.

Meteorologists (weathermen) in the United States usually express air pressure in inches of mercury (in-Hg), a measurement based on a mercury barometer. In its simplest form, this instrument consists of a glass tube sealed at one end and containing a vacuum, with the open end immersed in a tray of mercury. Air pressure on the surface of the mercury forces it up the tube to a height proportional to the air pressure, where its level can be read against an inch scale alongside the glass. At normal sea level conditions, air pressure can force the mercury up the tube about 29.9 inches (760 mm). This value is normal **barometric pressure**.

Automobile specifications frequently refer to vacuum measurements in inches of mercury. Vacuum in an engine is created as the pistons descend in the cylinder faster than the air can enter through the intake manifold, figure 2-11.

As a result, the air thins out to fill the cylinder, and the pressure decreases. Remember that automotive vacuum gauges usually read zero at normal atmospheric pressure. A manifold vacuum of 19 inches (480 mm) really corresponds to a true absolute pressure of about 11 inches (280 mm) of mercury.

HEAT FLOW

Heat energy is present in any substance as long as the temperature of that material is above absolute zero. This heat moves from object to object in specific ways.

Whenever there is a temperature difference between two objects, heat flows from the warmer object to the cooler object until the

Atmospheric Pressure: The pressure caused by the weight of the earth's atmosphere. At sea level, this pressure is 14.7 psi (101 kPa) at 32°F (0°C).

Vacuum: A pressure less than atmospheric pressure.

Barometric Pressure: Atmospheric pressure, as measured with a barometer.

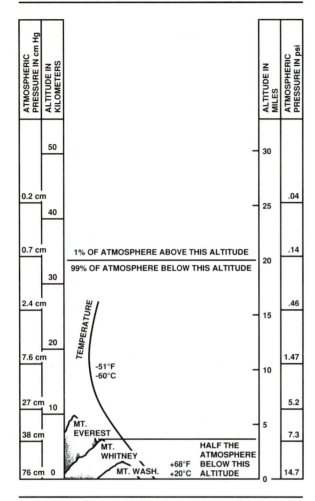

Figure 2-10. At an altitude of about four miles, atmospheric pressure is only half that found at sea level.

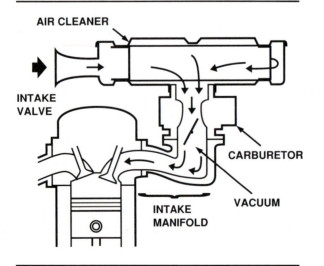

Figure 2-11. When a piston descends in the cylinder, it creates vacuum in the intake manifold.

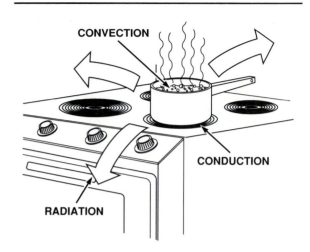

Figure 2-12. Heat can be transferred by convection, conduction, and radiation.

two objects are at the same temperature. There are three principle ways by which the heat flows from warmer objects to the cooler objects, figure 2-12:

• Conduction
• Convection
• Radiation.

Conduction
The form of energy transfer that occurs as heat moves through a substance, or from object to object by direct contact, is called **conduction**. If you heat one end of an iron bar with a torch, the other end of the bar also becomes hot as the heat is conducted through the bar. Place the hot iron bar on a cold anvil, and conduction warms the anvil wherever the iron bar contacts it. In conduction, heat energy is transferred between molecules without moving them from place to place.

Convection
Heat can be carried from one place to another by **convection**, in which a liquid or gas carries the heat from one place to another. The heating systems of modern houses transfer heat from a central furnace to each room by heating air and then blowing the warm air throughout the house. The liquid cooling system of an automobile engine carries heat from the cylinder head and engine block to the radiator by convection. In convection, heat energy is transferred by moving the molecules that carry it from place to place.

Radiation
When heat is moved from place to place without any transfer medium at all, the process is called **radiation**. A red-hot piece of iron will

melt a piece of wax placed next to it, even if the iron and the wax are both placed together in a sealed vacuum chamber. The heat is transferred from the iron to the wax as electromagnetic energy. Radio waves, X-rays, and infrared, visible, and ultraviolet light are all forms of electromagnetic energy. Solar energy from the sun heats the earth after traveling 93 million miles (149 million kilometers) through the vacuum of space. A microwave oven heats food inside without heating the air inside the oven. In radiation, heat energy is transferred in the form of electromagnetic radiation, without heating or moving molecules at all.

Humidity

The air we breathe is a mixture of nitrogen (78%), oxygen (21%), and lesser amounts of other gases in fixed proportions. Water vapor is a gas in the air that varies in concentration. **Humidity** refers to water vapor present in the air. The level of humidity depends upon the amount of water vapor present and the temperature of the air.

The amount of water vapor in the air tends to be higher near lakes or the ocean, because more water is available to evaporate from their surfaces. In desert areas with little open water, the amount of water vapor in the air tends to be low.

Even if water is available to evaporate, however, it may not do so if the air is saturated with water vapor. Warm air can hold greater amounts of water vapor than cold air, just as a container of warm water can dissolve more salt or sugar than a container of cold water. Polar regions can have very dry air even near open water because the very cold air is easily saturated with water vapor, and evaporation from the surface of the water stops.

Measuring humidity

Absolute humidity is a direct measurement of the actual weight of the water in a given volume of air. **Relative humidity** is the ratio (expressed as a percentage) of how much moisture is present in the air compared to how much moisture the air is theoretically capable of holding at that temperature. Because warm air can hold more moisture than cool air, the relative humidity within a sealed container of air holding a fixed amount of water vapor falls as the temperature rises, and rises as the temperature falls. The absolute humidity inside that container stays the same, as long as no water vapor condenses to liquid.

As moisture-holding air cools, the relative humidity rises to 100%, and the air becomes

saturated with water. This temperature is called the **dew point** of the air for that absolute humidity. If the air cools any further, water condenses out of the air as a liquid. Water vapor in the air also condenses if it contacts a cold surface, such as the inside of a cold automobile windshield.

Relative humidity is commonly measured with a hygrometer or a psychrometer. A **hygrometer** depends on a sensitive element that expands and contracts depending on the humidity. Hygrometers typically resemble a clock, with the scale reading from 0 to 100% relative humidity. Permanent-recording hygrometers may be constructed so that an ink pen or electric stylus makes a continuous record on a rotating paper disc or paper-covered drum.

A **psychrometer** uses two thermometers, one of which has the bulb covered in a cotton wick soaked in distilled water from a built-in reservoir, figure 2-13. The wick keeps the bulb of

Conduction: The transfer of heat through a substance or between objects by direct molecular contact.

Convection: The transfer of heat from place to place by the circulation of a gas or a liquid.

Radiation: The transfer of heat as pure energy, without heating the medium through which it is transferred.

Humidity: Water vapor in the air.

Absolute Humidity: A measurement of the actual weight of water in a given volume of air.

Relative Humidity: The ratio of how much moisture the air actually holds at a particular temperature compared to how much it could hold.

Saturated: A condition in which air holds as much water vapor as possible without forming water droplets at a given temperature and pressure.

Dew Point: The temperature at which air becomes 100% saturated with moisture at a given absolute humidity.

Hygrometer: A device used to measure relative humidity containing a humidity-sensitive element.

Psychrometer: A device used to measure relative humidity containing a wet and a dry thermometer.

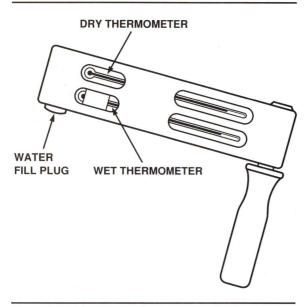

Figure 2-13. A sling psychrometer can be used to measure relative humidity.

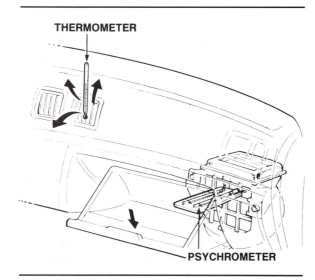

Figure 2-14. Honda recommends measuring humidity with a small wet-and-dry bulb psychrometer inserted into the evaporator vent. Because the evaporator is blowing air, the wet bulb's temperature will drop, but the dry bulb will read the temperature of the airflow.

the "wet thermometer" wet so that it can be cooled by evaporation. To take a relative humidity reading, the psychrometer is placed in an airflow for a certain time, figure 2-14. Sling psychrometers are spun around in the air a certain number of times. Water evaporates from the cotton wick at a rate inversely proportional to the relative humidity of the air: faster if the humidity is low, and slower if the humidity is high. The "dry thermometer" registers ordinary air temperature. The higher the

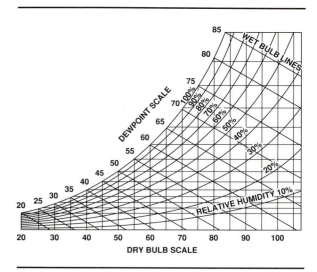

Figure 2-15. A psychrometric chart can be used to derive humidity, dew point, or temperature, if the other two are known.

relative humidity, the closer the readings of the two thermometers, and the lower the humidity, the greater the difference. The different temperatures indicated by the wet and dry thermometers are compared to a chart, which gives the relative humidity. Sling psychrometers have been used by field meteorologists for many years. The name comes from the design of older instruments, in which an open housing containing the thermometers was whirled around the head. For HVAC service, some manufacturers provide a tool with the two thermometers fixed to a small board. This is slipped into the evaporator outlet, and the air conditioner fan provides the necessary airflow.

The psychrometric chart
A psychrometric chart, figure 2-15, shows the relationship between humidity, dew point, and temperature for a gas, in this case, water vapor. Different substances have different charts. Charts for such materials as Refrigerant 12 tell the air conditioning technician what to expect in terms of refrigeration system performance at given temperatures and humidity levels. The *Shop Manual* discusses psychrometric charts and their use in detail.

HEATING AND COOLING IN AN AUTOMOBILE

So far in this chapter, we have discussed heat, temperature, pressure, and humidity. We now relate these topics to the automotive heating, ventilation, and air conditioning (HVAC) system.

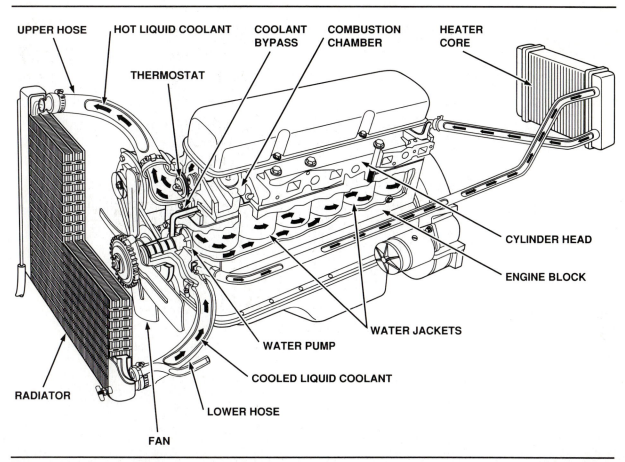

UPPER HOSE   HOT LIQUID COOLANT   COOLANT BYPASS   COMBUSTION CHAMBER   HEATER CORE

THERMOSTAT

CYLINDER HEAD

ENGINE BLOCK

WATER JACKETS

WATER PUMP

COOLED LIQUID COOLANT

RADIATOR

LOWER HOSE

FAN

Figure 2-16. In a typical automotive cooling system, the coolant circulates constantly between the radiator and the engine's water jackets.

Heat Exchangers in an Automobile

The study of heating and cooling is really the study of how to move heat. Heating systems move heat *to* the passenger compartment, and air conditioning systems remove heat *from* the passenger compartment. **Heat exchangers** are used to move heat between automobile components. An excellent example of a heat exchanger is the automotive radiator.

The radiator

The most obvious source of heat in the automobile is that produced by the engine during operation. This heat must be removed from the engine cylinder head and block as it is produced, or the engine overheats and will eventually fail.

The automotive cooling system, figure 2-16, transfers heat by conduction and convection. Heat is first conducted through the metal cylinder head and engine block and into the water jackets. Circulating engine coolant absorbs the heat and transfers it by convection to the radiator. Heat is transferred by conduction into the radiator metal and is absorbed into the air

Heat Exchanger: A component in which heat is transferred from one medium (such as hot coolant) to another (such as the surrounding air) through conduction.

■ A Filter For The Ozone Layer

Here's a tip from General Motors when servicing an AC system after one of their compressors has failed. The standard shop practice has been to clean the screen or change the orifice tube, flush the condenser, evaporator, and the lines with R-11, then backflush with R-12 so the R-11 doesn't damage the compressor. The problem with this procedure is the evaporator: because of its many bends and baffles, debris collects inside that cannot be easily and effectively flushed out. Besides, this procedure pumps a considerable quantity of refrigerant directly into the atmosphere.

The new recommended procedure is to install an in-line filter at the outlet of the condenser. This traps the debris that would otherwise be flowing through the system.

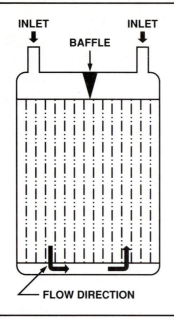

Figure 2-17. A heater core works like a small radiator, transferring heat from the engine coolant to the air flowing through it.

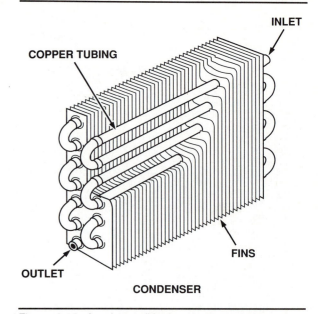

Figure 2-18. An air conditioning system condenser transforms the gaseous R-12 into a liquid by transferring heat to the airstream flowing between the fins.

moving between the radiator fins, raising the air temperature. This warm air is then removed by convection away from the car.

Heat exchangers require a **temperature gradient** to function. An automobile radiator can transfer coolant heat into cold air more efficiently than it can transfer heat into warm air. If the air temperature around a radiator were equal to the temperature of the engine coolant, then no heat would be transferred. If the air were *warmer* than the coolant, then the heat exchanger would operate in the other direction. The engine coolant would absorb heat from the air.

The performance of heat exchangers is also related to the surface area exposed to the regions being cooled and warmed. Radiators and engine castings of air-cooled engines are usually constructed with cooling fins to expose greater surface area to the cooling air. In this design, heat is conveyed directly to passing air, without the use of a liquid coolant.

The heater core
The **heater core**, figure 2-17, is constructed like a small radiator, with inlet and outlet tubes attached to a finned core. Like a radiator, fins increase the surface area. The heater core transfers heat from engine coolant to the air blown between the fins. The warm air is blown through the passenger compartment to heat it.

The air conditioning system condenser
In the air conditioning system, heat is removed from the compressed, gaseous refrigerant in order to return it to a cooler liquid state. This is the job of the **condenser**, figure 2-18. Although it is a heat exchanger, the condenser differs from the radiator or the heater core in that it is constructed to circulate high-pressure gas and liquid Refrigerant 12 instead of low-pressure liquid coolant. Numerous small, thin fins give the condenser maximum heat transfer capability.

The air conditioning system evaporator
The **evaporator**, figure 2-19, absorbs heat from the air that is blown through it, lowering the air temperature to cool the passenger compartment. The evaporator:

• Is constructed so that the refrigerant evaporates or boils as it enters.
• Supplies a surface through which the liquid refrigerant absorbs latent heat of vaporization as it changes state to a gas.
• Removes water vapor from the air entering the passenger compartment by condensing it and draining it outside.

Warm air from the passenger compartment (or from outside the car) is blown between the fins of the evaporator. Conduction through the evaporator transfers the heat from the air to the evaporating refrigerant inside. The cooled air is then circulated to the passenger compartment.

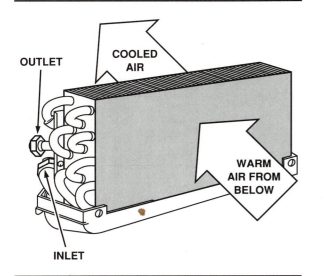

Figure 2-19. An air conditioning system evaporator removes heat from the air entering the car by transferring it to the vaporizing R-12.

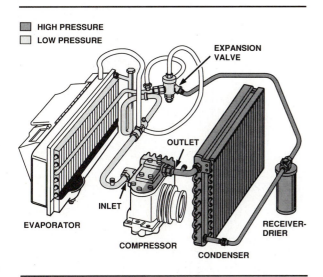

Figure 2-20. There are six main parts of a typical air conditioning system.

The Refrigeration System

Heat cannot be destroyed, but it can be transferred. The automotive air conditioning system removes heat from the passenger compartment, and transfers it to the airstream outside the car. It also removes moisture from the air passing through it, channeling it to a drain that leads outside the car.

The refrigeration system operates in a **closed-loop**. The same refrigerant is used over and over again as it circulates through the system. The mechanical refrigeration system consists of six principle parts, figure 2-20:

● Compressor

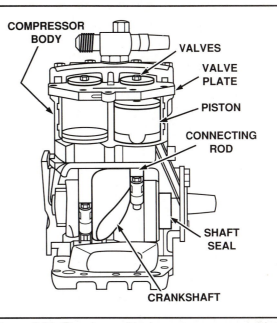

Figure 2-21. The air conditioning compressor provides the mechanical force needed to pressurize the R-12.

● Condenser
● Receiver-drier or accumulator
● Expansion device
● Evaporator
● Refrigerant.

The compressor
The **compressor**, figure 2-21, is an engine-driven pump that increases the pressure ap-

Temperature Gradient: A situation in which an area of high temperature is connected to an area of low temperature, causing heat to flow from the hot to the cold area.

Heater Core: A heat exchanger in the HVAC system through which hot coolant passes and releases its heat by conduction.

Condenser: Part of the refrigeration system in which refrigerant vapor is changed to a liquid by removing heat from it.

Evaporator: The component in an air conditioning system that changes the liquid refrigerant to a vapor after removing its heat, which is discharged into the passenger compartment.

Closed-Loop: A system with no beginning or end. In a system, it is the continuous circulation of a material, such as refrigerant.

Compressor: One of the components of an air conditioning system that pumps the refrigerant and raises the pressure of the refrigerant vapor.

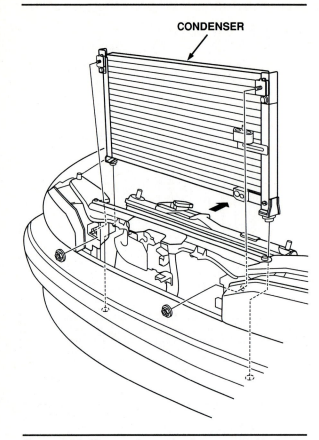

Figure 2-22. The condenser is often mounted in front of the radiator to take advantage of the constant airstream.

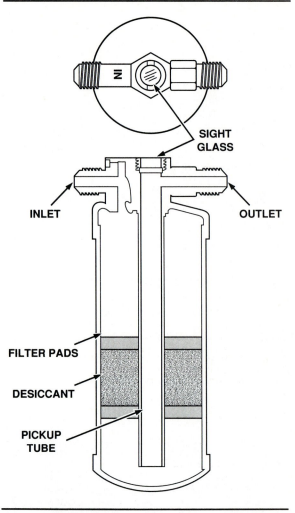

Figure 2-23. The receiver-drier is a reservoir for liquid R-12.

plied to the gaseous refrigerant and moves it through the system. As the refrigerant is compressed, its temperature rises. The boiling point of the refrigerant also rises under pressure, and the refrigerant is very nearly compressed to the point of being liquid. Several types of compressors are commonly used today by automobile manufacturers.

The condenser
The hot, gaseous refrigerant from the compressor is sent to the condenser. Outside air flows over the fins of the condenser, figure 2-22, and absorbs heat from the refrigerant. Enough heat is removed to lower the temperature below its boiling point (at that high pressure), and the refrigerant condenses to a liquid. As the gas condenses, it gives off the latent heat of vaporization it contained.

The receiver-drier or accumulator
The compressor and condenser are designed with enough capacity to keep more refrigerant liquid than is usually needed. This liquid is stored in one of two types of reservoirs. Some systems use a receiver-drier, figure 2-23, to

store refrigerant as a high-pressure liquid. Other systems use an accumulator to retain extra refrigerant as a low-pressure liquid until it evaporates.

These reservoirs also contain a **desiccant** to remove water vapor or moisture from the system. A desiccant is a chemical compound that absorbs water. This prevents moisture from freezing the expansion device, or combining with the refrigerant and the refrigerant oil to form corrosive acids.

The expansion device
An expansion device consists of a valve or restricted orifice that meters the release of the refrigerant from its liquid, high-pressure state to its gaseous, low-pressure state. The expansion device controls the rate at which refrigerant expands inside the evaporator. There are several different kinds of expansion devices, figure 2-24.

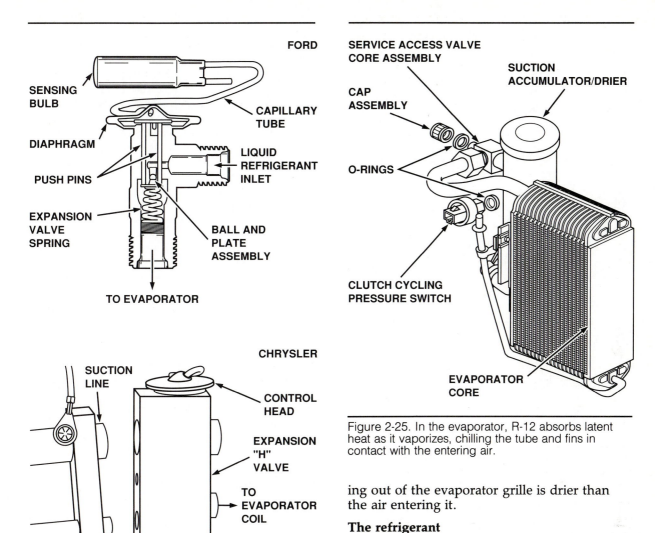

FORD

SENSING BULB

CAPILLARY TUBE

DIAPHRAGM

PUSH PINS

LIQUID REFRIGERANT INLET

EXPANSION VALVE SPRING

BALL AND PLATE ASSEMBLY

TO EVAPORATOR

CHRYSLER

SUCTION LINE

CONTROL HEAD

EXPANSION "H" VALVE

TO EVAPORATOR COIL

Figure 2-24. Two types of thermostatic expansion valves. These devices or a calibrated orifice provide the restriction against which the compressor pumps.

SERVICE ACCESS VALVE CORE ASSEMBLY

SUCTION ACCUMULATOR/DRIER

CAP ASSEMBLY

O-RINGS

CLUTCH CYCLING PRESSURE SWITCH

EVAPORATOR CORE

Figure 2-25. In the evaporator, R-12 absorbs latent heat as it vaporizes, chilling the tube and fins in contact with the entering air.

The evaporator
The evaporator is a heat exchanger containing the chamber into which the boiling refrigerant vaporizes, figure 2-25. When a liquid evaporates, it must absorb latent heat of vaporization. In a refrigeration system, this heat is absorbed from warm air blowing across the surface of the evaporator, figure 2-19. The air is cooled, and it is then blown into the passenger compartment.

The evaporator is also where moisture is removed from the passenger compartment air. As moist recirculated or outside air passes over the cold evaporator fins, water vapor condenses from the air and drips to the bottom of the evaporator housing. From there it flows through a drain onto the ground. The air passing out of the evaporator grille is drier than the air entering it.

The refrigerant
Refrigerant 12, or R-12, is a nearly ideal refrigerant, because it:

• Does not react with materials used in the system.
• Is nonflammable and nonexplosive.
• Is reusable and soluble in oil.
• Evaporates at a very low temperature (–21.7°F at zero psi; –5.7°C at zero kPa).

The R-12 used in automotive air conditioning systems is similar to the refrigerant used in home refrigerators and air conditioners. R-12 has a very high specific heat, and a high heat of vaporization, so a small amount can absorb and give up a great deal of heat during temperature and state changes. This allows air conditioners to have a high cooling capacity in a small size.

Desiccant: A drying agent in the receiver-drier of an air conditioning system, used to remove moisture.

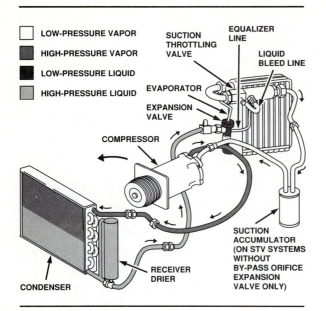

◻ LOW-PRESSURE VAPOR
▨ HIGH-PRESSURE VAPOR
■ LOW-PRESSURE LIQUID
▦ HIGH-PRESSURE LIQUID

Figure 2-26. Wide pressure variations exist throughout the air conditioning system.

Many technicians refer to R-12 as "Freon." Freon is the registered brand name used by its inventor, the I.E. DuPont de Nemours Company. Much like the name "Kleenex" for facial tissues, "Freon" has become a generic term for the refrigerant dichlorodifluoromethane. Other trade names for refrigerant containing the same chemical compound include Aircon 12, Genetron 12, Prestone 12, and Freeze 12. The "12" indicates it is the same as R-12.

Air conditioning operation
The air conditioning system is pressurized at all times, even when it is turned off. When in operation, it creates a large pressure differential between the high side and the low side circuits, figure 2-26.

The air conditioning system is a continuous loop, but we can conveniently begin with the compressor.

The compressor pressurizes the gaseous R-12 by pumping against the restriction of the thermostatic expansion valve or fixed-orifice expansion tube. Hot, high-pressure refrigerant enters the high side circuit from the compressor outlet, and flows to the condenser.

In the condenser, the hot gas is cooled to below its boiling point at that pressure. It changes state and becomes a high-pressure liquid. The refrigerant gives up sensible and latent heat, which is transferred to the outside air.

From the condenser the liquid refrigerant enters the receiver-drier (in systems using an expansion valve), where the liquid is temporarily stored and any moisture and contaminants are removed.

Refrigerant then passes through a thermostatic expansion valve, or a fixed orifice expansion tube, into the low side circuit, where it expands to fill the greater space available and loses pressure. The decreased pressure lowers the boiling point to below the refrigerant's temperature. The refrigerant begins to boil and expand from a high-pressure liquid to a low-pressure gas. Metered amounts of this low-pressure refrigerant mist (a mixture of liquid and vapor) enter the evaporator, which is the vehicle's air cooler.

Because of its low boiling point, the refrigerant mist readily completes its vaporization and chills the evaporator coils by absorbing heat of vaporization from the air blowing into the passenger compartment. The low-pressure gas then flows to the inlet, or low side, of the compressor. In expansion tube systems, the gas enters the accumulator before flowing back into the compressor.

The system operates at varying internal temperatures and pressures, depending on the control settings and temperatures outside the automobile. Changes in engine speed also change the compressor speed, and affect its output.

SUMMARY

Matter is composed of elements, and the smallest identified particle of an element is an atom. Atoms are composed of protons and neutrons in the nucleus, and electrons orbiting around the nucleus. Matter on earth can be found as solids, liquids, and gases.

The melting point is the temperature at which solids melt to become liquids, and liquids freeze to become solids. The boiling point is the temperature at which liquids boil to become gases, and gases condense to become liquids. The melting point is essentially independent of pressure, but the boiling point increases as pressure increases.

The amount of heat in a substance is measured in calories, and the intensity of the molecular vibration in the substance is measured in one of three temperature scales: Fahrenheit, Celsius, or Kelvin.

Specific heat represents the number of calories required to cause a standard temperature change in a material. When a substance changes temperature, it absorbs or gives off sensible heat. At melting or boiling points, substances absorb or give off heat without changing temperature. This is called latent heat. Heat flows from warm objects to cool objects by one of three ways: conduction, convection, or radiation.

At sea level, the pressure of the atmosphere results in a weight of 14.7 pounds per square inch (760 mm-Hg). As altitude increases, the pressure decreases and the boiling point decreases.

Humidity is a measure of the amount of water vapor in the air. Absolute humidity is a measure by weight of water in a given volume of air. Relative humidity expresses the amount of water vapor in the air as a percentage of how much water vapor the air could possibly hold at that temperature.

Automobiles use heat exchangers to transfer heat between components in the engine and HVAC system, and to transfer heat to the air inside or outside the automobile. The modern automotive air conditioning system consists of a compressor, a condenser, a receiver-drier or accumulator, an expansion device, and an evaporator. Refrigerant 12 is a chemical compound that absorbs and gives up heat as it changes state between liquid and gas within the refrigeration system. The air conditioner uses this heat transfer to cool and dehumidify the passenger compartment.

Review Questions

Choose the single most correct answer.
Compare your answers with the correct answers on page 229.

1. An element is a form of matter that:
   a. Cannot be broken down chemically
   b. Has weight
   c. Occupies space
   d. All of the above

2. An atom consists of all of the following EXCEPT:
   a. Protons
   b. Molecules
   c. Neutrons
   d. Nucleus

3. Temperature is measured in:
   a. BTUs
   b. Calories
   d. Degrees
   c. None of the above

4. The temperature scale that uses zero degrees to correspond to absolute zero is:
   a. Celsius
   b. Kelvin
   c. Fahrenheit
   d. All of the above

5. Objects tend to expand when heated because:
   a. The intensity of the molecular vibration increases
   b. The intensity of the molecular vibration decreases
   c. The wavelength of the kinetic energy is broadened
   d. The kinetic energy is removed from the molecules

6. Compressing a gas:
   a. Increases the pressure and decreases the temperature
   b. Decreases the pressure and increases the temperature
   c. Decreases the pressure and decreases the temperature
   d. Increases the pressure and increases the temperature

7. Which of the following is true of specific heat?
   a. The higher the specific heat, the greater the heat transfer ability
   b. Water has a specific heat of 0
   c. It is based on the Kelvin scale
   d. It is the heat added to a material that causes a temperature change

8. The three states of matter are:
   a. Solid, liquid, and fluid
   b. Solid, vapor, and gas
   c. Solid, liquid, gas
   d. Liquid, vapor, and gas

9. Matter in its fluid state exerts pressure:
   a. Downward only
   b. Upward only
   c. In all directions
   d. Downward and to the sides

10. When heating a substance, latent heat is:
    a. The heat added to cause a change of state while the temperature stays the same
    b. The heat added that causes a change in temperature
    c. The amount of heat given off without changing state
    d. The number of calories needed to raise the temperature 1 degree Celsius

11. Fog and condensation form on the inside of a vehicle's windows when the inside glass temperature is colder than the interior air's _____ :
    a. Dew point
    b. Absolute humidity
    c. Relative humidity
    d. Greenhouse temperature

12. All of the following are true of atmospheric pressure EXCEPT:
    a. The higher the altitude, the lower the atmospheric pressure
    b. At high altitudes, water boils at a lower temperature than at sea level
    c. Atmospheric pressure is the result of the weight of air
    d. Atmospheric pressure at sea level is about 21.2 psi

13. The amount of water that air can hold depends on:
    a. Absolute pressure and temperature
    b. Absolute pressure and dew point
    c. Barometric pressure and temperature
    d. Barometric pressure and evaporation

14. A measurement of the actual weight of water in a given volume of air is:
    a. Absolute humidity
    b. Dew point
    c. Relative humidity
    d. Absolute pressure

PART TWO

Ventilation and Heating

Chapter Three
Ventilation, Heating, and
Engine Cooling Systems

Chapter Four
Ventilation and
Heating Controls

3

Ventilation, Heating, and Engine Cooling Systems

In previous chapters we examined the history of the automotive HVAC system, the need for heating, cooling, and ventilation of the passenger compartment, and some of the physical principles required to understand its operation. We now look at the basic parts of the heating and ventilation systems. In this chapter we discuss how the heating, ventilation, and engine cooling systems work together to maintain a comfortable environment for the driver and passengers.

FRESH AIR VENTILATION

The simplest way to improve the environment within a passenger compartment is to circulate fresh air within it. Circulating air of itself cools the human body, and removes air heated by solar radiation entering through the glass. Maintaining positive ventilation also lowers interior humidity and removes odors originating both within the car and penetrating into it from areas the car passes through. Positive air circulation through a ventilating system can also provide a convenient means of transferring heated or cooled air from other circuits in the HVAC system.

There are two means of generating an airflow through the passenger compartment:

- Through opened windows, cowl or wing vents, opened and closed manually
- Through a mechanical ventilation system, operated through an intake, a system of ducts, a blower, and various types of controls.

Open Windows for Ventilation

Opening windows is an effective way of ventilating a passenger compartment — sometimes too effective. Wing vents in the front windows of passenger cars were common from the early 1930s to the 1970s as a way to get more control over the entering airstream by deflecting some of the air away from an open window, and by providing the option of a much smaller window opening for situations requiring less airflow. Even with this control, however, the incoming air is unfiltered, and active ventilation exists only while the vehicle moves. The incoming air is also noisy, and open windows are inconvenient in the rain and in dusty areas. In addition, a major disadvantage is the extra fuel consumption that results from operating a vehicle with its windows down. Lowering the windows of a moving vehicle increases the **aerodynamic drag**, or resistance to forward motion caused by air, as the open windows scoop air into the passenger compartment in-

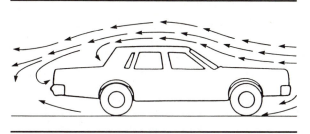

Figure 3-1. A moving vehicle forces the air aside, creating high and low pressure zones around it.

stead of permitting it to flow along the outside of the glass. This can significantly reduce fuel mileage.

Ram Air Versus Fan-Boosted Ventilation

The purpose of a mechanical ventilation system is to provide a controlled supply of fresh air to the passenger compartment. There are two types of mechanical systems currently in use:

- Ram air systems
- Fan-boosted systems.

The ram air effect
As a vehicle moves, the air it passes through is forced aside to allow the passage of the vehicle, figure 3-1. This flow of air over and around the body of the car creates areas of high air pressure that can be used for ventilation and cooling.

As the air flows over the hood of the vehicle, it forms a high-pressure area at the base of the windshield, created as the air is forced up and over the top of the vehicle. This high pressure forces (or rams) air through a **cowl air intake** mounted in this area, figure 3-2. The air is forced into ducts that lead to the passenger compartment of the vehicle. This is called the **ram air effect**. A cowl air intake usually consists of a grille or a row of louvers in the top of the cowl, flush with the rear of the hood. It is positioned above a horizontal air duct opening, or the ducts may simply draw air from around the trailing edge of the hood.

Once inside the vehicle, air is distributed from the cowl air intake to the various parts of the passenger compartment with ducts, hoses, and vents. Most vehicles have right- and left-side vents located at knee level under the dash, and many also have a center vent in the middle of the dash panel, figure 3-3. The center vent may have horizontal and vertical slats to enable the driver to control the direction of the airflow. Some systems have an additional

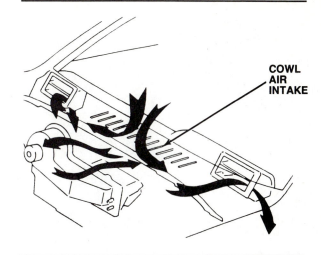

COWL AIR INTAKE

Figure 3-2. Ram air is forced into the cowl air intake at the base of the windshield by a zone of high pressure.

control that redirects most of the airflow from the center vent to a floor-directed vent.

As the fresh ram air enters the vehicle, it pressurizes the passenger compartment slightly and forces out the air already inside the car.

Aerodynamic Drag: The resistance to an object's forward motion caused by the obstruction of and friction with the surrounding air.

Cowl Air Intake: The inlet vent at the base of the windshield that admits ram air into the HVAC system.

Ram Air Effect: Forced circulation of ventilating air by opening the HVAC system to a high-pressure area caused by the forward motion of the vehicle.

■ **For Summer Rain And Slow City Traffic**

For a few years immediately following the Second World War and before the advent of true air conditioning, Pontiac offered the Fisher "Venti-Heat" accessory. This used a thermostat-controlled blower in the engine compartment to force warm, fresh air through heater vents in the back seat area and two vents on the dashboard. The thermostat controlled the air temperature automatically to maintain a driver-selected level. The blower could also be used to defrost the windshield. The system had several settings: "For winter", "For de-icing", "For summer rain storms or slow city traffic", and "For unpleasant outside odors."

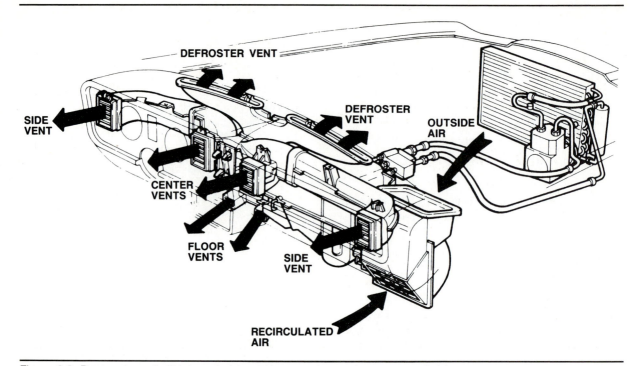

Figure 3-3. Duct systems built into a dashboard have outlets at the center and sides.

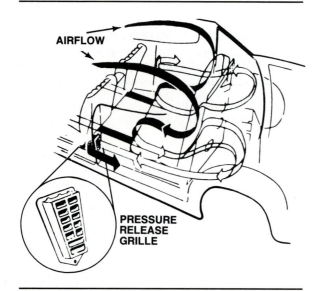

Figure 3-4. Fresh air forced into the passenger compartment pushes stale air outside through the pressure release grille.

This is done on some vehicles through a **pressure release grille** mounted in the door pillar, figure 3-4. Other vehicles have a similar air outlet mounted under and behind the rear seat.

Fan-boosted ventilation systems
The ram air system requires the vehicle to be rolling forward to work. With this system

alone, airflow will be weak or nonexistent at low speeds. Fan-boosted ventilation systems are better for low-speed operation, especially in urban areas where stop-and-go traffic is common. The main difference is that the pressure required to cause airflow is provided by an electric fan or blower built into the system. The same fan can boost ventilation when the heater, defroster, or air conditioning system is in use.

The fan-boosted system uses an elecric blower assembly, figure 3-5, and uses the same ducting and ventilation registers as the heater and air conditioning systems. In some vehicles, the fan runs constantly on a low setting for positive ventilation whenever the ignition is on, even if the control head has an OFF setting. When the heating or air conditioning system is engaged, the driver has the option of increasing the airflow by turning up the fan setting.

THE HEATING SYSTEM

There are two primary reasons to heat the interior of an automobile:

• To warm the windows of the vehicle
• To improve the comfort of the passengers.

Warming the vehicle's windows is important so that ice and mist can be removed upon engine warm-up, and to prevent them from reforming so they do not obscure the driver's

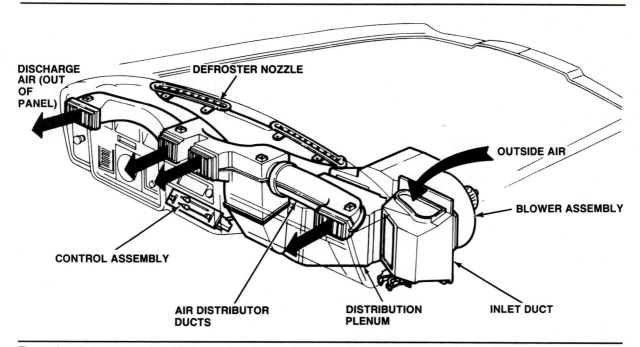

Figure 3-5. A fan-boosted ventilation system forces air through the vents even when the vehicle is not moving.

vision. The heater defroster is one of the most important safety systems in the automobile. Heating and defrosting systems are used throughout the year when the temperature falls below a comfortable level or when the windows inside the passenger compartment mist due to high humidity.

Heating System Operation

Most cars use heat from the engine for the heating system of the vehicle. On air-cooled engines, the heat is taken from air that has passed over the hot engine, using sheet metal heat exchangers and extensive ductwork and shrouding, figure 3-6. On cars with liquid-cooled engines, this heat is taken from the engine coolant.

The simplest style of heater, figure 3-7, is an expanded part of the engine cooling system. In this system, waste heat from combustion is removed by coolant circulating through the **water jacket** inside the engine block, figure 3-8.

The basic heater system uses a heater control valve, figure 3-9, to regulate the flow of the hot coolant from the water jacket into the HVAC system. Heater control valves can be controlled manually (by a cable), electrically, or (most commonly) by vacuum motors. The hot coolant is carried by the heater hose to the heater core, usually located under the dashboard of the automobile. The water pump on the engine circulates coolant throughout the heating system.

Simply warming the passenger compartment air can be accomplished quietly with a small flow of air. Defrosting, on the other hand, goes quicker if there is a large airflow to spread the heat across the entire windshield. Very early HVAC systems were built with a single-speed blower, but most vehicles have multiple-speed blower motors.

The airflow that the blower can produce depends on the speed of rotation and the size of the fan. Blowers are used to move either passenger compartment air (recirculation) or outside air (fresh) through the heater core to warm the air. This warm air is then distributed throughout the passenger compartment.

Temperature regulation

There are three principle ways to adjust the temperature of the air that enters the passenger compartment:

• By controlling the rate at which coolant flows through the heater core (coolant control)

Pressure Release Grille: An air vent inside the passenger compartment that prevents pressure from building up inside the vehicle while the HVAC system is operating.

Water Jacket: The passages in the engine cylinder head and block that allow coolant to circulate throughout the engine.

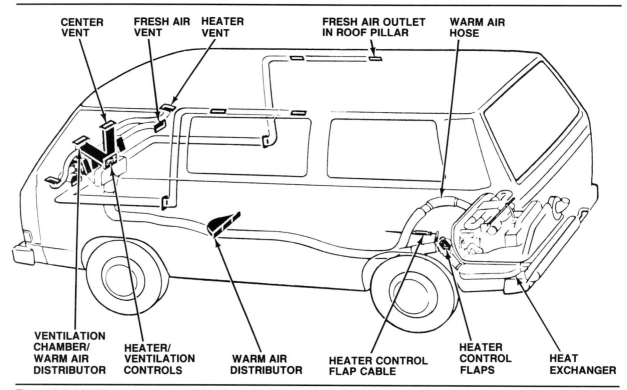

CENTER VENT   FRESH AIR VENT   HEATER VENT   FRESH AIR OUTLET IN ROOF PILLAR   WARM AIR HOSE

VENTILATION CHAMBER/ WARM AIR DISTRIBUTOR   HEATER/ VENTILATION CONTROLS   WARM AIR DISTRIBUTOR   HEATER CONTROL FLAP CABLE   HEATER CONTROL FLAPS   HEAT EXCHANGER

Figure 3-6. Heating systems used with air-cooled engines warm air in a heat exchanger in the engine compartment before blowing it into the passenger compartment.

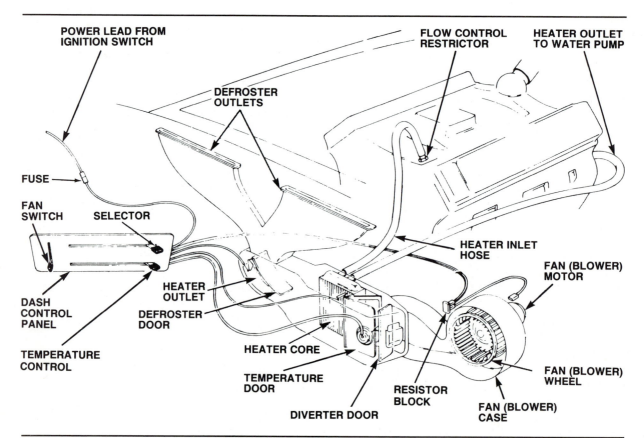

POWER LEAD FROM IGNITION SWITCH   FLOW CONTROL RESTRICTOR   HEATER OUTLET TO WATER PUMP

DEFROSTER OUTLETS

FUSE

FAN SWITCH   SELECTOR

HEATER INLET HOSE

FAN (BLOWER) MOTOR

HEATER OUTLET

DASH CONTROL PANEL   DEFROSTER DOOR

TEMPERATURE CONTROL

HEATER CORE

TEMPERATURE DOOR

DIVERTER DOOR   RESISTOR BLOCK   FAN (BLOWER) CASE   FAN (BLOWER) WHEEL

Figure 3-7. Heating systems used with liquid-cooled engines warm air by directing it through a heater core. The core is heated by the engine coolant circulated through the tubes inside it.

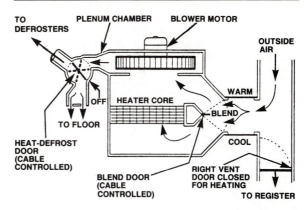

Figure 3-10. The blend door raises or lowers heater temperature by directing incoming air through or around the heater core.

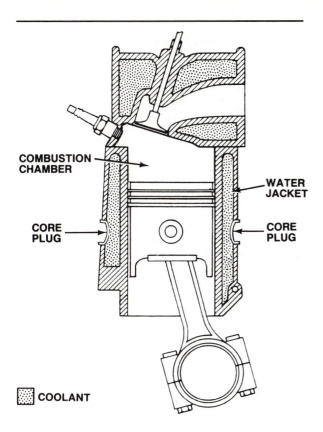

Figure 3-8. Coolant circulates through water jackets in the engine block and cylinder head.

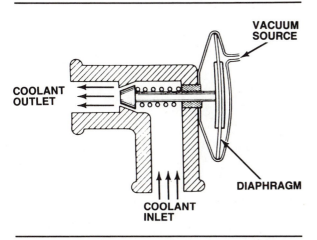

Figure 3-9. This heater control valve is opened by a diaphragm operated by modulated engine vacuum.

• By controlling the proportion of incoming air that passes or bypasses the heater core (air control)
• By using a combination of coolant control and air control.

The thermostat in the engine cooling system maintains the coolant at a constant temperature. A heater control valve varies the rate at

which coolant flows through the heater core. Increasing or decreasing the flow rate increases or decreases the rate at which heat can be transferred to the passenger compartment air. This, in turn, controls the temperature of the air passing into the passenger compartment.

The second method does not use a heater control valve. Instead, airflow through the heater core is controlled by blend doors that blend fresh air with heated air. This is called a **blend air** system, figure 3-10. This system controls the temperature of the air passing into the passenger compartment by blending fresh, unheated air with heated air that has passed through the heater core. The position of the blend door determines how much of the air from the blower fan will go through the heater core and how much will bypass it. By changing the proportion of the air that is heated, the blend door controls the temperature of the air that leaves the duct system.

The same blend door can be used to control interior cooling levels as well. All of the cooled airflow passes through the air conditioning evaporator. A portion of the air may be routed by the blend door back through the heater core where it is rewarmed. The cold air stream and the warmer air stream are then remixed in the **plenum chamber** before distribution to the

Blend Air: A type of HVAC system that controls air temperature using a door directing incoming air through or around the heater core.

Plenum Chamber: The largest part of the air conditioning duct system. When operating it is filled with air at a slightly higher pressure than the surrounding air.

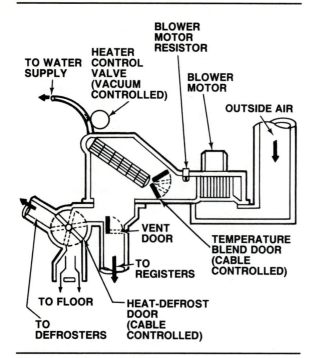

Figure 3-11. This combination system uses blend doors to control air circulation, and also turns the heater control off when the air conditioning system is set to MAX.

The third method is a combination system that uses a heater control valve to control coolant flow through the heater core, and blend doors to control the airflow around it, figure 3-11. In this system, the heater control valve shuts off all coolant flow through the heater core when the air conditioning setting is on MAX, and allows coolant flow in all other settings. The doors operate in the same way as the method just described. Most modern vehicles use this combination system, although many carmakers call it a blend-air system.

Air distribution system
The air distribution system of the vehicle takes the warm air from the plenum chamber and directs the heat either to the defroster system or to the passenger heating system.

The forced-air defroster system, figure 3-12, directs heated air through ducts on the top of the dashboard near the base of the windshield. Heating the windshield removes mist and ice.

The passenger heating system, figure 3-13, directs warm air through a register directed at the passenger's feet, and through vents

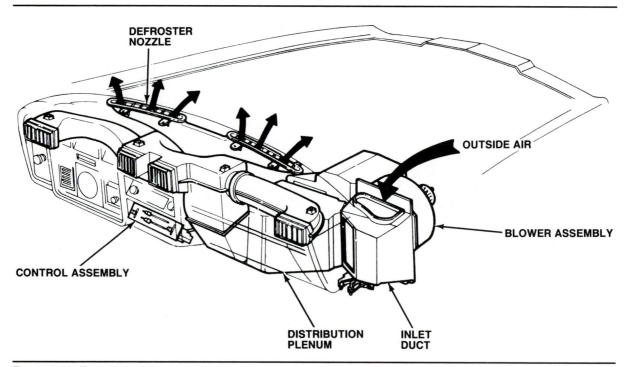

Figure 3-12. Forced-air defroster system.

passenger compartment. Ford used this system for many years, and General Motors uses this method on some base-level pickup trucks.

mounted on the center and on either side of the dash. Some cars also have ducts in the rear seat area.

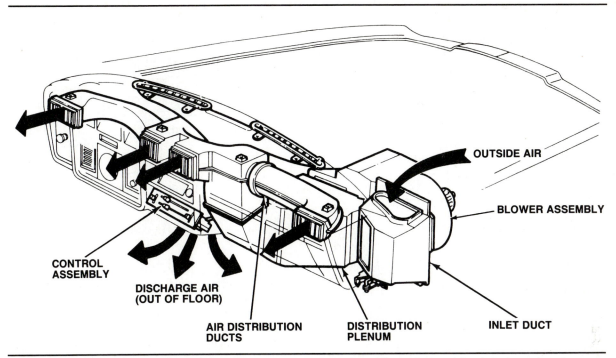

Figure 3-13. Passengers can direct air into the passenger compartment through a variety of ducts and vents.

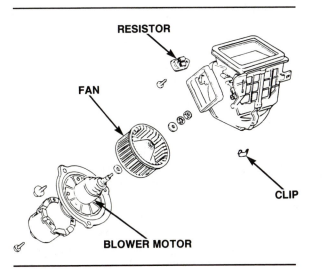

Figure 3-14. An electric motor drives the heater blower.

Heating System Components

Heating systems range from simple systems with manual controls and a 2-speed blower, to the automatic computer-controlled systems (often called Climate Control) that combine all heating, venting, and air conditioning functions. In this chapter, we will discuss only the heating portions of the systems.

A typical heating system consists of the:

- Blower motor
- Heater core

- Heater control valves (on some systems)
- Heater hoses
- Ducting and doors
- Plenum chamber.

Blower motor
A blower motor, figure 3-14, is used to circulate the air needed for heating, defrosting, and air conditioning.

Most blower motors are permanent-magnet, variable-speed, direct current motors. The speed of the blower can be changed by one of two methods:

- Varying electrical resistance at the switch
- Varying electrical resistance at the motor.

In the first system, motor speed is increased by increasing the voltage in the circuit. This can be used for multiple-speed motors or variable-speed motors. On a multiple-speed motor (one with several distinct speeds), a switch mounted on the instrument panel controls the blower operation, figure 3-15. Typically, the switch controls blower speed by directing the electric current to the motor through or around various coils on a **resistor**

Resistor: An electric circuit that resists current flow, used to lower the voltage applied to another device such as a motor.

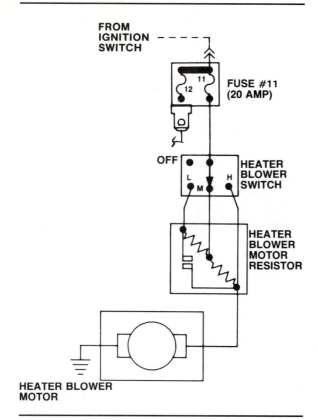

FROM
IGNITION
SWITCH

FUSE #11
(20 AMP)

OFF

HEATER
BLOWER
SWITCH

HEATER
BLOWER
MOTOR
RESISTOR

HEATER BLOWER
MOTOR

Figure 3-15. The blower control switch routes current through paths of varying resistance to control motor speed.

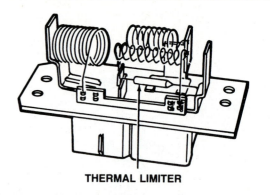

THERMAL LIMITER

Figure 3-16. Blower motor resistors are installed on a block near the motor. Some resistors have a thermal limiter.

block, figure 3-16. The resistor block may be a part of the switch assembly, or mounted remotely from the switch.

When the driver selects a low blower speed, the current is routed to the motor through several resistor coils (or a single high resistance coil) on the resistor block. The high resistance lowers the voltage available to the motor, resulting in a low speed. When a higher speed is selected, current flows through fewer of the resistors (or through a single low-resistance resistor), which causes the motor to run faster. The highest switch position usually bypasses all the resistors, giving the highest blower speed.

Some units use a large variable resistor called a **rheostat** to control the voltage to the blower motor, which permits the driver to choose any speed between the lowest and the highest. Because rheostats are bulky and expensive, their use has been limited primarily to aftermarket units.

Some newer HVAC systems have variable-speed motors. In these systems, the speed of the blower motor is changed by varying the

resistance electronically. This has two main advantages. By controlling the speed of the motor electronically, there are no resistor blocks to heat up. This reduces heat and wasted power. The second advantage is that the applied voltage can be smoothly varied by the electronic circuit for infinite speed control of the motor.

The second major type of blower motor, figure 3-17, changes speeds by changing the number of windings that are used to run the motor. These usually are 2-speed motors. When low speed is desired, the fan switch directs power to the grounded brush and the low-speed brush. When higher speed operation is desired, the switch supplies power to the high-speed brush instead. Changing brushes changes the number of windings in the motor actually being used. This changes the blower speed and fan output.

The heater core
The heater core, figure 3-18, is a heat exchanger similar to a radiator, but differing in its size and configuration. The heater core is much smaller than the radiator. The radiator disposes of its excess heat into the air stream that flows through the engine compartment. The heat leaving the heater core is directed into the passenger compartment where it is used to warm the interior and the passengers.

The amount of heat transferred by a radiator or heater core depends upon its surface area. Increasing the surface area that contacts the air increases the thermal transfer to the air. Like radiators, heater cores generally are of a honeycomb or cellular design to increase the surface area. Coolant flows through the tubes, allowing the heat to be absorbed by conduction and disposed of by convection.

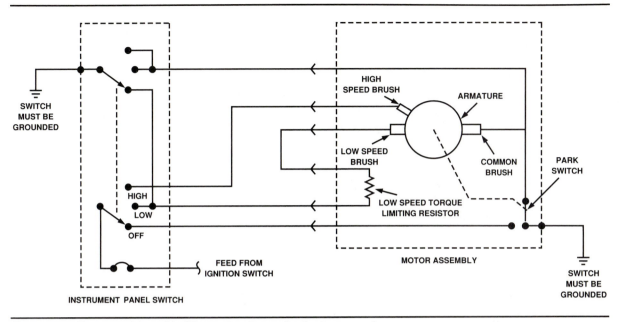

Figure 3-17. Two-speed fan with different brush sets for the two speeds.

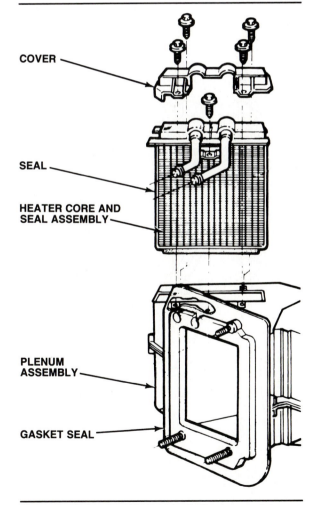

Figure 3-18. The heater core is similar to a radiator, but is mounted within the heater ductwork.

Heater control valves

A heater control valve (sometimes called the coolant control valve or the water control valve) controls the rate of coolant flow through the heater core. The valve is on the heater inlet hose and may be located near the engine, in the heater case, or on the fenderwell. The valve works much like a faucet or petcock except that it can be controlled by cables, vacuum, or an electric solenoid.

The cable-operated heater control valve, figure 3-19, is controlled from the passenger compartment by a wire cable. When the driver slides or rotates the temperature control switch, the motion is relayed directly to the valve by the wire. This method works unless the valve sticks or the cable binds. If that happens the extra force needed to move the temperature control lever can break the mechanism.

The vacuum-operated heater control valve, figure 3-20, depends upon a vacuum motor modulated by intake manifold vacuum to change the position of the valve. While these valves are more expensive to manufacture, they operate more smoothly than the cable type, and a friction-prone cable is eliminated. Vacuum motors are discussed in depth in the next chapter.

Rheostat: A continuously-variable resistor used to control current.

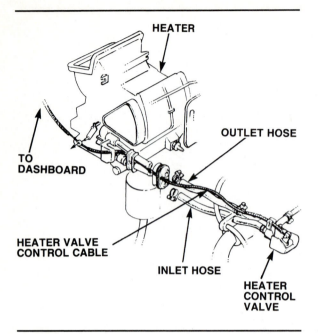

Figure 3-19. The manually operated heater control valve is controlled from the dashboard by a cable.

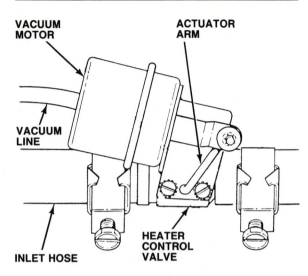

Figure 3-20. The vacuum-operated heater control valve is controlled by a vacuum motor.

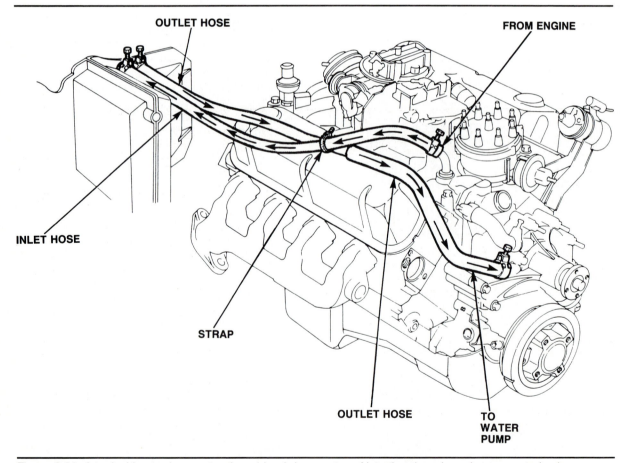

Figure 3-21. A typical heater hose setup for a blend door system. Note that there is no heater control valve.

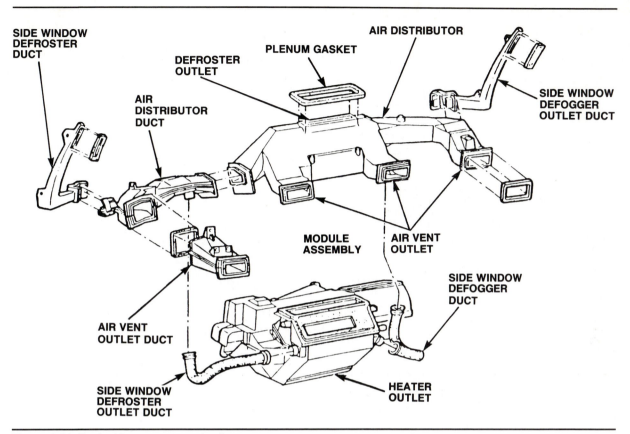

Figure 3-22. Typical heater system ducting.

Heater control valves that are opened and closed by an electric current activating an electromagnet are sometimes used. Electric heater control valves are uncommon, but they offer an advantage over vacuum systems in that they cannot develop a vacuum leak.

Heater hoses
Heater hoses are used to conduct coolant from the engine to the heater core and the control valve, figure 3-21. These hoses must withstand the heat of the coolant and the heat of the engine compartment. They also must be able to resist oil, gasoline, and vibration.

The most common type of heater hose is made of neoprene-type materials with reinforcing cords built into the hose parallel to the length of the hose. Premium quality hose or metal pipes are used in systems where the hose is routed near the exhaust manifold. Premium hose is manufactured with an extra braided nylon outer sheath.

Ducting and doors
The ducting system of the automobile directs the flow of heated, cooled, or vented air to various outlets within the passenger compartment. In the past, ducting was made of corrugated, foil-covered paper tubing. Modern ducting consists of molded, glass-impregnated plastics.

The flow rate or heat of the incoming air is regulated by doors mounted at the intake ends of the ductwork, figure 3-22. These doors are controlled by vacuum, electricity, or cables, and will be covered in detail in Chapter 4. Because they can be moved to the closed position to block airflow, some trade manuals refer to the doors as "defroster valves" or "vent valves." At the outlet ends of the ducts are grilles through which the air must pass. These plastic grilles generally have slats that can be moved to direct the flow of air away from or toward the occupants without restricting the flow.

The plenum chamber
The largest piece of ductwork is called the heater vent module, or heater case assembly, figure 3-23. This assembly is the mounting place for the heater core, the blend door, and the various vent doors and registers that determine the destination of the air.

The heater case assembly forms a plenum chamber. A plenum is a box or other similarly shaped structure through which a fluid passes, such as the plenum chamber beneath multiple

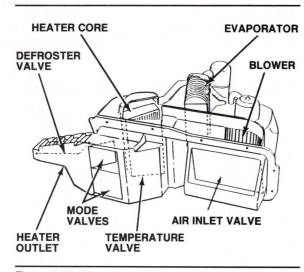

Figure 3-23. Heater vent module or heater plenum.

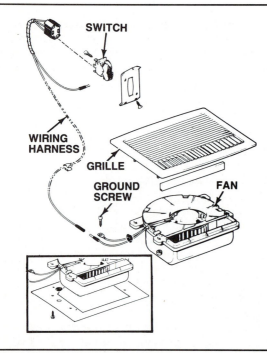

Figure 3-24. Some older cars used a defogger fan to blow air at the inside of the rear window.

Figure 3-25. Electric grid defroster in the rear window.

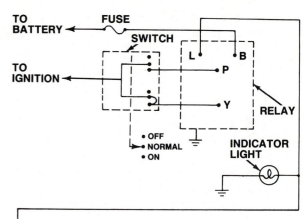

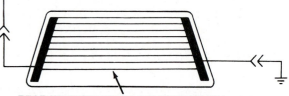

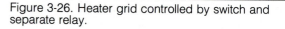

Figure 3-26. Heater grid controlled by switch and separate relay.

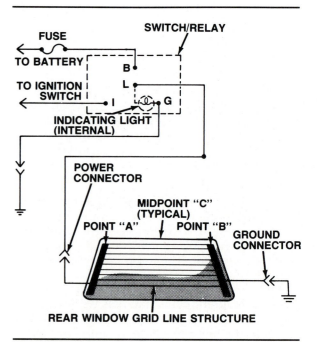

Figure 3-27. Heater grid controlled by combination switch-relay.

carburetors, where air-fuel charges from the different carbs are mixed. The air enters from the cowl air intake. While the air is in the plenum chamber, heat may be added from the heater core or withdrawn by the evaporator core. After the air is processed in the plenum, it is distributed through ductwork to the various parts of the passenger compartment.

The position of the internal doors in the plenum are controlled by cables, vacuum motors, or electrically operated motors and solenoids.

DEFROSTERS AND HEATED WINDSHIELDS

So far we have discussed the fan-type defroster system that is part of the heating system. However, there are two other types of defrosters. Technically, neither of these is part of an automotive HVAC system, but they still are important. They are the fan-type rear window defogger, and the electrical grid defroster bonded to or imbedded inside the window glass.

Rear Window Defogger and Defroster

Some older vehicles have a rear window defogger, figure 3-24, with a motor-driven fan similar to that used in the heating system but mounted behind the rear seat near the rear window. The driver controls it with a switch that routes motor current through circuits of varying resistance, like the heater blower discussed earlier. Heat is provided electrically by a length of resistance wire in the defogger unit. The resistance wire is connected in parallel with the motor so that it heats when the

■ **From Front To Back**

This early air conditioning system, on a 1953 Oldsmobile, used most of the familiar features of a modern system. The arrangement, however, was novel. The air intakes were scoops in each rear fin. There was an outlet above each door in the ceiling panel for the air-

conditioned air, and return air inlets just below the rear window. The system used the heater's 2-speed blower. The blower was not part of the air conditioning system, so it merely moved the air backward through the car to the return air inlets.

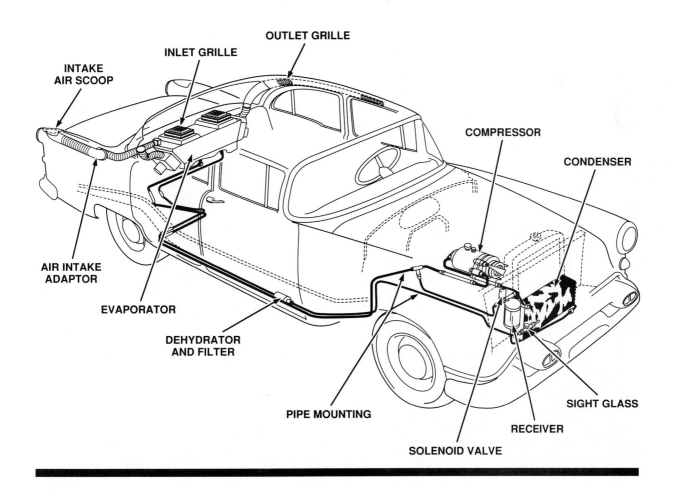

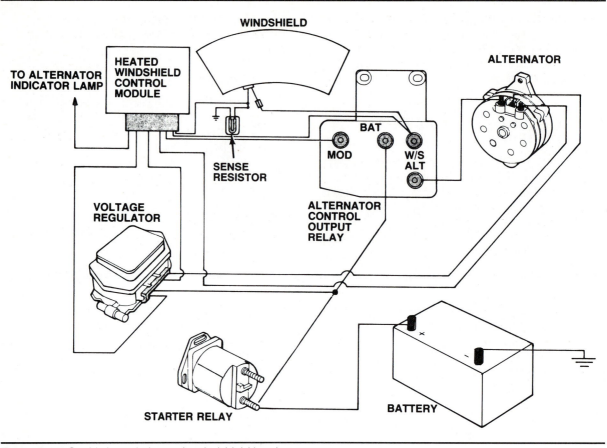

Figure 3-28. Sophisticated electronic windshield-heating system.

motor is running at either high or low speed.

Many newer vehicles have a defroster in the rear window. A defroster is a grid of electrical heating conductors that is bonded to the rear window glass, figure 3-25. The defroster grid is sometimes called a defogger. Current through the grid may be controlled by a separate switch and a relay, figure 3-26, or by a switch-relay combination, figure 3-27.

Most newer models have a **solid-state** timing module that switches the defroster current off automatically. In a modern Climate Control system, this often is controlled by the computer.

Heated Windshields

Some late-model cars have a front windshield containing a conductive material that can be heated to rapidly melt frost and ice. The standard 3-layer laminated windshield has a silver and zinc oxide layer applied to the back of the outer glass layer, to form an electrical conductor within the windshield. Silver buss bars at the top and bottom of the windshield connect the conductive layer to the power and the

ground circuits. We will cover the operation of a system manufactured by Ford to explain the operation of a fairly sophisticated heated windshield system. Figure 3-28 shows the components of this system:

- Conductive windshield
- Alternator output relay
- Control module
- ON/OFF switch
- Sensing resistor.

Before the heated windshield will operate, the system must be on, the engine must be running, and the interior temperature of the vehicle must be under 40°F (4°C).

The control module contains a **thermistor**, or temperature-sensitive resistor, to sense in-car temperature and to prevent system operation when the temperature exceeds 40°F (4°C). It also contains a timing function to limit system operation to 4-minute cycles. When the three operational conditions are met, the module signals the driver by turning on an indicator lamp. At the same time, it turns off the charging system voltage regulator and switches the alternator output from the car's electrical sys-

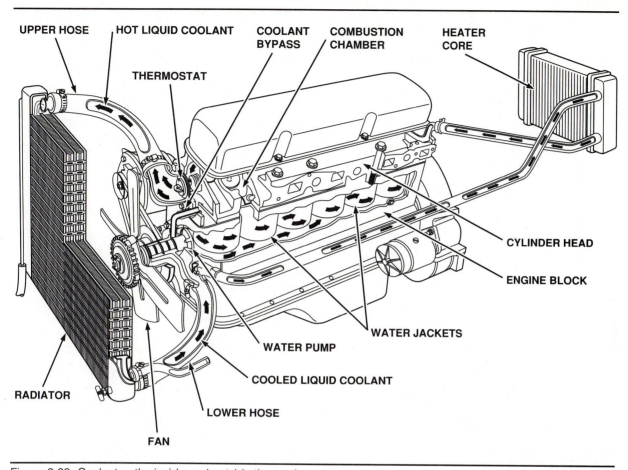

UPPER HOSE   HOT LIQUID COOLANT   COOLANT   COMBUSTION   HEATER
                                   BYPASS   CHAMBER   CORE

THERMOSTAT

CYLINDER HEAD

ENGINE BLOCK

WATER JACKETS

WATER PUMP

COOLED LIQUID COOLANT

RADIATOR

LOWER HOSE

FAN

Figure 3-29. Coolant paths inside and outside the engine.

tem to the windshield power circuit to energize the power relay, then turns the regulator back on to restore alternator output. This connects the windshield power circuit to the alternator output terminal through the power relay.

Once the engine is running and the battery is disconnected from the starting circuit, alternator output drops to about 12 volts. Sensing this drop, the voltage regulator causes the alternator to produce its maximum output, from 30 to 70 volts, depending upon engine rpm. The control module prevents alternator output from exceeding 70 volts. While the system is operating, the module also monitors battery voltage. If the battery voltage drops below 11 volts, the module denies power to the power relay and reconnects the car's electrical system to the alternator.

The heated windshield module is also linked to the engine computer by the same wiring that transmits the air conditioning compressor ON signal. If the windshield system is turned on and the vehicle is not in gear, the windshield module signals the engine computer to increase engine speed to about 1,400 rpm, ensuring enough output from the alternator. Once the vehicle is shifted into gear, the engine computer resumes its normal idle speed control function. Since they are both carried on the same circuitry, an air conditioning signal will override a heated windshield signal if they occur at the same time.

A sensing resistor connected to the module prevents system operation with a cracked or damaged windshield. The module monitors the voltage across a resistor and shuts off the system if it detects a voltage drop. A 15-ampere fuse in the fuse panel protects the low-voltage control circuit; a fusible link at the

Solid-State: In electronics, consisting chiefly of semiconductor devices and related components.

Thermistor: An electronic component whose resistance to electric current changes rapidly and predictably as its temperature changes.

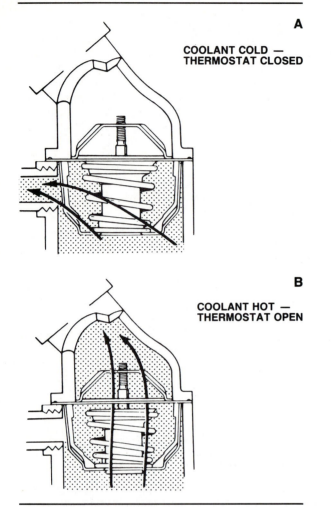

A

**COOLANT COLD —
THERMOSTAT CLOSED**

B

**COOLANT HOT —
THERMOSTAT OPEN**

Figure 3-30. With a cold engine, the thermostat stays closed (A). As the engine is warmed, the thermostat opens (B).

alternator output control relay protects the high-voltage power circuit.

Heated windshields draw a great deal of electric current. To avoid overloading the charging system, manufacturers sometimes install a second alternator, which provides current only to the windshield heater.

THE ENGINE COOLING SYSTEM

When the air-fuel mixture in a combustion chamber burns, the cylinder temperature can soar to 6,000°F (3300°C). During the complete 4-stroke cycle, the average temperature is about 1,500°F (800°C). Only about one-quarter to one-third of this heat energy is turned into mechanical energy by the engine. The remaining heat must be removed by other means to maintain engine efficiency and prevent overheating.

About half of this waste heat remains in the combustion gases, and is removed through the exhaust system. The other half of this waste heat energy is absorbed by the metal of the engine block, which is then cooled by the cooling system. The engine cooling system, in turn, can recycle much of this waste heat through the passenger compartment heating system.

Proper operation of the cooling system is essential. If the excess heat is allowed to build up in the engine, then:

• Engine oil temperature will rise, reducing viscosity and engine lubrication, and decomposing the oil.
• The incoming air-fuel mixture will become too hot and reduce engine efficiency.
• Excessive cylinder head temperatures can cause damaging pre-ignition or detonation.
• Metal engine parts can expand to the point of damage, seizure, or total engine failure.

Operation of the Cooling System

The liquid coolant is constantly circulated through the engine, and absorbs heat from the metal engine castings. The coolant is then circulated outside the engine into a radiator, which is exposed to the air stream. The passing air absorbs the heat from the coolant, and the coolant is returned to the engine to repeat the cycle. The greater the temperature difference between the coolant and the air stream, the more heat the air can absorb, and the more efficient the system becomes.

There are two flow paths for the coolant. Outside the engine, coolant circulates through hoses and the radiator, figure 3-29. Inside the engine, coolant circulates through the pump and the water jacket passages. To keep the engine running within an optimum temperature range, coolant flow is distributed between these two paths. The distribution is controlled by the thermostat, a temperature-sensitive valve that regulates coolant flow within the engine and the radiator circuits.

When the engine is cold, it must be warmed quickly to its ideal operating temperature. To speed the warm-up, the thermostat stays closed when the coolant is cold, figure 3-30, position A. This prevents the coolant from circulating through the radiator. Instead, the water pump pushes it through a passage that bypasses the radiator hose inlet, and returns it to the engine.

When the engine is warmed up, the thermostat opens, and coolant circulates through the radiator, figure 3-30, position B. This removes much of the heat energy from the coolant before it circulates back through the engine. The

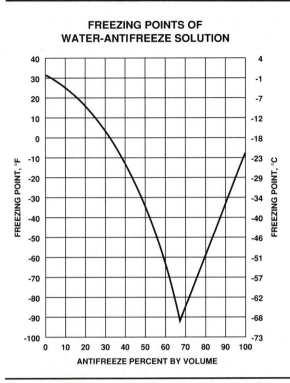

FREEZING POINTS OF WATER-ANTIFREEZE SOLUTION

Figure 3-31. Up to a concentration of 68 percent, adding antifreeze extends the lower temperature limit of engine coolant by protecting against freezing.

system may be designed so that the thermostat also seals the bypass circuit when it opens, forcing all the coolant to flow into the radiator.

Engine Coolant

Early cooling systems used plain water as engine coolant. With its high specific heat and thermal conductivity, plain water can transfer heat quite well. However, it has disadvantages when used in a cooling system:

• Iron, steel, and aluminum engine parts react with water to form rust and corrosion, which weaken parts, clog water jackets, and slow heat transfer from the coolant to the engine castings.
• Using hard water introduces minerals to the cooling system, which clogs water jackets with thick scale deposits, and also reduces heat transfer.
• When the car is not running and the system is not pressurized, water will freeze at its normal freezing point of 32°F (0°C). The expansion of water as it freezes can crack radiators, fittings, and even engine blocks.

To prevent freezing and retard development of rust and scale, early motorists added many substances to the water in their cooling systems. Many of these did work, but had various

drawbacks. Salt, calcium chloride, and soda were used as antifreezes, but formed acids in the coolant and corroded the engine and radiator. Adding sugar or honey to the cooling system also prevented freezing, but only at concentrations so high that the syrup was difficult to circulate through the engine. Kerosine and engine oil were sometimes used because of their low freezing points, but were flammable and caused the rubber hoses to deteriorate.

Methanol (wood alcohol) or ethanol (grain alcohol) were much more successful. Alcohols work well as antifreezes; a 50/50 mixture of either methanol or ethanol will protect against freezing to –20°F (–29°C). However, alcohols boil at lower temperatures than water and will therefore evaporate from the engine fairly quickly. To maintain freeze protection, the alcohol concentration must be tested periodically and enough fresh alcohol added to bring the protection up to the necessary level.

At one time, glycerine was also popular for use in cooling systems, as the first "permanent antifreeze" (permanent in that it did not evaporate like the alcohols). Concentrated glycerine boils at 227°F (108°C), and a 50/50 mixture protected against freezing as well as alcohol. Glycerine antifreezes were marketed partially diluted with water and with added corrosion inhibitors.

Modern cooling systems use a mixture of water and a permanent **ethylene glycol** antifreeze, producing a much better coolant than either water or antifreeze alone. Commercially-available antifreezes are about 96 percent pure ethylene glycol, 2 percent added water, and 2 percent additives. Ethylene glycol does not transfer heat as well as water, but the greater temperature range within which an ethylene glycol-water mixture remains a liquid more than makes up for this disadvantage.

Concentrated ethylene glycol freezes at about –8°F (–22°C), but a 50/50 mix of ethylene glycol and water resists freezing down to a temperature of –34°F (–37°C), figure 3-31. Maximum protection against freezing is given by a solution of 68 percent antifreeze. Concentrating the antifreeze any more than this causes the coolant freezing point to rise, instead of fall. The freezing protection of concen-

Ethylene Glycol: A chemical compound that forms a good engine coolant when mixed with water, increasing the coolant's resistance to both freezing and boilover.

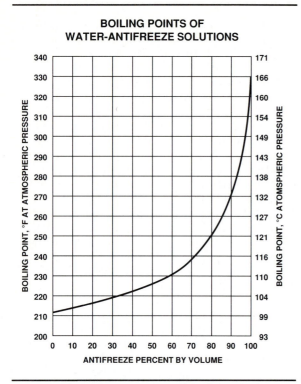

Figure 3-32. Adding antifreeze also extends the upper working temperature limit of engine coolant by protecting against boiling, even without a radiator pressure cap.

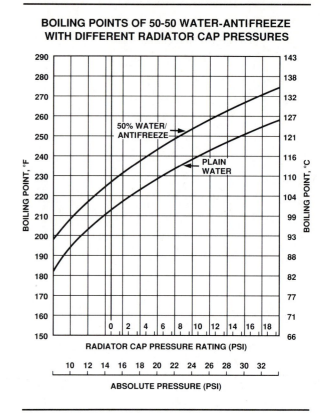

Figure 3-33. Pressurizing the cooling system provides protection against boilover for both water and antifreeze-based engine coolant.

trated, 100% antifreeze is no better than that of a 35-percent solution in water.

Because of the high temperature at which antifreeze vaporizes, mixing it with water in the coolant also protects against coolant boilover. Boiling is harmful because the gases form steam pockets in the water jacket. Steam in the cooling system absorbs much less heat than liquid, so localized hot spots form that can warp or crack castings. In addition, steam pressure forces coolant out of the radiator, reducing efficiency even further. A cooling system filled with water and ethylene glycol resists boiling to significantly higher temperatures than one filled with plain water. Concentrated antifreeze boils at 330°F (165°C), and a 50/50 mix resists boiling up to 226°F (108°C), figure 3-32. Pressurizing the system with a sealed radiator cap improves the system further, figure 3-33. In fact, many modern temperature warning lamps are calibrated for high coolant temperatures obtainable only with antifreeze-based coolant. Plain water used with these systems can boil without activating the warning light.

Antifreeze usually contains rust inhibitors, antifoaming agents, and sometimes water-soluble lubricants. It may also contain small

particles designed to seal minor leaks in the cooling system.

Although 50 percent antifreeze is the industry standard, some manufacturers recommend only a 33-percent solution or less. Less than a 50-percent solution protects from freezing but does not give the corrosion protection available with a 50-percent solution.

Cooling System Components

Most automotive engines use a liquid cooling system. A typical system, figure 3-34, includes the:

- Radiator
- Engine cooling fan
- Radiator pressure cap
- Coolant recovery tank
- Water pump
- Thermostat
- Water jacket
- Thermostat-controlled bypass
- Core plugs, or freeze plugs
- Coolant hoses
- Coolant recovery system.

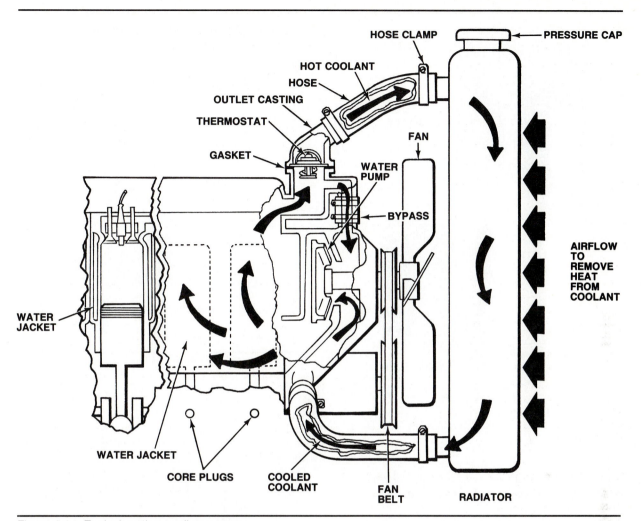

HOSE CLAMP — PRESSURE CAP

HOT COOLANT

HOSE

OUTLET CASTING

THERMOSTAT

GASKET

FAN

WATER PUMP

BYPASS

AIRFLOW TO REMOVE HEAT FROM COOLANT

WATER JACKET

WATER JACKET

CORE PLUGS

COOLED COOLANT

FAN BELT

RADIATOR

Figure 3-34. Typical engine cooling system.

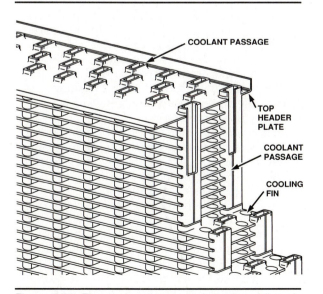

COOLANT PASSAGE

TOP HEADER PLATE

COOLANT PASSAGE

COOLING FIN

Figure 3-35. The coolant passages (tubes) and fins of the radiator core.

The radiator

The radiator is a heat exchanger. It absorbs heat from the hot coolant exiting the engine and transfers it to the cooling air stream passing through the radiator. Its efficiency is fairly high because it exposes a large amount of surface area to the surrounding air.

Radiator cores are made of thin metal tubes, usually copper, bronze, or aluminum, with cooling fins attached, figure 3-35. Coolant flows through the tubes and transfers its heat to the radiator metal. The air flowing past the radiator tubes and fins absorbs this heat. The number of tubes and fins in a radiator, and their condition, determine the unit's heat-transferring capacity.

To keep a steady stream of coolant flowing into and out of the core, two large reservoirs called header tanks are connected to opposite ends of the tubes. Header tanks are usually

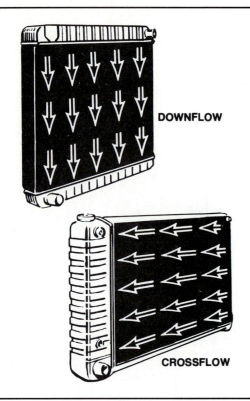

Figure 3-36. Older cars usually have downflow radiators. Crossflow radiators permit lower hoodlines for styling reasons.

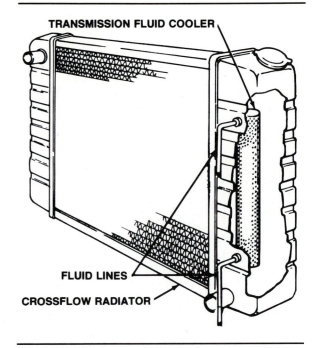

Figure 3-37. The transmission fluid cooler is installed in one of the radiator tanks.

constructed from brass, copper, and aluminum, but some modern header tanks are molded plastic.

There are two styles of radiator construction:

• Downflow radiators, figure 3-36, have vertical tubes and tanks at the top and bottom of the core.
• Crossflow radiators, figure 3-36, have horizontal tubes and a tank on either side of the core. These generally are wider and shorter than the downflow type.

Most radiators are fitted with a draincock at or near the bottom. This faucet-like fitting is used to drain the cooling system for periodic maintenance. Radiators without a draincock must be drained by removing the lower radiator hose.

On vehicles with automatic transmissions, one of the header tanks usually contains a transmission oil cooler, figure 3-37. The pump in the transmission forces hot transmission fluid through the lines and into the coil in the outlet tank. Waste heat from the transmission is absorbed by the coolant surrounding the coil, and the cooled fluid is then returned to the transmission.

The radiator fan

At highway speeds, airflow through an unobstructed radiator is usually great enough to absorb excess engine heat. Unfortunately, driving conditions and vehicle designs are not always so ideal. Automobiles must also endure stop-and-go driving in hot weather, with hills, towing, and air conditioning each adding to the heat load the radiator is expected to dissipate.

To increase the airflow through the radiator when the vehicle is not moving, manufacturers mount a fan in front of or behind it to force a stream of air through the core, figure 3-38. Until the advent of front-wheel-drive (FWD) cars, the fan was usually mounted on the same shaft as the water pump impeller, and was driven by the same belt.

Electric fans have become more common in recent years because of the flexibility they offer in automobile design, figure 3-39. Transverse engines in FWD vehicles cannot be connected directly to a radiator fan if the radiator is installed in front, behind the grille. Electric fans, however, can be mounted to the radiator wherever it is located. Another advantage of the electric fan is that it can be controlled directly with a thermostat. Whenever a sensor detects heat above a certain level in the radiator, it can switch on the fan. The fan need only run until the temperature is reduced below the desired level.

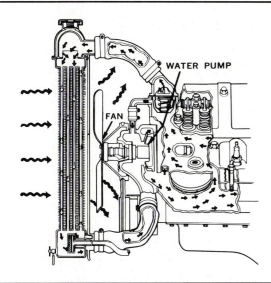

Figure 3-38. The engine-driven fan draws air into the engine compartment through the radiator core.

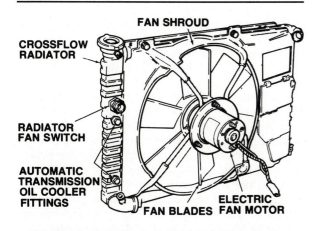

Figure 3-39. Electric fans can be mounted directly to the radiator or its shroud.

Typically, an electric fan is not disabled by turning off the ignition key. These fans can and will switch on if the sensor detects a high enough temperature. This can happen even though the vehicle has been turned off and the engine is not running. Technicians should temporarily disconnect the power lead to the fan when working in that area, figure 3-40. Be sure to reconnect it when the service work has been completed.

The simplest fans have rigid blades. These work quite well when used with the thermostatic controls, but on conventional belt-driven fans they are noisy and absorb a measurable amount of engine horsepower at higher speeds. To increase fuel economy and decrease noise, manufacturers have developed several alternative designs.

Figure 3-40. Always disconnect the power lead to an electric fan before working near it.

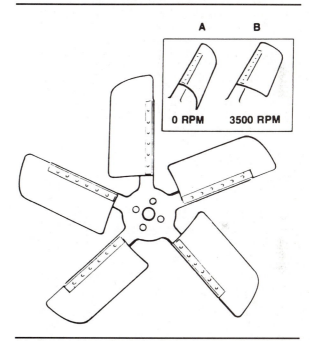

Figure 3-41. The flexible blades of this fan change shape to reduce drag as the engine speed increases.

The most basic of these is the flex-blade fan, figure 3-41. At low rotational speeds, the curve

■ **One Firebird, Two Fans**

The 1987 Pontiac Firebird with the V-8 engine has two radiator fans. The electronic control module (ECM) controls the driver-side fan. It turns on the fan at under 35 mph if the air conditioning is turned on or if the coolant reaches 226°F (108°C). At speeds greater than 35 mph, the fan responds only to coolant temperature. The passenger-side fan is controlled by a coolant temperature switch between cylinders 6 and 8, but does not respond to the AC load. It turns on the fan if the coolant temperature reaches 238°F (114°C).

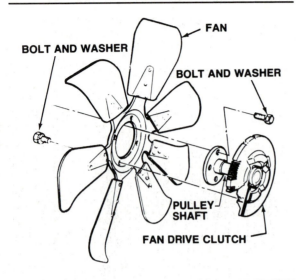

Figure 3-42. Clutch fans have a fluid-drive that controls the speed of rotation.

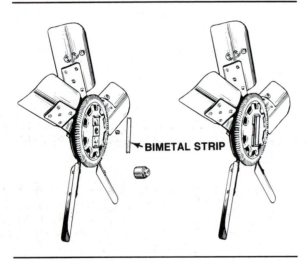

Figure 3-43. The bimetallic temperature sensor spring controls the amount of silicone that is allowed into the drive which, in turn, controls the speed of the fan.

of the fan blades pulls air through the radiator core. As fan speed increases, the resistance of the air flattens the blades slightly, and the fan requires less horsepower to turn than one with rigid blades. Although this also reduces the amount of air the fan can move with each rotation, both the fan and the vehicle itself are moving fast enough to maintain a strong airstream through the radiator.

Another way to avoid power loss and excess noise is the clutch fan, or fluid-drive fan, figure 3-42. This device allows the fan to rotate fast enough when needed to keep the engine cool, but slips when not needed to prevent wasting power.

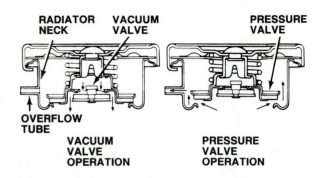

Figure 3-44. Radiator caps used in pressurized systems have two valves that keep system pressure between upper and lower limits. An additional gasket is used in systems with coolant recovery tanks.

There are two types of fan clutches:

• Centrifugal type
• Thermostatic type.

Both types use a silicone-fluid coupling much like a torque converter. Above a certain speed, the torque required to rotate the fan exceeds the amount that the viscous fluid coupling can transfer without slipping. The fan then slips harmlessly.

The centrifugal-type fan clutch uses **centrifugal force** to engage and disengage the fluid coupling. The thermostatic-type fan clutch depends upon a **bimetallic temperature sensor** spring attached to a valve controlling the flow of silicone, figure 3-43. When the air flowing through the radiator is warm, the spring permits more fluid to enter the coupling. This causes the fan to spin to a higher speed, closer to that of the water pump pulley, drawing more air in through the radiator. When the airflow is cool, the spring retracts the valve and allows greater slippage of the fan.

Radiator pressure cap

As explained in Chapter 2, the temperature at which a liquid boils depends on the nature of the liquid and the pressure applied to it. To raise the boiling point and thus obtain greater thermal capacity from the vehicle cooling system, the system is kept sealed and pressurized. The pressure comes from the expansion of the coolant as it warms.

The radiator cap must keep the system pressurized, vent any excess pressure, and allow atmospheric pressure to re-enter the system as the coolant cools and contracts after the engine is shut off. The cap, figure 3-44, contains two valves. A pressure relief valve allows the pressure in the system to rise 7 to 18 psi (88 to 124 kPa) above normal atmospheric pressure before the coolant is allowed to escape. This can

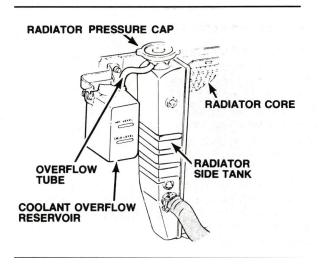

Figure 3-45. Most radiator caps are mounted on one of the radiator header tanks.

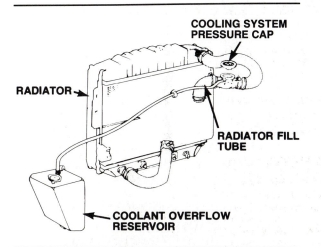

Figure 3-46. Some radiator caps are mounted away from the radiator to lower the radiator profile.

raise the temperature at which the coolant boils to 260°F (127°C) or more. The vacuum valve allows outside air to enter the system when the engine cools. These pressure caps are usually on the top or side tank, figure 3-45, but occasionally can be found in unusual locations such as on a special hose section, figure 3-46.

Radiator caps designed for use with coolant recovery systems have an extra gasket inside the sealing lip to create a vacuum seal. These are discussed more fully with coolant recovery systems.

Water pump
The water pump uses centrifugal force to circulate the coolant. It consists of a fan-shaped impeller, figure 3-47, set in a round chamber with curved inlet and outlet passages. The

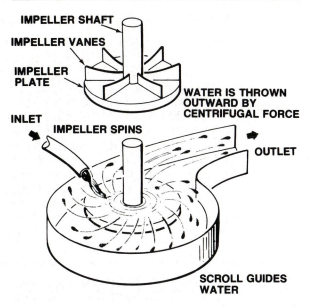

Figure 3-47. The water pump impeller is driven by the engine. Its spinning blades apply centrifugal force to move the engine coolant.

chamber is called a scroll because of these curved areas. The impeller, figure 3-48, is driven by a belt from the crankshaft pulley and

Centrifugal Force: The natural tendency of objects, when forced to move in a curved path, to move away from the center of rotation.

Bimetallic Temperature Sensor: A device that uses two strips of different metals welded together. When heated, one side will expand more than the other, causing the strip to bend, which makes or breaks a pair of contact points.

■ **Hupmobile Leads The Way**

We take them for granted now, but when the sealed radiator cap was first introduced, it was Big News. In 1934, the Hup Motor Car Corp. of Michigan, called it "the most important change since the advent of the water pump" when it installed the new caps on the Hupmobile Sedan, Coupe, and top-of-the-line Victoria.

The sealed radiator caps were set to release at 3.5 psi (24.1 kPa). This, coupled with a sealed radiator overflow pipe, eliminated a vacuum within the system and raised the boiling point to about 225°F (107°C). Engineers had discovered that this minor change led to reduced water loss, quicker engine warm-up, and less loss of antifreeze.

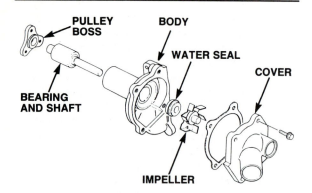

Figure 3-48. Exploded view of a typical water pump mounted behind the crankshaft pulley.

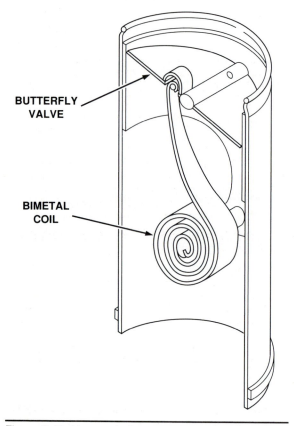

Figure 3-49. Very early thermostats used a bimetallic spring coil spliced into the radiator hose.

spins within the scroll. Coolant from the radiator or bypass enters the inlet and is picked up by the impeller blades. Centrifugal force flings the coolant outward, and the scroll walls direct it to the outlet passage and the engine. Because the water pump is driven by the engine, coolant circulates whenever the engine is running.

Figure 3-50. Aneroid-bellows thermostats cannot be used in modern pressurized cooling systems because the bellows would respond to system pressure as well as temperature.

Modern water pumps require so little attention that they are easy to neglect. Centrifugal pumps are inefficient unless they spin rapidly and evenly, so worn or loose drive belts will cause poor cooling performance. Early water pumps required periodic lubrication, but modern pumps are lubricated for life at the factory. The pump shaft is sealed to prevent coolant from leaking into and past the bearings.

Thermostats
The **thermostat** is a temperature-sensitive valve that regulates the flow of coolant between the engine and the radiator. When the coolant is cold, the thermostat is completely closed. The coolant circulates through the water jacket and bypass circuit, and not the radiator. This permits the engine to warm up rapidly. As the coolant temperature rises, the thermostat opens and the coolant is directed into the radiator to be cooled. When coolant temperature falls, the thermostat closes slightly, and decreases the flow of coolant through the radiator. The thermostat's position varies during normal operation, but it is rarely open completely. Operating conditions that could open the thermostat completely include long uphill climbs, idling in heavy traffic, extremely hot days, or selection of a thermostat with too low a temperature rating for the engine.

The earliest thermostats used a simple bimetallic spring coil to control a butterfly valve regulating the rate of coolant flow through the radiator, figure 3-49. These early thermostats were a great improvement, but were vulnerable to corrosion. A much more rugged design incorporated an **aneroid bellows**, figure 3-50. The bellows was composed of thin metal and contained a small amount of volatile liquid, such as alcohol. An internal vacuum held the bellows closed when cold. As the coolant warmed, the liquid inside the bellows vapor-

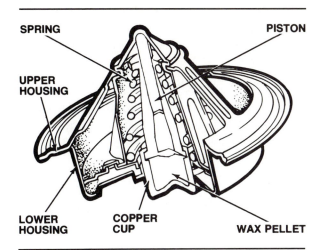

Figure 3-51. A cross section of a wax-actuated thermostat.

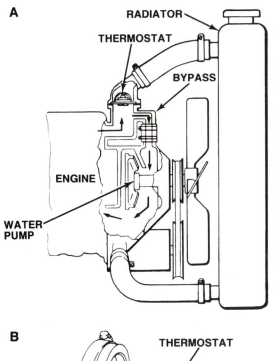

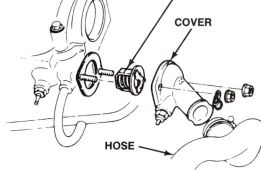

Figure 3-52. Typical thermostat locations.

ized, increasing the internal pressure and expanding the bellows. The expanding bellows opened a valve, admitting coolant into the radiator circuit. These thermostats functioned quite well in the open, unpressurized systems for which they were designed. They are not suitable for use in modern sealed systems with a pressure radiator cap because cooling system pressure counters the internal vapor pressure, and tends to hold them closed as the coolant warms.

All late-model thermostats are wax-actuated, figure 3-51. A sealed chamber in the thermostat is filled with wax that is solid when cold, but melts and expands when heated. When the wax is cold, a spring holds the thermostat closed. As the coolant temperature nears the thermostat rating, the wax melts and expands, overcoming spring tension to open the thermostat. This type of thermostat will work consistently under different system pressures.

Most thermostats are mounted in a metal housing at the top of the engine, figure 3-52. Thermostats are available with different opening temperatures. Common settings are in the range of 180° to 195°F (82° to 90°C). Thermostats should be fully open at 20 degrees Fahrenheit (11 degrees Celsius) higher than their rated temperature. Replacement thermostats must have the correct opening temperature for the system to work correctly. Selecting one

Thermostat: A device that automatically responds to temperature changes in order to activate a switch or regulate a valve.

Aneroid Bellows: A temperature sensor with accordion-shaped pleats in its surface, containing a small amount of volatile liquid. Temperature changes cause the bellows to expand or contract, as more or less of the liquid inside vaporizes.

■ **Thermostat By Wire**

If the cooling system thermostat is recessed into the water outlet casting, sometimes it can be tough to keep it in place when reinstalling the outlet. To make it easier, thread a piece of stiff wire through the outlet casting, through the leg openings in the thermostat, and then back through the outlet. By pulling on the wire ends, you can hold the thermostat in place while reattaching the outlet casting. Remove the wire before installing the hose.

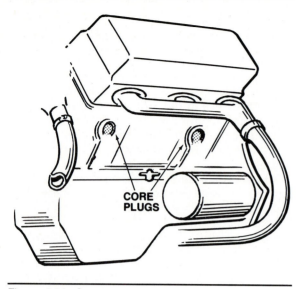

Figure 3-53. Core plugs are pressed into holes in the cylinder block.

rated at too low a temperature prevents the engine from warming up completely, and can cause poor gas mileage, reduced engine performance, sludge formation in the crankcase, and severe engine wear. A thermostat with too high a setting may cause various problems including engine ping or detonation, increased oil consumption, and reduced engine life.

Thermostats can be damaged by the corrosion and scale that builds up in the cooling system. This material will cling to the central plunger of the thermostat, causing erratic and sticky valve movement. A thermostat that sticks shut can cause serious engine damage by allowing the engine to overheat. A thermostat that has stuck open prevents the engine from warming up, and causes reduced engine performance as well as preventing normal operation of the heater/defroster.

The thermostat must never be left out of the cooling system after service. Without the thermostat, coolant temperature is regulated only by the overall efficiency of the cooling system, and the engine will likely never reach normal operating temperature. In addition, designers position coolant passages in the engine — such as the bypass circuit — to work properly with a thermostat in place. Running an engine without the thermostat can disrupt the correct coolant flow patterns and cause local overheating in the cylinder head, even though the coolant temperature gauge might indicate the coolant temperature to be too low. The correct thermostat maintains the engine within its most efficient operating range, ensures that engine temperature is even from place to

place, and permits coolant into the radiator only when engine temperature is high enough to require it.

Water jacket, core plugs, and thermostat bypass

Nearly all of the heat produced in an engine is the product of the combustion, or burning, of the fuel. Naturally, the hottest parts of an engine are those parts exposed to the burning fuel. Passages are designed into the block and cylinder head castings to allow the coolant to pass through areas near the exhaust valves, and combustion chambers. These coolant passages, when taken together, are called the water jacket.

Coolant enters and leaves the engine at the points where the radiator hoses attach. In some engines, water distribution tubes receive coolant at the front of the engine and distribute it near each valve seat. Holes in this tube allow all areas to receive equal amounts of coolant. Water jacket transfer holes between the block and the head are often different sizes to force incoming coolant toward the rear of the engine. The water jacket holes punched in the head gaskets are usually carefully sized to restrict coolant transfer at the front of the engine and force it toward the rear.

Core plugs, figure 3-53, sometimes incorrectly called freeze plugs, seal the holes used by the foundry to remove core sand from the inside of the block. These are round discs of sheet metal pressed into openings on the sides of the engine block, figure 3-54. These plugs may pop out if the coolant freezes, but they are not totally effective because frozen coolant also is likely to crack the block. The best way to prevent freeze damage is to use the correct amount of antifreeze in the coolant.

The thermostat bypass circuit permits coolant to flow through the water pump and back into the engine when the thermostat is closed. The bypass can be an external hose or a drilled or cast passageway within the engine or water pump body. In some designs, the thermostat closes the bypass circuit as it opens the passage to the radiator, forcing all the coolant through the radiator when the engine is warm. Other systems leave the bypass open, and split the flow between the bypass and the radiator circuits whenever the engine is running.

Some engines have a spring-loaded bypass circuit. When the cold engine is first started, the thermostat remains closed. Coolant pressure builds enough to open a spring-loaded bypass valve installed just below the thermostat. This allows the coolant to circulate

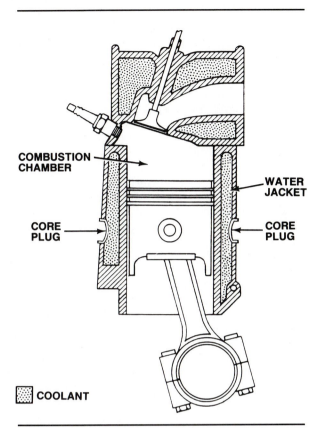

COMBUSTION CHAMBER

WATER JACKET

CORE PLUG

CORE PLUG

COOLANT

Figure 3-54. The core plugs seal the water jacket after the casting sand has been removed.

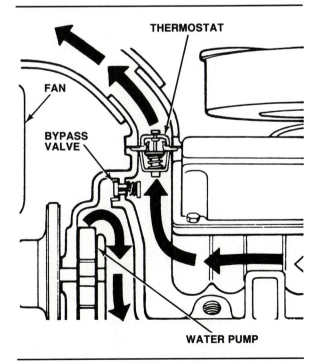

THERMOSTAT

FAN

BYPASS VALVE

WATER PUMP

Figure 3-55. Some engines use a spring-loaded bypass valve that opens under coolant pressure when the thermostat is closed.

through the bypass channel, figure 3-55, and back into the engine block. When the operating temperature is reached, the thermostat opens, and coolant circulates through the radiator.

Coolant recovery system
As the engine coolant warms, it expands. If the cooling system is completely filled with coolant, it will lift the pressure relief valve in the radiator cap and overflow onto the ground. In the past, this was prevented by leaving a large airspace in the radiator. Modern vehicles with crossflow radiators use a coolant recovery tank instead, and fill the radiator completely with coolant, figure 3-56.

A coolant recovery tank is a simple plastic reservoir, usually bolted to the firewall, connected to the radiator through the overflow

Core Plug: Also called a freeze plug. A shallow metal cup inserted into the engine block to seal holes left by manufacturing. These cups are designed to pop out if the coolant in the block freezes, but do not offer complete protection.

■ **Tracer Two-Stage Thermostat**

Over the years, several variations on the standard cooling system thermostat have been introduced. With the 1989 Mercury Tracer, Ford Motor Company has brought out another one. This is a two-stage unit that is said to provide better coolant temperature control with less fluctuation and quicker warm-up. This thermostat uses a small sub-valve in addition to the main valve. During cold weather operation, only the sub-valve opens to control engine coolant temperature in the range of 185° to 190°F (85° to 88°C). During warm weather operation, the main valve opens to permit increased coolant flow through the radiator, preventing coolant temperature from exceeding 190°F (88°C).

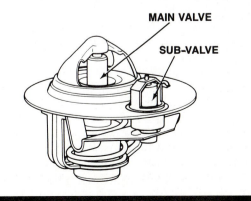

MAIN VALVE

SUB-VALVE

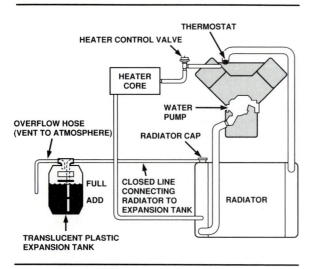

Figure 3-56. The coolant recovery system.

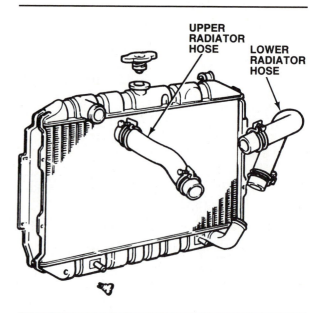

Figure 3-57. Radiator hoses must be large enough to carry the coolant when the thermostat is fully open.

tube, and kept about half full of coolant. The overflow tube leaves the radiator filler neck above the level of the relief valve, but below the outer sealing gasket. The tube enters the reservoir from the bottom, or through a cap with a plastic tube that extends to the bottom.

As the coolant in the radiator expands and pushes the relief valve in the radiator cap open, it flows through the overflow tube into the reservoir. When the engine is stopped and cools, the coolant in the radiator contracts and opens the vacuum valve. Instead of air, however, the vacuum valve siphons coolant through the overflow tube from the recovery tank, back into the radiator. Radiator caps designed for coolant recovery systems have an additional gasket that isolates the vacuum valve from the atmosphere. This is necessary to ensure that coolant is drawn back into the system from the tank, rather than air from outside the cap.

The coolant level in the recovery tank rises and falls with engine temperature, but the radiator and the engine cooling system are always kept completely full. By excluding air from the cooling system, rust formation and corrosion are greatly reduced. Keeping the air out of the cooling system also raises the thermal efficiency of the system by ensuring that air and foam are not circulated with the coolant, and prevents entrained air bubbles from eroding the water jackets.

Hoses and sensors
In addition to the major parts of the system, there are minor parts that are also important to the operation of the system. The upper and lower radiator hoses, figure 3-57, must be large

enough to handle the maximum flow of coolant occurring when the thermostat is fully open. The smaller heater hoses divert a portion of the coolant to and from the heater core.

Sensors that monitor the cooling system are an important control element used to provide information to the engine control computer. Most computerized engine controls read the coolant temperature sensor for information used to set the fuel-air ratio. These will be discussed in detail in Chapter 4.

Cooling Systems for Air-Cooled Engines

So far, the discussion of the cooling system has dealt only with liquid-cooled engines. The cooling system of an air-cooled engine, figure 3-58, is quite different in construction. Cooling fins are cast into the engine block, cylinders, and cylinder heads. A fan, driven by the engine, forces outside air through ductwork and over these fins to cool the engine. Typically, a bellows-style thermostat regulates engine compartment temperature by opening or closing additional air ducts, which raise or lower the rate at which cooling air passes through the engine compartment. The exhaust system also frequently contains heat exchangers to transfer heat from exhaust gases to a separate fan-driven heating circuit. In Volkswagens, these heat exchangers are constructed in one piece with the stamped steel covers surrounding the exhaust pipes, with internal finning to absorb

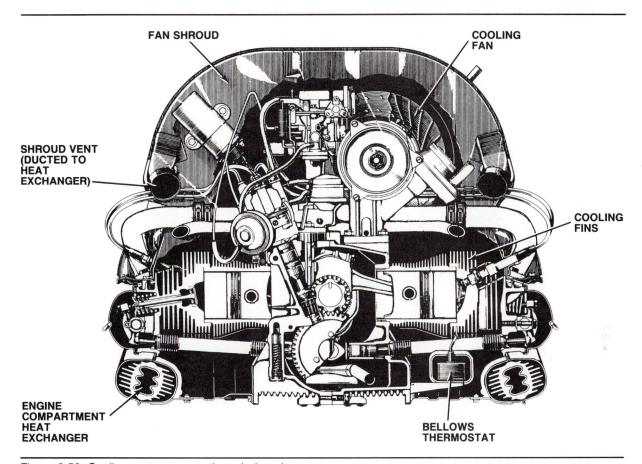

FAN SHROUD

COOLING FAN

SHROUD VENT (DUCTED TO HEAT EXCHANGER)

COOLING FINS

ENGINE COMPARTMENT HEAT EXCHANGER

BELLOWS THERMOSTAT

Figure 3-58. Cooling system on an air-cooled engine.

heat from the exhaust pipe. Air is blown over the fins and then transferred to the passenger compartment.

SUMMARY

A fresh air ventilation system is essential for passenger comfort and driver safety. It relies on a supply of fresh air provided by ram or fan-boosted intakes. Ram air is the air pushed into the intake vents by the forward motion of the car. Fan-boosted air is drawn in by the blower motor.

The heating system warms the windows and passenger compartment to ensure unobscured visibility and passenger comfort. In cars with liquid-cooled engines, some of the waste heat generated by the engine is carried by the coolant through the heater core and into the passenger compartment to warm the inside air. The temperature is regulated by controlling either the rate of coolant flow through the heater core (heater control valve system), or by mixing warmed air from the heater core ductwork

with unwarmed air (blend air system). Some systems combine the two methods. Heater control valves are controlled by vacuum, cables, or electricity, as are the blend doors that direct fan-boosted airflow.

The pressurized cooling system absorbs excess engine heat into the liquid coolant flowing through the water jacket in the engine castings. The water pump circulates the coolant, and coolant flow between the engine and the radiator is regulated by the wax-actuated thermostat on or near the engine block. The hot coolant flows through the radiator, which transfers the heat to the air stream moving through the radiator, and returns to the engine. Airflow is enhanced by an electric or engine-driven fan mounted between the engine and the radiator. The coolant expands as it warms, opening the radiator cap and venting the excess coolant into the recovery system. As the coolant cools, vacuum draws coolant back into the radiator from the coolant recovery tank.

Review Questions

Choose the single most correct answer.
Compare your answers with the correct answers on page 229.

1. Waste heat from combustion is removed from the engine through the:
   a. Heating system
   b. Water jacket
   c. Manifold
   d. Heater control valve

2. Air temperature regulation is accomplished by:
   a. Varying the ratio of heated air to unheated air
   b. Varying the flow of coolant through the radiator
   c. Changing the vent positions
   d. Combination of b and c

3. Controlling blower motor speed can be done by:
   a. Varying the electrical resistance at the switch
   b. Varying the electrical resistance at the motor
   c. Changing the number of windings in the motor
   d. All of the above

4. What is the *main* advantage of a pressurized cooling system in a vehicle?
   a. It lowers the boiling point of the coolant
   b. It raises the boiling point of the coolant
   c. It prevents evaporation of the coolant
   d. None of the above

5. Which of the following is *not* true of ethylene glycol antifreeze?
   a. It transfers heat better than water
   b. It remains a liquid through a wide temperature range
   c. It may contain additives
   d. Pure antifreeze freezes at 0°F (−18°C)

6. A radiator's ability to transfer heat depends on:
   a. The airflow past it
   b. The number of tubes and fins
   c. The condition of the tubes and fins
   d. All of the above

7. Which of these fans drains excessive engine power?
   a. Fluid-drive fan
   b. Electric fan
   c. Rigid-blade fan
   d. Clutch fan

8. Technician A says the engine thermostat is rarely open completely.
   Technician B says most late-model thermostats contain an aneroid bellows.
   Who is right?
   a. A only
   b. B only
   c. Both A and B
   d. Neither A nor B

9. Which of the following is *not* the job of the radiator cap?
   a. Pressurizes the system
   b. Vents excess pressure
   c. Allows atmospheric pressure to re-enter the system
   d. Opens under excessive temperatures

Ventilation and Heating Controls

No matter how efficient and versatile an automotive HVAC system is designed to be, it will not be used to its full potential if the controls are awkward or difficult to use. Control systems should be designed so that they are as simple and reliable as possible, and can be operated with minimal concentration from the driver. In this chapter, we will look at ventilation and heating control systems.

HVAC systems can be controlled through three basic types of systems:

- Manual
- Vacuum operated
- Electrically or electromagnetically operated.

With a manually operated system, the driver controls system operation directly, using slide switches or rotary knobs. In vacuum-operated or electrically operated systems, the driver moves a switch or knob to a given operating mode, and the switch or knob actuates remote vacuum or electrical devices that control the HVAC system components.

The components in a manually controlled system are mechanically operated by the driver. In spite of technological advances that enable engineers to build HVAC systems that practically run themselves, manual controls still are widely used in base-level cars because they are relatively inexpensive to manufacture.

Semiautomatic and fully automatic HVAC systems generally use a combination of vacuum-operated and electrical controls. In a semiautomatic system, many controls can operate without driver input. In a fully automatic system, the driver simply chooses a desired temperature. Sensors relay data about passenger compartment conditions to an automatic temperature control computer, which determines what the HVAC system must do to make those conditions match the driver's request. The computer then sends appropriate commands to the HVAC control devices.

This chapter explains the design and operation of the three types of HVAC controls. However, one element that is the same for all HVAC controls is the location of the driver-operated switches and knobs, so first we will take a look at this group of components, called the control head.

THE CONTROL HEAD

In the past, HVAC controls were simple, direct-operating devices, almost exclusively manually operated. Cowl and kick-panel ventilators were controlled by handles, levers and rods attached directly to the parts. Electrical switches that controlled the fan motors were

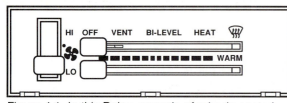

Figure 4-1. In this Delco example of a basic control head for manual heating and ventilation, all functions are mechanically controlled.

mounted to the heater housing, because that was where the fan was. Often a manual switch for the heater control valve was attached there as well. Gradually, these controls were centralized, both for convenience and styling. Both electrical switches and cable operated switches and controls were moved to the dashboard, first as individual units, and later mounted together.

All modern automotive heating, ventilation, and cooling systems use a **control head**, or control panel, figure 4-1, where the central controls are mounted. The control head usually is located in the center of the dashboard, within easy reach of the driver and the front-seat passenger, although it may be located to the left, accessible only to the driver. The exact appearance of the control head, as well as the assortment of controls mounted on it, varies from car to car. The control head illustrated in figure 4-1 is typical of those used in a basic blend-air HVAC system.

The Controls

The control head typically provides selector mechanisms or switches for:

- Blower motor control
- Temperature control
- Mode selection
- Fresh air or recirculated air selection
- Air conditioning control (if so equipped).

Blower control
The blower control is an electromechanical switch used to select the speed of the heater fan. Chapter 3 of this *Classroom Manual* discusses blower motor operation. Blower motors in older cars usually are 1- and 2-speed units, while those in newer cars may be 3-, 4-, or 5-speed or variable-speed units. The blower control switch may be a vertical or horizontal slide switch or a rotary-motion switch.

Some General Motors systems use a relay between the high switch position and the blower motor that limits the current passing through the control switch. Relays are discussed more thoroughly later in this chapter. Ford uses a **thermal limiter** in a resistor block,

with current flowing through the limiter at all blower speeds. If a faulty resistor block passes too much current, the temperature of the limiter rises. If the limiter reaches 100°F (38°C), it opens and turns off the blower motor. Blower motor speed resistors may be either remotely mounted or part of the switch at the control head. Remote resistor blocks generally are located in the HVAC airstream. This cools the resistors, which promotes a longer life for the unit.

Temperature control
The temperature control selector usually is a slide mechanism; it may slide vertically or horizontally. This slide generally has at least 3 inches (75 millimeters) of travel. Some older systems use a rotary-type control.

All blend-air systems (except automatic temperature control types) use a cable controlled by the temperature control selector on the control head. The other end of the cable is attached to a lever on the blend door at the plenum chamber, figure 4-2. Some older systems use a similar cable to operate the heater control valve, thus regulating the air temperature.

Mode selection
Most mode selection devices are slide mechanisms similar to the temperature selector and located in the control head. The driver uses the mode selector to select between VENT, HEAT, and DEFROST functions.

The mode selector controls the position of the air doors in the plenum. When the selector is in the VENT position, the doors allow air into the cowl air intake, through the plenum, and into the vehicle. In older systems, the VENT mode prevented airflow through the heater core. However, most newer systems have some temperature regulation even in the VENT mode, so the blend door directs some vent air through the heater core at all times. When the mode select lever is moved to the HEAT position, the blend door is moved to allow a portion of the vent or fan-boosted air to flow through the heater core. In the DEFROST

Control Head: The dashboard-mounted unit containing the controls for the heating, cooling, and ventilation system.

Thermal Limiter: A special circuit breaker in the blower motor resistor block that opens the circuit if the resistor block fails and excessive current begins to flow through it.

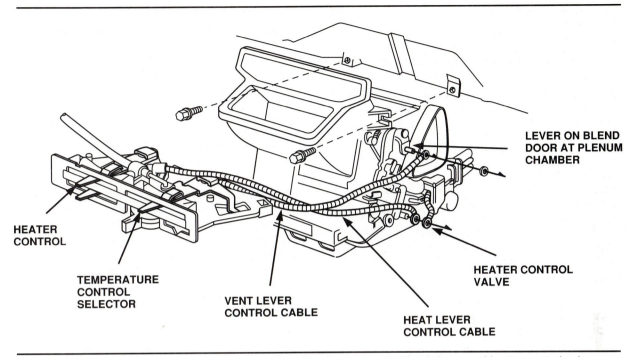

Figure 4-2. Cable controls originate at the control head and can operate blend doors and heater control valves remotely.

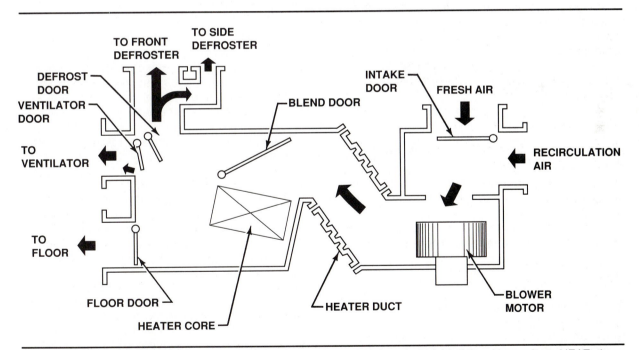

Figure 4-3. During DEFROST mode, the incoming air is directed at the windshield. If the driver selects HEAT, the air is also forced through the heater core.

mode, about 85 percent of the air is diverted through the defrost door, figure 4-3. Even when DEFROST is not selected, 10 to 20 percent of the heat is still directed through the defroster vents.

Some vehicles have a bilevel air discharge control. This control operates an air door that evenly splits the air between the center dash register and the floor register. The bilevel setting provides a more even air distribution pattern.

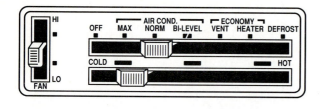

Figure 4-4. A basic electromechanical control head for a simple heater and air conditioning combination uses slide switches to select a heat or cooling level.

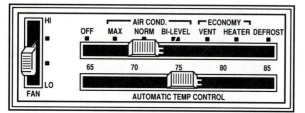

Figure 4-5. This middle-level air conditioning system uses a temperature setting slide to select an actual temperature, rather than a heat or cooling level.

Fresh air versus recirculated air

The recirculated air control operates an air door that determines the source of the air sent to the plenum. When the selector is in a fresh air position, air enters the HVAC system through the cowl air intake from outside the vehicle. When the selector is at the recirculate position, the air is taken from the passenger compartment.

When used in conjunction with air conditioning, the recirculate position is especially useful to rapidly cool the interior of a car that has been sitting in the hot sun. In this position, air that has already passed through the evaporator into the passenger compartment is directed back through the evaporator to be cooled even further. For this reason the recirculation control is common on air conditioned cars. Automobiles designed for add-on air conditioning systems rather than factory-installed systems have a recirculate control regardless of whether the air conditioner was ever installed.

Air conditioning controls

In addition to the heating and ventilation controls already mentioned, an air-conditioned vehicle has additional controls to operate the air conditioning. The type of controls used depends on the complexity of the air conditioning system.

A basic air conditioning system has a simple temperature control slide or rotary switch that adjusts the air-cooling level of the system between a cold and a hot setting, figure 4-4.

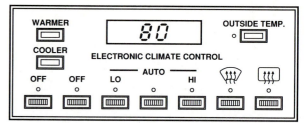

Figure 4-6. This premium Climate Control system control head can be much simpler to use. Many functions and selections are automatic.

Sometimes the control mechanism has one position for maximum cooling and another for "economy" operation.

A more sophisticated system, figure 4-5, has a temperature control setting that allows the driver to choose a specific temperature that the system maintains in the passenger compartment.

Some highly sophisticated air conditioning systems automatically control the:

• Air temperature and humidity (air is desiccated by passing it over the evaporator core first)
• Pattern of air distribution (by selecting the vents and the amount they open)
• Quantity of air (by selecting the blower speed).

Since so many factors are controlled automatically, the control head for such a complex system, figure 4-6, looks no more complicated than that for simpler systems.

MANUALLY CONTROLLED SYSTEMS

In manually controlled systems, the driver has direct control over the system through wire control cables linking the switches and knobs at the control head to the system components. These controls remain in widespread use in base-level cars because they are less expensive to manufacture.

The wire control cables, called **bowden cables**, consist of an outer sheath and an inner control wire or cable. Bowden cable controls work like the solid wire that operates the hand choke on older automobiles. The outer sheath is held in position, usually by brackets or a cable clamp mounted near each end, figure 4-7. The brackets maintain a fixed (but adjustable) distance between the control lever and the controlled element. Some cables are manually adjusted by sliding the bracket in its mount; others are adjusted by loosening the cable clamp, repositioning the cable sheath, and retightening the clamp. In the 1970s, the self-

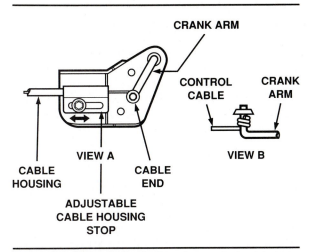

Figure 4-7. This adjustable Bowden control cable is set by sliding the portion of the bracket that holds the outer sheath in position.

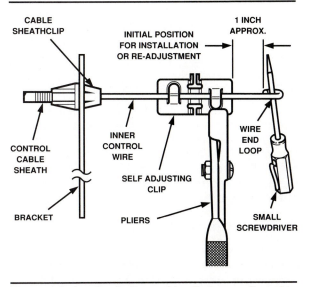

Figure 4-8. A self-adjusting cable clip is preadjusted to an overly-tight position during installation. It then slides to the correct position during initial operation.

adjusting cable was developed, figure 4-8. This cable uses a sliding clip, instead of a fixed cable end, that determines the distance between the end of the cable and the start of the cable sheath. The clip is held on the wire by friction, but slides along the wire to the correct position the first time the control is pulled or pushed against its stops.

The advantage to using solid wire controls, figure 4-9, is that the control lever can either push or pull on the inner wire to actuate the controlled component on the opposite end. This is especially useful to control components such as vent doors and heater coolant control valves, which must move in either direction.

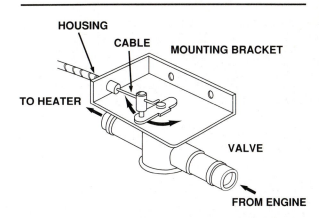

Figure 4-9. A solid wire control cable can move an actuating arm or other component in both directions. This cable both opens and closes the heater control valve.

Bowden Cable: A wire cable inside a rubber or metal sheath, used to provide remote control of a valve or control actuator.

■ **Heat By Hand**

Some of the very earliest hot-water automotive heaters used a heater control valve mounted on top of the engine block. On cold days, the driver had to stop the car, open up the hood, and manually turn on the flow of engine coolant. On hot days, he or she had to turn it off. Later, cable and vacuum-operated water valves were used and the driver no longer had to open the hood just to turn on the heat. Manual valves can still be found in the auxiliary heating systems of some modern trucks, where the heater circuits they control are needed only occasionally.

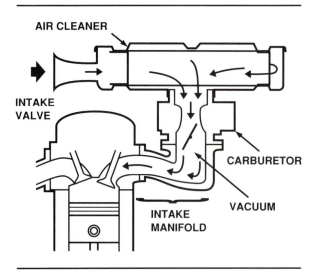

Figure 4-10. Downward movement of the piston creates a vacuum (low pressure) in the engine's intake manifold. The higher atmospheric air pressure then forces air into the engine.

VACUUM-OPERATED SYSTEMS

Vacuum-operated controls serve the same purposes as manual controls. Both types of controls translate driver input into HVAC system operation. With manual controls, the driver provides the input by moving control levers or knobs, and the control cables transfer this action directly to the HVAC mechanisms. With vacuum-operated systems, the driver operates switches that in turn use stored engine vacuum to provide control input to the HVAC system. The vacuum operates **actuators** that translate the input into a mechanical action, such as changing the position of blend doors, or opening and closing a heater control valve.

The Source of the Vacuum

Air, like any gas, always attempts to move to and fill a region of lower pressure. Since either pressure or vacuum can be used to move air through a hose, either pressure or vacuum can be used to power the air-operated actuators of the HVAC system. In either case, a source of pressure or vacuum is required.

For pressure to be used, a pressure source would have to be added, such as an engine-driven compressor. This would add to the weight, complexity, and expense of the automobile.

On the other hand, a vacuum source is readily available on gasoline engines. As the intake valves in the cylinders open and the pistons move downward on the intake stroke, piston movement pulls air into the engine, figure 4-10, creating a vacuum in the intake manifold,

relative to outside air pressure. This **manifold vacuum** is used to control the signal circuits and actuators of some HVAC control systems. Manifold vacuum can be tapped easily from fittings in the intake manifold or from the carburetor body or base, and typically varies from 0 to about 26 in-Hg (0 to 700 mm-Hg) in normal engine operation.

Diesel engines operate without throttles, and raise or lower engine speed by regulating the amount of fuel injected. Because the intake manifold is not restricted by a throttle plate, diesels do not have useable manifold vacuum. Rather than design and install different actuators, manufacturers simply add an accessory belt-driven vacuum pump to the diesel engine, and run their standard HVAC actuators from the pump.

Vacuum Control Devices

Vacuum control devices, or actuators, usually can be divided into three general groups:

• Vacuum motors
• Vacuum valves and switches
• Vacuum reservoirs and delay valves.

Vacuum motors are run by engine vacuum, and operate a mechanical component, such as a blend door, outside air door, or defrost door. Vacuum valves and switches are actually electric or thermostatically operated switches that regulate or redirect vacuum in the vacuum lines. Vacuum reservoirs and delay valves are used to delay or smooth out the operation of another actuator.

Vacuum motors

A **vacuum motor** often is called a power servo or a vacuum pot. It is used to automatically control an air door by responding to a varying vacuum signal from a vacuum **transducer**. The transducer is an electric vacuum valve that converts an electrical signal from a switch or other component into a vacuum signal that is routed to the vacuum motor through hoses. A vacuum motor either is normally open or normally closed. A normally-open motor controls a device that must stay open when the vacuum is released. A normally-closed motor is used with a device that must stay closed when vacuum is released. Normally-open vacuum motors are not interchangeable with normally-closed types.

To prevent a vacuum system failure from becoming a vehicle safety problem, most modern HVAC vacuum devices are normally open and operate in a fail-safe mode of full heat and full defrost. For example, a heater coolant control

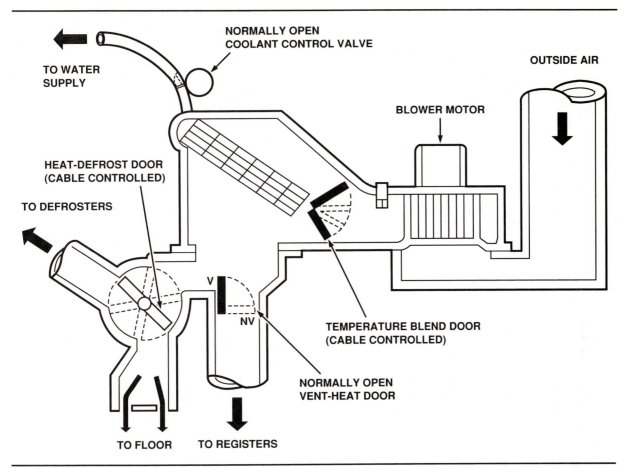

Figure 4-11. The normally open vacuum motor in the heater hose of this blend door system permits normal heater operation even if the vacuum line breaks or the control head mechanism fails.

valve that is operated by a normally-open vacuum motor, figure 4-11, still delivers heat to the heating and defrost systems even if the vacuum line breaks. Having hot coolant circulating too rapidly through the heater core is safer than not having any. Similar thinking is used in designing blend doors. Should a vacuum line deteriorate, the spring in the vacuum motor pulls the door into the fail-safe position (either open or closed) chosen by the designers.

There are four basic types of vacuum motors:

• Single-diaphragm, two-position
• Single-diaphragm, variable-position
• Double-diaphragm, three-position
• Double-action.

A single-diaphragm, two-position motor, figure 4-12, consists of an outer housing with a diaphragm suspended inside it, a pull rod linked to the diaphragm, and a spring. The diaphragm is exposed to outside air pressure on the pull rod side through a small vent hole.

Actuator: Special component such as a vacuum motor or solenoid that translates a vacuum or electrical signal into the physical movement to operate an HVAC valve, door, or flap. Typically an actuator performs an on/off function.

Manifold Vacuum: Low air pressure in the intake manifold of a running engine, caused by the descending pistons creating empty space in the cylinders faster than the entering air can fill it.

Vacuum Motor: An actuator that provides mechanical control of an HVAC component by using vacuum to create movement of a rod, lever, or crank.

Transducer: A vacuum valve that converts (transduces) an electrical signal into a vacuum signal, which is then used to control another vacuum device such as a vacuum motor.

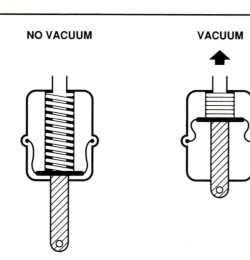

Figure 4-12. The single-diaphragm, two-position vacuum motor is either fully on, or fully off.

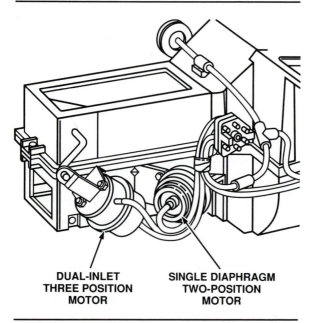

Figure 4-13. The single-diaphragm, two-position vacuum motor is often used simply to open and close an air door, while a dual-inlet, three position motor can provide intermediate positions.

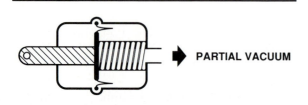

Figure 4-14. A single-diaphragm, variable-position vacuum motor is similar to the two-position motor, but is operated by adjustable vacuum from a separate vacuum valve. It can hold a door or valve in any intermediate position.

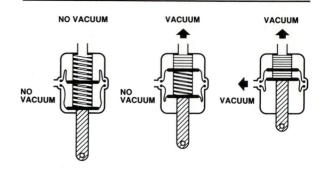

Figure 4-15. A double-diaphragm, three-position vacuum motor uses vacuum from two sources to adjust a pull rod to any of three distinct positions.

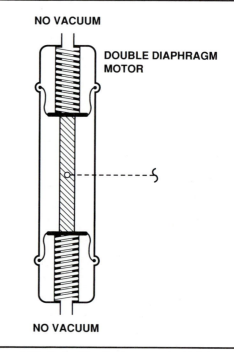

Figure 4-16. A double-diaphragm, dual-inlet vacuum motor moves the pull rod in two directions, with an "at rest" position in the middle.

When no vacuum is applied to the diaphragm, the spring holds the rod at its outermost position. Applying vacuum forces the diaphragm back toward the vacuum inlet, and the pull rod moves with it. The rod has only two positions: fully in or fully out. Typically, this type of vacuum motor controls an air door, figure 4-13, pulling it either open or shut.

A single-diaphragm, variable-position vacuum motor, figure 4-14, is controlled by a separate vacuum valve that meters the amount of vacuum applied. The pull rod can be in any position from fully in to fully out, depending upon the amount of vacuum acting on the diaphragm. General Motors uses this type of vac-

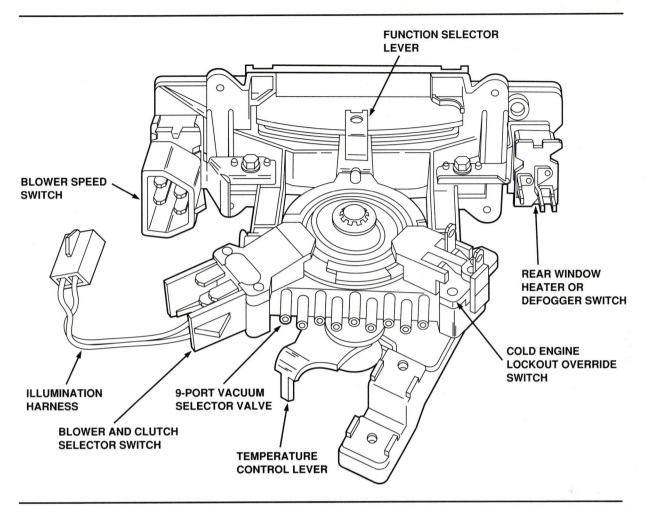

FUNCTION SELECTOR
LEVER

BLOWER SPEED
SWITCH

REAR WINDOW
HEATER OR
DEFOGGER SWITCH

ILLUMINATION
HARNESS

9-PORT VACUUM
SELECTOR VALVE

COLD ENGINE
LOCKOUT OVERRIDE
SWITCH

BLOWER AND CLUTCH
SELECTOR SWITCH

TEMPERATURE
CONTROL LEVER

Figure 4-17. A vacuum valve selector routes vacuum to and from the various actuators when the driver selects different operating modes. This example is incorporated into the control head.

uum motor in some of its systems to control the position of various airdoors.

A double-diaphragm, three-position vacuum motor, figure 4-15, has two diaphragms and two vacuum ports. When no vacuum is applied, the pull rod is fully extended. Applying vacuum to one port pulls the rod in halfway. Applying vacuum to both ports at the same time pulls the rod in all of the way.

A dual-inlet, double-action vacuum motor, figure 4-16, can be operated by vacuum in two directions. When no vacuum is applied, the pull rod is in the center ''at rest'' position. Applying vacuum to one end pulls the rod to that end; applying vacuum to the opposite end pulls the rod in that direction. These motors typically are used to control a bidirectional door such as an air conditioner-heater bilevel door.

Vacuum valves
For vacuum controls to operate properly, vacuum must be applied to some actuators and

not to others, for the various selections chosen by the driver. For example, if air conditioning is desired, vacuum must be applied to the actuators that move the blend door.

Vacuum valves are used to route vacuum to specific actuators, depending on the mode selected. Carmakers use various types of vacuum

■ **Low Coil Output**

A customer brings a car into your shop for air conditioning service. You discover the compressor clutch and bearings are burned and the seals have failed. Of course, you will replace those parts. But what was the cause? Check for low output voltage from the coil. If this is the case, there may not be enough voltage to create the magnetic field needed to pull in the armature. This will cause the clutch to slip, resulting in clutch, seal, and bearing failure.

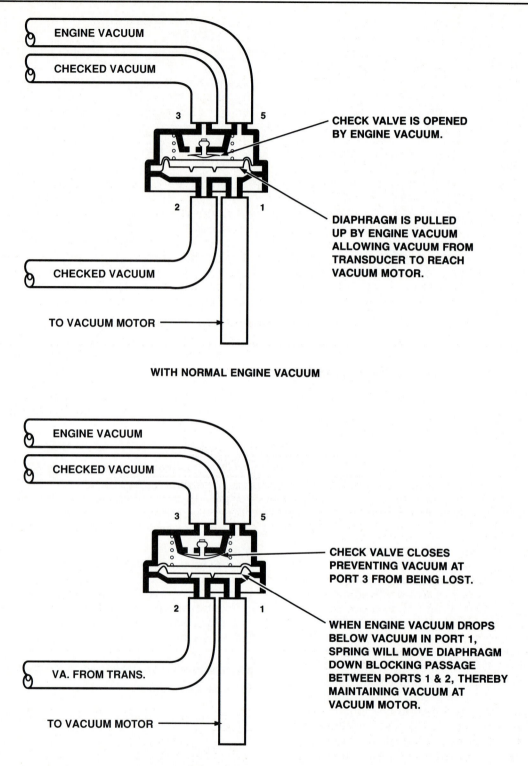

ENGINE VACUUM

CHECKED VACUUM

3   5   CHECK VALVE IS OPENED
                      BY ENGINE VACUUM.

                      DIAPHRAGM IS PULLED
2   1   UP BY ENGINE VACUUM
                      ALLOWING VACUUM FROM
                      TRANSDUCER TO REACH
CHECKED VACUUM   VACUUM MOTOR.

TO VACUUM MOTOR →

WITH NORMAL ENGINE VACUUM

ENGINE VACUUM

CHECKED VACUUM

3   5   CHECK VALVE CLOSES
                      PREVENTING VACUUM AT
                      PORT 3 FROM BEING LOST.

2   1   WHEN ENGINE VACUUM DROPS
                      BELOW VACUUM IN PORT 1,
                      SPRING WILL MOVE DIAPHRAGM
                      DOWN BLOCKING PASSAGE
                      BETWEEN PORTS 1 & 2, THEREBY
VA. FROM TRANS.   MAINTAINING VACUUM AT
                      VACUUM MOTOR.

TO VACUUM MOTOR →

WITH LOW ENGINE VACUUM

Figure 4-18. A check relay vacuum valve maintains the driver-selected vacuum applied to a vacuum motor even if engine vacuum falls. Without it, normal changes in engine vacuum would operate the vacuum motors independently of the controls.

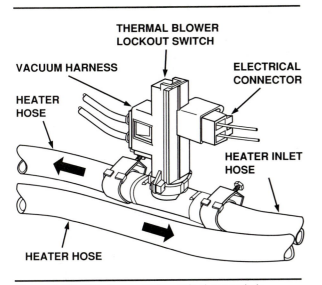

THERMAL BLOWER
LOCKOUT SWITCH

VACUUM HARNESS

ELECTRICAL
CONNECTOR

HEATER
HOSE

HEATER INLET
HOSE

HEATER HOSE

Figure 4-19. This thermal blower lockout switch regulates both an electric blower motor and a vacuum-operated air door in relation to engine coolant temperature.

tem or by electrically operated vacuum solenoids in a fully automatic system. These solenoids are described in detail later in this chapter. As the selector position changes, different vacuum outlet ports are covered and uncovered inside the valve body. When a vacuum port is uncovered, vacuum from the reservoir is applied to the actuator connected to that port, which causes the actuator to change position.

A check relay vacuum valve, figure 4-18 is used to maintain vacuum at the reservoir to prevent unwanted operation during low manifold vacuum conditions, such as full throttle acceleration or hill climbing. Normal manifold vacuum pulls up the diaphragm and opens the check valve, allowing vacuum from the transducer to reach the vacuum motor. When manifold vacuum drops, spring pressure pulls the diaphragm down to block the passage between

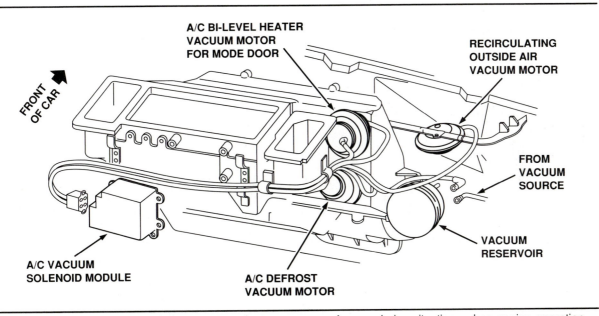

A/C BI-LEVEL HEATER
VACUUM MOTOR
FOR MODE DOOR

RECIRCULATING
OUTSIDE AIR
VACUUM MOTOR

FRONT OF CAR

FROM
VACUUM
SOURCE

A/C VACUUM
SOLENOID MODULE

A/C DEFROST
VACUUM MOTOR

VACUUM
RESERVOIR

Figure 4-20. A vacuum reservoir or vacuum tank stores vacuum for use during situations when engine operation cannot supply it.

valve selectors, but all operate on the same general principles. A vacuum valve, figure 4-17, has an inlet port connected by a vacuum hose to intake manifold vacuum. The hose often is routed through a vacuum reservoir. Outlet ports on the valve body are connected to HVAC system actuators, and vacuum is routed through the outlet ports to the actuators when the ports are open.

The opening and closing of the outlet ports is controlled by levers in a semiautomatic sys-

ports A and B, and the check valve closes to prevent a vacuum loss at port C.

Some vacuum valves in an HVAC system must operate independently of any driver input, usually in response to certain engine operating conditions. One example is the thermal blower lockout switch used by Ford, figure 4-19. This is a combination vacuum valve and single-pole single-throw electrical switch with a thermal element in contact with the engine coolant. When coolant temperature reaches

EASY FLOW DIRECTION

VACUUM CHECK VALVE

NO FLOW DIRECTION

Figure 4-21. A one-way vacuum check valve opens to permit high manifold vacuum to draw down the pressure inside the vacuum reservoir, but closes whenever manifold vacuum decreases.

approximately 120°F (49°C), the electrical switch contacts close to permit operation of the HVAC blower, and to energize a vacuum solenoid that causes the outside/recirculation door to move to the outside position.

Vacuum reservoirs
The level of vacuum in the intake manifold depends upon engine speed and throttle position. In normal operation, vacuum readings can vary continuously between zero and about 25 in.-Hg (635 mm-Hg) of vacuum. If this varying vacuum were applied directly to the vacuum actuators, their operation would vary from very little movement to sharp, harsh action. This inconsistent actuator operation could cause inconsistent HVAC component operation. For example, air doors could flap back and forth as the vacuum level oscillates.

This is also why manufacturers no longer use vacuum motors to power the windshield wipers, as was common on passenger cars until the 1960s. When climbing a hill, the low

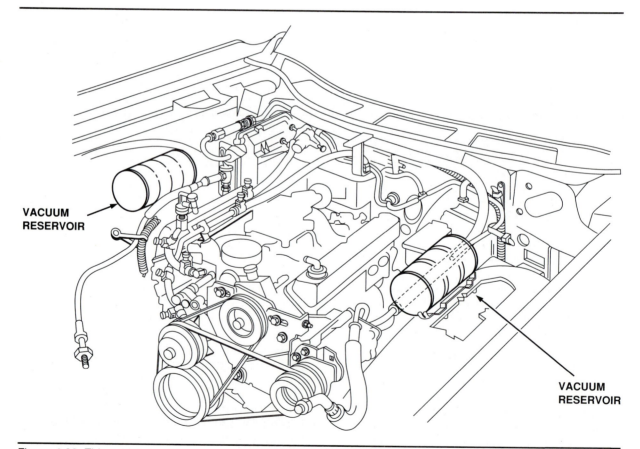

VACUUM RESERVOIR

VACUUM RESERVOIR

Figure 4-22. This vehicle uses two vacuum reservoirs to maintain sufficient system vacuum to operate the vacuum actuators several times.

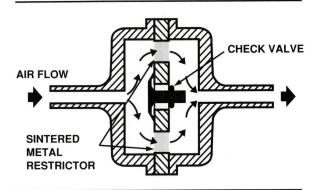

Figure 4-23. A vacuum line restrictor acts like a damper to slow the operation of a vacuum component.

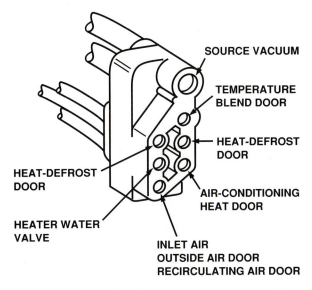

Figure 4-24. Vacuum harness connectors simplify connecting different vacuum harnesses on the assembly line.

manifold vacuum caused the wipers to sweep back and forth very slowly, and at full throttle they would stop completely. When coasting down the other side in gear, the high manifold vacuum caused the wipers to speed up to several times their normal speed. Needless to say, this could be fairly distracting.

A vacuum reservoir, figure 4-20, eliminates this potential problem by storing vacuum for HVAC use when manifold vacuum decreases. When engine vacuum is high, air is pulled from the reservoir through a one-way **check valve**, figure 4-21, to create a vacuum in the reservoir equal to that in the intake manifold. When the engine vacuum drops, the check valve closes, storing the vacuum level in the reservoir.

Most systems have just one or two main reservoirs; others may have additional small reservoirs or tanks used in the system, figure 4-22. Reservoirs usually are large enough to operate the control through several cycles. By the time several cycles are done it is likely that the engine vacuum will have risen enough to once again store a vacuum in the reservoir.

Restrictors may be placed in the vacuum lines leading to certain actuators to limit the vacuum application, figure 4-23. This has the effect of slowing or slightly delaying the actual movement of the actuator, which results in smoother, less abrupt action.

Vacuum lines

A vacuum control switch might have as many as nine different outlet ports, connected to the system actuators by vacuum lines. Often, vacuum lines are bunched together and routed behind the dash as a unit, much like a wiring harness. Vacuum harnesses connect in only one way to their mating connectors to prevent reversed or mismatched vacuum lines during

assembly or service, figure 4-24. They are often color-coded.

Vacuum hoses and hose assemblies generally are made of neoprene-type synthetic rubber or plastic tubing. These materials are flexible enough to ensure excellent sealing of the connections. Vacuum hoses deteriorate, however, if exposed to excess vibration, engine heat, oil, or other chemicals.

Reading Vacuum Diagrams

Diagrams for vacuum systems are similar to wiring diagrams for the electrical system (which are discussed later in this chapter). A vacuum diagram is especially needed with late-model engines. Vacuum line routing and connections can vary a great deal on a given engine during a single model year. For instance, one diagram may apply only to engines sold in California, with a different diagram used for other states.

Vacuum diagrams differ among carmakers, but all provide the same information. Most manufacturers supply a different diagram for each of the possible operating conditions. This way, the technician can determine what the

Check Valve: A valve that permits fluid or vacuum flow in one direction but prevents it in the opposite direction.

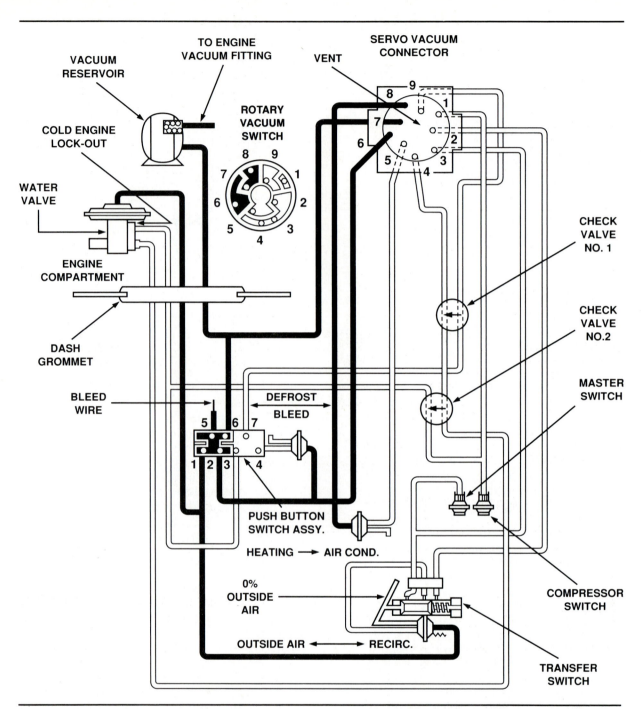

Figure 4-25. Blacked-in hoses on a typical Chrysler vacuum diagram indicate applied vacuum for a particular HVAC setting.

system operating conditions should be for a given circumstance. Many diagrams list the color-coding on the vacuum lines for identification. For example, a typical Chrysler diagram, figure 4-25, illustrates in heavy black lines where vacuum is present when the controls are set for no heat and no outside air. This diagram shows that the vacuum closes the

normally-open coolant valve and moves the air door to select recirculation. Devices such as the master switch and the compressor switch are not operated because no vacuum is applied to their actuators.

Figure 4-26 is a diagram of a typical General Motors late-model fully automatic air

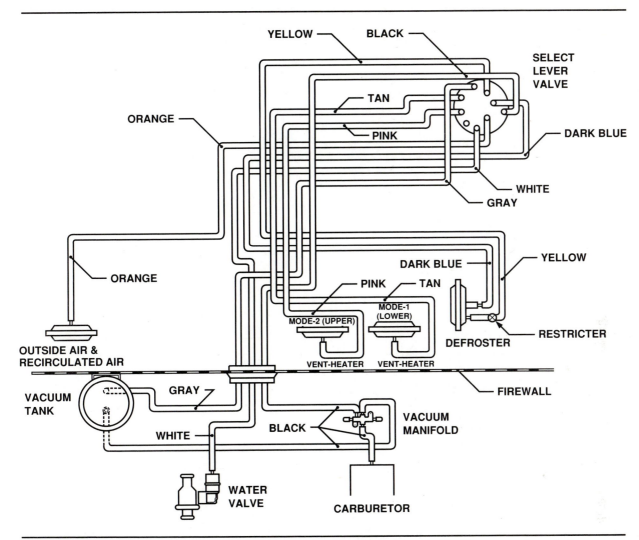

Figure 4-26. Typical General Motors vacuum diagram shows color markings to identify vacuum lines during service.

conditioning system with several vacuum components:

- Three single-diaphragm, two-position motors
- A double-action motor
- A vacuum solenoid module
- A vacuum reservoir, or tank
- A one-way check valve inside the vacuum reservoir.

A typical Ford diagram is shown in figure 4-27. Vacuum is distributed from a seven-port vacuum valve selector, shown at the bottom of the diagram.

ELECTRICALLY OPERATED CONTROLS

Most semiautomatic and fully automatic systems use both vacuum-powered and electrically operated devices to control the operation of

■ **Computer Connections**

Today's sophisticated engine and accessory computers and control modules don't often fail, but there are exceptions. The earlier analog-type modules were trouble-prone because they were susceptible to electrical interference and heat or vibration from the engine compartment. The switch to digital computers reduced computer failures considerably.

Still, it often appears that a control module has failed. But before throwing it away and replacing it with a new one, consider this: experts say that 90 percent of the computers returned as defective are actually not defective at all. The problem very often is simply a faulty connector.

To check this out, always clean and test the connectors, then recheck the module. They are much cheaper than the computer.

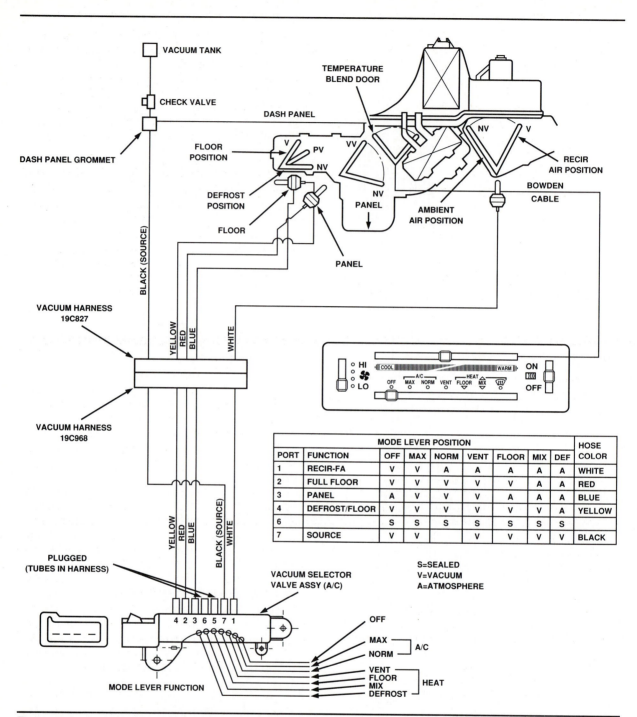

Figure 4-27. A comprehensive Ford vacuum diagram, showing a 7-port vacuum valve selector, the control head, plenum, and ducting.

the system. There are at least two advantages for electrically operated controls:

• Electrical controls are more versatile in their movements. Electric motors and servomotors can produce rotary motion more easily than a vacuum device.

• Electrical controls often are smaller and more compact.

Electrical wires and even printed circuit boards can be used to control the system. These wires are smaller and easier to install behind the dash than comparable vacuum lines.

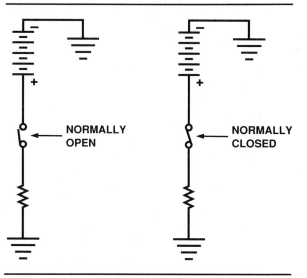

Figure 4-28. These symbols for normally-open and normally-closed switches are used on electrical system diagrams.

Basic Electrical Components

The electrical devices used to control HVAC systems are typical of other automotive electrical systems. These devices include:

• Switches
• Relays
• Solenoids
• Servomotors
• Circuit protection devices.

Electrical current, whether used to operate the HVAC system or for other purposes, needs a complete path to flow through. This path is called a **circuit**. A circuit is a circular path from a power source, such as a car battery, to and through any number of electrical devices, and back to the power source. If there is any break in the circuit, no current can flow through it. The electrical devices that follow act as parts of the HVAC electrical circuits.

Switches

Switches are used in automotive electrical systems to start, stop, or redirect current flow. They can be operated manually by the driver or remotely through mechanical linkage. Manually operated switches allow the driver to control the operation of the HVAC system components. A remotely operated switch is controlled indirectly by the driver or the passengers.

There are many types of switches, but all have common characteristics. They all depend upon physical movement for operation. A simple switch contains one or more pairs of contact points; one of each pair is stationary and

the other is movable. When the switch is operated, the movable points contact the stationary points to complete the circuit.

Some switches are designed so that the contact points are normally open (NO) in the "at rest" position and switch operation closes them to allow current flow, figure 4-28. In other switches, the contact points are normally

---

Circuit: A electrical path composed of wiring, switches, and other electrical components that leads to and from a power source through the component operated by the electric current. A series of vacuum lines and vacuum-operated components is sometimes called a vacuum circuit; unlike electricity, vacuum does not require a complete loop leading back to the power source.

■ **Tran(sfer) + (Re)sistor**

The word, "transistor," was originally a business trademark, used to describe an electrical part that transferred electric signals across a resistor.

Transistors are used to control current flow in a solid-state electronic system. In this way, they work like a mechanical relay, but with no moving parts and a high degree of reliability.

A transistor is a three-element semiconductor. The three parts are the base, the emitter, and the collector. The emitter and the collector are the outer layers, and the base is the inner layer. The two outer layers consist of a material that has either a negative charge (called N-material) or a positive charge (called P-material). The middle layer has the opposite charge. Thus, a transistor is said to be an NPN or a PNP transistor.

Most transistors either allow current flow across the area where the two types of materials are joined (called the junction), or they prevent the current flow. In the first case, the transistor is said to have a forward bias; in the second case, it is said to have a reverse bias.

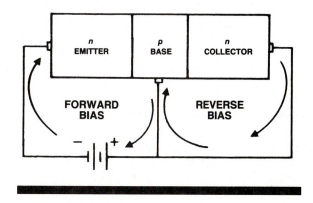

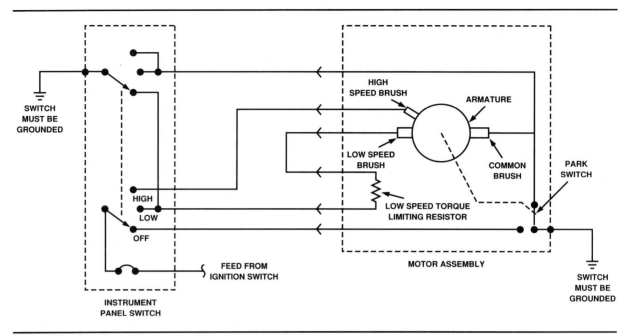

Figure 4-29. Switches are shown schematically on circuit diagrams to simplify interpretation.

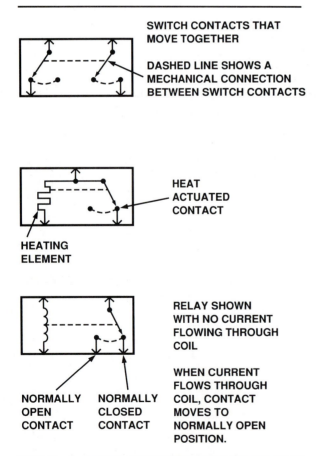

SWITCH CONTACTS THAT MOVE TOGETHER

DASHED LINE SHOWS A MECHANICAL CONNECTION BETWEEN SWITCH CONTACTS

HEAT ACTUATED CONTACT

HEATING ELEMENT

RELAY SHOWN WITH NO CURRENT FLOWING THROUGH COIL

WHEN CURRENT FLOWS THROUGH COIL, CONTACT MOVES TO NORMALLY OPEN POSITION.

NORMALLY OPEN CONTACT

NORMALLY CLOSED CONTACT

Figure 4-30. The straight dashed line connecting parts inside a switch symbol indicates that movement of one affects the other. The curved dash line indicates which circuits are closed by the movable contact.

closed (NC) in the ''at rest'' position, allowing current flow until the switch is operated.

A switch may be locked in the desired position, or it may be spring-loaded so that a constant pressure is required to keep the points out of their normal position. Switches with more than one set of contact points can control more than one circuit.

Switches are shown in simplified form on electrical diagrams so that current flow through them can be easily traced, figure 4-29. Triangular contact points on the diagrams generally indicate a spring-loaded return, and circular contact points indicate a locking-position switch. A dashed line between the movable parts of a switch means that they are mechanically connected and operate in unison, figure 4-30.

In addition to manually operated switches, HVAC electrical circuits use various other switch designs. Oil pressure and vacuum switches respond to changes in pressure. Switches designed to sense engine coolant temperature contain a bimetallic strip that flexes as it heats or cools, opening or closing the switch contacts, figure 4-31.

Relays
A **relay**, figure 4-32, is a type of remotely controlled switch that uses an electromagnet to physically move the contacts that open and close the switch. It allows a small amount of current to control a much larger current. A simple relay contains an electromagnetic coil in

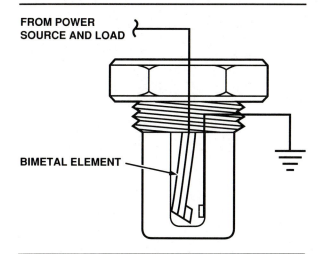

FROM POWER SOURCE AND LOAD

BIMETAL ELEMENT

Figure 4-31. This bimetallic temperature sensor switch is screwed into the water jacket, exposing the end to the coolant. Expansion and contraction of the bimetallic element closes and opens the ground circuit.

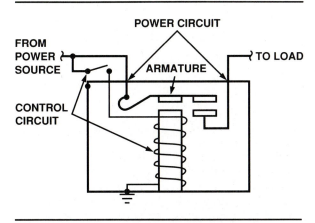

POWER CIRCUIT

FROM POWER SOURCE

TO LOAD

ARMATURE

CONTROL CIRCUIT

Figure 4-32. A relay uses a low-amperage control circuit to open and close a high-amperage power circuit.

series with battery voltage and a switch. Near the electromagnet is a flat blade, or armature, of some material which is attracted by a magnetic field. The armature pivots at one end and is held away from the contact point at the other end by spring pressure.

To activate the relay, the driver closes the switch, and a small current is passed through the coil, creating a magnetic field which moves an armature to open or close a set of contact points in a separate, high current circuit. The low current circuit through the coil is the control circuit. The high circuit through the armature is the power circuit. The power circuit, up to 30 amperes in an automobile, may be used to operate such accessories as heater blower motors or air conditioning compressor

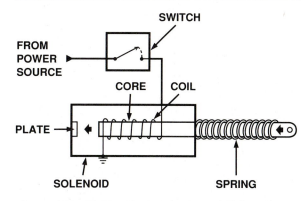

SWITCH

FROM POWER SOURCE

CORE   COIL

PLATE

SOLENOID   SPRING

Figure 4-33. Energizing a solenoid pulls the movable plunger into the coil. Spring pressure pulls the plunger out when the switch is turned off.

clutches. The small control current is switched remotely, usually from the dashboard. This eliminates the need to run the heavy current leads to a large switch mounted on the dashboard. The relay itself can be mounted remotely near or as part of the component it controls.

Solenoids and other actuators
A **solenoid** is a 2-position linear-motion actuator often used to control air doors, water valves, and other single-motion devices. It operates much the same as a relay, except that the solenoid core moves instead of the armature. This allows a solenoid to convert current flow into mechanical movement.

A solenoid, figure 4-33, consists of a cylindrical coil winding surrounding a sliding, spring-loaded iron plunger. When the switch is closed and current flows through the coil, it creates a magnetic field that attracts the plunger, drawing it against spring pressure into the center of the coil. When the current flow

Relay: An electromagnetic switch that uses a low amperage circuit to open and close separate contacts that control a high amperage circuit. Typically, a relay permits a light-duty dashboard switch to operate a component requiring much more current.

Solenoid: An electromagnetic actuator consisting of a moveable iron core or shuttle that slides into a cylindrical coil when current is applied, and is forced back out by a spring when current is cut off. Typically, a solenoid is used to physically move a valve or door attached to the core.

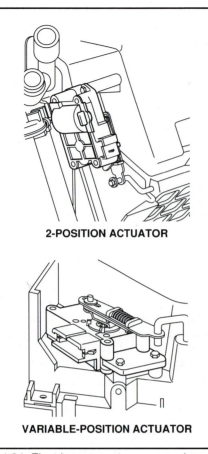

2-POSITION ACTUATOR

VARIABLE-POSITION ACTUATOR

Figure 4-34. Electric servomotors are used as actuators to control the operation of doors and valves.

stops, the magnetic field disappears and spring pressure returns the plunger to the at-rest position.

Servomotors
An electric **servomotor**, figure 4-34, is a cross between a motor and a solenoid. However, while a solenoid produces movement in a straight line, a servomotor produces rotation along a circular path. A servomotor can be constructed to position the actuating arm at any position between fully extended and fully retracted.

Some computer-controlled HVAC systems use a DC servomotor, figure 4-35. This servomotor is actuated by the computer to provide variable control to the blend door.

Circuit protection devices
Because all conductors have some resistance to the flow of electric current, passing current through a conductor always raises its temperature. The amount of heat generated depends on the size (gauge) of the conductor, its resistance, and the amount of current. If the wire carries too much current, the heat will damage

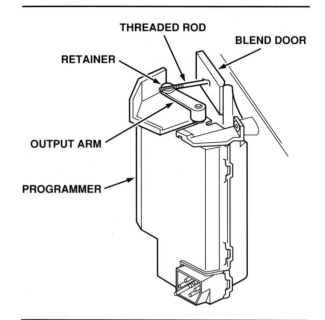

Figure 4-35. A DC servomotor provides variable control to the blend door in this Cadillac Climate Control system.

the insulation, the conductor, nearby wires, or other electrical devices.

For this reason, circuit protection devices are needed to keep circuitry from being overloaded with current. Automotive electrical systems use three types of protectors, figure 4-36:

- Fuses
- Circuit breakers
- Fusible links.

An automotive fuse is a fine metal strip of zinc housed in a glass cartridge, on a ceramic body, or inside a blade-type plastic plug. A fuse can carry a specified current without damage. At any higher current than the rated capacity, the metal strip will melt, opening the circuit and preventing damage to other electrical devices in the circuit. Fuses are rated by their current capacity. It is the *rate* of current (measured in amperes), not the amount (measured in volts), that causes a fuse to burn out, or blow. As long as the current passing through a fuse is within the limit tolerated by its design, a fuse can operate with varying voltages. Automotive fuse ratings generally range from 0.5 to 35 amperes. Fuses are made in a range of standard sizes. All domestic and most foreign carmakers use blade-type fuses introduced by General Motors in 1977.

Circuit breakers are mechanical units that use different rates of expansion in heated metals to protect circuitry. Unlike fuses, they will last through repeated uses. They are used

BLADE TYPE FUSE

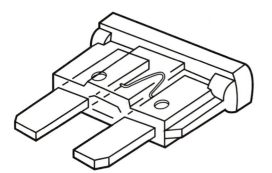

CIRCUIT BREAKER

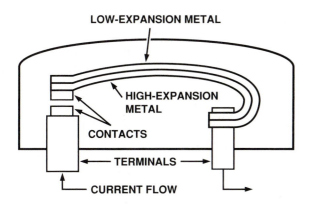

FUSIBLE LINK

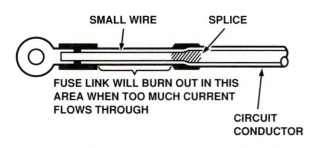

Figure 4-36. The three types of circuit protection devices.

in circuits where temporary overloads are more frequent and where power must be restored rapidly. Circuit breakers consist of a set of contact points, one on a fixed mounting and the other on a bimetallic strip. As current flows across the bimetallic strip, the metals heat and expand at different rates. If too much current flows, the expansion becomes great

enough to bend the strip and open the contact points, stopping the current. In Type I circuit breakers, the strip cools in a few seconds and the points close. In Type II circuit breakers, the contacts remain open, and a button pops out of the breaker case to indicate that the circuit is broken. Once the source of the problem has been corrected, the breaker can be reset by pressing the button.

Fusible links are simply short lengths of smaller gauge wire installed in the circuit they are to protect. A current overload melts the strip before the rest of the circuit is damaged. Links usually are four gauge numbers smaller than the rest of the circuit wiring. For example, a circuit using 12-gauge wiring would be protected by a 16-gauge fusible link. The link is covered with a very heavy insulation which blisters and bubbles when the conductor melts, showing that the link has melted. Melted links are replaced by soldering or connecting a new one in place after the problem in the circuit has been corrected. Fusible links are used when it is awkward to run wiring from the voltage source to the fuse panel and back to the accessory. They also are used in circuits not otherwise protected and at junction connections or near a circuit splice.

Servomotor: An electric motor used for automatic control of a mechanical device, such as a blend door.

■ **Circuit Breakers As Test Aids**

Finding a problem in a circuit that keeps blowing fuses as fast as you put them in can be a real problem. You can keep the circuit operating long enough to locate the fault, however, by temporarily substituting a circuit breaker for the fuse. First obtain a circuit breaker in the ampere rating that matches the fuse. Solder two short leads with alligator clips to the breaker terminals. If the circuit breaker has spade terminals, you can crimp connectors to the leads instead. Then attach the clips to the fuse clips in the fuse panel. Operate the circuit. The breaker will pop on and off to keep the circuit working long enough for you to find the trouble spot. After fixing the problem, install a new fuse of the correct current rating.

If you keep several circuit breakers with different ampere ratings on hand, you will be ready to troubleshoot a variety of circuits.

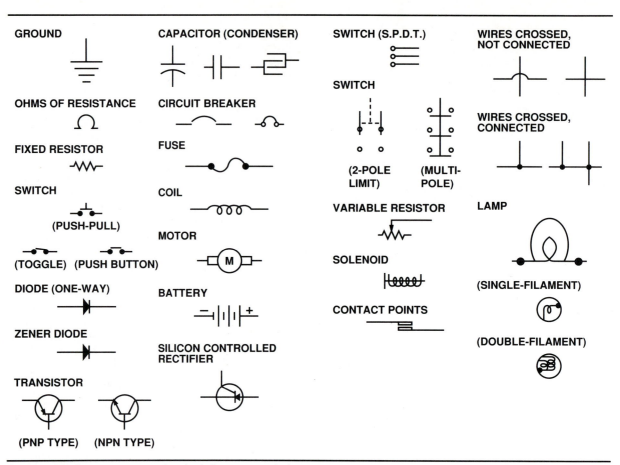

GROUND

OHMS OF RESISTANCE

FIXED RESISTOR

SWITCH

(PUSH-PULL)

(TOGGLE)   (PUSH BUTTON)

DIODE (ONE-WAY)

ZENER DIODE

TRANSISTOR

(PNP TYPE)   (NPN TYPE)

CAPACITOR (CONDENSER)

CIRCUIT BREAKER

FUSE

COIL

MOTOR

BATTERY

SILICON CONTROLLED
RECTIFIER

SWITCH (S.P.D.T.)

SWITCH

(2-POLE   (MULTI-
LIMIT)   POLE)

VARIABLE RESISTOR

SOLENOID

CONTACT POINTS

WIRES CROSSED,
NOT CONNECTED

WIRES CROSSED,
CONNECTED

LAMP

(SINGLE-FILAMENT)

(DOUBLE-FILAMENT)

Figure 4-37. Some common electrical diagram symbols.

Reading Electrical Schematics

To fully understand late-model HVAC systems, you must become familiar with the electrical circuits and components. When servicing electrically operated systems, you must be able to use the various types of diagrams to trace specific circuits and find electrical problems. There are three major types of diagrams:

- Circuit diagram
- System diagram
- Installation diagram.

A circuit diagram is a drawing that shows all of the different circuits in a complete electrical system. All the electrical information about a complete automotive circuit, including the switches, connectors, loads, and other devices, can be included in a single diagram. Wires generally are identified by color coding or by circuit numbers. Electrical components are identified by various symbols, figure 4-37. These symbols vary between carmakers.

Circuit diagrams use color coding, circuit numbers, and symbols that you must be able

to interpret. It is quicker and easier to diagnose and isolate an electrical problem using a circuit diagram than by working with the system diagram. You are not distracted or confused by wiring that is not part of the circuit on which you are working. A circuit diagram shows the paths that current takes in a properly functioning circuit.

A system diagram is a drawing of a circuit or any part of a circuit that shows how it works. You need to understand how the circuit is supposed to work before trying to determine why it is not working properly.

An installation diagram, or pictorial diagram, shows where and how wires and loads are installed in the automobile, figure 4-38. These diagrams can help you to locate the general harness or circuit within the car before you look at the circuit diagram for more detailed information.

Many electrical diagrams are indexed by grids. The diagram is marked into equal sections like a street map, with letters along the top and numbers down the sides. The diagram's index will list the letter and number for

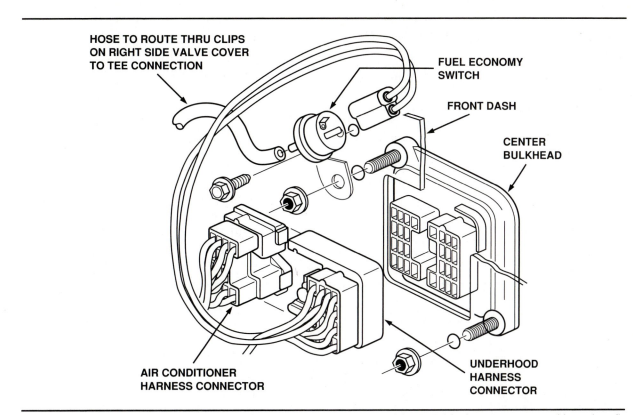

HOSE TO ROUTE THRU CLIPS
ON RIGHT SIDE VALVE COVER
TO TEE CONNECTION

FUEL ECONOMY
SWITCH

FRONT DASH

CENTER
BULKHEAD

AIR CONDITIONER
HARNESS CONNECTOR

UNDERHOOD
HARNESS
CONNECTOR

Figure 4-38. An installation diagram illustrates the actual appearance of the individual components and how they fit together.

each major part and many connection points. If the diagram is not indexed, you must find the part by its location on the automobile. Other electrical diagrams show the actual locations of the components.

Each division of General Motors incorporates a special troubleshooting section in its shop manual for a given vehicle. This section contains diagrams of the vehicle's entire electrical system. These schematics often are referred to as Valley Forge diagrams and are read from top to bottom. Some of the Ford diagrams are done in a similar style; these and the conventional horizontal diagrams and troubleshooting aids are included in its Electrical and Vacuum Troubleshooting Guide (EVTG) published for each vehicle in a model year.

■ Metric Wire Sizes

Look at a wiring diagram or a service manual for an imported car, and you may see wire sizes listed in metric measurements. For example, if you look at a wiring diagram for a Volkswagen Rabbit or Golf, you will see wire sizes listed as 0.5, 1.0, 1.5, 4.0, 6.0 and so on. Those numbers are the cross sectional area of the conductor in square millimeters (mm^2).

These metric measurements are not the same as circular-mil measurements. They are determined by calculating the cross section of the conductor with this formula:

$$\text{Area} = \text{Radius}^2 \times 3.14.$$

A wire with a 1 mm^2 cross sectional area actually has a 1.128 mm diameter.

The following table lists American Wire Gauge (AWG) sizes and equivalent metric wire sizes.

AWG Size (Gauge)	Metric Size (mm^2)
20	0.5
18	0.8
16	1.0
14	2.0
12	3.0
10	5.0
8	8.0
6	13.0
4	19.0

SUMMARY

In an HVAC system, the control head is the dashboard-mounted unit containing the various driver controls for the system. These include heat, defrost, ventilation, blower speed, and fresh air/recirculated air. If the vehicle has air conditioning, these controls also are located on the control head.

HVAC systems can be operated manually, with vacuum, electrically, or by a combination of electrical and vacuum.

Manually operated systems use Bowden cables to connect the levers at the control head to the various doors and other devices. Vacuum operated systems use engine manifold vacuum connected by hoses to vacuum motors and other vacuum devices. These actuators control the movement of the air doors and the heater coolant control valve. Electrically operated systems do the same thing with switches, relays, servomotors, and solenoids as actuators. Every electrical circuit has a fuse, fusible link, or circuit breaker to protect the circuit from current overload.

Carmakers provide diagrams or schematics of their vacuum and electrical systems. In complex, late-model systems, these can be invaluable aids in troubleshooting and repairing a problem with an HVAC system.

Review Questions
Choose the single most correct answer.
Compare your answers with the correct answers on page 229.

1. The control head typically contains all of the following *except*:
   a. Temperature selector
   b. Passenger compartment sensors
   c. Blower motor controls
   d. Mode selection

2. The job of a thermal limiter is to:
   a. Turn the blower on and off at preselected temperatures
   b. Provide the temperature control for the air conditioning system
   c. Limit current flow through the control switch
   d. Monitor coolant temperature

3. Vacuum-operated control systems use:
   a. Ported vacuum
   b. Manifold vacuum
   c. Absolute vacuum
   d. Venturi vacuum

4. Vacuum actuators include:
   a. Vacuum motors
   b. Vacuum switches
   c. Vacuum delay valves
   d. All of the above

5. Most vacuum motors:
   a. Are normally closed
   b. Respond to a vacuum transducer
   c. Both a and b
   d. Neither a nor b

6. A vacuum motor with two diaphragms and two vacuum ports is a:
   a. Single-action motor
   b. Double-action motor
   c. Three-position motor
   d. None of the above

7. Typical control system vacuum readings are:
   a. 0-10 in-Hg (0 to 250 mm-Hg)
   b. 0-20 in-Hg (0 to 500 mm-Hg)
   c. 0-30 in-Hg (0 to 750 mm-Hg)
   d. 0-40 in-Hg (0 to 1000 mm-Hg)

8. A relay:
   a. Uses an electromagnet
   b. Uses a large current flow to control a smaller current
   c. Contains an electric servomotor
   d. All of the above

9. A solenoid:
   a. Provides linear motion
   b. Has variable positions
   c. Contains a movable coil winding
   d. Converts mechanical movement into current flow

10. Fuses control the _____ of current flow.
    a. Temperature
    b. Amount
    c. Rate
    d. Speed

PART THREE

Air Conditioning

Basic Refrigeration Systems

All refrigeration systems perform certain basic tasks, which include cooling, dehumidifying, and removing dust from the air entering the passenger compartment. In this chapter, we will look at how automotive air conditioning systems handle these tasks. Understanding the general principles of air conditioning system operation will help you better understand the individual components and specific air conditioning systems covered in later chapters.

TYPICAL AIR CONDITIONING SYSTEMS

Automotive air conditioners cool the passenger compartment air by using refrigerant to absorb heat from the inside air and release it into the outside air. Air entering the passenger compartment is routed through the evaporator. While the air conditioner is running, liquid refrigerant is bled past a restrictor into the evaporator, where the low pressure causes it to boil at a low temperature. As you learned in Chapter 2, for the refrigerant to change state from liquid to vapor, it must absorb latent heat from the evaporator structure. Because of R-12's high specific heat, it absorbs a great deal of heat as it changes state. This cools the evaporator surface, through which the passenger compartment air flows. The air is dehumidified as water vapor in the air condenses on the cool evaporator surface and is removed through a drain passage in the housing. Airborne dust particles cling to the water on the evaporator surface in a manner similar to that of an oil-saturated engine air filter, and are drained with the condensed water. Meanwhile, the refrigerant vapor flows through the air conditioning system to the condenser, where it returns to a liquid and releases heat into the airstream outside the automobile.

This is the simplified version of the refrigerated air conditioning process that we covered in earlier chapters. The key points to remember are that both pressure and temperature changes can cause R-12 to change state between liquid and gas, and raising or lowering the pressure raises or lowers the boiling point of R-12. Releasing pressure from liquid refrigerant as it passes through an expansion device lowers its boiling point, permitting it to boil as it flows through the evaporator, absorbing heat. Applying pressure to the gaseous refrigerant with the compressor raises its boiling point, so that it condenses as it flows through the condenser, releasing heat.

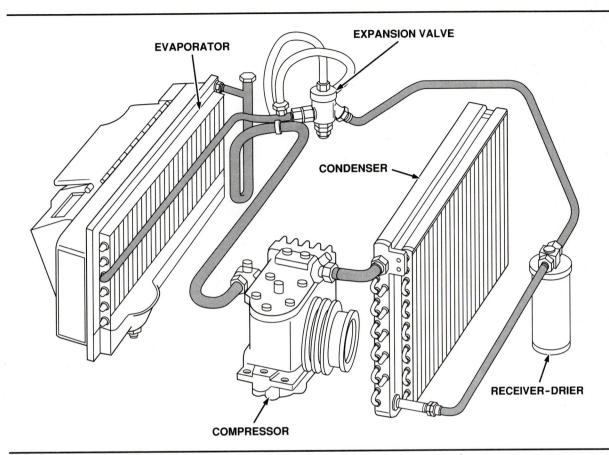

Figure 5-1. A typical automotive air conditioning system uses these five components. Some systems use an accumulator instead of a receiver/drier.

Air Conditioning System Components

All automotive air conditioning systems have at least five basic components through which the refrigerant flows, figure 5-1. These are the:

• Compressor
• Condenser
• Receiver-drier or accumulator
• Expansion device
• Evaporator.

Besides these major components, an air conditioner uses synthetic rubber hoses, metal lines, and various fittings to carry refrigerant through the system. Refrigerant is drawn into the compressor through the suction hose, and a high-pressure hose carries refrigerant from the compressor to the condenser. A small-diameter liquid line brings refrigerant from the condenser to the expansion device.

Two or more **service valves** also are part of the air conditioning system. Generally one is at the inlet and one at the outlet of the compressor. They do not affect system operation, and are used to gain access to the system dur-

ing servicing. There are two types of service valves:

• Schrader valves, which are somewhat similar to tire valves
• Stem-type valves, which require a special wrench for positioning.

High and Low Sides

An automotive air conditioning circuit can be divided into two portions: a **high side** and a

Service Valves: Schrader or stem-type valves near the inlet and outlet of the compressor, provided for service access to the refrigeration system.

High Side: The portion of the air conditioning system in which the refrigerant is under high pressure and at high temperature. It includes the compressor outlet, condenser, receiver-drier (if used), and expansion device inlet.

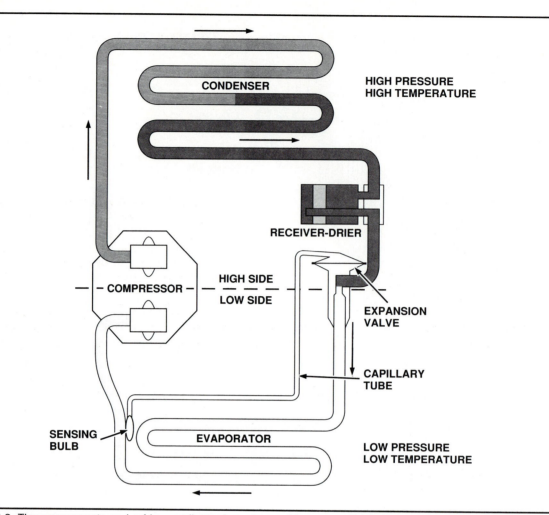

Figure 5-2. The components and refrigerant lines of an air conditioner are divided into the high side — high pressure, high temperature refrigerant — and the low side — low pressure, low temperature refrigerant.

low side, figure 5-2. These terms refer to the pressure of the refrigerant. Refrigerant in the high side is under high pressure, and in the low side it is under low pressure. Refrigerant occurs as both a liquid and a gas in both the high side and the low side, because in a running air conditioning system the temperature of the refrigerant changes even though the pressures are stable within each side of the system. The compressor and the expansion device divide the low side from the high side.

The high side

The **compressor**, figure 5-3, is the air conditioning system pump. It is belt-driven and controlled by an electromagnetic compressor clutch, figure 5-4. When the clutch is activated, electric current flows through the clutch field windings, activating the electromagnet. The magnet pulls the clutch hub into a pulley and locks it to the compressor mainshaft. A belt

from the engine drives the pulley, and thus when the clutch is engaged the belt also drives the compressor.

As it pumps, the compressor draws low-pressure, gaseous refrigerant from the accumulator (in a fixed-orifice expansion tube system) or from the evaporator (in a typical thermostatic expansion valve system). The compressor pressurizes the refrigerant, so that the refrigerant leaves it as a hot, high-pressure gas, figure 5-5. The high pressure also raises the temperature at which the gaseous refrigerant condenses to liquid. Remember that boiling point and condensation point are the same temperature; the difference is merely whether the change in state is from liquid to gas or gas to liquid. The high side of the air conditioning system starts at the compressor outlet, often called the discharge side of the compressor, and ends at the expansion device, discussed below.

INLINE COMPRESSOR

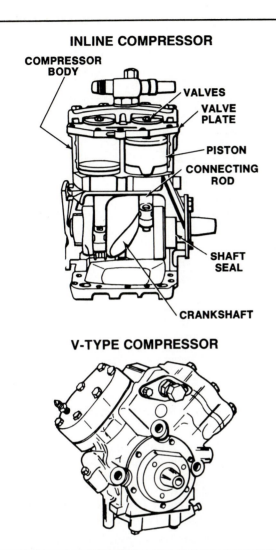

COMPRESSOR BODY

VALVES

VALVE PLATE

PISTON

CONNECTING ROD

SHAFT SEAL

CRANKSHAFT

V-TYPE COMPRESSOR

Figure 5-3. Air conditioning system compressors are designed in several styles.

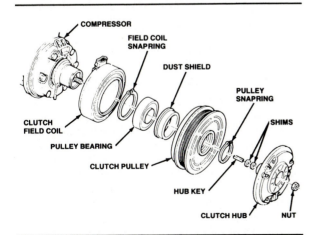

COMPRESSOR

FIELD COIL SNAPRING

DUST SHIELD

PULLEY SNAPRING

SHIMS

CLUTCH FIELD COIL

PULLEY BEARING

CLUTCH PULLEY

HUB KEY

CLUTCH HUB

NUT

Figure 5-4. Engagement of the compressor is controlled by an electromagnetic clutch.

After leaving the compressor, the high-pressure vapor enters the **condenser**, figure 5-6. This is a heat exchanger exposed to outside airflow. The condenser is made of copper tubing and fins and usually is located near the radiator, which it resembles. As the high-pressure refrigerant flows through the tubing, the airstream passing through the condenser fins removes heat from the high-pressure gas inside. Because of the high boiling point

Low Side: The portion of the air conditioning system in which the refrigerant is under low pressure and at low temperature. It includes the expansion device outlet, evaporator, accumulator (if used), and compressor inlet.

Compressor: The air conditioning system pump, belt-driven, controlled by an electromagnetic clutch. The compressor applies pressure to the refrigerant and pumps it through the system.

Condenser: A radiator-like tube-and-fin heat exchanger exposed to outside airflow. As gaseous refrigerant flows through the tubes, it condenses to liquid and releases heat that the airstream carries away.

■ Non-Metric Reminder

The temperature-pressure relationship of Refrigerant 12 has long been used by HVAC technicians in testing air conditioner operation. In a sealed air conditioning system that has been operating for a few minutes, the saturated gas pressure and temperature of the R-12 follow a fixed relationship. This means that when you know the refrigerant pressure, you can refer to the chart to determine its temperature. In this way you can tell if the temperature of the evaporator is cold enough to properly cool the air in the car, or to diagnose various problems. For U.S. mechanics, the pressure-temperature chart has always been in degrees Fahrenheit and pounds per square inch, and this leads to an easy rule-of-thumb for low-side testing:

Between about 20°F and 80°F, evaporator pressure in psi and evaporator temperature in degrees Fahrenheit should be about equal.

For instance, an evaporator pressure of about 30 psi should accompany an evaporator temperature of about 30°F. Of course, this rule does not apply when using metric units. Then it becomes 207 kilopascals and −1.1 degrees, hardly an easy-to-recall ratio.

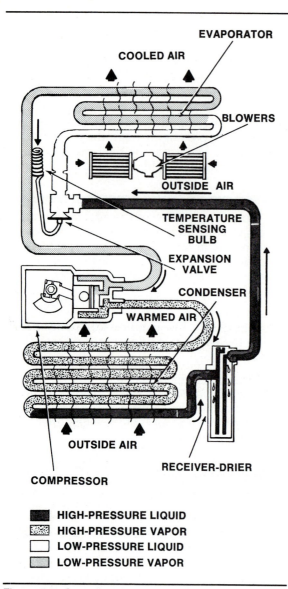

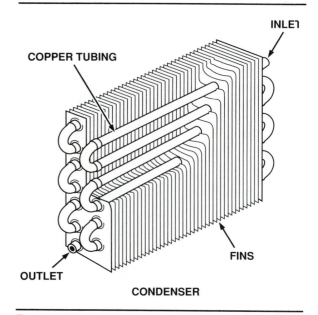

Figure 5-6. The condenser resembles a small radiator, but is designed to contain high-pressure gaseous and liquid refrigerant, rather than relatively low-pressure engine coolant.

assembly (such as receiver-dehydrator and filter-drier) but they all have the same purposes:

• Storing liquid refrigerant until it is needed
• Allowing any remaining gaseous refrigerant to change into liquid
• Removing any water from the refrigerant with a **desiccant**, or chemical drying agent.

Water must be excluded from the air conditioning system. If it mixes with refrigerant, the two substances form acids that damage the system components. A sight glass in the liquid line, frequently on the receiver-drier, allows the technician to examine refrigerant condition. From the receiver-drier, the refrigerant flows to the expansion device.

HIGH-PRESSURE LIQUID
HIGH-PRESSURE VAPOR
LOW-PRESSURE LIQUID
LOW-PRESSURE VAPOR

Figure 5-5. Once the air conditioner has run for a few minutes, liquid and gaseous refrigerant occur in both the high and low sides of the system.

■ Warm It First

For an air conditioning system to dry out any moisture inside, it must be warm. At 29 in-Hg of vacuum, water turns to steam at 87°F (737 mm-Hg and 35°C). At 28 in-Hg, it vaporizes at 101°F (711 mm-Hg and 43°C). A suggestion: at cold ambient temperatures, heat up the engine by running it for 30 minutes before testing or servicing the air conditioning system. If the system cannot maintain at least 29 in-Hg (737 mm-Hg) of vacuum, there is a leak.

caused by the high pressure, the pressurized refrigerant easily condenses to a liquid. As it changes state, the refrigerant releases heat to the condenser structure, and the airflow through the condenser carries the heat away. The refrigerant leaves the condenser as a warm, high-pressure liquid at about 100° to 140°F (40° to 60°C).

In a fixed-orifice expansion tube system, this warm liquid flows directly from the condenser to the expansion tube. In a variable-orifice thermostatic expansion valve system, it first flows to the **receiver-drier**, figure 5-7. Manufacturers use various names for this

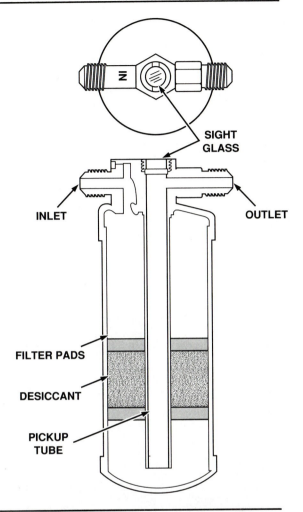

INLET

OUTLET

SIGHT GLASS

FILTER PADS

DESICCANT

PICKUP TUBE

Figure 5-7. The receiver-drier uses a desiccant, or chemical drying element, to remove moisture from the refrigerant. It is located between the condenser and the expansion valve.

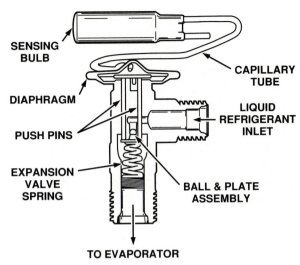

SENSING BULB

DIAPHRAGM

PUSH PINS

EXPANSION VALVE SPRING

CAPILLARY TUBE

LIQUID REFRIGERANT INLET

BALL & PLATE ASSEMBLY

TO EVAPORATOR

Figure 5-8. Refrigerant enters the expansion device as a high-pressure liquid. This Ford thermostatic expansion valve uses a spring-loaded valve controlled by a pressure diaphragm.

lower temperature, below the refrigerant's actual temperature. When that happens, the refrigerant begins to boil into a gas. Expansion devices are covered in detail in Chapter 7.

The low side
Lowering the pressure on the refrigerant lowers its boiling point substantially, so that the liquid continues to boil as it flows through the **evaporator**. The evaporator, like the con-

There are two basic types of expansion devices. Some systems use a **thermostatic expansion valve**, figure 5-8. This valve controls the flow of refrigerant into the evaporator in relation to evaporator outlet temperature. Other systems use an **expansion tube**, or fixed-orifice tube, which simply provides a constant restriction to refrigerant flow, figure 5-9.

The high-pressure side of the system meets the low-pressure side at the expansion device. The expansion device has a small orifice that provides the restriction in the line against which the compressor pumps. This is similar to the restriction that a narrow spray nozzle on a garden hose provides to pressurized water flow. As the high-pressure liquid refrigerant sprays through the orifice into the low-pressure area, the low pressure causes the refrigerant's boiling point to drop to a greatly

Receiver-Drier: The component between the condenser and expansion valve in which liquid refrigerant may be stored, gaseous refrigerant may change into liquid, and moisture is removed with a desiccant.

Desiccant: A chemical drying agent.

Thermostatic Expansion Valve: An expansion device that removes pressure from the refrigerant as it flows into the evaporator and controls the flow rate in relation to evaporator temperature.

Expansion Tube: Fixed-orifice tube; an expansion device that removes pressure from the refrigerant as it flows into the evaporator, but does not vary the flow rate.

Evaporator: A radiator-like tube-and-fin heat exchanger, exposed to airflow into the passenger compartment. As liquid refrigerant flows through the tubes, it vaporizes and absorbs heat from the air flowing between the fins.

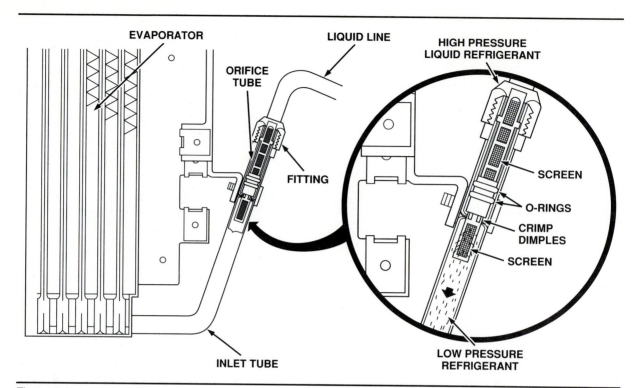

Figure 5-9. An expansion tube provides a restriction for the compressor to pump against, and is also carefully calibrated to meter the refrigerant flow into the low side of the system.

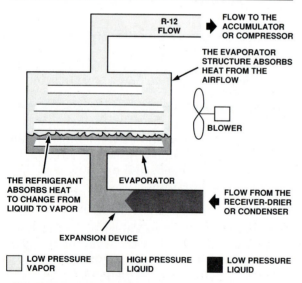

Figure 5-10. The evaporator is built into the air conditioning ducts in the passenger compartment. Refrigerant vaporizing inside chills its surface, and air is then blown over its fins into the passenger compartment.

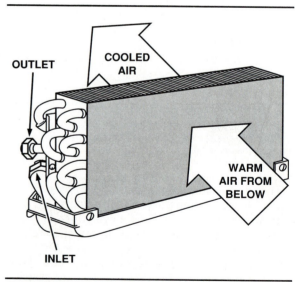

Figure 5-11. The vaporizing liquid refrigerant draws latent heat from the evaporator structure. In a correctly functioning evaporator, little or no liquid refrigerant passes out of the evaporator; all the R-12 should vaporize.

denser, is a heat exchanger. However, while the condenser transfers heat from the refrigerant to an airstream, the evaporator transfers heat from an airstream to the refrigerant, figure 5-10. The refrigerant absorbs latent heat as it vaporizes, and draws it from the evaporator structure, chilling its surface, figure 5-11. When the passenger compartment air is blown through the evaporator, it loses heat to the evaporator fins. This cools the air before it enters the passenger compartment. At the same

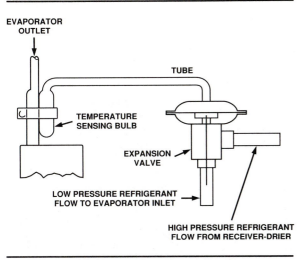

Figure 5-12. The temperature-sensing bulb of the expansion valve assembly is positioned close to the evaporator outlet, and enables the expansion valve to meter refrigerant flow into the evaporator according to outlet temperature.

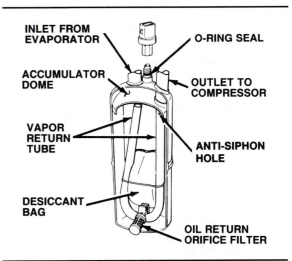

Figure 5-13. The accumulator, used in an expansion tube system, serves functions similar to those of a receiver-drier.

time, water vapor condenses and dust is trapped on the wet evaporator surface.

Ideally, all the refrigerant should evaporate inside the evaporator and leave as a low-pressure vapor. However, if a significant amount of liquid refrigerant is leaving the evaporator, we say that the evaporator is **flooding**. This can cause damage if liquid refrigerant reaches the compressor. On the other hand, if too little refrigerant enters the evaporator, it boils too quickly and can absorb no more heat and the system cannot provide maximum cooling. This is called **starving** the evaporator.

In a thermostatic expansion valve system, figure 5-12, a temperature-sensing bulb is positioned in close contact with the outlet of the evaporator. If the bulb senses a temperature that indicates evaporator flooding, the expansion valve reduces the amount of refrigerant entering the evaporator. If the temperature indicates a starving evaporator, the valve increases the refrigerant flow. Refrigerant leaving the evaporator in a thermostatic expansion valve system flows directly to the compressor intake port, often called the suction side of the compressor.

In a fixed-orifice expansion tube system, refrigerant leaving the evaporator flows to the **accumulator**, figure 5-13. The accumulator serves the same purposes as the receiver-drier in an expansion valve system. The accumulator:

• Stores gaseous refrigerant until it is needed.
• Allows any remaining liquid refrigerant to change into vapor.

• Removes any water from the refrigerant by means of a desiccant.

From the evaporator outlet or the accumulator, vaporized refrigerant is pulled into the compressor intake port. The compressor applies pressure to the refrigerant, and the air conditioning cycle begins again.

Evaporator Controls

So far, we have described a constant automotive air conditioning cycle, working at peak capacity, and providing a constant, maximum level of cooling. However, operating conditions are seldom constant, and the air conditioning system is often required to increase or decrease its output. Each of these changes alters the amount of heat the evaporator must

---

Flooding: An air conditioner malfunction, when too much liquid refrigerant leaves the evaporator without vaporizing.

Starving: An air conditioner malfunction, when too little liquid refrigerant enters the evaporator through the expansion device.

Accumulator: A component between the evaporator and the compressor inlet in which gaseous refrigerant may be stored, liquid refrigerant may change into vapor, and water can be removed from the refrigerant by means of a desiccant.

absorb, and requires modulating the flow of refrigerant into the evaporator:

• The compressor is belt-driven by the engine, and its output changes with engine speed. If uncontrolled, the high-side refrigerant pressure and system efficiency would go up and down with engine speed.
• The driver may select a temperature other than maximum cooling, requiring reduced output.
• When the car is standing still, airflow through the condenser drops, and reduces cooling efficiency.
• High **ambient temperature** raises the temperature of the air flowing through both the condenser and the evaporator, which reduces efficiency, and also typically causes the driver to select cooler air temperatures.
• When humidity is high, more water vapor condenses on the chilled evaporator. As this water vapor changes state to a liquid, it gives up a great deal of latent heat, which is absorbed by the evaporator fins. This heat is then transferred to the vaporizing R-12 inside the evaporator, along with the heat from the air passing over the fins into the passenger compartment. The result is that air conditioner operation providing good cooling on a dry day may be inadequate on a humid day.

Automotive air conditioning systems use modulating controls to compensate for these changing conditions and maintain the required evaporator temperature. These controls maintain evaporator temperature by regulating the pressure of the refrigerant inside it. Air conditioners use several types of evaporator controls, including:

• Cycling compressor clutches
• Variable displacement compressors
• Thermostatic expansion valves at the evaporator inlet
• Evaporator pressure control valves at the evaporator outlet.

These devices may be used singly or in combination with each other to achieve more precise control of evaporator operation.

Cycling compressor clutches
A **cycling compressor clutch** uses an electric switch operated by a thermostat to sense the temperature or pressure of the evaporator and engage or disengage the compressor clutch in response. When the evaporator temperature or pressure drops below a certain point, the switch disengages the compressor clutch. This stops the refrigeration process, because the compressor stops pumping refrigerant through

the system. When the temperature rises above the setpoint, the switch engages the clutch, the compressor begins pumping, and the cooling cycle resumes. Compressor clutches will be discussed in detail in Chapter 6.

Variable displacement compressors
A variable-displacement compressor regulates evaporator pressure, and therefore evaporator temperature, by changing the stroke of the pistons inside it in response to pressure changes in the low side circuit. Normally this system uses a pressure sensor positioned on the compressor near the suction port that monitors low side refrigerant pressure. When demand on the air conditioning system is high, the low side pressure will increase, reflecting a temperature increase in the evaporator. The compressor then increases its stroke volume to force more refrigerant into the evaporator to increase cooling performance. Compressors will be discussed in detail in Chapter 6.

Thermostatic expansion valves
Both cycling clutch systems and variable displacement compressors may also use a thermostatic expansion valve (TXV). The thermostatic expansion valve at the evaporator inlet operates first as a restriction to raise the high side pressure, and second as a modulating valve to assist the variable or cycling compressor operation in maintaining correct evaporator pressure. Its variable orifice responds to the temperature of the evaporator outlet to regulate evaporator temperature by increasing or decreasing the rate at which refrigerant enters from the system high side. The thermostatic expansion valve, and its variants, the H-valve or block valve, will be discussed in Chapter 7.

Pressure control valves
Systems with continuously-running, fixed-displacement compressors have often used a **pressure control valve** of one kind or another at or beyond the evaporator outlet that responds to and controls evaporator temperature by regulating the flow of the gaseous refrigerant out of the evaporator and into the compressor. Pressure is first sensed by a cell within the pressure valve that contains an absolute vacuum. This cell reacts to refrigerant pressure (and therefore temperature) inside the evaporator and operates the pressure control valve, figure 5-14. Whenever pressure decreases below a certain value, the valve closes and prevents refrigerant flow out of the evaporator. The compressor keeps running, and pressure in the evaporator builds. At a preset pressure point, the valve opens the line from

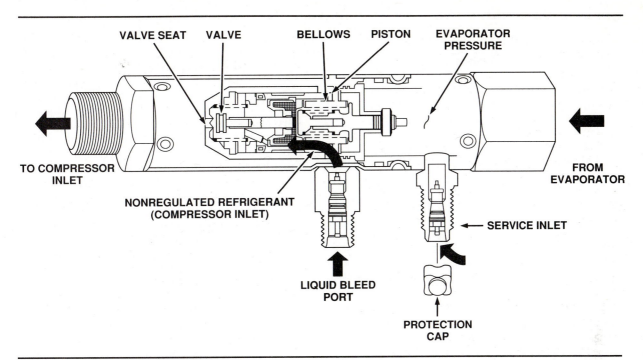

Figure 5-14. Although evaporator pressure control valve designs differ slightly among manufacturers, they all react to evaporator pressure to control refrigerant flow to the compressor.

the evaporator to the compressor, thus reducing evaporator pressure. This modulating action maintains output air temperature within the desired range.

The pressure regulator valves in common use have slight design variations, and each manufacturer uses its own term for its own valve:

• Chrysler: Evaporator pressure regulator (EPR or EPR II) valve, or evaporator temperature regulator (ETR) valve
• General Motors: Pilot-operated absolute (POA) valve
• Ford: Bypass orifice valve (BPO).

Many newer General Motors air conditioning systems use a Valves-in-Receiver (VIR) assembly, which combines the receiver-drier, sight glass, expansion valve, and a POA valve into one single unit. Some Ford systems use similar combination valves. The construction and operation of these evaporator outlet pressure regulators are explained fully in Chapter 7.

REFRIGERANT AND REFRIGERATION OIL

Two fluids are used in automotive air conditioning systems: refrigerant and refrigeration oil. Refrigeration oil lubricates the compressor and expansion valve. Refrigerant itself, as you

know, is the central element of the entire air conditioning process because it absorbs heat from the passenger compartment air and transfers it to the atmosphere.

Refrigerant 12

Currently, the refrigerant used in all automotive air conditioning systems is a chemical generically called **Refrigerant 12**, a term often

Ambient Temperature: The temperature of the air surrounding a component.

Cycling Compressor Clutch: An evaporator control device that uses a thermostatic switch to sense temperature in the evaporator fins and disengage or engage the compressor clutch in response.

Pressure Control Valve: An evaporator control device located between the evaporator and compressor that controls refrigerant flow into the compressor in response to pressure in the evaporator.

Refrigerant 12: Dichlorodifluoromethane (CCl_2F_2), abbreviated R-12; the refrigerant used in all current automotive air conditioning systems. It has a high specific heat and low boiling point, but is environmentally hazardous.

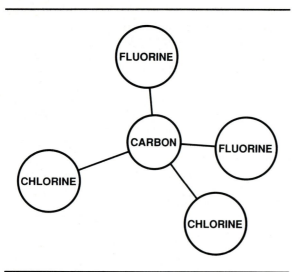

Figure 5-15. The chemical formula for Refrigerant 12 is CCl_2F_2. This means a molecule of R-12 has one atom of carbon (C), two of chlorine (Cl), and two more of fluorine (F).

abbreviated to R-12. It carries many trade names, including Aircon 12, Genetron 12, Prestone 12, Freeze 12, and Freon. The "12" indicates it is the same as R-12. R-12 is developed from carbon tetrachloride (CCl_4), a highly-toxic liquid once commonly used in fire extinguishers and cleaning fluids. A molecule of carbon tetrachloride consists of one atom of carbon and four atoms of chlorine. To form R-12 out of carbon tetrachloride, chemists replace two chlorine atoms with two fluorine atoms, producing **dichlorodifluoromethane** (CCl_2F_2), figure 5-15.

R-12 is an excellent refrigerant. First, it has a fairly high specific heat, so a relatively small amount can absorb and transfer large amounts of heat. Without this quality, the condenser and evaporator would have to be much larger, and would be more difficult to fit into an automobile without extensive design and styling modifications. Second, it has a low boiling point. Under normal atmospheric pressure, it boils at about –22°F (–30°C). These characteristics mean that R-12 can vaporize and absorb a great deal of heat at normal air temperatures. Additionally, R-12 is nontoxic, noncorrosive, soluble in oil and water, chemically stable, and easy to handle within a wide range of temperatures and pressures. R-12 is also compatible with normal metal and rubber materials used in the air conditioner. Of course, there are safety precautions you must observe when handling refrigerant, such as keeping it away from your eyes. These are outlined in Chapter 1 of the *Shop Manual*.

Even though R-12 is an excellent automotive refrigerant, widespread use has serious drawbacks. R-12 is a chlorinated fluorocarbon (CFC), and therefore any R-12 that escapes into the atmosphere contributes to the destruction of the earth's ozone layer, a very thin but very important part of the upper atmosphere that protects us from cancer-causing ultraviolet radiation. That is one reason why it is important the air conditioning system be leak-free. In fact, the government may soon require installed systems to be leak-free by law, and restrict the venting of air conditioners to the atmosphere during service. If so, future air

■ R-12: The End Of The Beginning

Refrigerant 12 has been the standard refrigerant in automotive air conditioners since 1955. In the near future, however, R-12 is likely to become scarcer, more expensive, and much more heavily regulated than it is now, as state and Federal government agencies eliminate it as an environmentally hazardous substance. By 1989, the Vermont Legislature passed a bill banning all CFC refrigerants by 1993. Other proposals concerned ending packaging of refrigerant in the 14-ounce cans popular with do-it-yourselfers, forcing sales in only the much more expensive 30 and 60 pound drums. In all, an estimated 18 states had over 70 separate pieces of pending legislation regulating or banning R-12. The Federal government suggested using the chlorofluorocarbon regulatory structure to generate revenue; either by auctioning the right to produce regulated CFCs, or by imposing a one- to two-dollar tax per pound of CFC manufactured. In the face of increasing regulation, expense, and the growing awareness of its hazardous nature, it is very likely that R-12 will eventually be banned entirely.

If phased out of new car air conditioning systems, recycling R-12 for older cars will become economically feasible as fresh R-12 becomes more expensive. Current estimates are that 30 percent of the R-12 now consumed by automobile dealerships is wasted by venting customer systems to the atmosphere, and could be recovered by recycling equipment. Current recycling equipment designs would cost between $3,000 and $7,000.

However, recycling brings up new questions, such as whether recycled R-12 would be acceptable to air conditioning system manufacturers or whether new types of refrigerants might be compatible with systems designed for R-12 use, making the purchase of expensive recycling systems unnecessary. As of this writing, Refrigerant 12 is still the only refrigerant recommended for automotive air conditioners.

Figure 5-16. Refrigerant is sold in bulk containers for professional use.

conditioning systems and service, like today's exhaust systems, would become subject to periodic inspection.

The legal issues may be irrelevant. By 1990, many domestic and foreign manufacturers required the service departments of their dealers to purchase and use R-12 recycling equipment, even without government regulations. Some went so far as to forbid their parts and service departments to sell R-12 in the smaller containers.

Special-purpose refrigerant

Some brands of R-12 contain special additives. One contains measured amounts of refrigeration oil, so oil can be added to the system along with the refrigerant. Another additive lubricates seals in contact with moving surfaces to improve the wiping action of the seal. Other additives include a sealer chemical that hardens with air contact, to plug pinhole leaks. Such leak sealers are effective only for very small leaks. Most leakage requires part repair or replacement.

Another common additive is leak-tracing dye. Refrigerant itself is difficult to detect directly, because it instantly vaporizes as it leaves a leak. Refrigerants with dyes should be added to a system only if it is at least 40 percent full. After the air conditioner is run for some time, the dye becomes visible as a red or blue streak on leaking hoses or fittings. Some dyes are visible under only black or ultraviolet light. However, most manufacturers do not recommend using dyes in the air conditioning system. Remember that doing so may void the system warranty.

Refrigerant containers

R-12 usually is sold in white containers, although you should not make a habit of relying on the color of a container to identify its contents. Be sure to read the label. Refrigerant is supplied for professional use in 30- and 60-pound (14- and 27-kilogram) bulk containers, figure 5-16. R-12 is also available in small cans, figure 5-17. These are generally 14-ounce (397-gram) cans, but they are often referred to as "pound cans," and are popular with do-it-yourselfers.

Never expose refrigerant cans to fire or flames. Burning refrigerant produces deadly phosgene gas, a gas that can harm you before you smell it. Moreover, the heat of a fire can make even an almost empty can explode, causing damage and possible injury. Dispose of

Dichlorodifluoromethane: The chemical name for Refrigerant 12, (CCl_2F_2).

■ Beyond R-12: Air Conditioners Of The Future

If R-12 is completely banned, air conditioning systems can certainly be produced that use other, non-hazardous refrigerants. Before they can be designed, however, a suitable replacement refrigerant must be found. One possibility is DuPont Company's HFC-134a, a non-CFC refrigerant that seems the most likely near-term, cost-effective replacement.

Unfortunately, 134a does not have nearly as much heat-exchange capability as R-12. Combined with its incompatibility with current refrigeration oils, this means that it cannot be used in systems designed for R-12. An effective 134a air conditioner will require:

● A larger condenser and evaporator
● A larger, more powerful compressor
● New high-pressure hose designs and seals
● Alternative refrigeration oils.

Incorporating the larger condenser and the heavier compressor assembly into the engine compartment of an automobile would likely have a great influence on styling and front-end design. This could easily reverse the aerodynamic styling trends of the 1990's, requiring much higher hoodlines and larger grille openings to permit enough airflow through the condenser to make the air conditioner work. Many of the current "cars-of-the-future" would become cars-of-the-past before being built, as manufacturers alter the front sheet metal in running changes to accommodate HFC-134a air conditioners.

Figure 5-17. Refrigerant may also be purchased in small "pound cans."

used refrigeration cans according to the manufacturer's recommendations on the side of the container.

Special-purpose fluids
Some refrigerant-like materials are available for purposes other than refrigeration. These include R-11 and R-22. These are not intended to be left permanently in the system. They are used to clean and flush the system to remove contaminants and moisture. If, for example, the compressor has had a major mechanical malfunction, small pieces of debris may be spread through the system. In this case, it is not enough just to replace the damaged compressor. Unless the particles are removed, they can damage or clog the repaired system as soon as it is started. Since R-12 is not designed for washing the inside of the air conditioning system, R-11 is used to flush away residue. R-22 can be used to pick up moisture so the system can be safely evacuated.

Refrigeration Oil

Lubricant in the air conditioning system:

• Lubricates the compressor and expansion valve
• Protects the inside of the air conditioning system
• Keeps seals in good condition.

The friction surfaces and bearings inside the compressor require lubrication to work properly and to ensure a long service life. Thermostatic expansion valves must be lubricated to stay in good condition. Lubricant coats the inside of the air conditioning system to prevent any corrosive substances from attacking the internal system components. The oil also keeps

seals soft and pliant, which reduces seepage from the system and aids system efficiency. In the compressor, for example, lubricant helps the piston rings seal tightly against their cylinder walls to prevent leakage, and apply maximum pressure to the refrigerant.

Refrigeration oil is a mineral oil especially formulated for air conditioning systems. Refrigeration oil is ideally suited for its purposes. It is virtually free of sulfur, so it does not damage rubber seals or form corrosive substances. It is nonfoaming, an important consideration since refrigeration oil flows through the entire system along with the refrigerant. Foam reduces system efficiency by displacing refrigerant. Refrigeration oil is wax-free, so it does not gum up the system, and its viscosity (thickness) stays the same even when its temperature varies due to the cooling process. Finally, refrigeration oil is dehydrated — it contains no dissolved water — to avoid contaminating the air conditioning system. However, as a result, it is hygroscopic and will absorb moisture from the air if left standing in an open or loosely sealed container.

Refrigeration oil is normally sold in cans that look similar to but are smaller than the "pound" refrigerant cans. These cans are charged with refrigerant as well as refrigeration oil, to provide pressure to feed the oil into the air conditioning system. Whenever the air conditioning system is discharged, some refrigeration oil is lost. Replacing system components such as the receiver-drier in which the oil accumulates also causes an oil loss. It is important to add refrigeration oil to the air conditioning system to compensate for these losses when you service the system.

CONTROL MODE AIRFLOW PATTERNS

Air conditioning system control modes and the exact airflow pattern created in each mode vary among systems. The following list of typical control modes describes airflow patterns in a representative air conditioning system:

• OFF. When the air conditioner is turned off, the:

— Outside air door is in "cold" position.
— Blend door is in "cold" position.
— Blower and compressor are not operating.
In some vehicles, the blower or compressor may operate even when the control is turned off.

• MAX — In the maximum setting, the air conditioning system reduces interior temperature as quickly as possible. Because this mode uses

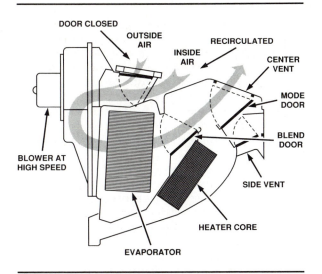

Figure 5-18. The airflow in a typical air conditioning system in the MAXIMUM air conditioning mode.

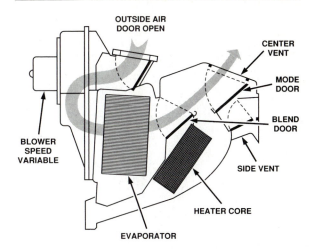

Figure 5-19. The airflow in a typical air conditioning system in the NORMAL air conditioning mode.

recirculated air, it does not flush stale vapors or odors from the vehicle. For this reason, the maximum setting should not be used continuously. At maximum, figure 5-18, the:

— Outside air door is closed.
— Mode door directs air to the center vent only.
— Blower motor is operated at high speed.
— Compressor is operating.

• NORMAL — This setting is used for most driving conditions. In the normal air conditioning mode, figure 5-19, the:

— Outside air door is open.
— Mode door directs air to the center vent only.
— Blend door position can be varied with the temperature control device.
— Blower speed can be varied with the blower control device.
— Compressor is operating.
— Heater core is operating.

• VENT — Ventilation. When the controls are at the ventilation setting, the airflow is the same as in the normal air conditioning mode, but the air conditioning system is not operating.

• BILEVEL — In the bilevel control mode, the cooled air circulates through the center vents and the floor vents at the same time. In this mode, figure 5-20, the:

— Outside air door is open.
— Mode door directs 60 percent of the air to the center vent and 40 percent to the floor-level vents.

— Blend door position can be varied with the temperature control device.
— Blower speed can be varied with the blower control device.
— Compressor is operating.
— Heater core is operating.

Refrigeration Oil: A mineral oil especially formulated for use as a lubricant in automotive air conditioning systems.

■ You'll Get A Charge Out Of This

When replacing an electronic component such as a control module, it is extremely important to eliminate electrostatic discharge. Many manufacturers now ship these parts in antistatic plastic bags. When handling these components, you must first sit in the car and touch a metal body part before opening the bag. This grounds you and removes any static electricity. Failing to take these precautions could shorten the lifespan of the component by as much as one-half.

Some technicians may suggest wearing an antistatic wrist band and grounding wire, similar to the ones often worn by computer operators. This is *never* a good idea for an automobile technician, where you might connect yourself to full battery current or wind the cord up in a cooling fan. Always sit down in the car and then touch a metal screw head or any other exposed metal grounded to the car body, before opening any antistatic containers. Touch a grounded point occasionally as you work, too.

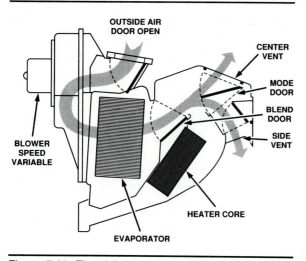

Figure 5-20. The airflow in a typical air conditioning system in the BILEVEL mode.

SUMMARY

An automotive air conditioning system uses five main parts through which refrigerant flows: the compressor, condenser, receiver-drier or accumulator, expansion device, and evaporator. The expansion device may be either a thermostatic expansion valve or an expansion tube. In the air conditioning high side, the refrigerant is under high pressure and at high temperature. In the low side, the refrigerant is under low pressure and at low temperature. Compressors are equipped with service valves, so that service technicians can gain access to the air conditioning system. One service valve is on the high side, and the other is on the low side. There are two types of service valves: stem-type and Schrader valves.

The belt-driven compressor draws in low-pressure refrigerant, compresses it, and sends high-pressure refrigerant to the condenser. In the condenser, the refrigerant changes states from a vapor to a liquid, releasing heat into the airstream. From the condenser, the refrigerant flows either to the expansion tube or, in an expansion valve system, to the receiver-drier, where any remaining vapor condenses and any water in the refrigerant is removed; then the refrigerant flows to the expansion valve. The expansion device removes pressure from the refrigerant.

From the expansion device, the refrigerant flows to the evaporator, where the refrigerant changes state from a liquid to a vapor, drawing heat from the evaporator structure and chilling it. The airflow into the passenger compartment is cooled as it flows between the chilled evaporator fins. Because moisture in the air condenses on the evaporator surface, water vapor in it condenses and is drained off.

If the refrigerant does not evaporate completely in the evaporator, the evaporator is "flooded". If the refrigerant evaporates too quickly, the evaporator is "starving". A thermostatic expansion valve uses a temperature-sensing bulb to modulate refrigerant flow into the evaporator in response to evaporator temperature.

In an expansion tube system, the refrigerant flows from the evaporator to the accumulator. The accumulator serves purposes similar to those of the receiver-drier, except that it allows liquid refrigerant to vaporize, instead of vice versa. From the accumulator, the refrigerant flows to the compressor inlet. In an expansion valve system, the refrigerant flows directly from the evaporator to the compressor. In the compressor, the refrigeration cycle begins again.

The two kinds of evaporator controls vary the cooling process to maintain consistent cooling in spite of varying conditions. The cycling clutch maintains a consistent temperature range by disengaging the compressor clutch whenever the evaporator temperature falls below the desired range and reengaging the clutch when the temperature rises. The pressure control valve modulates refrigerant flow from the evaporator to the compressor in response to evaporator pressure, keeping evaporator temperature within a desired range.

Refrigerant 12, or dichlorodifluoromethane (CCl_2F_2), is often called R-12. Its high specific heat and low boiling point make it suitable for use in an automotive air conditioning system, but it contributes to the destruction of the ozone layer of the atmosphere and may soon be banned. Special-purpose substances similar to R-12, such as R-11 and R-22, are available to clean and dry the air conditioning system during service.

Refrigeration oil is required to lubricate the compressor and expansion valve, protect the inside of the air conditioning system, and keeps seals in good condition.

Control modes and airflow patterns vary among air conditioning systems. Typically, in MAX mode, passenger compartment air is recirculated to cool the inside of the car quickly. In NORMAL mode, outside air is cooled and routed into the passenger compartment. In VENT mode, the refrigeration process is eliminated and unconditioned outside air is circulated into the passenger compartment. In BILEVEL mode, airflow is divided between the center dashboard vent and the vents at floor level.

Review Questions

Choose the single most correct answer.
Compare your answers with the correct answers on page 229.

1. Refrigerant leaves the compressor as a:
   a. Hot, high-pressure gas
   b. Cool, low-pressure liquid
   c. Hot, low-pressure liquid
   d. Cool, high-pressure gas

2. A receiver-drier:
   a. Stores excess refrigerant
   b. Traps moisture
   c. Allows refrigerant to condense
   d. All of the above

3. The evaporator is flooded when:
   a. Considerable liquid refrigerant enters it
   b. Considerable liquid refrigerant leaves it
   c. Evaporation is complete inside it
   d. The refrigerant cannot boil inside it

4. Technician A says a cycling compressor clutch responds to the temperature of the evaporator.
   Technician B says a pressure control valve on the compressor responds to evaporator pressure, and therefore temperature.
   Who is right?
   a. A only
   b. B only
   c. Both A and B
   d. Neither A nor B

5. Refrigerant 12:
   a. Has a low specific heat
   b. Has a high boiling point
   c. Is insoluble in oil and water
   d. None of the above

6. Refrigerant 12 is harmful because it:
   a. Destroys bacteria
   b. Destroys the ozone layer
   c. Is heavier than water
   d. Is corrosive to metal

7. Which of the following is *not* a feature of refrigeration oil:
   a. Nonfoaming
   b. Sulfur-free
   c. Variable viscosity
   d. Wax-free

8. Refrigeration oil can be lost when:
   a. Discharging the system
   b. Replacing the compressor
   c. A system leak occurs
   d. All of the above

9. In a typical air conditioning system, the BILEVEL mode divides the airflow:
   a. 60% to the dash and 40% to the floor
   b. 40% to the dash and 60% to the floor
   c. 50% to the dash and 50% to the floor
   d. 80% to the dash and 20% to the floor

10. In MAX AC mode:
   a. The coolant valve is closed
   b. The defroster door is open
   c. The outside air door is open
   d. The blower is disabled

6

Compressors and Compressor Clutches

The compressor is the air conditioning system pump, which circulates refrigerant though the system. Because refrigerant flow is restricted at the expansion device, the refrigerant pressure builds up within the condenser and refrigerant lines, creating the high pressure of the system's high side.

In this chapter, we will discuss how the compressor works with the condenser and evaporator to remove heat from the car. There are a number of compressor designs, and we will examine the most popular compressors in use. Additionally, we will discuss compressor clutches and how they work.

COMPRESSOR, CONDENSER, AND EVAPORATOR INTERACTION

An automotive air conditioning system is a closed-loop system. The compressor is the heart of this system. The human heart takes in blood through one valve and pumps it through another to circulate it through the body, where it undergoes changes such as having oxygen added to or taken from it. In a similar way, the compressor takes in heat-laden, vaporized refrigerant from the low side of the air conditioning system and forces it into the high side to circulate through the system. As it circulates, the refrigerant changes from a gas into a liquid in the condenser and from a liquid back to a gas in the evaporator.

Although the basic refrigeration process is explained in earlier chapters, we will review the causes and effects of the refrigerant's changes of state so as to better understand the compressor's role in that process.

There are two reasons the refrigerant changes back to a liquid inside the condenser tubing. The first is that the increased pressure raises the temperature at which the refrigerant gas will condense to a liquid (its boiling point), so that a smaller temperature drop in the gaseous refrigerant will cause it to condense. The second is that the airflow between the condenser fins and tubes cools it below that temperature. As the refrigerant condenses, the latent heat that it absorbed when it changed into a gas inside the evaporator is released to the condenser and carried away by the airflow.

The expansion device in an automotive air conditioning system restricts the flow of refrigerant from the high side to the low side, figure 6-1. Because of this restriction, refrigerant can pass through the expansion device at the rate forced by the compressor only if the pressure is increased. This is similar to increasing water pressure in a garden hose by restricting it with

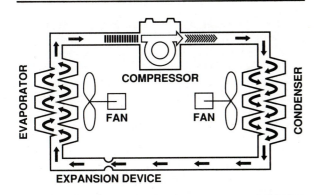

Figure 6-1. Refrigerant flowing through an automotive air conditioning system changes pressure and temperature at both the compressor and the expansion device.

a spray nozzle — the pressure builds up behind the nozzle until the spray is fast enough to balance the pressure. And like a garden hose, refrigerant compression does not take place only within the compressor. The compressor's pumping action pressurizes the refrigerant throughout the system high side. The area in which the refrigerant is compressed starts at the compressor outlet and ends at the orifice inside the expansion device.

Increasing the pressure on any liquid raises its boiling point, and increasing the pressure on any gas raises its condensation point (for any one substance, these are the same temperatures). Refrigerant 12 is no exception. For example, at atmospheric pressure, refrigerant has a boiling point of –22°F (–29°C). At 120 psi (830 kPa), it has a boiling point of 100°F (38°C). The latter is a normal air conditioning high side pressure when the air temperature outside is 70°F (21°C). When this outside air blows through the condenser fins, the refrigerant temperature inside the condenser soon falls below 100°F (38°C), and the R-12 condenses from a gas to a liquid.

Remember that these temperatures and pressures are examples only. At 80°F (27°C) ambient air temperature, the high side pressure might be 150 psi (1,035 kPa) or more, and the refrigerant's boiling point would be correspondingly higher. However, at any temperature, the general principles described remain the same. *Increasing its pressure or decreasing its temperature cause the refrigerant to condense.*

The effect of refrigerant condensation is that the heat that the refrigerant absorbed as it boiled in the evaporator is now released, and the refrigerant cools. The heat is transferred from the refrigerant into the metal condenser by conduction and then from the condenser

into the airflow by convection. When refrigerant reaches the system restriction, it is a warm liquid, ready for use in the low side of the system.

Once the liquid refrigerant sprays through the expansion device, it is no longer pressed against the restriction, and so pressure is removed from it. Pressure is further reduced by the suction action of the compressor inlet, at the other end of the low side. This pressure drop lowers the boiling point of the refrigerant so that it promptly begins to boil in the evaporator. For example, at 30 psi (207 kPa), which is a normal low-side pressure, refrigerant boils at 32°F (0°C). An airflow through the evaporator at this or any higher temperature will cause the refrigerant to boil. *Decreasing its pressure or increasing its temperature cause the refrigerant to boil.*

As the refrigerant boils, it absorbs latent heat from the metal evaporator as it turns into a gas. The heat is transferred from the evaporator to the refrigerant by conduction. In turn, the evaporator absorbs heat from the air flowing between its tubes and fins by convection as the air flows into the passenger compartment.

Without the pressurized refrigerant flowing from the compressor, the refrigeration process will stop. If the compressor is not pumping refrigerant against the restriction, the pressure does not build up in the high side, the refrigerant does not condense, and no heat is dumped into the outside airflow. In the low side, with no suction against the restriction to create a low pressure and draw the refrigerant through the evaporator, the refrigerant does not boil, and no heat is removed from the air flowing into the passenger compartment. Thus, when the air conditioner compressor is

■ Controlling Evaporator Flow By Hand

Before thermostatic controls, hand valves were used to regulate evaporator and passenger compartment temperature. In the late 1950s, the popular Mark IV air conditioning system used the manually-operated SelecTrol valve to regulate the flow of refrigerant through the evaporator. Basically, this was a simple faucet mounted on the suction line next to the evaporator. A knob on the dashboard was connected to the valve by a cable. Turning the knob counterclockwise opened the valve to allow full refrigerant flow through the system and ensure maximum cooling. A bypass orifice allowed a continuous small flow of refrigerant and oil, even with the valve closed.

turned off, the refrigerant pressure and temperatures take several seconds to gradually equalize throughout the system until there is no longer any difference between the low side and the high side. When the compressor is turned back on, the pressure and temperature differences between the refrigerant in the high and the low side build up until the air conditioner is fully functional.

TYPES OF COMPRESSORS

Over the years, well over two dozen air conditioning compressors have been used by numerous manufacturers. However, all fall into one of three designs:

• Positive-displacement piston
• Variable-displacement piston
• Rotary-vane.

Most HVAC compressors are positive-displacement piston designs. A positive-displacement piston compressor is one that displaces a constant, uniform volume of refrigerant for each revolution or operating cycle, just as a piston-driven internal combustion engine takes in and exhausts the same volume of gases with each operating cycle.

A variable-displacement piston compressor is one that displaces a volume of refrigerant that varies with the changing load on the air conditioning system. The two designs currently used both alter cylinder displacement by increasing or decreasing the piston stroke.

A rotary-vane compressor has no pistons at all. Instead, it uses a rotor with sealing vanes spinning inside an elliptical chamber, similar to many power steering pump designs. Only one design is currently used, but its efficiency is very high for its size.

All current compressors are belt driven from the engine, and all are engaged and disengaged using an electromagnetic clutch. The operation of compressor clutches is explained in detail later in this chapter. For now, it is important to understand that because the compressor is driven by a belt from the engine, it absorbs engine horsepower when operating. Even an efficient compressor can use a significant portion of a small four-cylinder engine's power, detracting noticeably from the car's performance. Compressor design variations result from the ongoing engineering goal of providing an efficient pump in a smaller, lighter unit that uses less engine power.

The compressor body provides the housing for all other compressor parts. It contains the cylindrical bores in which pistons move or the elliptical chamber in which an impeller turns, the space in which the crankshaft or swashplate operates, the inlet and outlet ports through which refrigerant flows, and attachments for mounting the compressor in the car. Front and rear heads may be part of the compressor body assembly. They generally are installed using gaskets or O-rings to seal the compressor.

Positive-Displacement Piston Compressors

A piston-type compressor has an intake stroke just like that of a four-stroke automobile engine, figure 6-2. Just as the intake stroke of an engine's piston creates a low-pressure area that draws the air-fuel mixture into the cylinder head, so the intake stroke of the compressor piston creates a low-pressure area to draw gaseous refrigerant into the compressor, figure 6-3.

The similarity ends here, however. In an automobile engine, the compression stroke compresses the air-fuel mixture inside a sealed cylinder, with both the intake and exhaust valves closed.

Compression takes place differently in the two-stroke piston-type air conditioning compressor. Because the discharge valve does not resist compression, the refrigerant gas is compressed simultaneously throughout the entire high side of the air conditioning system. At the end of the compressor piston's intake, or suction, stroke, the maximum possible charge of evaporated refrigerant has been drawn in. The piston begins its compression, or discharge, stroke and this pressure shuts the suction valve and opens the discharge valve at the same time. The charge of refrigerant gas is pushed out of the compressor into the high-side line towards the condenser, and ultimately the expansion device.

The restriction caused by the expansion device is what results in pressurizing of the refrigerant. The piston forces gaseous refrigerant into the high-side lines and condenser faster than the liquified refrigerant can spray through the restriction. As a result, the high-side essentially "backs up," and pressure increases throughout the system between the discharge port and the expansion device.

Internal components
The major internal components of a piston compressor, figure 6-4, are the reed valves, pistons and rings, and the piston drive mechanism.

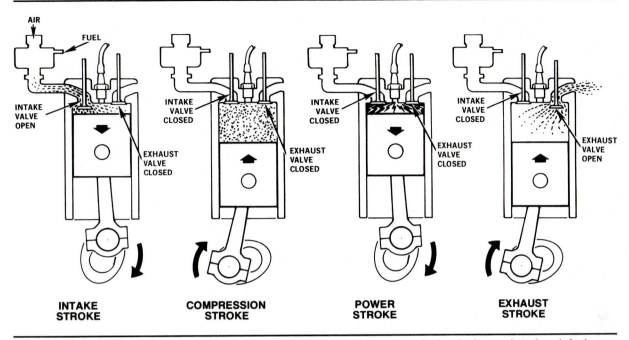

Figure 6-2. A typical compressor has an intake stroke similar to this engine cylinder. In the engine, the air-fuel mixture is drawn in on the intake stroke, compressed on the compression stroke, ignited on the power stroke, and released on the exhaust stroke.

■ A Pistonless Compressor

Engineers at Sanden International USA and General Electric have developed what may be the next-generation of automotive air conditioning compressors. This experimental version departs from traditional compressors in several important ways. First, it uses a spiral-channel design instead of pistons. This is quite similar to the G-Lader superchargers used on some Volkswagen models, derived from a design patented in France in 1905. The spiral is considerably more efficient than the piston, and reduces noise and wear.

In this design, concentric spiral ramps in both sides of a rotor mesh with similar ramps cast in the split housing.

The rotor moves around an eccentric shaft instead of spinning on its axis as in most compressor designs. Refrigerant drawn into the housing is squeezed through the spiral. This raises the pressure of the refrigerant, which is then forced through a cluster of ports in the center of the housing and into the discharge line.

Another innovation on this experimental design is that the compressor is driven by a 96-volt electric motor, rather than being belt driven from the engine. The compressor also is hermetically sealed to eliminate refrigerant leaks and seepage through porous rubber hoses.

VOLKSWAGEN G-LADER

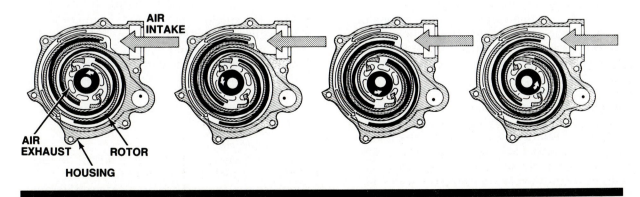

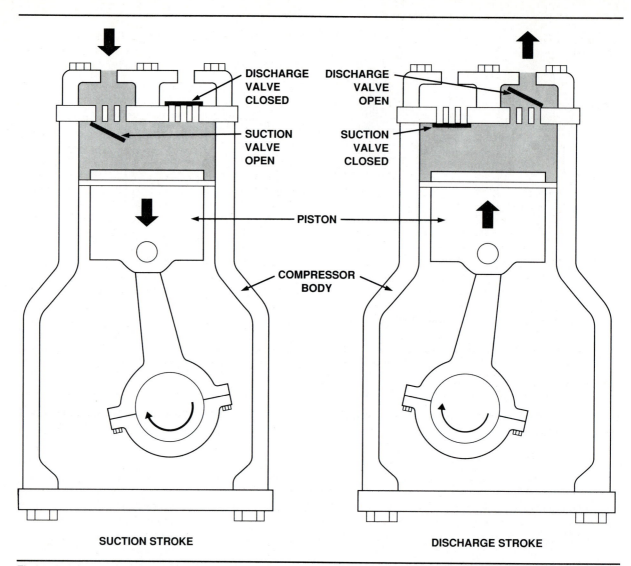

Figure 6-3. In a compressor, the piston's suction opens the intake valve to admit low-pressure R-12. On the piston's discharge, the pressure closes the intake valve and forces the R-12 out through the discharge valve.

Reed valves

All piston compressors use one suction valve and one discharge valve for each piston. The typical valve used in compressors is the reed valve: a one-way, flap-type check valve that is usually built into a valve plate sealing one or more cylinders, figure 6-5. The suction reed valve is located on the underside of the valve plate. When the suction created by the piston's downward stroke becomes strong enough, the suction reed valve bends, or flaps, off its seat, and gaseous refrigerant flows into the compressor. The refrigerant gas fills the partial vacuum created by the moving piston.

The discharge reed valve is on the top side of the valve plate, away from the piston. The partial vacuum in the cylinder also pulls the discharge valve tightly against its seat, sealing

off the system's high side from the cylinder during the suction stroke.

The reeds behave in exactly the opposite way during the piston's compression, or discharge. The increasing cylinder pressure pushes the suction valve tightly against its seat, sealing off the system's low side. The discharge valve on the opposite side of the valve plate, however, is unseated as the pressure in the cylinder increases. The piston pushes the refrigerant through the discharge valve, out of the compressor, and into the air conditioning system high side.

Pistons and rings

This basic two-stroke cycle depends upon the pistons and their sealing rings to provide an adequate seal against the high side refrigerant

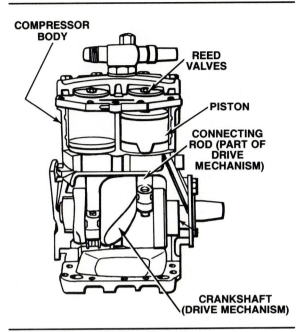

Figure 6-4. This two-cylinder compressor uses reed valves mounted to a valve plate, and two single-acting pistons mounted to a turning shaft.

vibration. Pistons have rings to seal the cylinders, similar to the compression rings in automobile engines.

Piston drive mechanisms

In some designs, a compressor crankshaft drives the pistons. Other compressors use a swashplate. With a crankshaft system, the pistons are attached to lobes or connecting rods on the shaft, which is powered directly by the compressor pulley. This is similar to an automobile engine crankshaft, except that it is the shaft that moves the pistons, not vice versa. By staggering the position of the lobes or connecting rods, the timing of the piston movement can be varied.

A **swashplate**, or axial plate, is a plate rigidly mounted to the crankshaft at an angle, figure 6-6. The pistons may be on one or both sides of the plate, and are attached to it so that the plate is free to rotate. As the pulley turns, the shaft and plate assembly rotate, forcing the pistons back and forth in their bores. In this way, the swashplate changes the rotating

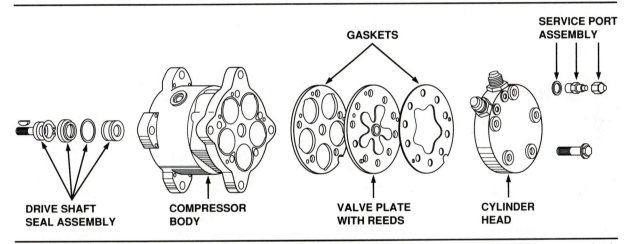

Figure 6-5. Reed valves on this Sanden SD compressor are placed beneath the star-shaped metal brace attached to the valve plate. The brace prevents the reeds from over-flexing.

pressure. As in the example, some compressors use only a single piston. Most piston compressors, however, have from two to six cylinders. The cylinders for these pistons may be arranged with parallel centerlines, radially, or in a V-type configuration, although the latter is seldom seen today. Usually, the action of each piston is opposite to the action of another piston. While one piston moves downward on its suction stroke, another moves upward on its compression stroke. This provides a constant flow of refrigerant through the compressor and also tends to lessen compressor

action of the shaft to a **reciprocating** action that provides driving force to each piston. Compressors that use a swashplate are called

Swashplate: Axial plate; an offset plate attached to the drive shaft of a piston compressor to drive the pistons.

Reciprocating: Back and forth or up and down movement.

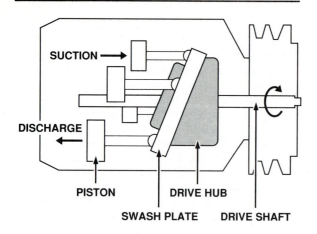

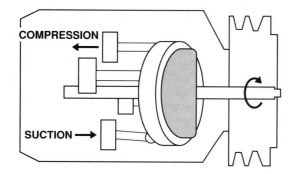

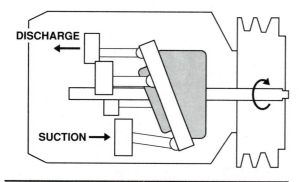

Figure 6-6. The swashplate, attached to the crankshaft at an angle, converts the pulley's rotary motion to axial motion, which drives the pistons in a reciprocating motion.

axial compressors, such as the General Motors 6-cylinder model. (A variation of the swash-plate is the wobble plate, described later. Manufacturers use this term to describe a variable-displacement swashplate, such as in the Chrysler C171 model.)

Square or parallel cylinder arrangements (Tecumseh/York)
The first compressors to see widespread automotive use were the two-cylinder, inline compressors made by York and Tecumseh, figure 6-7. The York version is aluminum, and the

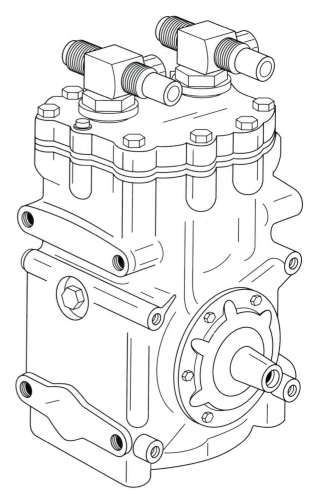

Figure 6-7. The venerable York and Tecumseh 2-cylinder inline compressors are quite similar. The design has inspired several imitations.

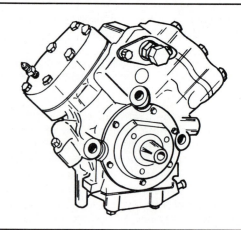

Figure 6-8. The Chrysler Air-Temp V-2 compressor was a popular V-twin design.

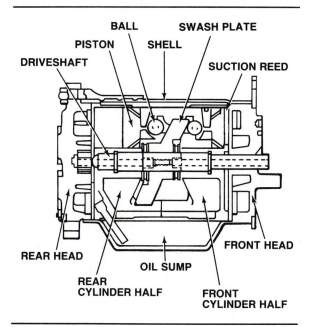

Figure 6-9. GM's Frigidaire A-6 axial compressor uses three double-acting pistons.

Tecumseh version is cast iron. These compressors have been used on some Ford and AMC vehicles, and aftermarket systems. Variations of this compressor have been made by some Japanese manufacturers as well, including Nippondenso and Sanden.

In this design, the two cylinder bores are parallel, and the reed valves are a part of a single head assembly. The compressor crankshaft operates the pistons through connecting rods. The crankshaft is supported in a housing held to the engine with mounting brackets. Typically, the pistons have one or two iron or steel piston rings, and the cylinder walls have steel inserts to provide a long service life for the compressor. This design is lubricated by oil splash from a sump at the bottom of the compressor.

V-type (Chrysler Air-Temp V-2)
The Chrysler Air-Temp V-2 is a two-cylinder, V-type compressor, figure 6-8, widely used on

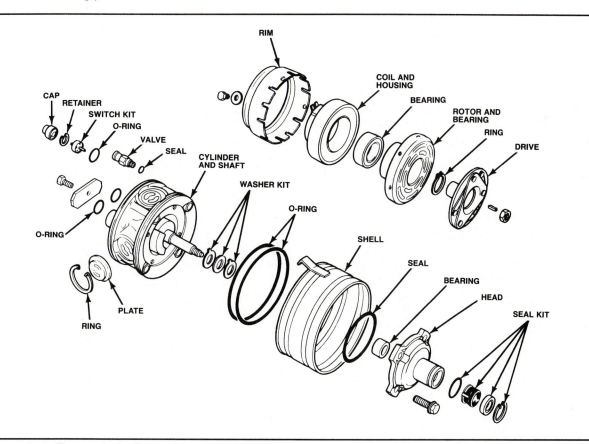

Figure 6-10. The 4-cylinder R-4 radial compressor was introduced by General Motors.

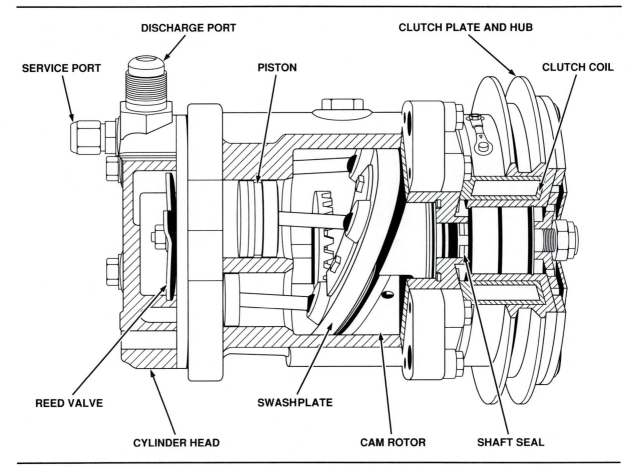

Figure 6-11. The Sankyo 5-cylinder compressor uses a swashplate to move the pistons.

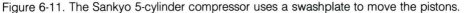

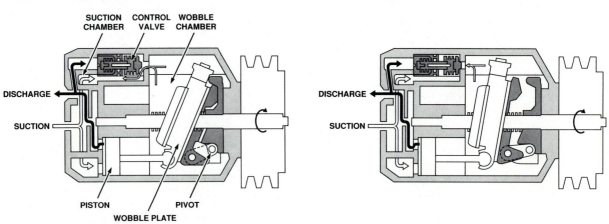

Figure 6-12. The Diesel Kiki CD-17 compressor varies the piston stroke, and therefore the discharge volume, by changing the angle of the wobble plate.

Chrysler cars through the early 1980s. Compared to earlier compressors, it offers superior balance and lower height. It also fits neatly into the valley of a V-8 engine, making it easier to mount in conjunction with the other belt-driven accessories in the engine compartment. It is lubricated by a rotor oil pump located under the rear cover plate.

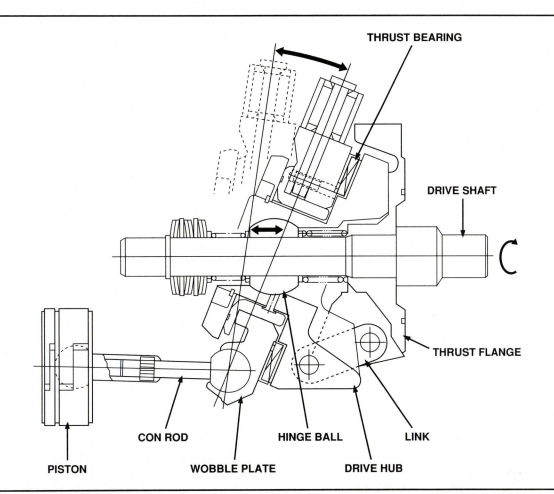

Figure 6-13. Instead of being rigidly attached to the driveshaft like a swashplate, a wobble plate is held to the driveshaft by a flexible ball joint.

This compressor is no longer widely used. It has been superseded by axial- and radial-piston compressors, as well as vane types, that are lighter and more powerful.

Axial type (Frigidaire A-6)
The General Motors Frigidaire A-6 is a six-cylinder axial compressor, figure 6-9. Compared to earlier two-cylinder compressors, its height is significantly lower. It uses three double-ended pistons driven by a swashplate. The three parallel piston bores are spaced evenly around the central axis of the compressor. Each of the six cylinders has its own set of reed valves for controlling the flow of refrigerant in and out of the cylinders.

Radial type (GM R-4)
The General Motors R-4 compressor, figure 6-10, is a four-cylinder, **radial** design. The four piston bores are positioned radially, 90 degrees apart, around the compressor crankshaft. An eccentric lobe on the crankshaft moves the compressor pistons up and down. This com-

pressor does not use an oil pump, but piston movement circulates lubricant.

Five- and seven-piston type (Sankyo)
The Sankyo five-cylinder and seven-cylinder compressors use a swashplate to drive the pistons, figure 6-11. They are lubricated by centrifugal force, using an oil deflector. High- and low-side service fittings are located on the cylinder head. These units are small, lightweight, consume little power, and are therefore ideally suited for downsized vehicles. They are quite common in both domestic and imported vehicles.

Variable-Displacement Piston Compressors
This type of compressor controls refrigerant pressure by varying the amount of gaseous refrigerant it takes in. Variable displacement is

Radial: Radiating from a common center.

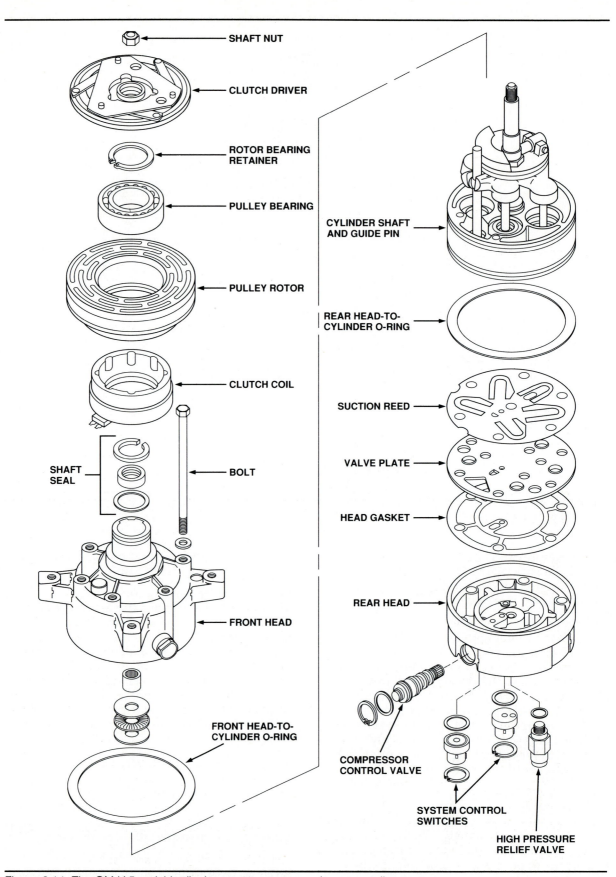

Figure 6-14. The GM V-5 variable-displacement compressor is a noncycling type.

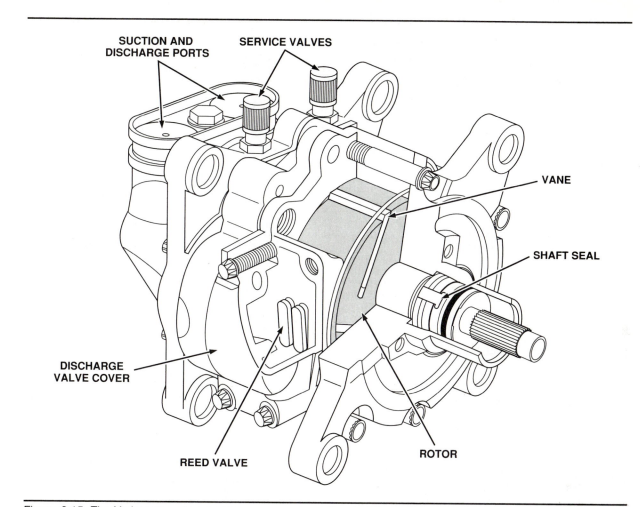

SUCTION AND
DISCHARGE PORTS

SERVICE VALVES

VANE

SHAFT SEAL

DISCHARGE
VALVE COVER

REED VALVE

ROTOR

Figure 6-15. The York rotary vane compressor operates without pistons at all, using a rotor with moveable vanes, spinning inside an elliptical housing.

accomplished by varying the piston stroke. The five pistons and bores are parallel, and spaced evenly around the axis of the crankshaft. The crankshaft has a variable-angle swashplate called a **wobble plate** attached to it, figure 6-12. It is similar to the swashplate used in a positive-displacement compressor. However, the angle that the plate makes with the crankshaft is variable because it is attached to the shaft by a flexible joint, figure 6-13.

A bellows-actuated control valve located in the rear head controls the wobble plate angle in response to the pressure differential between the suction area ahead of the piston, and the crankcase area behind it. The valve senses when suction pressure is above a preset control point, and then opens to bleed refrigerant from the crankcase into the compressor suction side, decreasing the pressure differential. When there is no pressure differential, the angle of the swashplate is steeper, providing longer piston strokes and maximum displace-

ment. When suction pressure falls to the control point, the valve bleeds gas from the discharge side back into the crankcase and closes the crankcase-to-suction side line. This reduces the angle of the swashplate, providing shorter piston strokes and less displacement.

The Chrysler C171 compressor and the General Motors V-5 compressor, figure 6-14, are variable displacement, five-cylinder compressors that were introduced in 1985. Refrigerant temperature is maintained by varying the output, not by cycling the clutch. The pistons and compressor body are aluminum, and the crankshaft is relatively short and lightweight, resulting in a lightweight compressor. The piston bores receive a special silicon treatment to eliminate the need for cast iron liners.

Wobble Plate: A variable-angle swashplate used in a variable-displacement compressor.

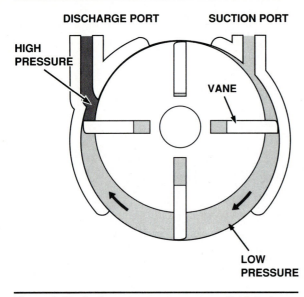

Figure 6-16. As the rotor turns, gaseous R-12 is drawn into the space between each pair of vanes, compressed, then expelled through the discharge port.

Rotary-Vane Compressors

Instead of shaft-driven pistons in bores, the York rotary compressor, figure 6-15, uses a shaft-mounted rotor turning inside an elliptical chamber to draw in and discharge refrigerant. The rotor has four slots in it, 90 degrees apart, each containing a movable vane or blade, figure 6-16. As the impeller turns in the chamber, the vanes move in and out to stay in contact with the chamber wall.

Because the chamber is elliptical, rotor and vane rotation creates a low-pressure area at the suction port into which gaseous refrigerant flows. The next vane closes the gas off from the suction port and pushes it around the chamber to the discharge port. Again because of the chamber's shape, the gas is compressed to create a pressure that opens the discharge valve, and the gas flows into the air conditioning system high side. The discharge valve is the single valve used in this type of compressor. No suction valve is necessary because the rotary design prevents discharge pressure from contacting the suction port.

COMPRESSOR CLUTCHES

The compressor pulley is driven by a belt from the automobile engine. We mentioned in Chapter 1 that the very first air conditioning systems used a direct drive pulley system. The compressor pressurized the air conditioning system whenever the engine was turning, and

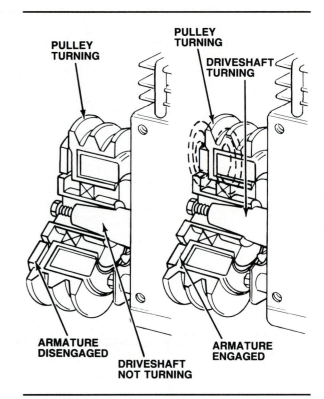

Figure 6-17. The electromagnetic clutch must be energized before any power from the drive belt can be applied to the compressor driveshaft.

the owner was required to remove the belt to turn the compressor off.

An electromagnetic clutch is used in all modern compressors to engage the pulley with the crankshaft when the air conditioner is turned on. When the clutch is energized by electric current, the pulley engages with the compressor, figure 6-17. When the current stops, springs in the clutch disengage the compressor from the pulley, and the pulley freewheels. The two types of electromagnetic compressor clutches are:

- Stationary field
- Rotating field.

A stationary field clutch has a magnetic **field coil** mounted on the end of the compressor, figure 6-18. Electric current passing through the windings creates a magnetic field that attracts the pole piece of the compressor clutch. Bringing the two parts of the clutch assembly together locks the pulley to the compressor crankshaft. This type of clutch has fewer parts and is more reliable and widely used than the older rotating field type.

In a rotating field clutch, figure 6-19, the magnetic coil is mounted within the pulley. Brushes that ride on commutator-like slip rings

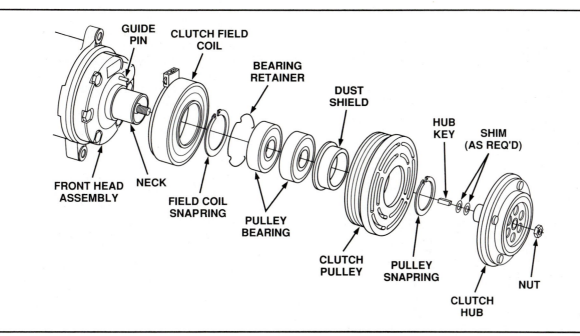

Figure 6-18. In a modern stationary field clutch, the field coil is firmly bolted to the compressor, and does not itself rotate.

conduct current to the winding to create the magnetic field that engages the clutch.

The compressor clutch is also used in many systems to control system pressure, engaging and disengaging the compressor. These are called **cycling clutch** systems. In variable-displacement systems, system pressure is controlled by the wobble plate instead, as it alters piston stroke inside the cylinders. Compressor clutches for these systems remain engaged, turning the compressor continuously as long as the air conditioning system is being used. Some other systems also maintain compressor engagement whenever the air conditioning system is on; these use evaporator control valves, instead of a cycling clutch, to maintain system pressure.

Compressor Clutch Electrical Circuit

The electrical circuit that provides power to the electromagnetic compressor clutch contains a fuse and may contain various temperature or pressure switches and other clutch controls, figure 6-20. The fuse, generally 25 amperes, is in the main fuse panel. An additional fusible link may be installed in the clutch circuit. In most systems, for electric current to flow through the clutch circuit and engage the clutch, the dashboard control must be set for the MAXIMUM air conditioning, NORMAL air conditioning, BILEVEL, or DEFROST mode. The reason that many air conditioners operate in the defrost mode is to dehumidify the air.

Field Coil: A magnetic coil fastened to the front of a compressor, used to engage and disengage the compressor clutch. Current applied to the coil produces a magnetic field that pulls in an armature to engage the clutch.

Cycling Clutch: A pressure-control system that maintains air conditioning refrigerant pressure by engaging and disengaging the compressor with its electromagnetic clutch.

■ Tempo/Topaz Clutch Slippage

The Ford 1983-87 Tempo and Mercury Topaz suffer burned-up compressor clutches. Why? In the original design of their air conditioning circuits and harnesses, excessive voltage drops were allowing only 10.5 to 11 volts to be applied to the compressor clutch. Low voltage at the clutch kept it from engaging fully, causing slight clutch slippage. Eventually, the slippage caused the clutch to burn up.

If you find a Tempo or Topaz with a damaged compressor clutch, check the clutch application voltage at the clutch connector. If it is below 12 volts, order the relay and wiring harness assembly that Ford released to fix the problem. The harness splices into the main harness to provide the relay control circuit. The relay gets connected directly to battery voltage and applies that voltage directly to the clutch when energized.

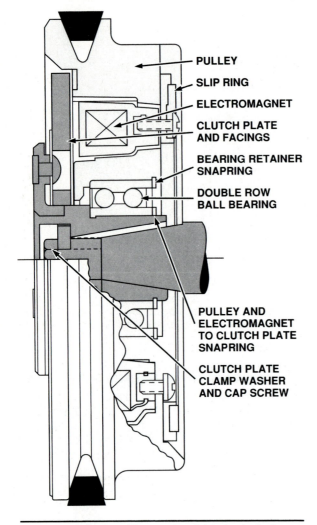

PULLEY

SLIP RING

ELECTROMAGNET

CLUTCH PLATE
AND FACINGS

BEARING RETAINER
SNAPRING

DOUBLE ROW
BALL BEARING

PULLEY AND
ELECTROMAGNET
TO CLUTCH PLATE
SNAPRING

CLUTCH PLATE
CLAMP WASHER
AND CAP SCREW

Figure 6-19. In the older rotating field clutch design, the field coil spins with the pulley. Electrical contact is made through slip rings on the back of the coil assembly.

Cycling clutch controls

In a system that uses a cycling clutch, the compressor cycles on and off to control evaporator temperature. Turning the compressor on and off in this manner directly controls evaporator core pressure and also prevents ice from building on the coils.

One of two types of switches is used to control a cycling clutch. One monitors evaporator temperature, and the other monitors evaporator pressure. Because the relationship between the temperature and pressure of R-12 is predictable, either can be used to control the compressor operation. This switch engages or disengages the compressor by closing or opening the electrical circuit that powers the electromagnetic clutch. It generally is wired in series with the clutch field coil. When evapora-

tor pressure or temperature rises to a set point, the switch closes, current flows through the circuit, and the clutch engages. When low-side pressure or temperature drops below the set point, the switch opens, the circuit is broken, and the clutch disengages.

In a fixed-orifice expansion tube system, a typical pressure-controlled cycling clutch switch opens when low-side pressure is about 25 psi (170 kPa) and closes when low-side pressure is about 45 psi (310 kPa). In a thermostatic expansion valve system, the switch typically opens when low-side pressure is 10 to 15 psi (70 to 100 kPa) and closes when low-side pressure is 25 to 30 psi (170 to 205 kPa).

Other electric clutch controls

Other types of electric compressor clutch controls alter compressor action in response to system and vehicle conditions. These may include a:

• Power steering pressure or cutout switch that opens when high power-steering loads are encountered.
• Wide-open-throttle (WOT) switch that opens during full acceleration.
• Pressure-sensing switch in the transmission to override the WOT switch if the transmission is in high gear.
• Anti-dieseling relay to prevent dieseling (engine run-on) when the engine is shut off.
• High-pressure switch that opens when head pressures exceed a preset limit.
• Low-pressure switch that opens when the refrigerant charge is low.
• Feedback circuit to the engine computer to control idle speed and engine timing when the air conditioner is operating.

Another element of the clutch circuit is the compressor clutch **diode**, placed in parallel with the windings of the magnetic clutch. This diode protects other electrical circuits from voltage spikes. Voltage spikes are generated by the collapsing of the magnetic field in the clutch winding when the clutch is turned off. These spikes, measuring up to 1,200 volts, are similar to spikes created by the ignition coil. However, while voltage spikes in the ignition coil are used to provide the sparks for ignition, voltage spikes created by turning off the compressor clutch serve no useful purpose and may, in fact, damage sensitive electronic cir-

Diode: An electronic semiconductor device that acts as a switch. A diode allows current flow in one direction but not the other.

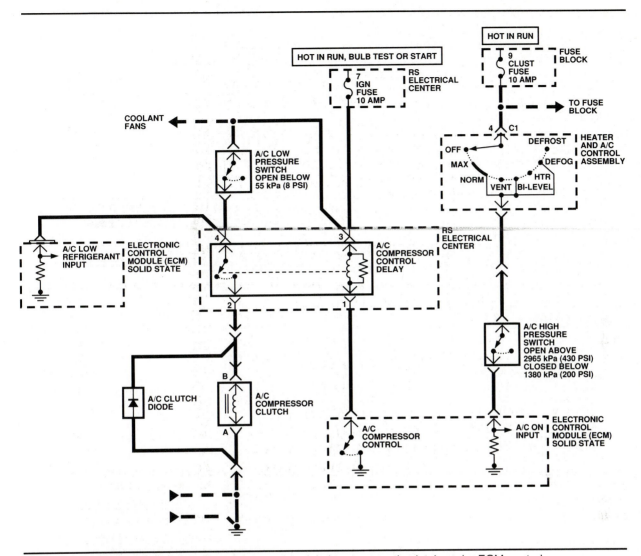

Figure 6-20. The electrical circuit for a typical late-model electromagnetic clutch under ECM control.

cuits, such as those found in the compressor clutch control. The diode suppresses these spikes before they can cause damage.

SUMMARY

The compressor provides the pressure to circulate refrigerant through the system and works with the condenser and evaporator to apply and remove pressure. If the compressor stops pumping, the refrigeration process stops. There are three categories of compressors: positive displacement piston, variable displacement piston, and rotary-vane. All are belt-driven and all are engaged and disengaged by an electromagnetic clutch.

The piston of a piston compressor draws in refrigerant gas from the low side during its suction stroke and pushes the gas out of the compressor into the high side as it returns on

its discharge stroke. The gas is pressurized in the high side by being pushed against the restriction at the expansion device. The major components of a piston compressor are the pistons and rings, piston drive mechanism, and reed valves. Cylinders may be arranged parallel, radially, or in V-type configurations. The piston drive mechanism is either a crankshaft, swashplate, or a pivot-mounted swashplate called a wobble plate. Each piston uses two reed valves: a suction valve and a discharge valve.

Compressors have been manufactured in many designs. The first compressors to see widespread automotive use were the two-cylinder, inline compressors made by York and Tecumseh. The Chrysler Air-Temp V-2 is a two-cylinder, V-type compressor, widely used on early model Chrysler cars. The General Motors Frigidaire A-6 is a six-cylinder, axial compressor with swashplate drive. The General Motors R-4 compressor is a four-cylinder, radial compressor driven by a crankshaft. The Sankyo five- and seven-cylinder compressors use a swashplate to drive the pistons.

The Chrysler C171 compressor and the General Motors V-5 compressor are variable displacement, five-cylinder compressors. This type of compressor controls refrigerant pressure by varying the amount of gas it takes in, accomplished by increasing or decreasing piston stroke with a wobble plate. The angle of the wobble plate is controlled by a bellows-actuated control valve.

The York rotary-vane compressor uses a shaft-mounted rotor turning inside an elliptical chamber to draw in and discharge refrigerant.

No suction valves are required in these compressors.

The two types of magnetic compressor clutches are stationary field clutches and rotating field clutches.

A fuse protects the clutch power circuit. One of two types of switches is used to control a cycling clutch. One monitors evaporator temperature, and the other monitors evaporator pressure.

Other switches in the electrical system affect compressor clutch operation in response to system and vehicle conditions. The compressor clutch diode suppresses voltage spikes generated by the collapsing of the magnetic field in the clutch winding before they can cause damage.

Review Questions

Choose the single most correct answer.
Compare your answers with the correct answers on page 229.

1. Refrigerant condenses inside the condenser because:
   a. Increased pressure raises its boiling point
   b. Airflow around the condenser cools it below its boiling point
   c. Both a and b
   d. Neither a nor b

2. Which of the following is *not* a major component of most compressors?
   a. Pistons and rings
   b. Reed valves
   c. Clutch
   d. Pressure relief valve

3. Technician A says all automotive air conditioning compressors are belt driven and all use an electromagnetic clutch.
   Technician B says the major categories of compressors are the rotary, inline, and variable-displacement types.
   Who is right?
   a. A only
   b. B only
   c. Both A and B
   d. Neither A nor B

4. The earliest common compressors were the:
   a. Inline 2-cylinder model
   b. V-type model
   c. Rotary model
   d. 6-cylinder model

5. An EPR valve is commonly found on the:
   a. York 2-cylinder compressor
   b. GM 6-cylinder compressor
   c. Chrysler Air-Temp compressor
   d. None of the above

6. The swashplate converts:
   a. Rotary motion to axial motion
   b. Axial motion to rotary motion
   c. Axial motion to radial motion
   d. Centrifugal motion to rotary motion

7. The GM Radial R-4 compressor has:
   a. An oil pump and a pressure relief valve
   b. An oil pump and a superheat switch
   c. No oil pump and an eccentric lobe on the crankshaft
   d. No oil pump and a swashplate on the crankshaft

8. The rotary vane compressor does *not* use:
   a. Pistons
   b. Reed valves
   c. Cylinders
   d. Any of the above

9. The variable displacement compressor uses:
   a. Five pistons
   b. A swashplate
   c. A wobble plate
   d. An impeller

10. Technician A says the stationary field clutch is the most common compressor clutch today.
    Technician B says the stationary field clutch has more parts than the rotating field clutch, and is less reliable.
    Who is right?
    a. A only
    b. B only
    c. Both A and B
    d. Neither A nor B

11. Which of the following have been widely used to control evaporator temperature?
    a. Suction throttling controls
    b. Evaporator thermostatic controls
    c. Cycling clutch controls
    d. All of the above

12. Compressor controls *do not* include which of the following?
    a. WOT switch
    b. Power steering cutout switch
    c. Throttle position sensor
    d. Anti-dieseling relay

13. When the air conditioning is off, the compressor operates in the _____ mode to dehumidify the air.
    a. NORM
    b. DEFROST
    c. RECIRCULATE
    d. BILEVEL

14. Voltage spikes in the compressor clutch circuit are controlled by a:
    a. Relay
    b. Thermistor
    c. Diode
    d. Switch

15. A pressure-operated electrical switch generally is wired in _____ with the _____.
    a. Series; field coil
    b. Parallel; field coil
    c. Series; ground circuit
    d. Parallel; ground circuit

7

System Component Description

In previous chapters, we explained the theory of refrigeration and discussed the refrigeration systems used in automotive cooling. We described the construction and operation of the compressor and the compressor clutch, which pressurizes the refrigerant and circulates it through the system. In this chapter, we will discuss the components used to regulate air conditioner operation by maintaining an even evaporator temperature and pressure, in spite of changes in the temperature or humidity of the air passing through the evaporator.

First, we will cover the metering devices that regulate evaporator efficiency by controlling the rate at which liquid refrigerant enters the evaporator: thermostatic expansion valves, and fixed-orifice expansion tubes, figure 7-1.

Next, we will cover the devices that regulate evaporator temperature by controlling the rate at which gaseous refrigerant leaves the evaporator. We will also cover the combined valve assemblies that use one component to perform several of these functions.

Finally, we will cover the other refrigeration system components: condensers, evaporators, receiver-driers and accumulators, and refrigerant lines and hoses. The electrical operating controls that affect the operation of the compressor are covered in Chapter 8.

EXPANSION DEVICES

The expansion device is the connection between the high and the low sides of the air conditioning system. Its functions are to:

• Provide a restricted **orifice** in the circuit, which permits the compressor to create the pressure differences forming a high and a low side.
• Meter the refrigerant that enters the evaporator, either to a constant rate, as with fixed-orifice expansion tubes, or to variable rates, as with thermostatic expansion valves.

A restriction in the air conditioning circuit is critical to the operation of the refrigeration cycle, by separating the high and the low sides of the system. The compressor pressurizes all the refrigerant between its discharge port and the restriction. As the high-pressure liquid refrigerant sprays through the orifice, it enters the low-pressure evaporator and boils, chilling the evaporator. The low-pressure gaseous refrigerant then leaves the evaporator and returns to the compressor, where the cycle repeats.

Correct metering of the refrigerant entering the evaporator is critical. The rate at which liquid refrigerant enters must be carefully bal-

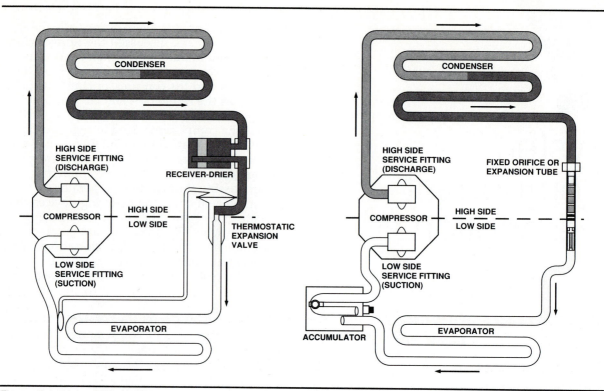

Figure 7-1. Air conditioning systems can be divided into thermostatic expansion valve types (left) or the fixed-orifice expansion tube types (right).

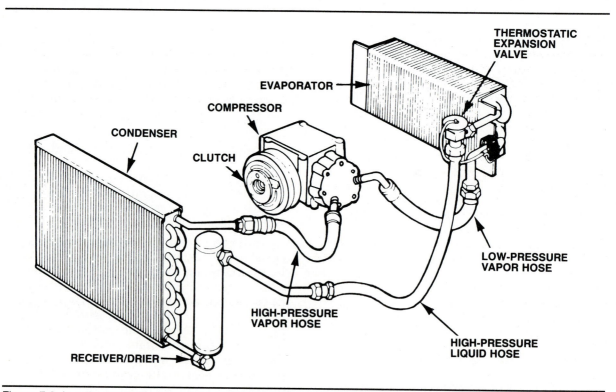

Figure 7-2. In a thermostatic expansion valve (TXV) system, the TXV both meters the refrigerant and serves as the flow restriction.

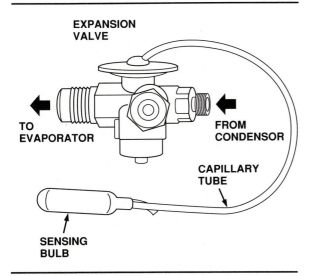

Figure 7-3. A typical Ford thermostatic expansion valve consists of the valve body and the remote sensing bulb.

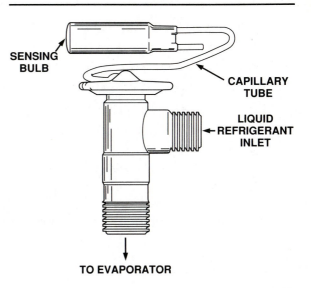

Figure 7-4. Expansion and contraction of the fluid in the sensing bulb actuates the diaphragm to open and close the valve.

anced against the rate at which airflow temperature, humidity, and other variables cause it to vaporize and flow to the compressor suction port.

If liquid refrigerant enters the evaporator too slowly, the evaporator starves. In a starving evaporator, not enough R-12 enters to absorb heat from the evaporator, and the evaporator temperature will rise.

If refrigerant enters too rapidly, the evaporator floods. The temperature of a flooded evaporator also rises, because the high pressure of the liquid R-12 permits higher temperatures to be reached before the refrigerant boils.

The two main types of expansion devices are the thermostatic expansion valve (the H-valve is a similar variation), and the fixed-orifice expansion tube. Combination valves combine the operation of the expansion device with other functions, and are covered later in this chapter.

Thermostatic Expansion Valves

The thermostatic expansion valve, figure 7-2, actively compensates for changes in operating conditions by balancing liquid refrigerant flow into the evaporator to refrigerant flow out of it. When increasing demand for cooling begins to boil the refrigerant to a gas faster than liquid refrigerant enters, the thermostatic expansion valve permits more refrigerant to enter to remove the extra heat. This maintains the correct amount of refrigerant as a liquid in the evaporator, ensuring the most efficient cooling without either too much or too little refrigerant passing through the evaporator.

Thermostatic Expansion Valve (TXV) systems, figure 7-3, use a temperature-sensitive device located on the evaporator in combination with a pressure-sensitive diaphragm to control the size of a variable orifice. This regulates the rate at which liquid refrigerant can flow into the evaporator, figure 7-4. Many thermostatic expansion valve systems use additional evaporator outlet (suction) pressure controls such as suction throttling valves or evaporator pressure regulators to aid in the control of system pressure. These devices are covered later in this chapter.

The key to the thermostatic expansion valve operation is the variable orifice. In the thermostatic expansion valve system, the outlet from the high-pressure side to the low-pressure side of the system is a variable-diameter hole in the thermostatic expansion valve. A **pintle valve** or metering ball-and-seat is used to increase or decrease the size of the orifice, figure 7-5. In this way the thermostatic expansion valve controls how rapidly refrigerant is allowed into

Orifice: A small hole, or opening, in a valve, tube, or pipe.

Pintle Valve: A ball-and-seat valve inside a thermostatic expansion valve assembly. The ball-shaped pintle is attached to a normally closed diaphragm, which opens and closes the valve in response to pressure changes.

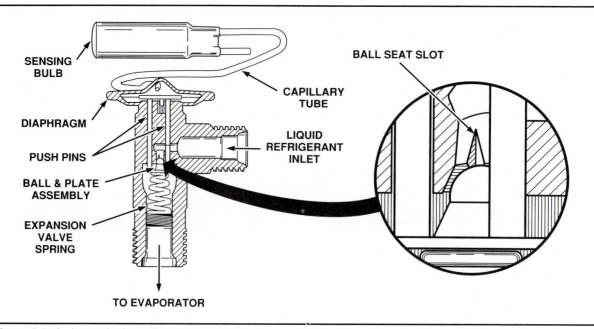

Figure 7-5. A slot cut in the ball seat permits a small amount of refrigerant and refrigerant oil to pass through even when the valve is closed.

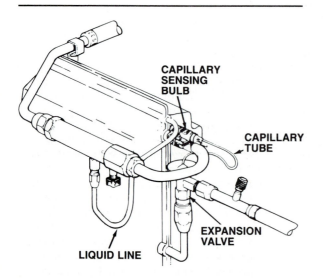

Figure 7-6. The capillary bulb is attached near the evaporator outlet to sense evaporator temperature.

the evaporator. To ensure that some refrigerant and refrigeration oil always circulates through the system, some thermostatic expansion valves have a slot cut into the pintle or ball, figure 7-5. This prevents the valve from closing completely.

Evaporator outlet temperature
The thermostatic expansion valve controls the refrigerant flow in response to the temperature of the evaporator outlet, measured by a re-

motely mounted sensing bulb and **capillary tube**, figure 7-6. The bulb is mounted at the end of the tube, insulated from ambient temperature, and in direct contact with the outlet of the evaporator. It may be clamped to the outlet pipe or mounted inside a passage near the outlet of the evaporator. The bulb and tube contain a temperature-sensitive gas such as R-12 or carbon dioxide. The rise or fall of the evaporator outlet temperature causes this gas to expand or contract, resulting in a rise or fall of the pressure inside the capillary.

This outlet-temperature-sensitive pressure is applied to one side of the spring-loaded diaphragm inside the thermostatic expansion valve, figure 7-7. As the capillary tube warms, the gas inside expands, forcing the diaphragm downward. The diaphragm magnifies this pressure and uses it to crack the valve open by pushing the pintle away from its valve seat. This increases the size of the orifice and allows more refrigerant into the evaporator, increasing the cooling capacity.

When the evaporator cools in response to the boiling of the added refrigerant, the gas in the capillary contracts. This relieves the pressure on the thermostatic expansion valve diaphragm, closing the valve, reducing refrigerant flow. The valve constantly opens and closes slightly to maintain the temperature of the evaporator outlet within a narrow range, admitting liquid refrigerant at the maximum rate at which it can leave as a gas.

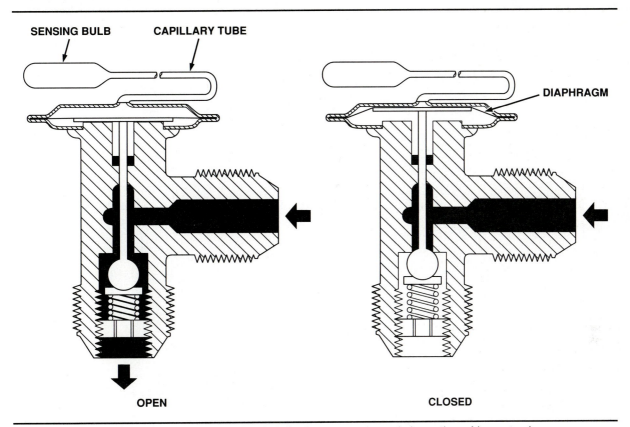

SENSING BULB   CAPILLARY TUBE

DIAPHRAGM

OPEN   CLOSED

Figure 7-7. Pressure pushing on the spring-loaded diaphragm opens and closes the refrigerant valve.

Internal versus external equalization

As explained above, thermostatic expansion valve diaphragm operation depends on a pressure differential. Pressure on the top of the diaphragm is applied through the capillary tube. The equalizing pressure on the underside of the diaphragm can be internal (from the evaporator inlet) or external (from the evaporator outlet):

• An internally equalized thermostatic expansion valve has a passage that permits evaporator inlet pressure to reach the underside of the diaphragm, figure 7-8.
• An externally equalized thermostatic expansion valve has an extra line mounted to the underside of the diaphragm housing, figure 7-9. This line monitors the outlet pressure of the evaporator. The connection can be either at the outlet of the evaporator or at the outlet of the evaporator pressure control device.
By sensing the outlet rather than the inlet pressure, the externally equalized system responds directly to the pressure drop across the evaporator. This is more effective, particularly on larger evaporators.

Superheat

Once the refrigerant in the evaporator turns completely to a gas, it can absorb no more latent heat of vaporization. However, it can still absorb some amount of sensible heat from the evaporator, which *will* cause its temperature to rise (sensible heat was discussed in Chapter 2). When the gaseous refrigerant that leaves the evaporator is warmer than the liquid refrigerant that entered it, it is said to be **superheated**. Superheat is usually measured as the actual temperature difference between the refrigerant at the inlet and at the outlet of the evaporator. Typical values for superheat in a correctly-running evaporator are between 4° and 16°F (3° and 10°C).

Capillary Tube: A long, narrow tube used to transmit internal gas pressure from a remote sensing bulb to a thermostatic expansion valve diaphragm.

Superheat: The sensible heat absorbed by the refrigerant after it has completely vaporized as it passes through the evaporator.

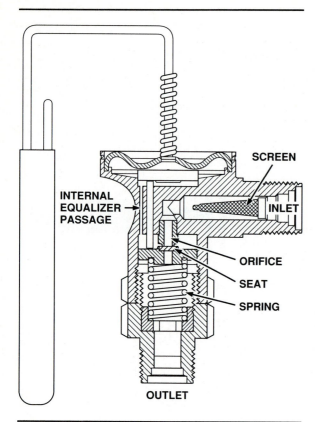

Figure 7-8. An internally equalized TXV channels evaporator inlet pressure to the underside of the diaphragm.

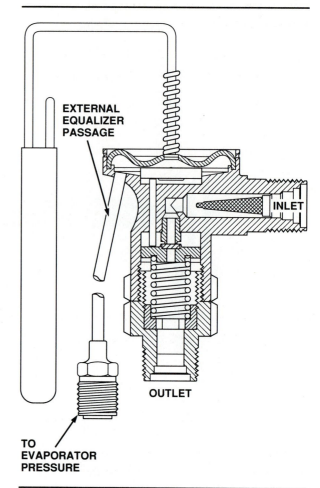

Figure 7-9. An externally equalized TXV channels evaporator outlet pressure to the underside of the diaphragm.

Superheat is important because it ensures that all (or almost all) the refrigerant vaporizes before leaving the evaporator. Uncontrolled liquid R-12 in the system low side can cause severe damage if it reaches the compressor. Liquids are not compressible, and a charge of liquid in a compressor cylinder will destroy the reed valves, at the very least. In order for the temperature of the refrigerant to begin rising, it must have completed the change of state to a gas. Maintaining a certain level of superheat is an easy way to ensure complete refrigerant evaporation.

Note that this applies only to thermostatic expansion valve systems, most of which use a receiver-drier in the line leading to the evaporator. Fixed-orifice expansion tube systems use an accumulator in the line leading from the evaporator, which collects liquid refrigerant and prevents it from reaching the compressor. In these systems, small droplets of liquid pass out of the evaporator with the vapor in normal operation.

Different evaporators operate with different normal amounts of superheat, and the thermostatic expansion valve is designed to work with that particular evaporator temperature

range. Designers calibrate the thermostatic expansion valve to the expected superheat differential by varying the tension of the spring that holds the pintle valve closed against the diaphragm, figure 7-5. The setting of the superheat spring determines the operating temperature difference between the inlet and the outlet of the evaporator. A stronger spring will hold the inlet orifice closed until a higher temperature is reached at the evaporator outlet, while a weaker spring will permit the orifice to open at lower temperatures.

It is important to check the serial number of the thermostatic expansion valve when replacing it. Even though it may look identical to other thermostatic expansion valves used by the same manufacturer, the superheat calibration in the thermostatic expansion valve is likely to be different. Correct operation of the air conditioning system may not be possible if the wrong thermostatic expansion valve is installed.

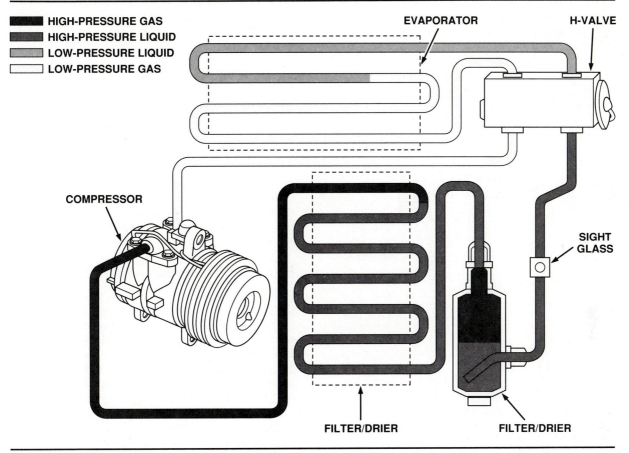

Figure 7-10. This typical Chrysler system uses an H-valve as the expansion device.

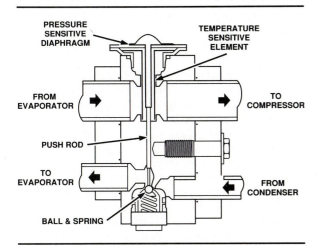

Figure 7-11. An H-valve combines the temperature-sensing and pressure-regulating functions of earlier expansion valves into a single assembly.

H-Valves

The H-valve is a variation of the thermostatic expansion valve, and is widely used by Chrysler and other carmakers, figure 7-10. It includes both the temperature-sensing and

pressure-sensing functions of the thermostatic expansion valve, but uses no external tubes. Ford calls its version a block valve, while Chrysler refers to it as an H-valve. Both are more rugged, easier to install, and cheaper than the conventional thermostatic expansion valve.

The H-valve has two refrigerant passages which form the legs of the "H", figure 7-11. The lower passage is the refrigerant line from the condenser to the evaporator, and contains the ball and spring valve. The upper passage is the refrigerant line from the evaporator to the compressor, and contains the temperature-sensing element. A push rod connects the diaphragm of the temperature sensor located at the top of the block to the valve ball at the bottom.

In operation, the refrigerant flow is controlled by the position of the diaphragm at the top. The diaphragm position depends on the temperature of the gaseous refrigerant at the evaporator outlet, registered by the temperature sensor. When the temperature sensor is cooled below a preset value, pressure within it

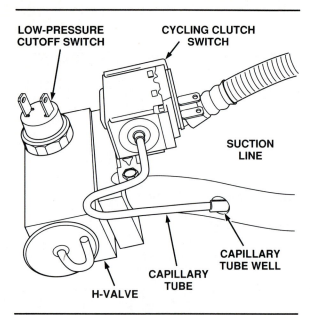

Figure 7-12. In this Chrysler system, a low-pressure cutoff switch and a cycling clutch switch are mounted on the H-valve.

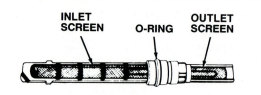

Figure 7-13. The restriction inside the expansion tube separates the high-pressure and low-pressure sides of the system.

The suction line sensing cycling clutch switch detects the evaporator outlet temperature and cycles the compressor clutch to control system cooling. This capillary device does not directly control the metering orifice.

Fixed-Orifice Expansion Tubes

Like thermostatic expansion valves, fixed-orifice expansion tubes (sometimes simply called orifice tubes) provide a restriction that separates the high-pressure and low-pressure sides of the system, figure 7-13. Liquid refrigerant flows from the condenser through the liquid line to the orifice where it undergoes rapid expansion and changes from a warm, high-pressure liquid to a cold, low-pressure liquid and gas mixture.

As with the thermostatic expansion valve system, the refrigerant changes state between a liquid and gas because the pressure in the evaporator is so much lower than in the refrigerant line upstream from the orifice. The result is that the refrigerant begins to vaporize quickly, and absorbs the latent heat from the evaporator structure.

The orifice tube is located in the evaporator inlet line, figure 7-14, and contains a calibrated tube made of plastic or metal and a mesh screen or other type of filter on both the input and output ends, figure 7-15. The screen prevents contaminants in the refrigerant from reaching the orifice. Crimp dimples in the evaporator inlet tube prevent the orifice tube from falling into the evaporator, and one or two O-rings on the tube form a seal so that all refrigerant flows through the orifice.

Fixed-orifice expansion tubes are delicate, and should be replaced whenever debris enters the system. There is no service to the tube; it is replaced when required, and some manufacturers recommend that it be replaced automatically whenever the system is opened for service. In many cases, it cannot be removed from the liquid line, so the entire line must be replaced as an assembly. In other cases, a special tool is used to remove the tube from the line, figure 7-16.

drops, causing the valve to close. When the sensor is warmed above a certain value, pressure rises and the valve opens.

The bottom of the diaphragm senses the evaporator pressure through the internal passage around the thermal element. As evaporator pressure increases, the diaphragm flexes upward, pulling the thermal element and push rod away from the ball seat of the valve. The valve spring forces the ball into the tapered seat and the liquid refrigerant flow is reduced. As the pressure falls, the diaphragm flexes downward again to open the valve, allowing more refrigerant to flow.

The internal sensing element produces the required pressure on top of the pressure-sensing diaphragm. As the cool refrigerant passes the thermal element, the gas above the diaphragm contracts and allows the valve spring to close the valve. When heat from the passenger compartment is absorbed by the refrigerant, it causes the gas to expand and the push rod again forces the valve to open, allowing more refrigerant to flow so that more heat can be absorbed.

Some H-valves include two additional sensor switches mounted on the valve body, figure 7-12. The low-pressure cutoff switch is mounted in the block and senses high-side system pressure. The switch prevents damage to the compressor by keeping it from operating when the refrigerant level is low or when the ambient temperature has fallen below freezing.

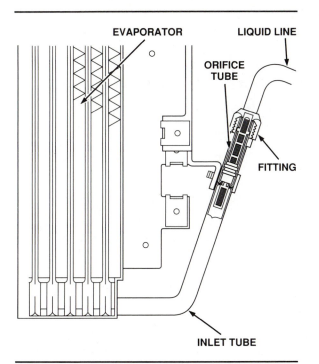

Figure 7-14. The expansion tube is usually located on the evaporator.

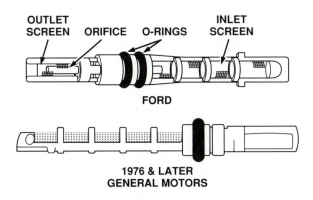

Figure 7-15. Some orifice tubes can be replaced as separate assemblies.

Orifice tube systems do not use receiver-driers. Instead, an accumulator collects refrigerant droplets leaving the evaporator, and ensures that only refrigerant gas reaches the compressor. The accumulator is mounted in the outlet line from the evaporator. The General Motors Cycling Clutch Orifice Tube (CCOT) and Fixed-Orifice Tube Cycling Clutch (FOTCC) and the Ford Fixed-Orifice Tube (FFOT) systems are typical, figure 7-17. These systems generally rely on a thermostat at the evaporator inlet or a pressure switch on the accumulator to cycle the compressor clutch on and off at about 32°F (0°C). However, systems with a variable compressor are non-cycling.

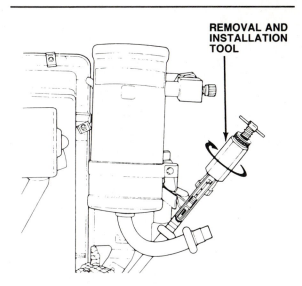

Figure 7-16. Some Ford orifice tubes require a special removal tool.

EVAPORATOR TEMPERATURE CONTROLS

A variety of specific evaporator temperature controls have been used with air conditioning systems. Cycling compressor clutches and variable-stroke compressors were discussed in Chapter 6. The role of the thermostatic expansion valve was discussed in the previous section. We now discuss the remaining evaporator control devices. These are broken down into their primary applications below.

Orifice Tube System

In fixed-orifice expansion tube systems, the orifice is always open, with no valve and no temperature-sensing or regulating capacity. In older systems, the compressor cycles on and off to regulate the refrigerant entering the evaporator by varying the pressure in the system high side. The compressor can be controlled by a pressure switch mounted on the accumulator, a temperature switch mounted on the evaporator inlet, or by an ambient switch, most often mounted to the evaporator. The ambient switch prevents compressor operation if the ambient temperature is below about 50°F (10°C).

Late-model GM Variable-Displacement Orifice Tube (VDOT) systems also use a fixed-orifice tube. As discussed in Chapter 6, the refrigeration cycle is controlled by varying the compressor displacement instead of cycling the compressor. This is done with a bellows-actuated control valve mounted in the rear of the compressor.

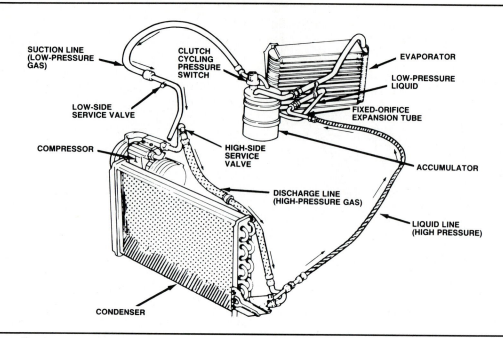

Figure 7-17. This typical Ford fixed-orifice tube (FFOT) system works in essentially the same way as the General Motors CCOT system.

Expansion Valve System

Thermostatic expansion valve systems are very efficient at balancing the pressures and temperatures of vaporizing refrigerant in order to extract the most latent heat, and therefore keep the evaporator as cold as possible. Normally, this is an advantage, as they can cool the interior of a warm car very rapidly by removing the maximum amount of heat from the air entering the passenger compartment.

However, sometimes the system is too efficient. Water vapor normally condenses on the fins and tubes of the evaporator. A thermostatic expansion valve can chill the evaporator to below 32°F (0°C), freezing the water. This reduces airflow through the coil, which reduces the amount of heat absorbed by the evaporator. This makes the evaporator even colder, resulting in even more frost forming. This cycle continues until the evaporator core becomes clogged with frost, a condition known as **freeze-up**. The air conditioning system can provide little or no additional cooling until it is turned off long enough for the frost to melt and drain away.

To compensate, designers often add several types of evaporator temperature regulating devices to these systems to modulate temperature further. Temperature and pressure-sensitive cycling clutch controls were discussed in Chapter 6. Another approach to this problem is to run the compressor all the time, but restrict the refrigerant flow in the suction line between the evaporator and the compressor. Because these devices throttle the flow of refrigerant to the compressor, they are called suction throttling devices.

Suction throttling devices

Thermostatic expansion valves control the rate at which liquid refrigerant enters the evaporator by measuring and responding to the temperature of the evaporator outlet — which is a reliable indicator of refrigerant pressure. This ensures that the evaporator remains at the correct temperature for proper air conditioner operation under various conditions that alter the amount of heat it must remove from the airflow. Other systems perform the same task by regulating the rate at which gaseous refrigerant leaves the evaporator, often as supplementary components.

Older HVAC designs use various suction throttling devices, while some later versions incorporate combination valves, discussed in the next section. Various devices with different names have been used:

- Suction throttling valve (STV)
- Pilot-operated absolute valve (POA)
- Evaporator pressure regulator (EPR and EPR II)
- Evaporator temperature regulator (ETR).

A typical suction throttling device, figure 7-18, is mounted near the outlet of the evaporator. These valves work by throttling (restrict-

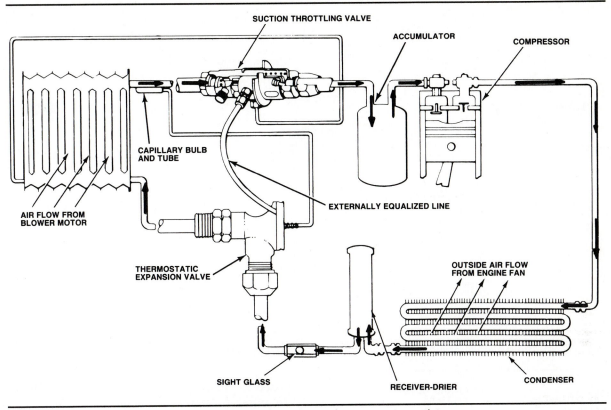

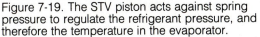

Figure 7-18. A suction throttling device is usually located near the evaporator outlet.

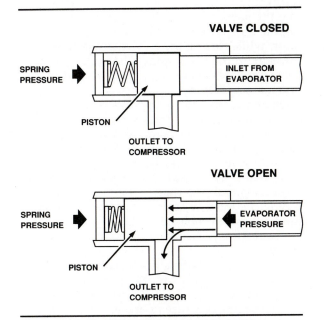

Figure 7-19. The STV piston acts against spring pressure to regulate the refrigerant pressure, and therefore the temperature in the evaporator.

ing) the evaporator suction (outlet) pressure to keep it at a constant level of about 27 to 32 psi (185 to 220 kPa) at sea level. Because of the pressure-temperature relationship of R-12, this creates an evaporator temperature of 29° to 33°F (–2° to 1°C). When evaporator pressure drops below this level, the valve closes to reduce refrigerant flow. Above this pressure, the valve opens to increase refrigerant flow. When the temperature averaging effects of the evaporator's mass are taken into account, this generally is enough to prevent evaporator freeze-up.

Systems with suction pressure regulating devices have compressors that operate continuously as long as the outside temperature remains above about 50°F (10°C).

Suction Throttling Valve (STV)
The Suction Throttling Valve (STV) regulates the temperature of the evaporator by limiting the minimum evaporator outlet pressure. By preventing freeze-up of the evaporator, the STV ensures maximum cooling.

The STV is a diaphragm-operated, piston-type valve, figure 7-19. The piston is balanced

Freeze-Up: Clogging of an evaporator core with frost, resulting from its temperature dropping below the freezing point of water. Freeze-up results in very poor cooling until the ice is melted off.

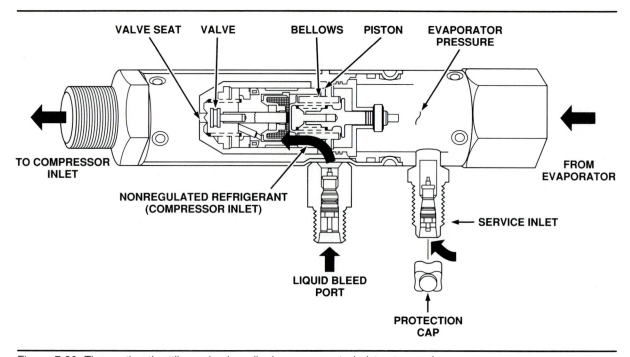

Figure 7-20. The suction throttling valve is a diaphragm-operated piston-type valve.

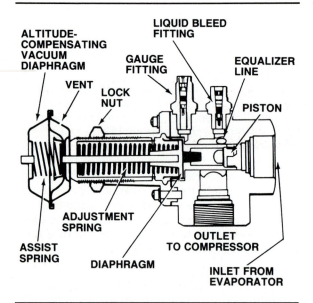

Figure 7-21. This typical suction throttling valve uses an altitude-compensating vacuum diaphragm.

by two opposing forces: evaporator pressure at one end, and a combination of atmospheric and spring pressure on the other end. Flow through the valve depends on the location of the piston. On one end of the piston, spring pressure plus atmospheric pressure are applied to one side of a diaphragm, figure 7-20. These pressures act to close the valve. On the opposite end of the piston, a diaphragm is ex-

posed to the evaporator outlet pressure. When the outlet pressure is high enough, it acts on the diaphragm to open the valve. This allows refrigerant to flow out of the evaporator and into the suction side of the compressor. Opening the STV reduces the pressure in the evaporator, while closing the STV increases the pressure in the evaporator. The cycling of the valve regulates evaporator pressure and therefore its temperature.

One problem with early STVs was that they allowed atmospheric pressure to be applied to one side of the diaphragm, making the valves altitude-sensitive. This problem was overcome by adding an altitude-compensating vacuum diaphragm, figure 7-21. The diaphragm can be turned manually to change the pressure opposing the internal spring. Another variation used a bowden cable controlled by the driver to change the pressure supplied by external springs.

Some systems have a dual evaporator-pressure limiting feature. When the driver sets air conditioning to MAX, the STV maintains an evaporator pressure of at least 28 psi (193 kPa). In less than maximum cooling conditions, the minimum pressure may be controlled at a higher level, such as 32 psi (221 kPa). This feature prevents high-altitude freeze-up of the evaporator.

The low-side service port often is part of the STV. The oil bypass line and the equalization line for some types of thermostatic expansion valves also may be attached to the STV.

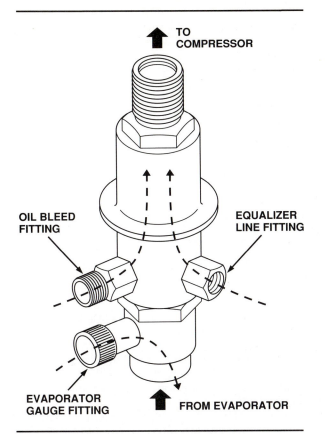

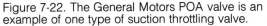

Figure 7-22. The General Motors POA valve is an example of one type of suction throttling valve.

STVs were common on General Motors vehicles until the mid-1960's, when they were replaced by pilot-operated absolute valves.

Pilot-Operated Absolute (POA) Valve
The **pilot-operated** absolute valve, figure 7-22, is a special type of suction throttling valve commonly used on many General Motors and Ford systems. While most manufacturers refer to it as a POA valve, its full name is Pilot-Operated Absolute Suction Throttling Valve (POASTV).

The POA valve, like the STV, controls evaporator pressure by restricting the evaporator outlet to keep the pressure from falling too low. Unlike the STV, the POA valve is not referenced to atmospheric pressure, but rather to a vacuum captured inside a brass bellows. This ensures more exact temperature regulation. It also eliminates the need for the dual pressure-control system in the STV that prevents high-altitude freeze-up of the evaporator.

An equalizer line connects the thermostatic expansion valve to the POA valve. This line permits the outlet pressure of the POA valve to be imposed on the diaphragm of the expansion valve. When the outlet pressure of the

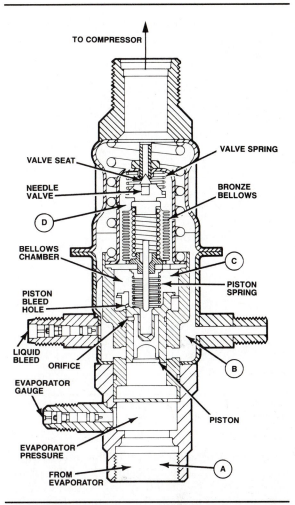

Figure 7-23. In a POA valve, a bronze bellows holds a nearly perfect vacuum to be used as the reference vacuum.

POA valve drops below a preset limit, this decrease in pressure is transmitted to the diaphragm of the expansion valve through the equalizer line. This causes the expansion valve to open and flood the evaporator with refrigerant and oil, assuring lubricant to the compressor through the oil bypass line, and increasing the evaporator pressure. This only occurs when the compressor capacity becomes greater than the evaporator output and the resulting drop in POA valve outlet pressure.

In a typical POA valve, figure 7-23, refrigerant enters the valve at point A. This pressure

Pilot-Operated: Referring to a smaller internal valve (the pilot valve) that regulates the movement of the larger valve into which it is placed.

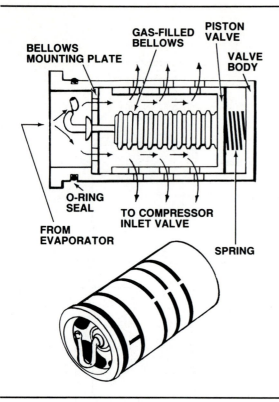

Figure 7-24. This early EPR valve uses a gas-filled bellows to regulate evaporator outlet pressure.

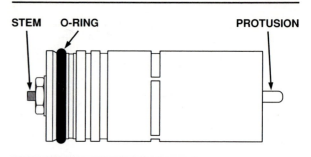

Figure 7-25. The later pilot-operated EPR valve can be identified by the protrusion from one end.

is applied through a screen to the lower side of the piston ring. The opposite side of the piston is loaded by a calibrated spring. When evaporator pressure exceeds the minimum level, the valve opens to allow the flow of refrigerant into the main section of the valve at point B.

This flow occurs because the evaporator pressure applied to one side of the piston exceeds the combined pressure of the spring and the pressure in the area behind the piston at point C.

As the valve is forced open, evaporator pressure slowly flows through the bleed holes in the piston into the area (point C) behind the piston. As the pressure in area C equalizes with the pressure in area A, the force applied by the spring moves the valve toward the closed position.

It is at this point that the pilot valve is used to further control or modulate evaporator pressure. The area (point D) surrounding the pilot bellows and the needle valve is connected by a pilot hole to the area above the piston. This pilot hole equalizes the pressure in areas C and D. As pressure builds up in C and allows spring pressure to close the valve, pressure also builds up in area D.

Raising the pressure in area D collapses the bellows with the entrapped vacuum. This

moves the pilot valve from its seat, opening that orifice to refrigerant flow.

Opening the pilot valve reduces the pressure on the bellows with the result that the valve closes. When the pressure is reduced in area D, it also is reduced in area C. The evaporator pressure once again is enough to open the valve against the spring pressure.

The operation of this valve prevents the pressure in the evaporator from falling below the required minimum of 28-32 psi (193-221 kPa). It does this without requiring altitude compensation.

As with the STV, the two low-side Schrader valve fittings are mounted on the POA valve. One is the oil bleed line. The other is a service port. These ports cannot be used interchangeably. The equalization line for the thermostatic expansion valve also is attached to the POA valve.

Evaporator Pressure Regulator (EPR)
Evaporator Pressure Regulator (EPR) valves are STVs that perform much the same functions as the POA valve. The biggest difference is that the valve piston is controlled by a gas-filled bellows, figure 7-24. EPR valves prevent evaporator outlet pressure, measured at the compressor inlet, from falling below about 22 to 26 psi (152 to 179 kPa) by restricting the outlet. A calibrated spring holds the valve closed in opposition to the outlet pressure from the evaporator. The EPR valve allows refrigerant flow when openings in the piston align with openings in the valve body. A bypass in the valve allows continuous compressor operation even when the valve is closed.

The EPR valve is mounted in the suction port of the compressor. It is necessary to remove the suction line and fittings to gain access to it. Air conditioning systems with EPR valves use an auxiliary service fitting to allow outlet pressure of the evaporator to be read on one side of the EPR while compressor suction pressure is read on the other side.

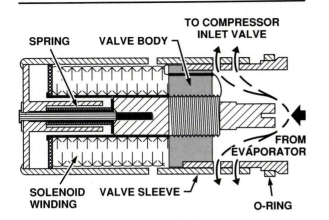

Figure 7-26. The ETR valve has a solenoid that responds to an electrical signal from a switch on the evaporator.

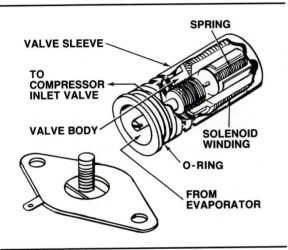

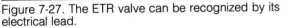

Figure 7-27. The ETR valve can be recognized by its electrical lead.

Chrysler has used several versions of the EPR valve. Chrysler air conditioning systems from 1961 to 1969 used a bellows-type EPR valve. A pilot-operated EPR valve was used on 1970-72 models, figure 7-25. In this version, a built-in pilot device actuated the main valve.

The ETR valve
From 1967 through 1974, Chrysler used an Evaporator Temperature Regulator (ETR) in place of the EPR valve on its automatic air conditioning systems. The ETR, figure 7-26, is a normally-open solenoid-type valve.

Like the EPR valve, the ETR valve is located in the suction side of the compressor. It can be easily identified because it is a solenoid-operated device with a wire lead, figure 7-27. The ETR valve is either on or off depending on whether the solenoid is energized.

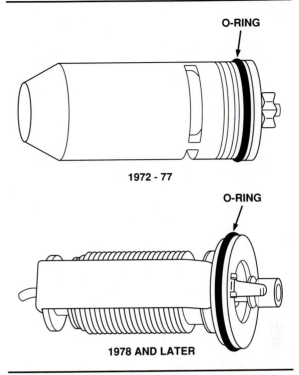

Figure 7-28. Chrysler introduced redesigned EPR II valves in 1972 and 1978.

Operation of the ETR is controlled by a thermal switch in the evaporator. If the temperature sensor indicates that evaporator freeze-up may occur, the valve is closed to raise the evaporator pressure and temperature. This does two things:

• It blocks the flow of refrigerant, which relieves the load on the compressor and saves energy.
• It raises the pressure in the evaporator to keep it from getting too cold.

EPR II
In 1972, Chrysler dropped most ETR valves and returned to the use of an EPR valve. Like the earlier EPR valve, the improved EPR II valve, figure 7-28, has the bypass that allows continuous compressor operation. The bullet-shaped EPR II valve fit all earlier vehicles including those originally using an ETR. A redesigned EPR II valve was used on 1978 and later models.

COMBINED VALVE ASSEMBLIES

Newer vehicles combine more than one control element into a single valve. These valves may combine the functions of the thermostatic expansion valve and the suction throttling device, fixed-orifice expansion tubes, refrigerant storage and desiccant devices, and evaporator

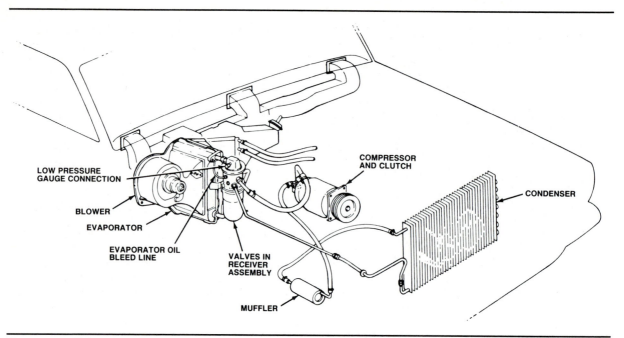

LOW PRESSURE
GAUGE CONNECTION

BLOWER

EVAPORATOR

EVAPORATOR OIL
BLEED LINE

VALVES IN
RECEIVER
ASSEMBLY

MUFFLER

COMPRESSOR
AND CLUTCH

CONDENSER

Figure 7-29. This typical General Motors air conditioning system uses a VIR assembly to control evaporator pressure.

pressure controls. This reduces the number and size of components and the number of connections needed, which reduces the cost and complexity of the overall system. These devices include the:

- Valves-in-receiver (General Motors)
- Evaporator-equalized valves-in-receiver (General Motors)
- Combination valve (Ford)
- Mini-combination valve (Ford).

The Valves-in-Receiver (VIR) Assembly

The Valves-In-Receiver (VIR) assembly usually is mounted next to the evaporator, figure 7-29. It combines four elements:

- Thermostatic expansion valve (TXV)
- Pilot operated absolute (POA) valve
- Receiver-drier
- Sight glass.

The operation of the VIR is a combination of the individual actions of these four components, figure 7-30. The thermostatic expansion valve cartridge meters the refrigerant into the expansion area. The POA valve throttles evaporator outlet pressure to prevent evaporator freeze-up. The receiver-drier stores liquid refrigerant and traps any moisture it may contain. The sight glass aids the technician in troubleshooting the system.

There are five connections to a typical VIR installation:

- High-pressure liquid line inlet from the condenser
- Metered low-pressure outlet to the evaporator
- Low-pressure evaporator outlet line
- Oil return line from the evaporator
- Low-pressure suction outlet to the compressor.

Several connections are eliminated by placing all of these elements in a single housing. The equalizer line is a drilled hole that connects the diaphragm cavity to the evaporator outlet pressure found in the POA valve cavity. The thermostatic expansion valve capillary tube and bulb are eliminated because evaporator outlet pressure is applied directly to one side of the thermostatic expansion valve diaphragm. Making the sight glass a part of the VIR assembly eliminates the need for separate mounting connectors for the sight glass elsewhere in the system.

All components of the VIR can be serviced separately. However, due to limited access, it may be necessary to remove it as a unit for service. Removing the inlet connector valve at the top of the assembly allows replacement of either the POA capsule or the thermostatic expansion valve capsule. The lower shell containing the receiver-drier can be removed to replace the desiccant bag.

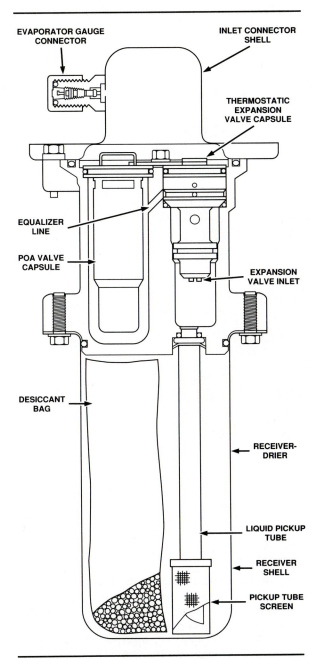

EVAPORATOR GAUGE CONNECTOR

INLET CONNECTOR SHELL

THERMOSTATIC EXPANSION VALVE CAPSULE

EQUALIZER LINE

POA VALVE CAPSULE

EXPANSION VALVE INLET

DESICCANT BAG

RECEIVER-DRIER

LIQUID PICKUP TUBE

RECEIVER SHELL

PICKUP TUBE SCREEN

Figure 7-30. This VIR assembly combines the functions of a TXV, POA valve, receiver-drier, and sight glass (not shown).

Evaporator-Equalized Valves-in-Receiver (EEVIR) Assembly

General Motors used the VIR assembly until 1975, when it introduced the Evaporator-Equalized Valves-In-Receiver (EEVIR). The EEVIR works much the same as the VIR assembly. The changes were an effort to control the evaporator temperature more smoothly

during normal operation by eliminating surges that occurred during some operating modes.

On the VIR, the equalizer port was located between the POA capsule cavity and the expansion valve. In the EEVIR, the port is internal to the expansion valve capsule, figure 7-31. Also, the EEVIR assembly has no top O-ring. Direct sensing of evaporator outlet pressure improved the reaction speed to changes in evaporator pressure resulting in smoother temperature control.

Another feature of the EEVIR is a moisture-sensitive sleeve visible through the sight glass port. The sleeve is made of a chemically treated litmus paper that is normally blue. If moisture is detected in the system, acid in the sleeve turns the sleeve pink. If the sleeve has turned pink, it indicates that the system should be discharged, the desiccant replaced, and the system repaired, evacuated, and recharged.

Identifying a VIR and an EEVIR

An EEVIR assembly can be substituted for a VIR assembly if the complete units are exchanged. It is not recommended that an early-model VIR be installed into a late-model system.

There are two components of the EEVIR assembly which *must not* be interchanged with the VIR assembly:

- The valve housing
- The expansion valve capsule.

Also, on the original VIR, the expansion valve has an O-ring in the upper groove which must not be used in an EEVIR. If you are unsure, consult a shop manual or parts catalog.

It is not difficult to tell the difference between the VIR and the EEVIR. The earlier VIR assembly (pre-1975) has a:

- Black label
- Internal drilled passage between the POA and the TXV
- Three O-rings
- Silver-colored valve housing and expansion valve.

By contrast, the EEVIR:

- Is used on 1975 and later models
- Has a red label or red dot on the sight glass
- Has only two O-rings
- Uses a gold-colored expansion valve capsule
- Has a gold-colored valve housing or has the letter "E" stamped below the sight glass.

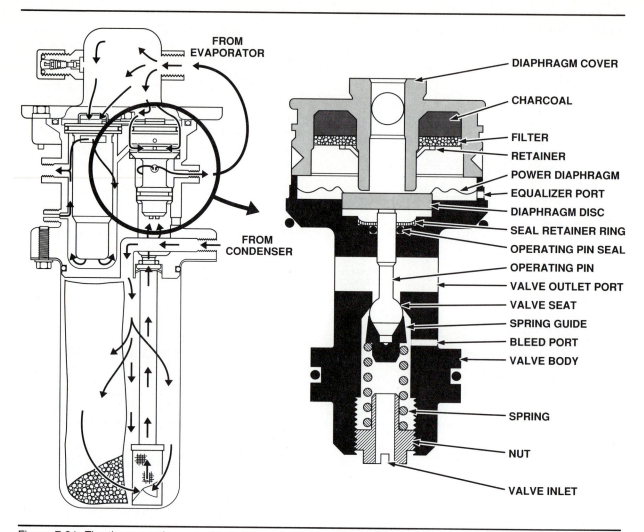

FROM EVAPORATOR

FROM CONDENSER

DIAPHRAGM COVER
CHARCOAL
FILTER
RETAINER
POWER DIAPHRAGM
EQUALIZER PORT
DIAPHRAGM DISC
SEAL RETAINER RING
OPERATING PIN SEAL
OPERATING PIN
VALVE OUTLET PORT
VALVE SEAT
SPRING GUIDE
BLEED PORT
VALVE BODY
SPRING
NUT
VALVE INLET

Figure 7-31. The thermostatic expansion valve portion of the General Motors EEVIR uses a simple pintle valve.

Ford Combination Valve

The Ford combination valve, figure 7-32, combines the functions of an H-block thermostatic expansion valve and an STV into a single assembly. Unlike the VIR or EEVIR assemblies used by General Motors, the "combo" valve does not incorporate the receiver-drier as part of the assembly. Like the GM assembly, the combination valve is mounted near the evaporator.

The early Ford combination valves, like the early VIRs, had an equalizer port between the thermostatic expansion valve and the STV. Later-model combination valves used a notched seat in the thermostatic expansion valve to apply evaporator outlet pressure to the underside of the diaphragm. The earlier models are referred to as external-equalized combination valves. The later valves are called by-pass orifice (BPO) combination valves.

In the Ford combination valve, both evaporator outlet temperature and evaporator pressure are sensed internally. This eliminates the need for a separate capillary tube and bulb.

The combination valve, figure 7-33, consists of four main components. The STV manifold housing serves as both the connection to the air conditioning compressor hose and one side of the mounting housing of the STV assembly. The STV itself screws into one side of the expansion valve housing. The evaporator manifold plate serves as both the evaporator inlet and outlet connection.

In some versions, the expansion valve block attaches directly to the evaporator, eliminating a manifold assembly used on other models. In other models, the evaporator liquid bleed passages are internal, similar to the externally equalized combination valve. These combination valves have an external line leading to the

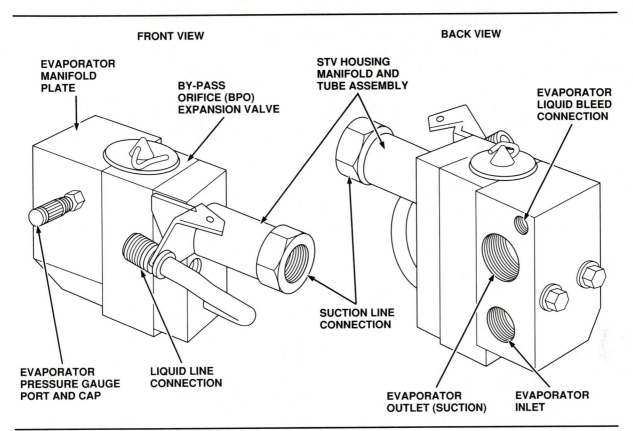

FRONT VIEW

BACK VIEW

EVAPORATOR
MANIFOLD
PLATE

BY-PASS
ORIFICE (BPO)
EXPANSION VALVE

STV HOUSING
MANIFOLD AND
TUBE ASSEMBLY

EVAPORATOR
LIQUID BLEED
CONNECTION

SUCTION LINE
CONNECTION

EVAPORATOR
PRESSURE GAUGE
PORT AND CAP

LIQUID LINE
CONNECTION

EVAPORATOR
OUTLET (SUCTION)

EVAPORATOR
INLET

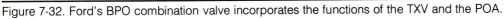

Figure 7-32. Ford's BPO combination valve incorporates the functions of the TXV and the POA.

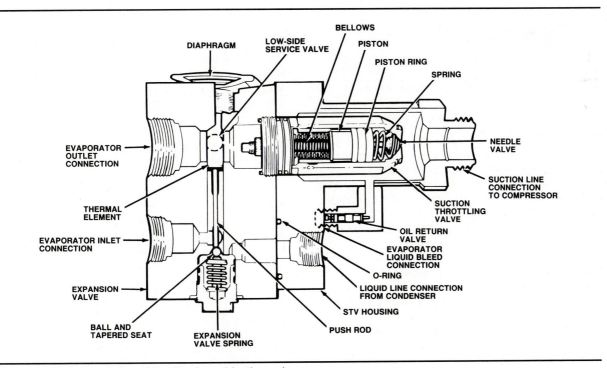

DIAPHRAGM

LOW-SIDE
SERVICE VALVE

BELLOWS

PISTON

PISTON RING

SPRING

EVAPORATOR
OUTLET
CONNECTION

NEEDLE
VALVE

SUCTION LINE
CONNECTION
TO COMPRESSOR

THERMAL
ELEMENT

SUCTION
THROTTLING
VALVE

EVAPORATOR INLET
CONNECTION

OIL RETURN
VALVE

EVAPORATOR
LIQUID BLEED
CONNECTION

EXPANSION
VALVE

O-RING

LIQUID LINE CONNECTION
FROM CONDENSER

STV HOUSING

BALL AND
TAPERED SEAT

EXPANSION
VALVE SPRING

PUSH ROD

Figure 7-33. Cross-section of the Ford combination valve.

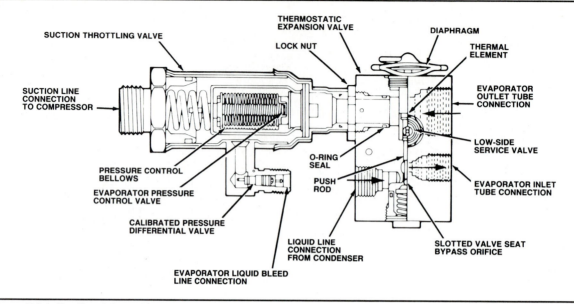

Figure 7-34. Ford's mini-combination valve works in the same way as a separate BPO H-valve and suction throttling valve.

suction side of the STV. The pressure differential valve is installed in the fitting on the STV housing. Also mounted on the combination valve is an evaporator outlet pressure service port. This port has an uncalibrated Schrader valve. The liquid bleed line port is pressure calibrated.

The BPO combination valve is identified by its serial number and its silver color. The earlier, externally equalized valve, was gold colored. Unlike GM's VIR/EEVIR, the two Ford combination valves are not interchangeable.

Ford Mini-Combination Valve

The mini-combination valve, figure 7-34, is similar to earlier combination valves in design and operation. However, it is smaller and more compact, and weighs less than the earlier versions. The H-block expansion valve portion of the mini valve connects directly to the evaporator core tubes, thus eliminating the evaporator manifold plate. The suction throttling valve screws directly into the expansion valve body, eliminating the STV housing manifold. The expansion valve seat is slotted, making it a bypass orifice-type expansion valve. The mini valve operates in the same manner as a separate BPO H-valve and suction throttling valve.

CONDENSERS AND EVAPORATORS

Condensers and evaporators are two of the four heat exchangers in an automotive air

conditioning system, figure 7-35. (The other two — radiators and heater cores — were covered in Chapter 2.)

Condenser and evaporator functions are opposite, figure 7-36. In the condenser, heat is *removed from* the high-pressure refrigerant gas and released into the passing airstream, figure 7-37. Removing heat under high pressure permits the refrigerant to condense to a liquid. In the evaporator, heat is removed from the passenger compartment air and *added to* the low pressure refrigerant liquid. Adding heat under low pressure forces the refrigerant to boil back to a gas.

Condenser and Evaporator Construction

Evaporators and condensers are similar, and fairly simple in construction. Both consist of:

• Tubes to carry the refrigerant
• Fins to increase surface area
• Inlet and outlet connections for the refrigerant.

Heat is exchanged in the tubes and fins of the condenser or evaporator. Heat transfer is improved by using a relatively large surface area of thin metal in contact with a small flow of refrigerant. Condenser designs vary. The tubes may be round, or flat with internal chambers, figure 7-38. The tubes are the direct link between the refrigerant flowing through them and the fins between which the air flows.

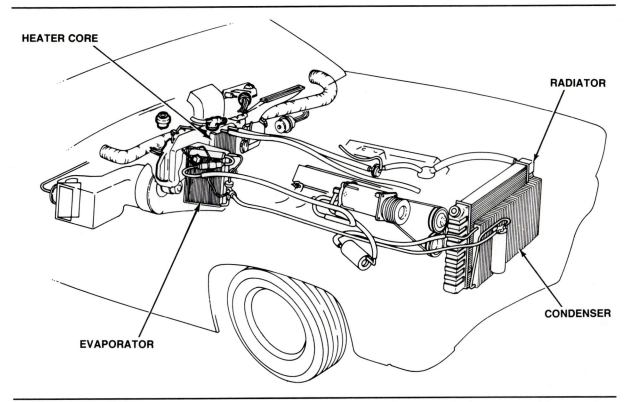

Figure 7-35. The heat exchangers in an automotive HVAC system are the radiator, the heater core, the evaporator, and the condenser.

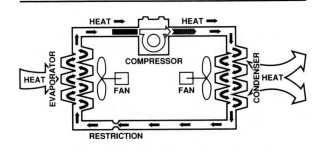

Figure 7-36. The condenser and the evaporator both transfer heat between an airstream and the refrigerant, but in opposite directions.

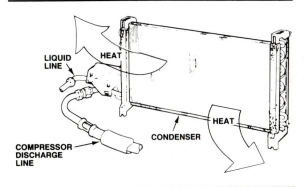

Figure 7-37. The airflow through the condenser removes heat from the refrigerant.

The thin, sheetmetal fins are mounted between the tubes to increase the surface area. In a condenser, the fins transfer heat from the tubes to the passing air. In an evaporator, the fins transfer heat from the passing air to the tubes. Because air has a much lower specific heat than R-12, the same volume of air cannot carry as much heat. To compensate, the surface area of the fins in contact with the air is much greater than the surface area of the tubes in contact with the refrigerant. This ensures that enough air is in contact with the metal condenser or evaporator to transfer heat fast enough for efficient operation.

The fins can be similar to those used in a radiator or they may be spikes or shards of thick aluminum foil. These maximize the amount of available surface area without making the fins so fragile that they can be easily bent or matted.

The inlet and outlet connectors join the condenser or evaporator to the hoses that connect it to the system, figure 7-39. These may be tubing nuts with O-rings, flare joints, or spring-lock quick-connections. The thermo-

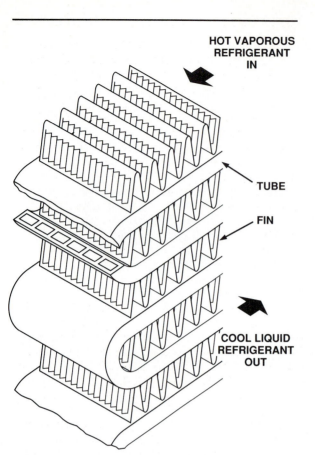

HOT VAPOROUS
REFRIGERANT
IN

TUBE

FIN

COOL LIQUID
REFRIGERANT
OUT

Figure 7-38. One condenser design uses flat,
extruded tubes.

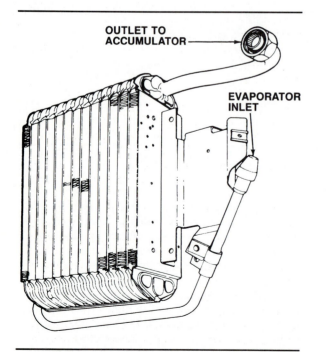

OUTLET TO
ACCUMULATOR

EVAPORATOR
INLET

Figure 7-39. The inlet and outlet connections on this
evaporator are threaded-coupler wedge connectors.

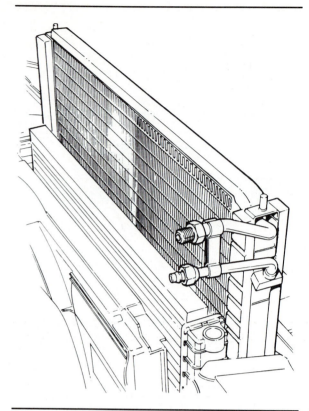

Figure 7-40. The condenser is usually located between
the front of the engine's radiator and the grille.

static expansion valve or the fixed-orifice expansion tube is usually located in the inlet to
the evaporator.

The Condenser

The condenser is usually located in front of the
engine's radiator, where a strong flow of ram
air can be counted on to draw heat from the
high-pressure refrigerant, figure 7-40. As with
the radiator, air is drawn through the condenser by the fan when the vehicle is not
moving.

Hot, high-pressure refrigerant gas enters the
condenser from the compressor at the top, figure 7-41, and liquid is removed from the
bottom. To encourage even and smooth refrigerant flow, the tube is bent into a serpentine
path. This allows the condensed liquid refrigerant to run along the bottom of the horizontal
tubes while gaseous refrigerant flows along the
top until it, too, condenses.

The refrigerant entering the condenser is almost 100 percent gaseous, and hot — normal
high side temperatures on a 95°F (35°C) day
might be 230°F (110°C). The heat in the refrigerant is that which the evaporator removed
from the air entering the passenger compartment as the refrigerant boiled.

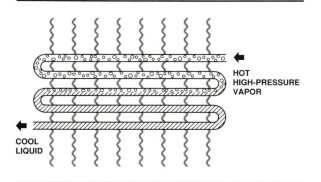

Figure 7-41. Refrigerant enters the top of the serpentine condenser tube as a gas. When it finally exits at the bottom, it has all condensed to a liquid.

The temperature of the gaseous refrigerant as it enters the condenser is much higher than its temperature as it left the evaporator, because the compressor has reduced the volume by pressurizing it. Pressurization does not add heat, but the same amount of heat that had been dispersed through a large volume of refrigerant gas is now concentrated in a much smaller space.

When the refrigerant condenses, it gives off this latent heat of vaporization that it absorbed as it boiled in the evaporator. This is the heat carried away by the air flowing between the condenser tubes and fins. The refrigerant leaves the condenser as a much cooler, high-pressure liquid, at about 100° to 140°F (40° to 60°C), and flows into the high-side refrigerant lines.

The Evaporator

The evaporator is located within the ductwork that connects the ram air intake with the ventilation outlets for the passenger compartment, usually behind or beneath the dash. In blend-air systems, the heater core will also be located within the same ductwork to enable the heated and cooled air to be mixed, and to permit the evaporator to dry air intended for the defroster outlets.

Warm, high-pressure refrigerant liquid enters the evaporator through the fixed-orifice expansion tube, or through the thermostatic expansion valve. As the pressurized refrigerant sprays through the restricted orifice, it enters the low-pressure evaporator and immediately begins to boil. The evaporator is at lower pressure because the refrigerant flow from it to the suction side of the compressor is unrestricted, unlike the line leading from the compressor outlet to the expansion device. (Of course, this pressure may be modulated by

the suction throttling devices discussed earlier). As it boils, it absorbs latent heat of vaporization from the evaporator, chilling it, and therefore the air blowing into the passenger compartment.

Under high heat-load conditions, all the liquid refrigerant is vaporized and only gas flows toward the compressor. Under light heat-load conditions, vaporization may be incomplete and some liquid may leave the evaporator. This may occur in a thermostatic expansion valve system even if the valve remains fully closed, because of the small slot cut into the pintle valve to ensure compressor lubrication. In fixed-orifice expansion tube systems and some thermostatic expansion valve systems, this liquid is trapped in an accumulator on the evaporator discharge line.

Evaporators also are used to control humidity. When warm, humid passenger compartment air passes over the cold evaporator, the temperature of the air is lowered. This lowers the moisture-carrying capability of the air, and the moisture condenses on the cold evaporator surface and is drained away outside of the vehicle.

When warm HVAC output temperatures are selected, this cooled, dehumidified air is reheated by passing it through the heater core. The dehumidified air increases passenger comfort by increasing the rate at which perspiration can evaporate, and reduces fogging of the passenger compartment windows. The DEFROST setting in air conditioned cars uses the evaporator specifically to speed operation by drying the air to be blown against the windshield.

There are two main evaporator designs, the single-pass type and the multipass type. In the single-pass evaporator, refrigerant flows directly from the inlet to the outlet. In the multipass type, flow is directed back and forth across the evaporator before reaching the outlet. Most evaporators today are the multipass type.

The single-pass evaporator, figure 7-42, typically has 12 or 14 plate-fin sections. It is used with the fixed-orifice expansion tube refrigeration system.

The multipass evaporator, figure 7-43, resembles the single-pass type from the outside. Inside, however, partitions control the flow pattern to maintain high velocity. This prevents excess oil from collecting in the evaporator core. The liquid collects when the compressor is off, but is forced out when the flow starts again.

A typical multipass evaporator has 12 plate-fin sections. The mixture of refrigerant and oil

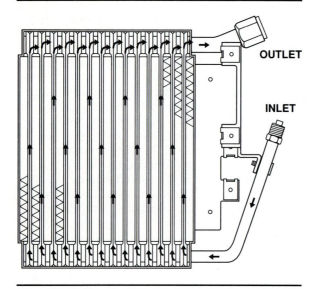

Figure 7-42. The single-pass evaporator is usually used on fixed-orifice tube systems.

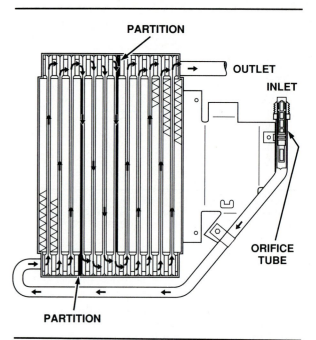

Figure 7-43 The multipass evaporator uses internal partitions to increase the speed of refrigerant flow.

enters the core at the inlet near the bottom, and is routed so that it flows upward through the partitioned first three plate-fin sections. The next four plate-fin sections are partitioned to force the refrigerant to flow downward toward the bottom of the evaporator. The refrigerant then flows over to the remaining five plate-fin sections, where it is forced to flow up and out through the outlet tube. The velocity of the refrigerant flow in this multipass pattern eliminates the need for the oil bleed line normally used on models with suction throttling valves to ensure adequate compressor lubrication.

RECEIVER-DRIERS AND ACCUMULATORS

Air conditioning systems contain more refrigerant than is needed at any one time. This surplus is kept in reserve to make sure the system is always adequately supplied, and to ensure adequate circulation of refrigerant oil through the system. The reserve refrigerant is stored in assemblies called receiver-driers and accumulators.

Receiver-Driers

The receiver-drier is mounted in the high side of the system between the condenser and the thermostatic expansion device, figure 7-44. Receiver-driers are used in systems with thermostatic expansion valves.

General Motors and some other manufacturers call this device the receiver-dehydrator.

The term **dehydrator**, like the word drier, refers to its role in removing moisture from the refrigerant. The receiver-drier:

• Removes moisture from the refrigerant
• Traps contaminants or debris before they can enter the TXV or evaporator
• Stores excess refrigerant
• Ensures that only liquid refrigerant enters the TXV during normal operation
• On some systems, locates the pressure relief valve and low-pressure cutoff switch
• On some systems, locates the sight glass.

The receiver-drier outlet fitting to the evaporator is usually located near the top of the assembly, figure 7-45. Refrigerant entering the assembly separates into liquid droplets that fall to the bottom and gas that rises to the top.

The outlet fitting to the thermostatic expansion valve may be located at the side, bottom, or top of the receiver-drier tank. Regardless of location, the outlet is connected internally to a pickup tube so that the refrigerant leaving the receiver-drier comes from near the bottom to the tank. This ensures that only liquid refrigerant will be supplied to the thermostatic expansion valve.

Before the droplets of refrigerant can reach the pickup tube, they pass through pads or bags of desiccant. Filter screens and filter pads also are commonly used between the inlet and outlet of the receiver-drier. The desiccant and

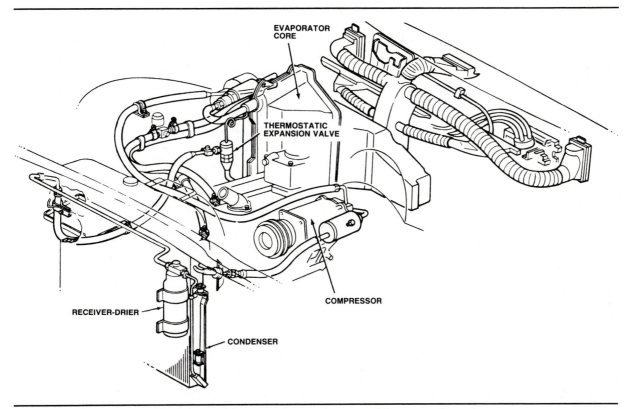

Figure 7-44. The receiver-drier is located between the condenser and the expansion valve.

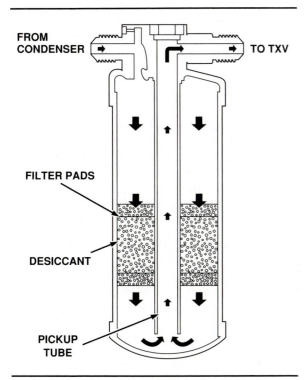

Figure 7-45. The main job of the receiver-drier is to remove moisture from the system and trap debris.

the filters prevent any solids from reaching the thermostatic expansion valve and clogging its orifice.

Receiver-driers are also convenient locations upon which to attach other components, such as sight glasses or pressure relief valves, figure 7-46.

The amount of moisture the desiccant can hold is directly proportional to its temperature. There are several materials that can serve as a

Dehydrator: A device with a desiccant to remove moisture from the refrigerant, also called a receiver-drier.

■ No Alcohol For The Desiccant

Some aftermarket companies recommend adding alcohol to the refrigeration system to remove moisture without changing the desiccant. This is *not* recommended by the carmakers because the alcohol may destroy the desiccant, releasing debris that could clog screens and filters. Using alcohol may actually release the water that had been trapped.

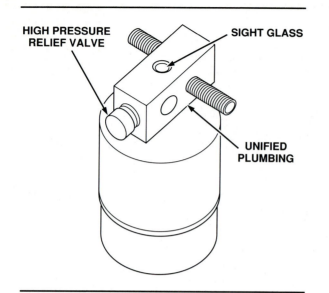

Figure 7-46. This receiver-drier has a one-piece multi-plumbed fitting at the top, which also contains the sight glass and a pressure relief valve.

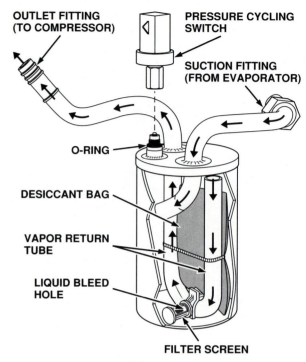

Figure 7-47. Some systems used a pressure cycling switch on the accumulator.

desiccant. A commonly used material is silica gel. This fine, off-white, granular powder attracts and holds moisture. During manufacturing it is baked dry and packaged in a porous bag. The silica gel protects the system by trapping the moisture that would otherwise combine with the refrigerant to produce system damaging acids.

The amount of desiccant determines how much moisture can be absorbed from the system. When the moisture level exceeds that amount, the system components will be endangered, and the desiccant must be replaced.

The receiver-drier serves as a reservoir or holding tank for the stored refrigerant. Having more refrigerant in the system than can actually be used at any moment ensures instant response to suddenly increased heat loads on the system. It also ensures that all parts of the system are continuously supplied with refrigerant oil. Because it is the last component upstream of the thermostatic expansion valve, the receiver-drier is a common place to locate the sight glass. Some General Motors and Chrysler systems use the receiver-drier to locate the pressure cutoff switch, and, on some models, the high-pressure relief valve, figure 7-46.

Accumulators

The accumulator is another type of storage device, mounted in the low side of the system between the evaporator and the suction side of the compressor, figure 7-47. The accumulator:

• Prevents liquid refrigerant from entering the compressor
• Removes moisture from the refrigerant
• Traps debris before it can enter the compressor
• Stores excess refrigerant
• Ensures a supply of oil to the compressor
• On some systems, locates the low-side service port.

Accumulators most commonly are found on cycling clutch systems using fixed orifices. The Ford thermostatic expansion valve system with a POA valve used in the late 1970s, used a suction-side accumulator on the low-pressure side of the system to protect the compressor. The function is similar to that of a cycling clutch accumulator.

Gaseous refrigerant enters the accumulator from the evaporator, figure 7-48. The angle of the inlet pipe ensures that any liquid droplets will fall to the bottom of the accumulator. Any debris passing through the system also falls to the bottom of the accumulator. This gaseous refrigerant circulates through the desiccant bag inside the accumulator. The desiccant absorbs

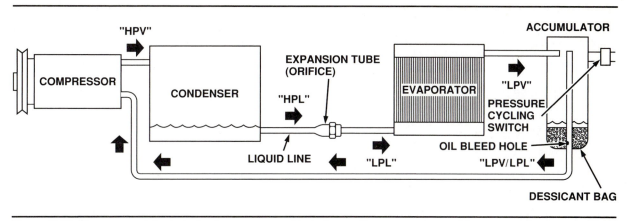

Figure 7-48. The accumulator is in the low-pressure side between the evaporator and the compressor.

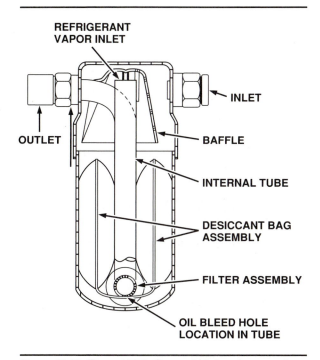

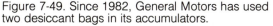

Figure 7-49. Since 1982, General Motors has used two desiccant bags in its accumulators.

any moisture that may be present. The refrigerant is drawn into the accumulator outlet which is connected to the suction side of the compressor.

General Motors updated its accumulator design in 1982 to add more desiccant, figure 7-49. Earlier models should have the newer accumulator fitted when replacement is needed.

At the bottom of the accumulator is a small wire mesh strainer that allows only liquid refrigerant and liquid refrigerant oil to pass through. On the other side of the strainer, a small orifice leads into the suction line. Since the amount of oil or refrigerant allowed

through the orifice is small, it does not damage the compressor. This feature ensures that lubricating oil will always be available to the compressor.

The accumulator usually is located at the outlet of the evaporator, but it can be located anywhere between the evaporator outlet and the compressor inlet. Refrigerant that is still liquid when it reaches the accumulator will remain there until it evaporates.

REFRIGERATION HOSES, CONNECTIONS, AND OTHER ASSEMBLIES

The major assemblies of an HVAC system are located near the front of the vehicle (condenser), on the engine (compressor) and behind the dash (evaporator and heater core). Refrigerant lines connect these assemblies to the control devices (such as the TXVs, STVs, and VIRs). The hoses and lines must:

• Contain the refrigerant and prevent contamination of the system by outside air.
• Prevent system damage that could result from vibration and differing rates of thermal expansion between the components.
• Conduct the pressurized refrigerant from one assembly to another throughout the refrigeration loop.
• Allow the system to be disassembled for repair and replacement of components.
• Resist damage from high pressure, rapid temperature changes, and constant vibration.

Types of Refrigeration Lines and Hoses

There are two basic types of refrigeration lines, figure 7-50. Rigid lines are pipes made of copper, steel, or aluminum. Flexible lines are

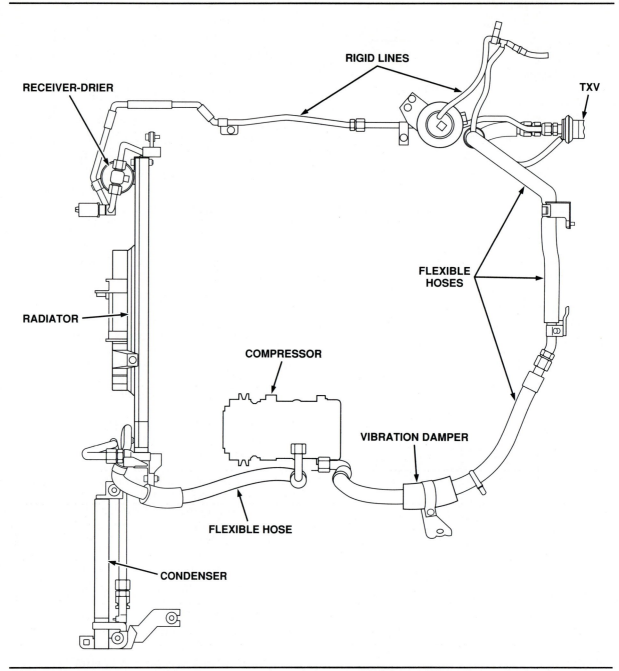

Figure 7-50. Rigid lines and flexible hoses are both used in air conditioning systems.

made of reinforced rubber or nylon hose with high-pressure connectors at either end.

Rigid lines
Most modern air conditioning systems use rigid lines in locations with sharp turns or reduced clearance, figure 7-51. These lines are used to connect parts of the system that are rigidly mounted. The most common application is the line between the condenser and the receiver-drier.

Metal tubing comes in standard sizes, figure 7-52. Note that the allowable torque for fittings on aluminum or copper tubing is far less than for steel lines.

Flexible hoses
Flexible refrigeration hoses are used to link parts of the system that vibrate or move in relation to each other. Lines to and from the compressor contain flexible sections to allow relative movement between the engine-

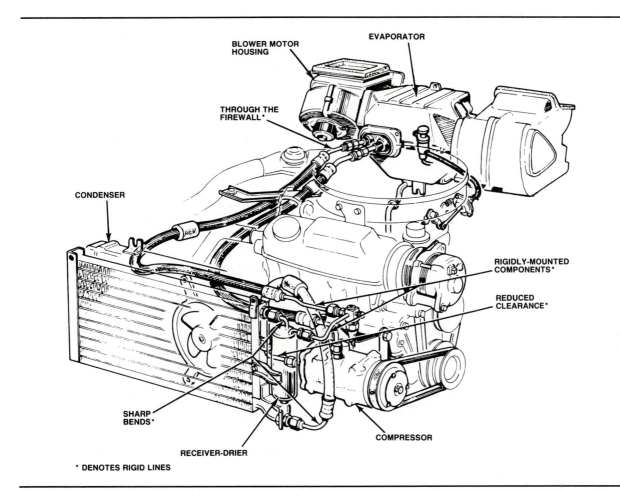

BLOWER MOTOR HOUSING

EVAPORATOR

THROUGH THE FIREWALL*

CONDENSER

RIGIDLY-MOUNTED COMPONENTS*

REDUCED CLEARANCE*

SHARP BENDS*

RECEIVER-DRIER

COMPRESSOR

* DENOTES RIGID LINES

Figure 7-51. Rigid tubing is used when there is reduced clearance, sharp bends, or rigidly mounted components.

METAL TUBE OUTSIDE DIAMETER	THREAD AND FITTING SIZE (inches)	STEEL TUBING TORQUE		ALUMINUM OR COPPER TUBING		NOMINAL TORQUE WRENCH SPAN (inches)
		FT. LB.	Nm	FT. LB.	Nm	
1/4	7/16	10-15	14-20	5-7	7-9	5/8
3/8	5/8	30-35	41-48	11-13	15-18	3/4
1/2	3/4	30-35	41-48	15-20	20-27	7/8
5/8	7/8	30-35	41-48	21-27	29-37	1-1/16
3/4	1-1/16	30-35	41-48	28-33	38-45	1-1/4

Figure 7-52. Torque specifications for rigid refrigerant line.

mounted compressor and other body-mounted components.

A flexible hose, figure 7-53, generally is of multilayer construction. Typically it consists of a synthetic rubber hose body with nylon reinforcing threads. A common design begins with a core hose of hypalon rubber, and overcoat it with a nitrile rubber for heat and abrasion protection. Another synthetic rubber called Buna-N may be used for the inner core layer because of its resistance to attack from R-12.

General Motors has used a different type of flexible refrigeration hose since 1984. The Type-D Parflex hose is made of a nylon inner hose with a rubber overcoating. In some cases, there may be an outer layer to protect the line from abrasion and excess engine compartment heat. The layer can be a braided plastic or metal mesh, a layer of foam rubber, or both.

Flexible line is more expensive and less reliable than the rigid line. Stub lines, made of rigid line, often are used on assemblies such as

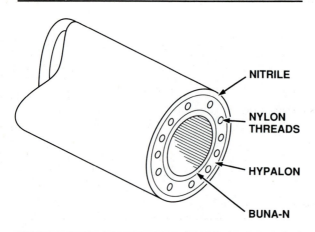

Figure 7-53. Construction of a typical flexible refrigerant hose.

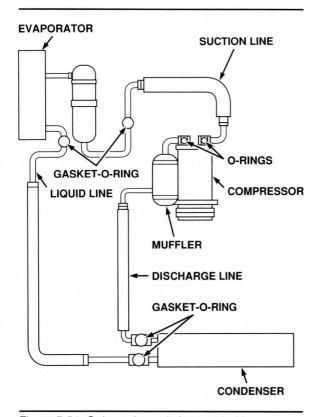

Figure 7-54. O-ring schematic for a typical late-model air conditioning system.

the compressor and the condenser to minimize flexible hose length.

If R-12 is banned as a refrigerant for automotive air conditioners, as now seems likely, alternative materials for flexible hoses will probably be required. The hose materials used for R-12 systems will likely not be compatible with alternative refrigerants.

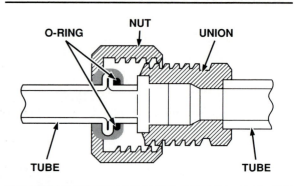

Figure 7-55. O-rings are usually made of neoprene rubber.

Refrigeration System Connections

Refrigeration system leaks could be greatly reduced if all of the lines between assemblies could be made as single-piece assemblies. However, detachable joints are used to make it easier to repair the system, figure 7-54. Both metal-to-metal and metal-to-rubber refrigeration joints must meet three requirements:

• The connection must be gas tight.
• The connection must be easy to disconnect and connect.
• The joints must withstand rapid and extreme temperature changes.

Two main types of refrigeration line connections are used:

• Flare fitting, or compression joint
• O-ring seal.

The flare fitting or compression joint depends on screw or wedge pressure created by tightening the threaded collar of the joint. A semisoft or compliant metal is chosen for the two halves of the fitting. Tightening the joint results in a gas-tight metal-to-metal seal.

The O-ring seal, figure 7-55, uses a fitting that butts the ends of the refrigeration line together inside a chamber formed by the connector. Between the line and the inside of the connector chamber, an O-ring is captured to form the needed seal. The O-rings usually are made of neoprene rubber and remain flexible over a wide range of temperatures. The proper seal of O-rings depends upon their being captured but not crimped by the connector. The O-ring must be lubricated with clean refrigeration oil before assembly to ensure a good seal.

A variation on the O-ring seal is Ford's spring lock connector, figure 7-56. It uses two O-rings mounted on the small end of the refrigeration line. The end of the joining refrigeration line is flared to slide over the two

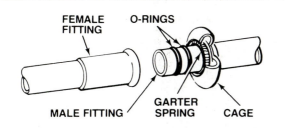

Figure 7-56. Ford's spring-lock coupling system.

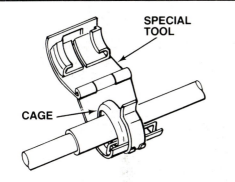

Figure 7-57. A special tool is needed to remove Ford's spring-lock connector.

O-rings. A circular garter spring holds the connection together. To disconnect the coupling, a special tool is required, figure 7-57.

Flexible hoses are connected to metal fittings by compression. The end opposite the flare or O-ring fitting, figure 7-58, is inserted into the inside diameter of the flexible hose. Circular ridges, called **sealing beads**, or barbs, are located on the insertion end. These circular ridges are larger in diameter than the inside diameter of the hose. Forcing the fitting into the hose compresses the beads against the inside of the hose.

In addition to the pressure caused by the sealing beads, the outside of the hose is compressed to improve the seal. This may be done by a hose clamp or by a crimped steel sleeve.

Service Valves

There must be some way for refrigerant to be added or discharged from the system, both during original assembly and for service. There are two types of valves used for this service: the Schrader valve and the stem valve. They commonly are found on the receiver-drier, accumulator, VIR, compressor, muffler, or on the lines themselves.

The Schrader valve
The most popular type service valve is the Schrader valve, figure 7-59. Schrader valves

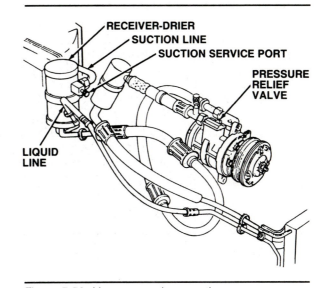

Figure 7-58. Hose-to-metal connections.

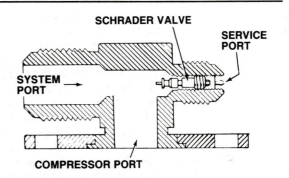

Figure 7-59. Schrader valves are the most common refrigeration service ports.

Sealing Beads: On a metal fitting, a ridge around the diameter of the fitting. This is inserted into flexible tubing to create a leak-tight connection.

■ **Hose Woes**

When you encounter a problem with deteriorated air conditioning or vacuum hoses or lines, naturally you will replace or repair them. But what caused the deterioration in the first place?

If the car is a transverse-mounted front-wheel-drive model, check the condition of the engine struts and motor mounts. If they are loose or worn, they may be allowing the engine to rock back and forth too much. This puts added stress on the hoses, particularly at the suction and discharge sides of the compressor. The flexing wears the hoses and lines out just as if they had been in service much longer.

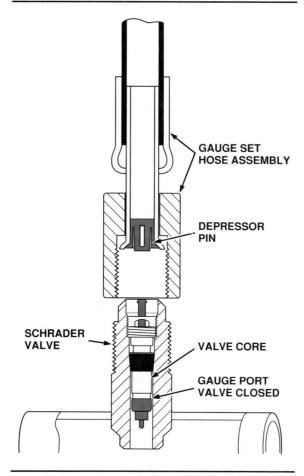

Figure 7-60. A depressor pin on the gauge set opens the Schrader valve.

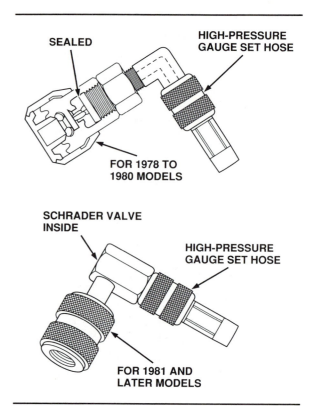

Figure 7-61. The stem-type service valve has three positions.

are held closed by internal pressure, although a small spring is included to keep the valve seated if the pressure is lost. When the service connection is made, the depressor in the end of the test hose presses on a small pin inside the valve, forcing the valve open, figure 7-60. The valve opens only when the service line connection is nearly complete, preventing contamination of the system or the unnecessary release of refrigerant.

The operation of the Schrader valve is often compared to a tire valve. However, the valves used in HVAC systems are more precise and of a higher quality than those used in tires.

In the past, many technicians have had difficulty finding the service ports and correctly identifying them as high side and low side. Incorrect connection may result in damage to the gauges and possibly to the air conditioning system. To prevent this, many systems built after 1976 have special high-side service ports that cannot be connected to the low-side service hose. General Motors systems use a differ-

ent thread on the high-side port. Service hose connections are screwed on, with the valve opening only when the connection is nearly complete. Ford systems require different sizes of quick-disconnect fittings, similar to an air hose coupling. Adapters are available for use with standard manifold gauge sets, figure 7-61.

The stem valve
The obsolete stem valve, figure 7-62, is a manually controlled valve system. The stem of the valve is turned in or out to open or close the valve.

The primary difference between the stem valve and the Schrader valve, beyond the manual control, is that the stem valve is a 3-position valve. In the back-seated position, refrigerant can flow from the compressor into the refrigerant line. This is the normal operating position for the valve and represents the fully open position.

In the mid-seated (cracked) position, the output pressure of the compressor is channelled not only to the refrigerant line but also to the pressure gauge port. This is the test position. The system can operate normally while the gauge registers system pressure.

In the front-seated position, the refrigeration hose is blocked off and only compressor out-

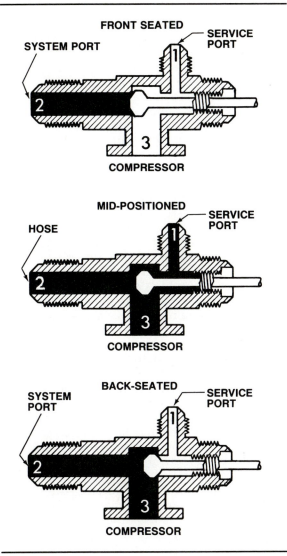

Figure 7-62. Ford uses adapters for the high-side gauge set.

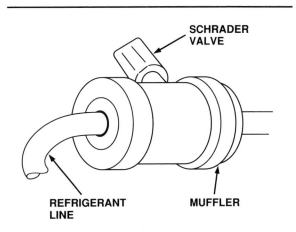

Figure 7-63. Mufflers are sometimes installed to quiet the compressor noises.

put pressure is directed into the pressure gauge test port. This isolates the compressor from the rest of the HVAC system. The front-seated position is the off position for the HVAC valve. *Never* attempt to operate the compressor with the service valve in the front-seated position. Front seating is only used to isolate the compressor oil level checks, repair, or replacement.

Mufflers

The air conditioning compressor can make quite a bit of noise as it pressurizes the refrigerant, both from the refrigerant itself, and from the vibrations in the high-pressure line. To quiet these noises, a refrigeration-type muf-fler is installed. The muffler, figure 7-63, is installed into the high side of the system at the outlet of the compressor. Since the noise can be transmitted through the metal of the line between the compressor and the condenser, this line often is covered with foam rubber tape to further reduce the noise.

Filters
An air conditioning system contaminated by compressor failure or other causes must be cleaned of all debris. This may be difficult because the debris may be spread throughout the many small areas of the air conditioning system. This is especially true of systems with serpentine evaporators, which have many turns in which debris can lodge. Some parts of the system cannot be effectively flushed. The compressor has many cavities in which debris may cling during cleaning, only to come loose

■ **Tightening Air Conditioning Hose Connections**

Special tools and precautions are recommended when tightening air conditioning lines and fittings. Many connections are made of aluminum. Tightening these too much can easily strip the threads, so be sure to follow the manufacturer's recommendations for proper tightening. Use a backing wrench to ensure that tightening the fittings does not twist the rigid lines used on some components. Continuing to tighten a leaking O-ring connector will not stop the leak. These connectors work because of the surface contact between the O-ring and the connector body. Further tightening may damage the threads or twist the line. Instead, install a new, properly lubricated O-ring.

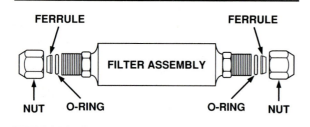

Figure 7-64. A liquid line filter can be a factory-installed item or an aftermarket item.

later. Even if the cleaning job is a thorough one, there always is the chance that some debris remains.

Because of all the difficulties, some manufacturers recommend installing an added filter, figure 7-64. This liquid line filter traps the debris before it can damage or clog the system. The filter generally is installed in the high-pressure liquid line between the condenser and the orifice tube, or between the condenser and the thermostatic expansion valve. It contains a screen and filter pad. The screen catches the larger particles and holds the filter pad. The pad catches the smaller particles and filters the refrigerant oil.

SUMMARY

Every air conditioning system uses either a thermostatic expansion valve or a fixed-orifice expansion tube to provide a restriction in the air conditioning circuit, which causes the refrigerant to change state from a liquid to a gas. These devices meter and regulate the refrigerant flow as it passes from the high-pressure side to the low-pressure side.

The variable-orifice Thermostatic Expansion Valve (TXV) is used on most systems with continuously-running positive-displacement compressors and many cycling-clutch systems with fixed displacement compressors. In a thermostatic expansion valve, a spring-loaded diaphragm responds to evaporator temperature and pressure to meter the refrigerant flow. Suction throttling devices are used on thermostatic expansion valve systems to help

regulate evaporator temperature variations and to prevent evaporator freeze-up. These controls have various names: Suction Throttling Valve (STV), Pilot-Operated Absolute (POA) Valve, Evaporator Pressure Regulator (EPR), and Evaporator Temperature Regulator (ETR). All do about the same task, and most are mounted near the evaporator outlet.

Newer thermostatic expansion valves may be combined with other devices into multipurpose components. The Valves-In-Receiver (VIR) and the Evaporator-Equalized Valves-In-Receiver (EEVIR) combine the TXV, the POA valve, a sight glass, and the receiver-drier. The combination valve and mini-combination valve combine the TXV and STV into an H-block.

The fixed-orifice expansion tube is used on late-model cycling clutch systems and continuously-running variable-displacement compressors. The tube is in the evaporator inlet line and contains no valve and no temperature or pressure-sensing capability.

Condensers and evaporators are both heat exchangers. The condenser permits the refrigerant to change state and release heat to the passing airstream. The evaporator permits the refrigerant to change state and absorb heat from the airflow entering the passenger compartment. Heat exchange takes place in the tubes and fins of the two components. Two types of evaporators are used: multi-pass and single-pass types.

The accumulator and the receiver-drier are refrigerant storage devices that also remove contaminating water from the system. Both use a desiccant to attract and hold the moisture.

The air conditioning system uses rigid metal refrigerant lines to link rigidly mounted components, and flexible rubber hoses to link parts that vibrate or move. Fittings generally are either flare fittings or O-ring connectors. Two types of valves are used to service the system: Schrader valves and stem valves. Other air conditioning system components include mufflers to quiet the noise of the compressor and filters to screen out possible internal contamination.

Review Questions

Choose the single most correct answer.
Compare your answers with the correct answers on page 229.

1. The evaporator temperature regulator (ETR) valve:
   a. Modulates
   b. Is usually partially open
   c. Is pressure regulated
   d. Is electrically operated

2. An externally equalized expansion valve in an air conditioning system is used to compensate for:
   a. Pressure drop across the evaporator
   b. Higher evaporator pressures
   c. Variations in high-side pressure
   d. Variations in compressor speed

3. Excessive moisture in an air conditioning system will freeze at the:
   a. Compressor
   b. Evaporator
   c. Receiver-drier
   d. Thermostatic expansion valve

4. Which of the following is *not* true?
   a. Most modern evaporators are the single-pass type
   b. Most condensers have a serpentine flow pattern
   c. In a condenser tube, gaseous refrigerant flows along the top
   d. Evaporator fins aid conduction

5. Which of the following systems typically uses a continuously running compressor?
   a. CCOT
   b. FFOT
   c. FOTCC
   d. TXV

6. A General Motors VDOT system uses:
   a. A thermostatic expansion valve
   b. A cycling clutch
   c. A variable-displacement compressor
   d. A variable-orifice tube

7. Which of the following occurs at the fixed-orifice tube?
   a. The pressure on the refrigerant is relieved
   b. The refrigerant evaporates quickly and completely
   c. The heat of latency is absorbed as the refrigerant changes state
   d. All of the above

8. A fixed-orifice tube:
   a. Has a temperature-sensing capability
   b. Has a pressure-sensing capability
   c. Usually is located in the evaporator inlet
   d. Has an internal valve

9. Which of the following is *not* a job of the thermostatic expansion valve?
   a. Meters refrigerant into evaporator
   b. Senses compressor outlet pressure
   c. Creates the pressure drop leaving the valve
   d. Varies refrigerant flow in response to changing heat loads

10. Technician A says the pintle valve or ball-and-seat varies the size of the orifice in a TXV.
    Technician B says evaporator inlet temperature determines how much refrigerant is allowed to pass through the TXV.
    Who is right?
    a. A only
    b. B only
    c. Both A and B
    d. Neither A nor B

11. A TXV senses evaporator temperature with:
    a. A thermostatic switch
    b. A capillary bulb and tube
    c. An ambient temperature switch
    d. An internal diaphragm

12. Technician A says an externally equalized TXV has a passage between the diaphragm housing and the evaporator outlet.
    Technician B says an internally equalized TXV has a vacuum line from the diaphragm housing to the evaporator outlet.
    Who is right?
    a. A only
    b. B only
    c. Both A and B
    d. Neither A nor B

13. Superheat is:
    a. The added heat absorbed by gaseous refrigerant below its boiling point
    b. The heat released by cooled refrigerant in the condenser
    c. The added heat absorbed by gaseous refrigerant above its boiling point
    d. The heat released by cooled refrigerant in the evaporator

14. Which of the following is *not* part of an H-valve:
    a. Temperature-sensing element
    b. Pressure-sensing element
    c. Diaphragm
    d. Superheat spring

15. Which of the following can result from evaporator freeze-up?
    a. The refrigerant may not properly evaporate
    b. Liquid refrigerant can be drawn into the compressor
    c. The air conditioning system produces little or no cooling
    d. All of the above

16. Suction throttling devices are used to:
    a. Prevent evaporator freezing
    b. Cycle the clutch less frequently
    c. Lower the suction pressure to the compressor
    d. Control the pressure of the refrigerant in the condenser

17. Which of the following suction throttling controls is referenced to an internal vacuum instead of to atmospheric pressure?
    a. STV
    b. POA
    c. EPR
    d. ETR

18. Which of the following suction throttling controls is generally mounted in the suction port of the compressor?
    a. STV
    b. Pressure cycling switch
    c. EPR
    d. ETR

19. Low-side service ports commonly are found on the:
    a. POA
    b. STV
    c. Accumulator
    d. All of the above

20. Which of the following is *not* true of a receiver-drier?
    a. Stores excess refrigerant
    b. Contains desiccant to trap moisture
    c. Contains the low-side service port
    d. All of the above

Air Conditioning System Controls

In addition to the thermostatic control in the passenger compartment, there are numerous additional controls that influence the operation of the air conditioning system, figure 8-1. These added controls can be divided into three categories:

• Controls that prevent damage to the air conditioning system.
• Controls that prevent air conditioning operation when engine power is needed for other purposes.
• Controls that prevent damage to other vehicle systems.

In this chapter we will cover the function and location of these controls. In the next chapter we will see how these controls are combined in semiautomatic and fully automatic systems, and in Chapter 10 we will look at representative systems used today by the carmakers.

PREVENTING COMPRESSOR DAMAGE

In certain instances, driver control must be overruled to prevent compressor operation. The compressor and other air conditioning components could be extensively damaged if:

• System pressure rises above or falls below safe limits.
• The supply of refrigerant or refrigeration oil is low.
• The system operates above or below specified temperatures.

Most compressor safety controls protect the system by interrupting electric current to the magnetic compressor clutch, figure 8-2. This may be done by directly interrupting power to the clutch or indirectly by interrupting power to the clutch control relay. The decision to interrupt power to the clutch or clutch relay may be made mechanically or electronically.

Ambient Temperature Sensing

Compressors must not operate when either the ambient or the compressor housing temperatures are too low. Temperature extremes may result in poor lubrication, tight tolerances, and part brittleness. Failures of reed valves, seals, gaskets, and piston rings may result.

Ambient air temperature is measured or sensed in two principal ways:

• Direct temperature sensing
• Pressure sensing.

Direct temperature sensing uses bimetallic or thermistor-type sensors. In the first type, the

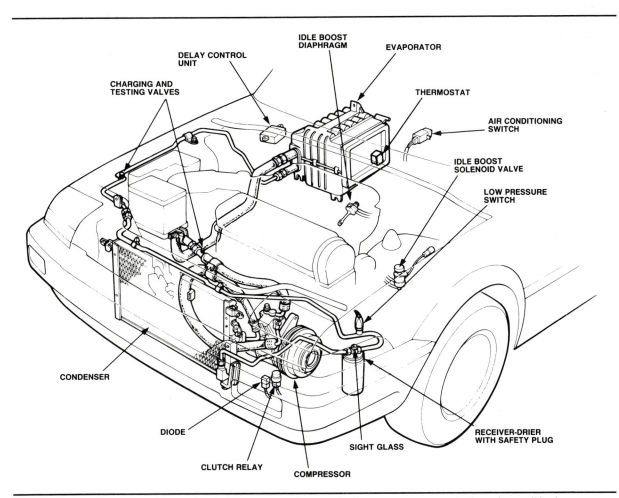

Figure 8-1. Numerous sensors and switches prevent damage to the compressor and other air conditioning components during high load or low refrigerant conditions.

movement of the bimetallic strip caused by the change in temperature is used to control other electrical or vacuum circuits that prevent or control compressor operation. These sensors were covered in detail in Chapter 4. A thermistor is a temperature-sensitive resistor. Changes in ambient temperature result in changes in electrical resistance. The resistance change can be converted into an electrical signal which is then used by the system control element.

Ambient air temperature can also be measured by using the standard relationship between the *pressure* of the refrigerant (R-12) and its *temperature*. If the pressure in the system falls too low, it can indicate that the outside air temperature is too low for safe compressor operation.

Ambient air sensing most often is used as an informational input to the control element of the air conditioning system. On some vehicles, it is used directly to prevent compressor operation.

Ambient temperature switch

The ambient temperature switch uses a temperature-sensitive bimetallic arm. The arm has electrical contacts mounted on it that must remain closed to complete the electrical circuit supplying power to the compressor clutch. The unit is preset to open the contacts when the temperature falls below the minimum value acceptable for reliable operation. This interrupts power to the clutch and prevents possible compressor damage. When rising ambient temperature reaches 32° to 50°F (0° to 8°C), the bimetallic arm closes the contacts, which completes the circuit and sends power to the compressor clutch.

The ambient temperature sensor switch is generally located in the engine compartment near the radiator or in the airstream entering the evaporator, figure 8-3.

Ambient temperature sensor

Thermistor-type ambient air temperature sensing devices commonly are mounted in the air

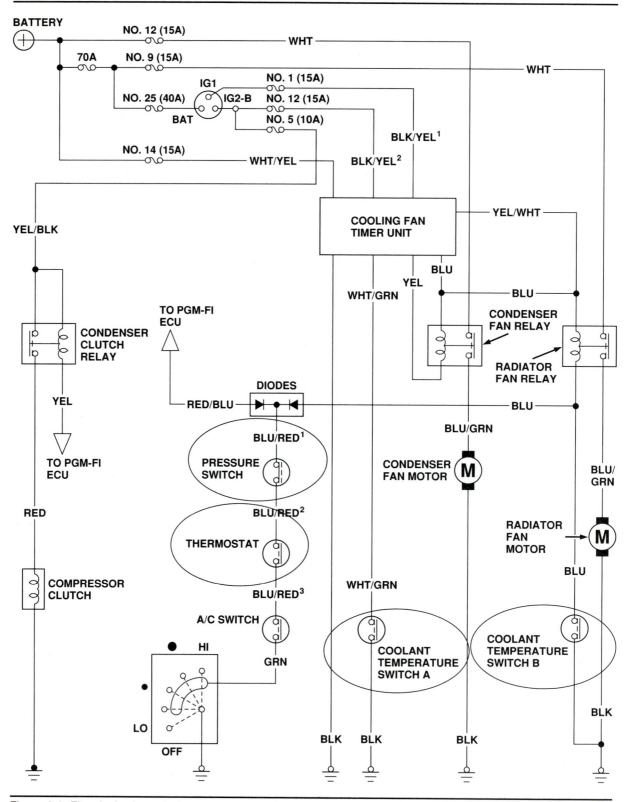

Figure 8-2. Electrical schematic for the 1990 Honda Accord showing the safety switches that signal the electronic control unit (ECU) to disengage the compressor clutch.

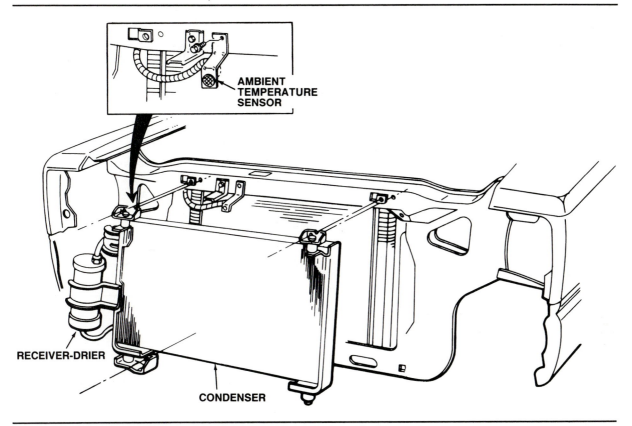

AMBIENT TEMPERATURE SENSOR

RECEIVER-DRIER

CONDENSER

Figure 8-3. Some ambient temperature sensors are mounted next to the condenser or compressor.

intake of the HVAC system. The Chrysler ambient temperature sensor is mounted on the rear surface of the evaporator-heater plenum. The ambient temperature sensor used on some late-model Mercury Cougar, Lincoln Mark VII and Ford Thunderbirds is located on the side of the air inlet duct and blower assembly, figure 8-4. In these representative installations, air is drawn from outside the vehicle through the cowl vents and passes over the sensor. The sensor measures the temperature of the air and sends this information to the computer. An in-car sensor, figure 8-5, measures the temperature of the passenger compartment. The programmer or computer reads the difference between the two measurements and signals the compressor (and sometimes the cooling fan) to vary air conditioning system operation accordingly.

Low-Pressure Sensing

Insufficient pressure in the low side of the system can indicate problems that can cause serious damage to the air conditioning system. Loss of lubrication is the leading cause of compressor failure. Most compressors depend

■ Energy Collapse And Voltage Spikes

Electrical solenoids convert electrical energy into mechanical movement. Solenoids are often used to produce the linear motion needed to change air door position, close water valves, and other similar functions.

One of the problems with solenoids is that when turned off, the falling current in the windings of the solenoid can act in a way similar to an ignition coil. The collapse of the magnetic energy that was stored when the current was flowing in the solenoid can induce voltage spikes in the solenoid coils.

To prevent damage to the rest of the electrical system, automakers usually include a reverse diode in parallel to the winding. When power to the coil is on, current flows through the winding unaffected by the diode because the diode is reverse biased. When power is turned off, the collapsing energy is blocked by the diode to prevent voltage spikes from entering the rest of the wiring system.

When servicing any solenoid or motor coil on an automobile, be sure to return the diode or capacitor, if used, to its correct location when reinstalling the solenoid. Failure to do so may result in electrical damage to the automobile.

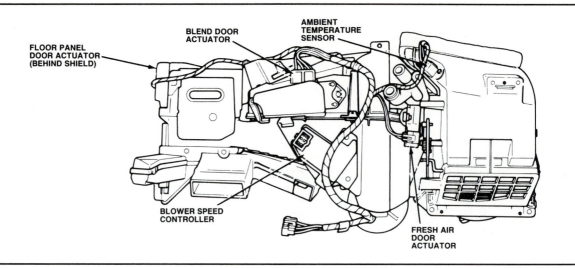

Figure 8-4. This ambient temperature sensor is located in the airstream to the evaporator.

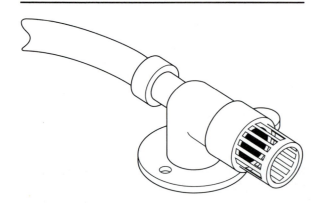

Figure 8-5. An in-car sensor draws passenger compartment air across a thermistor, which signals the programmer or ECU.

upon refrigeration oil, carried through the system by the refrigerant, for system lubrication. If a leak allows the refrigerant to escape, some or most of the refrigerant oil will be lost from the system and what oil remains will not be circulated. There are several pressure-detecting devices used to prevent the damage to the compressor that may be caused by low refrigerant levels. These include the:

• Low-pressure cutout switch
• High- and low-side temperature sensors
• Superheat switch and thermal limiter
• Pressure cycling switch.

Low-pressure cutout switch
Various types of low-pressure switches have been used. Carmakers call them cutout switches, cutoff switches, or pressure switches, but all work in essentially the same way. The low-pressure cutout switch, figure 8-6, is located

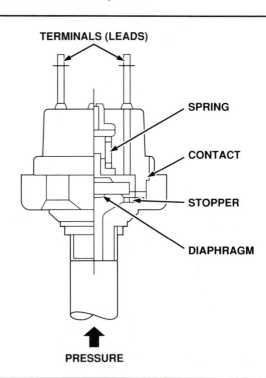

Figure 8-6. The low-pressure cutout switch senses low refrigerant pressure and converts this to an electrical signal.

on the high side of the system. Typically, the switch contacts are normally open at pressures below 20 psi (140 kPa) and closed at pressures above 30 psi (200 kPa). A diaphragm senses refrigerant pressure. When system pressure against the diaphragm overcomes spring pressure, the contacts close to complete the circuit. When pressure drops, the contacts open and the compressor clutch is de-energized.

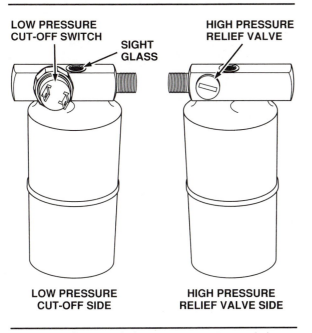

Figure 8-7. Some early low-pressure cutout switches were located on the receiver-drier.

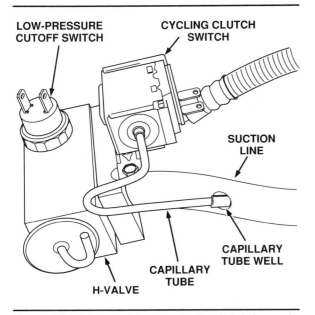

Figure 8-8. This low-pressure cutout switch is located on the H-valve.

On some models, the switch is located on the receiver-drier, figure 8-7. On 1979 and later Chrysler models the low-pressure cutout switch is part of the H-valve assembly, figure 8-8. American Motors and General Motors have used a device called a low-pressure cutoff switch or compressor-discharge switch. This switch was used on some CCOT systems with accumulators but without pressure cycling

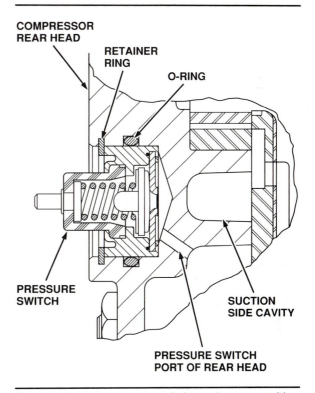

Figure 8-9. A low-pressure switch can be mounted in the rear head of the compressor.

switches. American Motors used this switch on 4-cylinder models built between 1980-86. Some General Motors systems use a low-pressure switch in the rear head of the compressor, figure 8-9.

High- and low-side temperature sensors
Because there is a known relationship between the pressure and the temperature of R-12 in an air conditioning system, it is also possible to measure the pressure by measuring the temperature of the system. General Motors uses these temperature sensors on some models equipped with electronic climate control.

The high-side sensor is located in the high-side line between the condenser and the orifice tube, figure 8-10. The low-side sensor is located in the low-side line between the orifice tube and the evaporator. Both sensors send input signals to the computer. The computer uses this information to block compressor operation if the pressure is too low, indicating a possible loss of refrigerant.

Superheat switch and thermal limiter
When the gaseous refrigerant that leaves the evaporator is warmer than the liquid refrigerant that entered, it is said to be superheated. The superheat condition may or may not indicate a fault in the air conditioning system. As

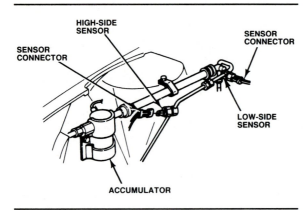

Figure 8-10. These high- and low-side temperature sensors are mounted in the line before and after the orifice tube.

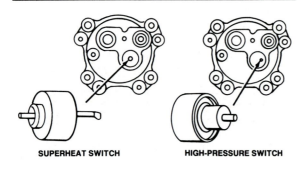

Figure 8-11. The superheat switch looks like the high-pressure switch that replaced it. They are not interchangeable.

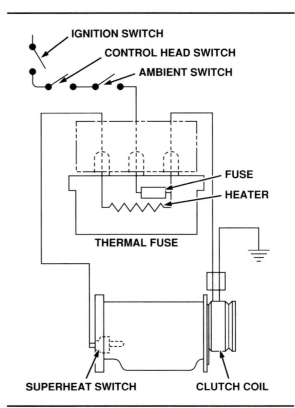

Figure 8-12. This electrical schematic for the superheat switch shows the thermal limiter (fuse).

discussed in Chapter 7, some systems are designed to operate with a specific amount of superheat — in the range of 4° to 16°F (3° to 10°C) — measured in the gaseous refrigerant at the evaporator outlet.

The presence of excessive superheat in the suction side indicates the amount of refrigerant entering the evaporator is too low, or that the temperature of the evaporator core is high. The latter may be normal. A car that has been parked in direct sunlight is likely to have a very warm evaporator and a very warm interior temperature as well. Until the air conditioning system can reduce the temperature of the evaporator and the interior, superheat in the refrigerant entering the compressor is normal.

Abnormal conditions that can be detected by measuring superheat include low refrigerant levels and partially frozen or blocked metering devices. The poor refrigerant flow that results from these situations can cause loss of lubrication to the compressor, and must be prevented.

A superheat switch is a temperature-pressure component mounted in the rear of

some GM 6-cylinder compressors, figure 8-11. It de-energizes the compressor clutch when a high-temperature, low-pressure condition is sensed. Most systems with superheat sensing use a type of time-delay fusing. This allows the superheat condition to continue for a period of time before the switch shuts off the compressor. When the superheat switch detects the predetermined combination of low pressure and high temperature in the suction line, it closes, allowing current through the heater resistor in the thermal limiter, figure 8-12. If the superheat condition continues long enough, the heat from the resistor will melt the thermal link. This breaks the electrical circuit to the magnetic clutch preventing further operation of the compressor. This thermal limiter is a "one-time" device and must be replaced if blown.

Intermittent superheat, resulting from conditions that are extreme but still in the normal range, does not allow the current to flow through the heater resistor long enough to melt the thermal link. Early model thermal limiters were found to be overly sensitive. Since 1975 the links that are installed have a higher melting point. This prevents temporary high temperature/low pressure situations from blowing the fuse.

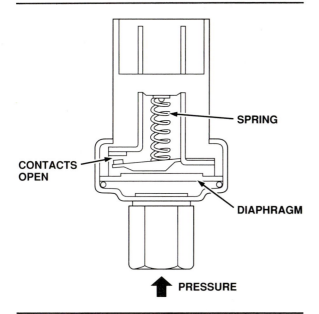

Figure 8-13. The pressure cycling switch operation is similar to the high-pressure switch.

The superheat switch, combined with a thermal limiter fuse, was used until 1978 on the GM A-6 compressor. It was replaced with a switch that was sensitive to high pressure only. This switch does not have a thermal sensing tube as a part of the assembly. Even though the pressure switch and the superheat switch look very similar, they are not interchangeable.

Pressure cycling switch
The pressure cycling switch is a multipurpose switch, figure 8-13. Its primary purpose is to cycle the compressor on and off in response to evaporator outlet pressure to prevent evaporator freeze-up. The switch also is used to prevent compressor operation when low refrigerant levels or low ambient temperature conditions are sensed.

Pressure cycling switches commonly are used on systems with orifice tubes. When the pressure at the outlet of the evaporator falls too low, indicating potential evaporator freeze-up, the switch opens to prevent engagement of the compressor clutch. Evaporator pressures also are low when ambient temperature conditions are too cold for safe compressor operation. The pressure cycling switch also opens under low-temperature, low-pressure conditions to protect the compressor.

Pressure cycling switches used by GM and Ford are mounted on the accumulator housing in the engine compartment, figure 8-14. These

switches are mounted in a Schrader valve and can be replaced without discharging the system.

Various versions of the pressure cycling switch have been used extensively on GM models since 1979. Because each switch cycles at a different pressure, it is important to replace a defective pressure cycling switch with the correct replacement part.

High-Pressure Sensing

When pressures on the high side of the system rise above safe levels, there is also a risk of damage. High-pressure conditions can be caused by:

- Internally blocked condensers
- Frozen or jammed magnetic clutches
- Faulty controls
- Inoperative fans, or shrouded condensers that result in high condenser temperatures
- Overcharged systems.

Abnormally high pressures can damage air conditioning system hoses, compressor reed valves, and compressor bearings. To prevent this condition, manufacturers install pressure relief valves and high pressure cutout switches.

The high pressure cut-out switch is an electrical switch that interrupts compressor clutch operation when the over-pressure condition is sensed. Preventing further operation of the compressor by opening the electrical circuit to the magnetic clutch prevents any further rise in system pressures.

Pressure relief valve
The pressure relief valve is a spring-loaded mechanical safety valve. When system pressure rises above the danger point, the pressure of the refrigerant overcomes the pressure of the calibrated spring inside the valve. The valve lifts from its seat and refrigerant escapes. The valve remains open only long enough to reduce the system pressure below the setpoint of the relief valve spring.

Pressure relief valves are mounted in the high side of the system, usually at the discharge port of the compressor, figure 8-15, in the high-pressure line, or at the receiver-drier, figure 8-16. If the pressure exceeds a preset level, typically 450 to 550 psi (3100 to 3800 kPa), the valve opens to release enough refrigerant to the atmosphere to lower the pressure. When the pressure falls below the setpoint of the valve, the valve closes. When the pressure relief valve cycles, both refrigerant and refrigerant oil are lost from the system. When the

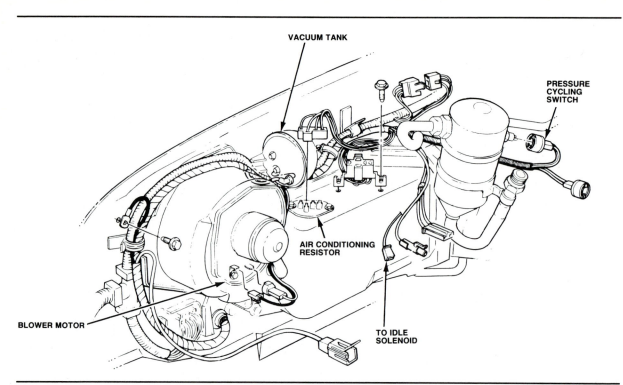

Figure 8-14. The pressure cycling switch is mounted on the suction accumulator.

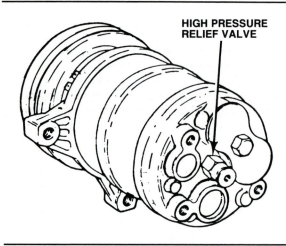

Figure 8-15. The pressure relief valve is mounted in the rear head of this 6-cylinder compressor.

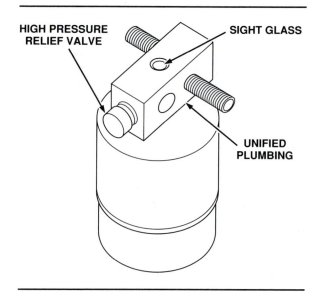

Figure 8-16. The pressure relief valve can also be located on the receiver-drier.

fault causing the pressure venting is repaired, the lost refrigerant and refrigerant oil must be replaced.

High pressure cutout switch
Both Chrysler and General Motors have used a high-pressure cutout switch to protect the compressor. It is mounted on the rear of the compressor and is wired in series with the low-pressure cutout switch and the ambient temperature sensor. The contacts in this electrical switch open to prevent current flow to the compressor clutch when system pressure rises above a certain level. The Chrysler switch opens at 375 psi (2600 kPa) and closes when system pressure falls below 250 psi (1700 kPa). The GM switch opens at 400 psi (2800 kPa) and closes at 290 psi (2000 kPa).

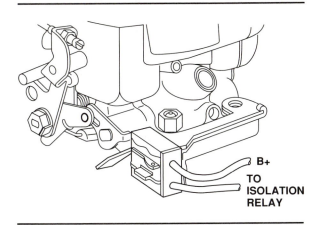

B+
TO
ISOLATION
RELAY

Figure 8-17. The WOT switch is connected to the throttle linkage.

COMPRESSOR DRIVEABILITY CONTROLS

Under some driving situations air conditioning compressor operation is undesirable, even though various system controls may be set for additional cooling. Driveability controls sense engine and vehicle operating conditions, and when conditions could lead to poor driveability they temporarily block operation of the compressor.

Driveability controls are most common on vehicles equipped with diesel or small-displacement gasoline engines. Diesel and 4-cylinder gasoline engines are not as well balanced or as powerful as larger 6- and 8-cylinder engines. As a result, the load of running the air conditioning compressor is significant at idle and during cold-start conditions. Compressor clutch cycling is especially noticeable at slow idle. Driveability controls are also commonly found on computer-controlled air conditioning systems. The goal of these systems is to produce a highly refined climate control that is unnoticeable to the driver.

Air conditioning operation may also be undesirable when the demand on the engine is high relative to engine speed, such as during parking, high speed acceleration, or periods of high alternator demand. Driveability controls prevent operation of the compressor during times when the power demand is high, but engine output is low.

Many different types of driveability controls have been used by different manufacturers. The following describe how representative controls operate. Check the appropriate shop manual before beginning work on a specific system.

Heavy-Load or Cold-Start Conditions

Carmakers use many types of switches and relays to prevent compressor operation during heavy-load, low-idle, or cold-start conditions. These include the:

- Wide-open throttle switch
- Low-vacuum switch
- Power steering pressure switch.

Wide-open throttle switch

The wide-open throttle (WOT) switch has been widely used with air conditioning systems. It can be mounted at the base of the carburetor, figure 8-17, or in the throttle linkage. The switch prevents compressor operation whenever the throttle is held wide open. The normally-closed switch opens when the accelerator pedal is moved to the full or nearly full open position. This prevents power from getting to the compressor clutch, removing the compressor as a load on the engine. More power is then available for vehicle acceleration. Opening the WOT switch also removes the heat load the air conditioning system places on the cooling system. This can improve engine cooling when climbing long grades.

On some cars, the WOT switch is connected in series with the air conditioning time delay relay. The switch de-energizes the relay to stop compressor operation when the switch opens. The compressor will not operate as long as the switch is open. When the switch closes, the time delay relay continues to prevent compressor operation for 5 seconds before allowing the compressor to return to normal operation.

On other cars, the WOT switch is wired in series with an isolation relay coil. This is similar to the time delay relay, except without the delay. The isolation relay acts as a switching device to open the compressor clutch circuit without affecting the engine idle speed.

On cars with automatic transmissions, a compressor cutout switch may be used to prevent compressor operation when the accelerator is depressed into the kickdown, or passing gear, range. Some models restore compressor operation after a short delay (6-10 seconds) while other systems delay compressor operation until the transmission shifts into higher gear.

A later variation is the throttle position sensor, figure 8-18. This sensor monitors the position of the throttle throughout its operating range instead of just sensing when the throttle is wide open. The information from the throttle position sensor is used by the body computer on some models to prevent clutch

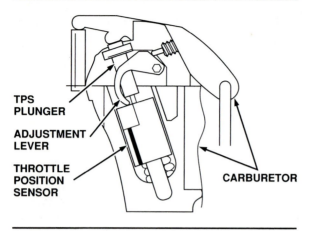

Figure 8-18. The throttle position sensor detects the driver's demand for power from the engine.

engagement when the throttle position indicates that full power is needed.

Low-vacuum switch

Intake manifold vacuum is a widely used indicator of engine loading. Some models use a vacuum-sensitive switch mounted on the intake manifold to prevent compressor operation when the intake manifold vacuum indicates high engine load conditions. The effect of the low-vacuum switch is the same as the WOT switch. Opening the switch removes the compressor load, making more power available for acceleration.

Power steering pressure switch

Power steering is most needed when the engine is operating at near idle speeds during parking maneuvers. During this time engine power output is at its lowest point.

The power steering pressure switch, figure 8-19, senses the pressure levels inside the power steering mechanism. This is a measurement of the amount of turning resistance being offered by the tires. When low-speed parking demands the most power, power steering pressures rise high enough to open the switch. When the pressure exceeds 300 psi (2070 kPa), the supply of power to the compressor clutch relay is interrupted. This leaves more power available to the power steering pump. This reduces the likelihood of the engine stalling or running roughly.

The power steering pressure switch is commonly mounted on the power steering pump, the rack-and-pinion steering assembly, or in the power steering pressure line.

Time Delay Devices

In many instances in air conditioning operation, it is desirable to allow the system either

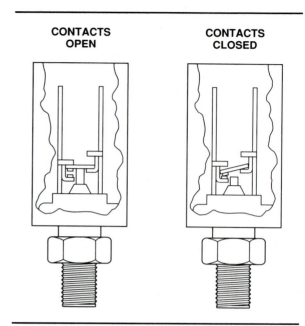

Figure 8-19. The power steering pressure switch reacts to fluid pressure.

to continue to run after the driver shuts it off, or to shut off even when the control is set to ON. Carmakers use a number of relays to handle these situations. They include the:

• Time delay relay
• Power brake time delay
• Anti-dieseling relay
• Electronic control module delay timer
• Constant run relay.

Time delay relay

The time delay relay, figure 8-20, is used on many newer cycling clutch systems. The time delay relay blocks operation of the compressor for a short time after the engine is started. It does this by preventing current from reaching the compressor clutch for 5 to 10 seconds after the engine has started or the air conditioning mode has been selected. This delay gives the engine time to purge the vapor fuel canister and time for the electrical system voltage to rise high enough to prevent compressor clutch chatter. The time delay also allows the engine to warm slightly before the air conditioning load is placed on the engine.

The time delay relay is usually located under the instrument panel near the steering column. On some vehicles the time delay relay is wired in series with the coolant temperature switch to block compressor operation if the vehicle overheats. It can also be connected to the wide-open throttle switch.

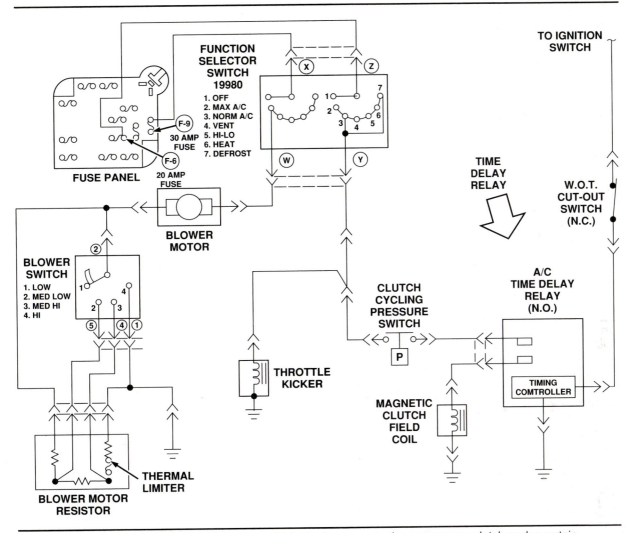

Figure 8-20. Schematic of the time-delay relay, which blocks power to the compressor clutch under certain conditions.

Power brake time delay relay

Power brake boosters depend upon intake manifold vacuum to operate the servo that boosts the power applied to the brakes. Ford has used a time delay relay that reduces the chance of the engine stalling due to a sudden change in intake manifold vacuum.

The power brake time delay relay is a solid-state electronic relay connected in series with the air conditioning relay, figure 8-21. Unlike electromechanical relays used in the clutch circuit, this relay is a timing device. When the brake light switch is closed by either momentarily or continuously depressing the brake pedal, the time delay will interrupt the air conditioning relay circuit for 3 to 5 seconds. Without battery voltage, the air conditioning relay coil magnetic field collapses and the relay contacts open, disengaging the compressor clutch.

The power brake time relay is typically found on Ford front-wheel-drive vehicles such as the Escort/Lynx and the Tempo/Topaz equipped with automatic transmissions.

Anti-dieseling relay

Dieseling, or engine run-on, is a result of hot carbon deposits in the combustion chamber. The deposits are capable of igniting the air-fuel mixture even after the engine has been turned off. Dieseling can lead to engine damage and always causes poor fuel combustion, resulting

---

Dieseling: A condition in which extreme heat in an engine's combustion chamber continues to ignite fuel after the ignition has been turned off.

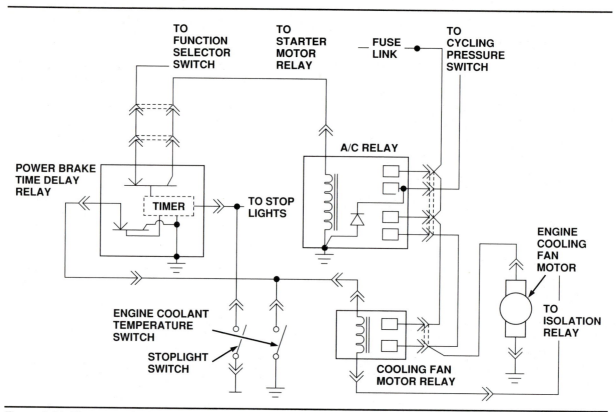

Figure 8-21. The power brake relay acts as a timer.

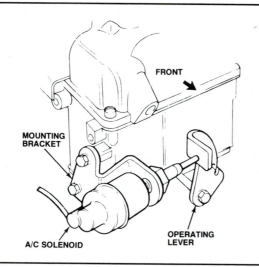

Figure 8-22. A throttle solenoid opens the throttle slightly when the air conditioning is on.

in unwanted emissions. Even though it may not be strictly true, dieseling is widely thought by consumers to be a sign of an engine that is badly out of tune. There have been several strategies to stop dieseling.

One method used by GM to prevent dieseling is to engage the air conditioning compressor clutch for a few seconds after the engine is shut off. The compressor load is enough to stall an engine prone to dieseling. The anti-dieseling relay typically engages the compressor clutch for 5 to 10 seconds after the engine is shut down.

Electronic control module delay timer
We stated earlier that the smaller capacity gasoline and diesel engines have poor power output at speeds near idle. For this reason many engines have used throttle solenoids on the carburetor to boost engine idle speed when the air conditioning mode is selected, figure 8-22. In late-model computerized systems, however, an electronic control module (ECM) delay timer is used to accomplish the same task of preventing roughness or stalling at idle with the air conditioning on. The delay timer prevents compressor clutch operation for 5 to 10 seconds to allow the engine to stabilize at the higher operating speeds caused by the idle set motor. The delay prevents sudden rough idling that might result if the compressor engages before the engine speed has stabilized at the higher setting.

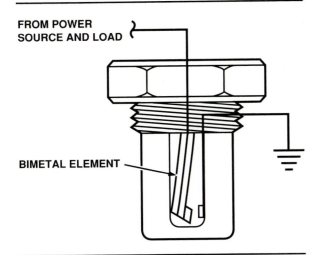

Figure 8-23. Most coolant high-temperature switches use a bimetal element.

Constant run relay

After a period of normal air conditioning operation, the temperature in the passenger compartment will stabilize. If the driver lets the vehicle idle, the compressor may cycle on and off as the system attempts to keep the passenger compartment at an even temperature.

This compressor cycling is often more noticeable to the driver than the minor temperature change that would occur if the cycling were delayed. The constant run relay prevents needless cycling for a period of time determined by the engine computer after the idle condition begins. Once the time delay is over, the computer returns control of the system to the thermostatic control mechanism. Then the clutch cycles normally to keep the passenger compartment cool. The constant run relay is intended to prevent rough idling while the vehicle is stopped for short periods of time such as at a stoplight.

One feature of this relay is that it allows current to operate the radiator fan while preventing operation of the magnetic clutch. This ensures adequate cooling during the period of interrupted clutch operation.

An example of the constant run relay is on some models of the 1987 Cadillac Fleetwood. The constant run relay prevents clutch cycling for 3 minutes after the engine returns to idle. The constant run relay also is used on some 1989 Buicks equipped with Electronic Touch Climate Control. When the engine is idling, the computer energizes the constant run relay through an electronic switch to ground. This effectively bypasses the pressure cycling switch. With the pressure cycling switch bypassed, the clutch cannot cycle for the 3 minutes the constant run relay is activated.

ENGINE COOLING SYSTEM CONTROLS

The air conditioning system increases the load on the engine cooling system, particularly during periods of high cooling system demand. The air passing through the radiator can only absorb a certain amount of heat, depending upon its temperature and density when it entered the front of the vehicle. If the air is first warmed by passing through the condenser, then the radiator efficiency will decrease.

In addition, simply running the compressor requires additional horsepower from the engine, and the heat from this source must also be removed from the coolant through the radiator.

There are two basic ways to prevent the air conditioning system thermal load from becoming a problem to the engine cooling system:

• Prevent air conditioning system operation when cooling system temperatures are abnormally high.
• Run the electric radiator fan longer or more frequently to lower coolant temperature.

Controls that Prevent Air Conditioning Operation

Several methods are used to interrupt air conditioning operation if the engine begins to overheat:

• A switch interrupts power to the compressor clutch.
• A sensor sends coolant temperature information to the computer for interpretation and action.

High coolant temperature switch

The high coolant temperature switch is wired to interrupt compressor clutch operation when the sensor indicates engine coolant temperature has become too high. Most high coolant temperature switches are the bimetallic type, figure 8-23. A typical switch, used by Audi, opens at 248°F (120°C) to prevent further compressor operation. The switch closes when the cooling system temperature falls below 223°F (106°C).

Coolant temperature sensor

On some models the coolant temperature sensor is used as an informational input to the engine computer or body computer. During periods of high heat load, the computer leaves the fan running longer. If the sensor indicates that the cooling system temperatures are still too high, the computer may shut off power to the magnetic clutch to prevent further system operation.

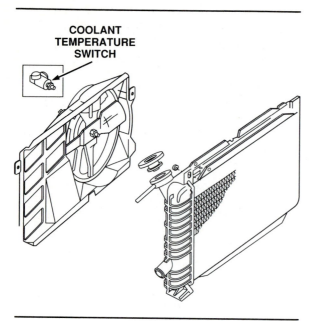

Figure 8-24. The coolant temperature fan switch on the radiator header tank reacts to coolant temperature.

Coolant temperature sensors may be located in the block or the cylinder head near the outlet for the top radiator hose. On other models the sensor may be located in a coolant passage in the intake manifold.

Cadillac has used electronic cooling fan control on its front-wheel-drive models. This system can turn the fan on and off as needed. At highway cruising speeds, when fan boosting is not needed, the computer turns off the fan.

Controls that Operate the Electric Radiator Fan

Some systems control the electric engine cooling fan to maintain even and low coolant temperatures when the air conditioner is running. There are several different ways:

• A temperature-sensitive switch can keep the fan running longer.
• A switch can control the fan in response to air conditioning system pressure or temperature.
• The fan can be kept on whenever the air conditioning system is on.

Coolant temperature fan switch

The coolant temperature fan switch (CTS) typically is mounted in the cylinder head or inlet radiator tank, figure 8-24. The CTS is a normally-open switch that closes when the temperature rises above a certain level. The primary use of the CTS is to control electric

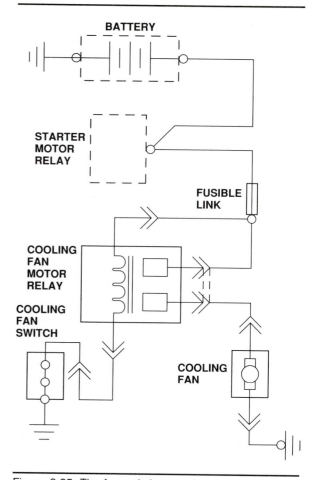

Figure 8-25. The fan switch controls the fan through the fan relay.

fan operation, figure 8-25, through the fan motor relay. On some models the CTS is bypassed by wiring the electric fan to operate constantly regardless of temperature when the air conditioning system is in operation. On other models the greater heat load on the cooling system will keep the CTS switch closed longer to increase fan running time.

Air conditioning system pressure fan switch
Some import cars use a fan control that turns on the radiator fan when refrigerant pressure or temperature rises above a certain level. This type of control system is designed to work in addition to the normal coolant temperature switch. When the air conditioning is turned off, fan control is handled by the CTS.

The high pressure switch used by Audi on the 5000 series closes to turn on the radiator fan when air conditioning high-side pressure rises above 200 psi (1380 kPa). The fan turns off when pressure falls below 170 psi (1170 kPa).

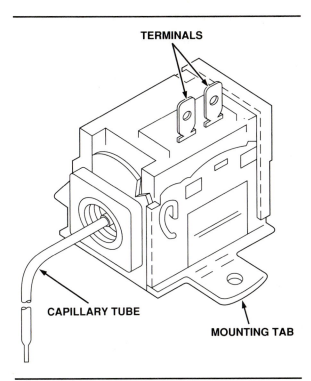

Figure 8-26. The thermostatic switch uses a capillary tube much like a TXV.

Air conditioning fan switch

The simplest way to ensure adequate cooling during the air conditioning mode is to wire the radiator/condenser fan in series with the air conditioning control switch. With this wiring system, the cooling fan runs constantly in the air conditioning mode. While this sometimes results in cooling that isn't necessary, it is an inexpensive way of ensuring adequate cooling during air conditioning operation.

Thermostatic Controls

We have already discussed various types of suction throttling and low evaporator pressure controls that are used to prevent the temperature of the evaporator from falling too low. Evaporator freeze-up prevents any further cooling of the passenger compartment because the frost blocks the flow of air through the evaporator.

There are many air conditioning operating conditions, however, that require less than maximum cooling. On some manual systems, a thermostatic control is used to regulate the temperature in the passenger compartment.

These devices sense the temperature of the evaporator and compare it to the cooling demand from the driver as indicated by the setting of the temperature slide or rotary switch.

Once the desired level of cooling is reached, the thermostatic switch will cycle the compressor clutch to prevent overcooling of the passenger compartment. Even if the driver places the setting on maximum cool, the suction pressure regulating device will override the thermostat to prevent evaporator freeze-up.

There are two principal types of thermostatic controls. The first uses a temperature-sensitive bimetallic element to determine the position of one of the two contacts of a switch wired in series with the compressor clutch. The position of the second contact is determined by the driver and is a function of temperature setting control position. By changing the gap between the contacts of the bimetallic switch, the temperature at which the contacts open or close is varied.

The second type of thermostatic control, figure 8-26, uses a capillary sensing tube. The bulb at the end of the capillary is attached to the evaporator much like the capillary of the TXV. Changing gas pressure in the capillary is

■ Make Mine Bimetal

A characteristic of all metals is that they expand and contract with changes in temperature. The rate of change with changing temperature is called the thermal coefficient of expansion. Each metal or metal alloy has a thermal coefficient that is unique to that material. Alloys of copper, steel, and nickel are commonly used to make bimetallic elements.

Bimetals are made by bonding two flat strips of different metals together under high pressure. At room temperature, the resulting strip of metal is flat. When the temperature changes, one side of the bimetal expands at a faster rate than the other. This causes the bimetal to curve away from the high-expansion side.

For practical applications, the bimetal is then formed into coils or strips. Coiled bimetals are used as thermal motors to create temperature-sensitive rotary motion. Common uses include thermostatic choke adjusters on carburetors.

Strip bimetals are used in turn-signal flashers and in a variety of different sensors. The coolant temperature switch uses a strip bimetal with an electrical contact mounted to one end. When the bimetal is cold, the contact is separated from a stationary contact, preventing completion of the electrical circuit to the compressor clutch. The curvature of the bimetal as it warms pulls the contacts toward each other. When the bimetal curvature is great enough to close the contacts, the temperature setpoint of the switch has been reached. This completes the electrical circuit to the clutch.

relayed to a bellows in the thermostat. The bellows works against the pressure of a spring whose tension is determined by the adjustment of the temperature control knob or slide. The result of the two competing inputs to a pivoting frame determines the position of one of the contacts of the switch wired in series with the compressor clutch. The second contact remains in a fixed position.

In comparison to the semiautomatic and fully automatic temperature control systems, the thermostatic controls are rather crude. The **hysteresis**, or difference in temperature between open and closed switch conditions, may be as much as 10° to 15°F (6° to 8°C). However, these thermostats do offer a limited type of temperature regulation.

SUMMARY

The air conditioning system places a heavy load on the engine, which can become a problem in certain conditions. Additional air conditioning controls are used to prevent damage to the air conditioning system or to other systems, and to prevent or limit air conditioning operation during high-load conditions.

Preventing damage to the air conditioning system is accomplished by sensing when the system pressure or temperature is too high or too low. Low system pressure also implies that the refrigerant and therefore refrigeration oil is too low. Temperature sensing is done with bimetallic sensors or thermistors. The bimetallic sensor uses two electrical contacts that open when a specified temperature is sensed. A thermistor provides a varying resistance in response to changing temperatures sensed. Ambient temperature sensors and switches may be either of these types.

Because there is a known relationship between the pressure and the temperature of R-12, the temperature of the system can be measured by sensing the pressure. Many switches operate on this principle. Some switches are in series with the compressor clutch, causing it to shut off when an out-of-limits condition is sensed. Others, such as the pressure relief valve, simply vent excess pressure to protect the compressor.

Another group of sensors and switches shuts off the compressor when the load on the engine is high. These conditions include slow idle, heavy uphill driving, or parking. These controls respond to wide-open throttle, low vacuum, or heavy demand on the power steering system. Similarly, a time-delay function is built in on many models that causes the air conditioning system either to run for a few seconds after the control has been turned off, or to prevent operation when it has been turned on. This is used to control dieseling, allow engine warm-up, or to prevent engine stall that could affect the power brakes.

A third group of controls protects the engine cooling system when a heavy demand is placed on it. Some of these controls prevent the air conditioning system from operating when coolant temperature is abnormally high. Others run the cooling system fan longer, or whenever the air conditioning is on.

Hysteresis: The failure of a device to return to its original value when the cause of the change has been removed.

Review Questions

Choose the single most correct answer.
Compare your answers with the correct answers on page 229.

1. Which of the following is *not* a category of air conditioning system control?
   a. Controls that prevent operation under certain conditions
   b. Controls that prevent damage to the compressor
   c. Controls that prevent engine operation
   d. Controls that prevent damage to other systems

2. The most common compressor safety control works by:
   a. Interrupting the flow of refrigerant
   b. Interrupting power to the magnetic clutch
   c. Varying the output of the compressor
   d. None of the above

3. Most ambient temperature sensors are:
   a. Thermistors
   b. Bimetallic-type
   c. Both a and b
   d. Neither a nor b

4. The major cause of compressor malfunctions is:
   a. Overpressure
   b. Underpressure
   c. Leaks in the compressor cylinder
   d. Loss of lubricant

5. Low-pressure cutout switches may be located:
   a. In the rear of the compressor
   b. On the receiver-drier
   c. On the H-valve
   d. All of the above

6. Superheat is a condition when R-12 is:
   a. Colder than needed for evaporation
   b. Warmer than needed for evaporation
   c. Warmer than needed for condensation
   d. Colder than needed for condensation

7. Technician A says that the pressure cycling switch responds to evaporator outlet pressure. Technician B says the pressure cycling switch responds to low refrigerant levels or low ambient temperatures.
   Who is right?
   a. A only
   b. B only
   c. Both A and B
   d. Neither A nor B

8. The pressure relief valve is:
   a. An electric solenoid
   b. A vacuum solenoid
   c. A spring-loaded valve
   d. A bellows-type valve

9. Air conditioning operation may be halted during periods of:
   a. Parking maneuvers
   b. High ambient temperatures
   c. Fast idle
   d. All of the above

10. The WOT switch is a:
    a. Compressor control
    b. Pressure control
    c. Air conditioning system control
    d. Driveability control

11. The anti-dieseling relay is a:
    a. Driveability control
    b. Time delay control
    c. Low-pressure control
    d. High-pressure control

12. The time delay relay:
    a. Is used on cycling clutch systems
    b. Prevents air conditioning operation for 30-45 seconds
    c. Is wired in series with the power steering switch
    d. Prevents evaporator freeze-up

13. The job of the constant run relay is to:
    a. Prevent dieseling after engine shutdown
    b. Prolong compressor operation during slow idle
    c. Prevent needless compressor cycling
    d. Bypass the evaporator temperature controls

14. Most engine coolant temperature switches are the:
    a. Thermistor type
    b. Bimetallic type
    c. Photovoltaic type
    d. Capillary tube type

15. The air conditioning thermal load is prevented from interfering with the cooling system by:
    a. Running the cooling fan longer
    b. Turning off the air conditioning when coolant temperature is high
    c. Increasing the idle speed when air conditioning is on
    d. All of the above

16. Hysteresis is the:
    a. Pressure difference between the high and low sides of the air conditioning system
    b. Temperature difference between the open and closed switch positions
    c. Time delay between the open and closed switch positions
    d. Continuous feedback signal from a sensor to the BCM

17. The power brake time delay relay is a:
    a. Mechanical device
    b. Solenoid-actuated device
    c. Solid-state electronic relay
    d. Cable-operated timer

18. Superheat switches are used on _____ compressors.
    a. Ford Variable-displacement
    b. Chrysler 2-cylinder inline
    c. GM 6-cylinder
    d. York radial

19. High air conditioning pressures can be caused by all of the following *except*:
    a. A leaking compressor front seal
    b. A jammed magnetic clutch
    c. A blocked condenser
    d. Faulty controls

20. Driveability controls are commonly found on vehicles with:
    a. V-8 engines
    b. 4-cylinder engines
    c. Dual cooling fans
    d. Manual HVAC controls

9

Automated Temperature Control

In earlier chapters we covered the basic components of heating-ventilation-air conditioning (HVAC) systems, including the basic control systems used to permit the driver to select a particular choice of operating mode. In this chapter we will cover the operation of semiautomatic and fully automatic climate control systems. There are many such systems available today. We will explain how these systems operate and the control mechanisms they use. Since nearly all late-model automatic systems are computer-controlled, you will learn what a computer is and how it operates. In Chapter 10, we will cover the operating details of representative automatic temperature control systems.

AUTOMATIC TEMPERATURE CONTROL

Beginning in the 1950s, carmakers have produced a wide range of HVAC systems to partially or fully control the passenger compartment temperature, humidity, and air circulation. Early efforts, of course, were crude by today's standards. Later, even the manual systems became fairly sophisticated. In a modern manual system:

• Temperature control is set and readjusted by the driver as often as necessary to maintain temperature control as ambient conditions change.
• Blower speed adjustment is manual.
• Air distribution control through dash and floor vents is manual.
• Mode selection is manual.

Today, most systems use automatic temperature control (ATC) that falls into one of two categories:

• Semiautomatic temperature control (SATC) systems that are programmer-controlled:

— Temperature control is manually set but automatically maintained regardless of changing conditions.
— Blower speed adjustment is manual.
— Air distribution through dashboard and floor vents may be manual but often is controlled by the programmer.
— Mode selection is manual.

• Electronic automatic temperature control (EATC) systems that are computer-controlled:

— Temperature selection is manually set, but automatically maintained for both heating and cooling, regardless of changing ambient conditions.

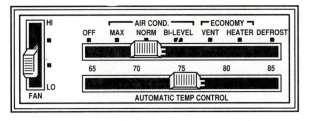

Figure 9-1. A typical control head on a SATC system has driver-operated fan, temperature, and air conditioning controls.

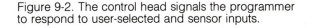

Figure 9-2. The control head signals the programmer to respond to user-selected and sensor inputs.

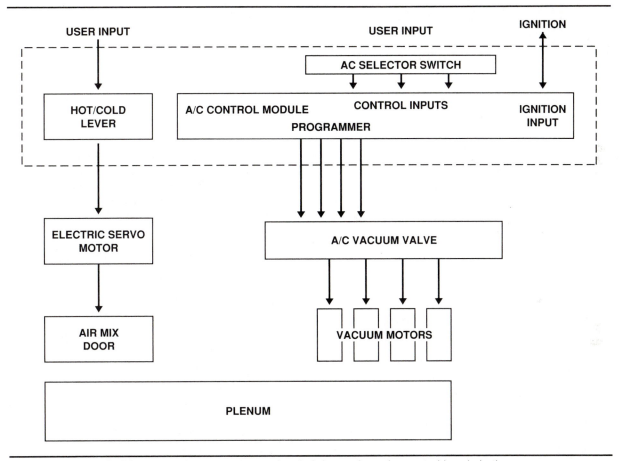

Figure 9-3. In this SATC system, the actuators receive their inputs from the control head via the programmer.

— Blower speed adjustment is automatic, and frequently combined with compressor clutch controls.

— Air distribution through dashboard and floor vents is automatic.

— Mode selection is semiautomatic or completely left to the computer.

— Information from numerous other vehicle systems is included in the ATC decision-making process.

On some systems, the distinction between semiautomatic and fully automatic is blurred. Some systems in the late 1970s were called au-tomatic; current terminology classifies them as semiautomatic. Some fully automatic systems use a programmer, and some semiautomatic systems use a computer but no programmer. The important distinction is whether the driver must take any action to control the temperature in the passenger compartment. If so, the system is semiautomatic; if not, it is fully automatic.

In the following discussion, we will cover programmer-controlled semiautomatic (SATC) systems and computer-controlled fully automatic (EATC) systems.

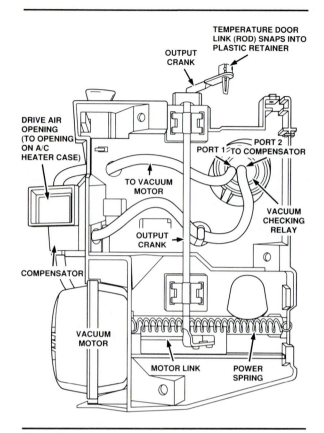

Figure 9-4. Early programmers were single units containing the vacuum controls.

SEMIAUTOMATIC TEMPERATURE CONTROL

In a semiautomatic system, the door positions and airflow must be controlled so that the passenger compartment remains at the desired temperature. This is done by the air delivery control system. This system contains four main components:

• Control head and temperature sensors
• Programmer or control assembly
• Blower speed and compressor power module
• Electrically or vacuum-operated actuators.

A typical semiautomatic system contains the same components as a manual system, but differs by the incorporation of a programmer. The actuators and doors are still moved through mechanical linkages and cables, and the blower speed is still set manually.

As in a manual system, the user must move a lever or press a button to activate the system, figure 9-1. Unlike a manual system, however, the user does not directly control the actuator. Instead, the motion provides input to the programmer, figure 9-2. The programmer then moves the cables or the vacuum selector valves. Once the user makes a selection, the

actual moving of the doors is left to the programmer.

The control head looks similar to those used in many manual systems. There are still levers and buttons to be selected. Many systems supply the control head with input from an in-car temperature sensor or air aspirator and an ambient temperature sensor. The control head is connected electrically to the programmer. The control head signals the programmer to respond to the user-selected input and the temperature data from the temperature sensors, figure 9-3.

The Programmer

The programmer adjusts the temperature of the air by controlling the blend air door position with either an electric motor or a vacuum motor. It also determines the airflow by selectively supplying current or vacuum to the actuators that move the different system doors. The programmer contains most of the temperature control components and usually is located in the passenger compartment on the air conditioning/heat module or directly behind the control head.

The term ''programmer'' originally referred to a vacuum assembly that could be installed and serviced as a unit. General Motors first introduced an assembly called a programmer in 1971. The GM system combined the vacuum servo, vacuum switches, and other control elements into a single assembly, figure 9-4. These systems were called ATC systems, even though by today's standards they were semiautomatic. These types of programmers serve as a chassis or mounting place for the system actuators. The temperature control decisions are made inside an electronic control module called an air conditioning controller which is a part of the control head. Most programmers contain the:

• Compensator assembly
• Vacuum motor
• Vacuum checking relay
• Output and control linkage.

The compensator is used to amplify a vacuum signal so it can control an actuator. This is done with a diaphragm-controlled vacuum valve. The control signal vacuum, often representing temperature conditions in the passenger compartment, is applied to one side of the diaphragm. The diaphragm is connected mechanically to a valve controlling a larger vacuum. Changes in the smaller vacuum result in changes to the higher vacuum. In this way, the smaller vacuum is amplified to the magnitude of the larger vacuum.

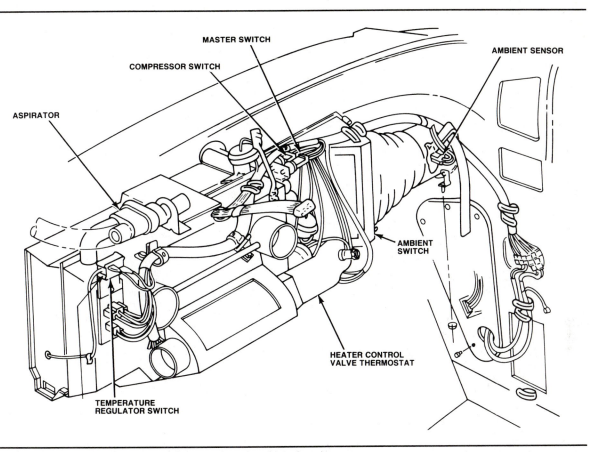

Figure 9-5. The air aspirator senses the temperature of interior air.

The compensator consists of a bimetallic sensor coil located in a stream of air that is drawn from the passenger compartment. The bimetallic coil expands and contracts as the flow of air rises and falls in temperature. Movement of the bimetallic coil determines the position of a vent valve that regulates the amount of vacuum applied to the servomotor.

The air stream through the ambient compensator is created by the **venturi effect**. A second hose is connected between the ambient compensator and the HVAC plenum. Air driven by the blower passes over the mouth of the opening to the ambient compensator. This creates a slight vacuum that draws the passenger compartment air through the compensator and over the bimetallic coil.

Most programmers use an air aspirator as the air temperature sampling device used by the compensator to sense passenger compartment air temperature. The aspirator is mounted to the HVAC plenum housing behind the dashboard, figure 9-5. A hose leads from the grille opening at the dashboard surface to the input of the aspirator. A second hose leads to the aspirator from the HVAC plenum. The air

flowing through the evaporator case creates a slight vacuum in the hose to the aspirator from the plenum that draws air through the hose coming from the passenger compartment.

The vacuum in the aspirator tube is satisfied by continuous flow of passenger compartment air through the device. Mounted in the aspirator housing is a bimetallic or thermistor-type temperature sensor. Because the airflow through the aspirator is continuous, the temperature sensor reading represents a constant monitoring of the passenger compartment air temperature. This information is sent to the control element.

Not all programmers are single, combined units. Chrysler uses a "programmer" that does function as a typical programmer, but is actually a collection of components.

Venturi Effect: The increase in speed and reduction in pressure of a gas as it passes through a restricted orifice, such as air through an aspirator.

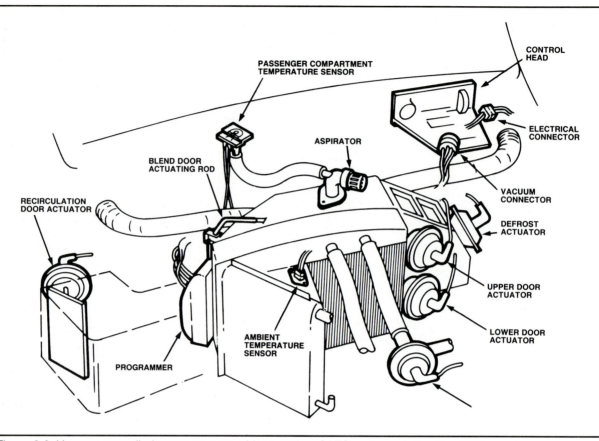

Figure 9-6. Vacuum-controlled actuators were widespread on SATC systems during the 1970s.

Actuators

The vacuum control system using a vacuum servo in the programmer to control blend door position was the most widely used SATC method during the 1970s, figure 9-6. The vacuum servo system uses sensors as information inputs to the amplifier. In the vacuum servomotor version, the electrical output signal of the amplifier is converted into a vacuum signal by a transducer.

The output voltage from the amplifier is used to regulate the position of a vacuum regulating valve inside the transducer. The solenoid-controlled valve converts the electrical output signal of the amplifier into a vacuum control signal. The vacuum control signal is used to determine the position of the vacuum servomotor.

General Motors, Ford, and Chrysler have all used systems of this type. Chrysler was the first to use the phrase Semi-Automatic Temperature Control (SATC). It was used through 1981. Many late-model air conditioning systems still use devices called programmers, but

these have become the housing for the electrical solenoids or motors, with system control given over to the computer.

Various types of vacuum actuators are used on SATC systems, and are connected to the mode pushbuttons or levers on the control head. Input vacuum is applied at all times; pushing a control device energizes the vacuum motor, which allows vacuum to pass to the appropriate door actuator. Output motion can be smoothly variable as in the case of a blend door control or it can simply open or close as in the case of a vent door position vacuum motor.

The primary vacuum-operated control in the system is the blend door servomotor. This is a large, calibrated vacuum motor, figure 9-7, that can be adjusted precisely to any point between fully extended and fully contracted. The motor moves the blend door to specific positions, depending on the vacuum levels applied to it. Often a vacuum diverter valve is included as a part of the vacuum servomotor. The vacuum diverter valve controls water valve operation and the recirculated/fresh air door.

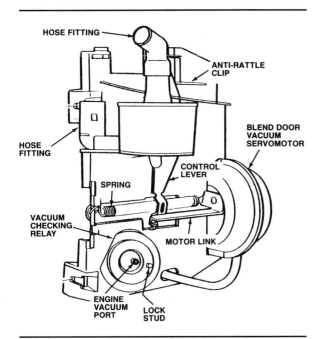

Figure 9-7. The blend door vacuum servomotor provides variable control to the door.

HOW A COMPUTER WORKS

Before you can fully understand how an electronic automatic temperature control (EATC) system works, you must understand how a computer works. Computers are the core of all late-model EATC systems, and understanding their operation will make troubleshooting and repairing those systems easier.

We often use the term ''computer'' without really understanding what it means. A computer is nothing more than a machine that receives information which it uses to make a series of decisions, and then acts as a result of the decisions made. A computer cannot think on its own; it does everything according to a detailed set of instructions called a **program**.

The earliest electronic computers and those in use today all use identical principles. They use voltage to send and receive information. As you know, voltage can be thought of as the electrical pressure which causes current flow, which does the real work in an electrical circuit. However, voltage can also be used as a signal. A computer converts input information or data into voltage signal combinations that represent number combinations. The number combinations can represent a wide variety of information — temperature, speed, pressure, or even words and letters. A computer handles or processes the input voltage signals it receives by interpreting what they represent

and then delivering data in computed or processed form.

Computer Functions

The operation of every computer, regardless of its size or the use to which it is put, can be divided into four basic functions:

1. Input
2. Processing
3. Storage
4. Output.

These basic functions are not unique to computers. The semiautomatic and manual control systems we've already covered had the same functions. However, we need to know how the functions work in a computer.

Input
The computer receives a voltage signal (input) from an input device. The device can be as simple as a button or a switch on an instrument panel. It can also be a sensor on an automobile engine. As discussed in Chapter 8, modern automobiles use various mechanical, electrical, and magnetic sensors to measure a variety of things, including vehicle and engine speed, coolant temperature, ambient air temperature, refrigerant pressure, and airflow. Each of these sensors transmits its information in the form of voltage signals which the computer can understand.

Processing
The computer receives input voltage signals and switches them through a series of electronic logic circuits according to programmed instructions. These processing logic circuits change the voltage signals, or data, into output voltage signals, or commands.

Storage
The program instructions for a computer are stored in its electronic memory. Some programs may require that certain input data be stored for later reference or future processing. In others, output commands may be delayed or stored before they are transmitted to devices elsewhere in the system. Computers use a number of different memory devices which we will look at later in this section.

Program: The instructions a computer needs to do its job. The program consists of mathematical instructions and may also include fixed data and require variable data from vehicle sensors.

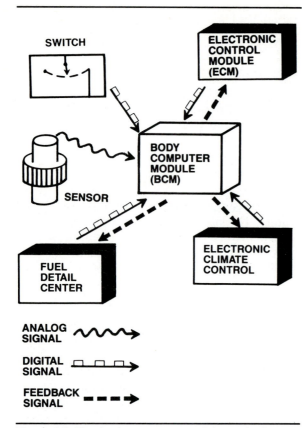

ANALOG SIGNAL

DIGITAL SIGNAL

FEEDBACK SIGNAL

Figure 9-8. The body computer module reads data from various input devices, while sending commands to other devices.

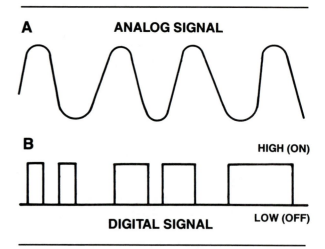

Figure 9-9. Signal patterns of analog and digital signals.

Output

After the computer has processed the input signal, it sends output voltage signals, or commands, to other devices in the system, such as an air door actuator or the compressor clutch. The output devices used on automobiles vary from a display on an instrument panel to a system actuator. The actuator is an electrical or mechanical device that performs the desired operation, whether it is adjusting engine idle speed, opening or closing an air door, or regulating airflow.

Computers can also communicate with, and control other computers through their input and output functions. This means that the output signal from one computer can be the input signal to another computer. For instance, on some 1986 and later GM cars, a body computer module (BCM) acts as a master control unit by managing a network containing all sensors, switches, and other vehicle computers, figure 9-8.

As an example, let's suppose the BCM sends an output signal to disengage the air conditioning compressor clutch. That same output

signal can become an input signal to the electronic control module (ECM) that controls engine operation. Based on the signal from the BCM, the ECM tells an actuator to adjust engine speed to compensate for the decreased load when the compressor is disengaged.

Analog and Digital Systems

A computer has to be told how to do its job. The instructions and data necessary to do this are called a program. Since a computer cannot read words, the information must be transmitted into a form the computer can understand — voltage signals. This can be done by using an analog or digital system.

Analog computers

The first automotive computer application was Chrysler's Electronic Lean-Burn (ELB) engine control system used from 1976 through 1978. Since it received, processed, and sent analog signals, it is called an analog computer. **Analog** means that the voltage signal or processing function varies continuously, relative to the field being measured or the adjustment required, figure 9-9, position A.

Most operating conditions affecting an automobile, such as temperature or speed, vary continuously, and are therefore analog variables. These operating conditions can be measured by thermistors or potentiometers acting as sensors.

If a computer is to measure engine speed changes from 0 rpm through 6500 rpm, it can be programmed to respond to an analog voltage that varies from 0 volts at 0 rpm to 6.5 volts at 6500 rpm. Any analog signal between 0 and 6.5 volts will represent a proportional speed between 0 and 6500 rpm.

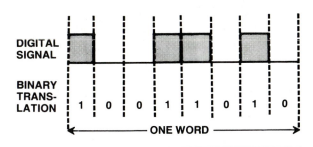
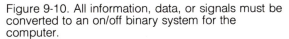

Figure 9-10. All information, data, or signals must be converted to an on/off binary system for the computer.

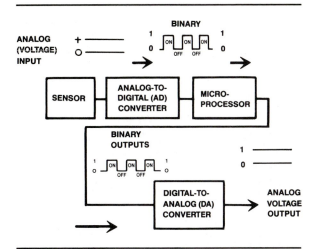

Figure 9-11. An analog-to-digital converter changes input signals into a binary system the microprocessor can understand.

Analog computers have several shortcomings, however. They are affected by temperature changes, supply voltage variations, and signal interference. They also are slower in operation, more expensive to manufacture, and more limited in what they can do than digital computers.

Digital computers

Digital computers first appeared on automobiles in 1980. **Digital** means that the voltage signal or processing function is a simple on/off, yes/no condition. The digital signal voltage is limited to two voltage levels. One is a positive voltage, the other is no voltage. Since there is no stepped range of voltage or current in between, a digital signal is a square wave, figure 9-9, position B.

Using our example dealing with engine speed, suppose that the computer needs to know that engine speed is either above or below a specific level, say 1800 rpm. Since it doesn't need to know the exact engine speed but only whether it is above or below 1800 rpm, the digital signal could be zero volts below 1800 rpm and one volt above 1800 rpm. A digital signal acts like a simple switch to open and close a circuit.

The signal is called "digital" because the on and off signals are processed by the computer as the digits or numbers 0 and 1. The number system containing only these two digits is called the **binary system**. Any number from any number system can be translated into a combination of binary 0's and 1's for the digital computer, figure 9-10.

A digital computer changes the analog input signals (voltage) to digital **bits** (binary *digits*) of information through an analog-to-digital (AD) converter circuit, figure 9-11. The binary digital number is used by the microprocessor in its calculations or logic networks to come up with the appropriate output signal. Since the output signal is a binary digital number, it often must go through a digital-to-analog (DA) converter

circuit to produce the voltage output to operate the actuator device, figure 9-11.

Analog-to-digital conversion

Earlier, we mentioned that most operating conditions affecting an automobile are analog variables. Engine coolant temperature is a useful example. Assume that the computer needs to know the exact coolant temperature within one degree. This requires analog input signals. Suppose our sensor measures temperature from 0 to 300 degrees and sends an analog signal that varies from 0 to 6 volts. Each 1-volt change in the sensor signal is therefore equivalent to a 50-degree change in temperature. If 0 volts equals 0 degrees and 6 volts equals 300 degrees, then:

    1.0 volt = 50 degrees
    0.5 volt = 25 degrees
    0.1 volt = 5 degrees
    0.02 volt = 1 degree, and so on.

Analog: A voltage signal or processing action that varies continuously with the variable being measured or controlled.

Digital: A voltage signal or processing function that has only two levels, on/off or high/low.

Binary System: A mathematical system containing only two digits (0 and 1) which allows a digital computer to read and process input voltage signals.

Bit: A digital input or output signal. One bit roughly equals one computer keystroke, or one discrete piece of information. The word comes from *binary digit*.

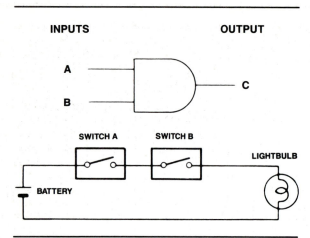

Figure 9-12. The symbol for an AND gate, and an electrical circuit that represents it.

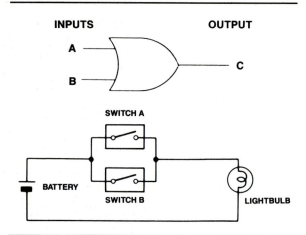

Figure 9-13. The representation and symbol for an OR gate.

For the computer to determine temperature within 1 degree, it must react to a sensor voltage change as small as 0.020 volt or 20 millivolts. For example, if the temperature is 125 degrees, the sensor signal will be 2.50 volts. If the temperature rises to 126 degrees, sensor voltage will increase to 2.52 volts. In reality, temperature does not pass directly from one degree to another. It passes continuously through all smaller increments, as does voltage as it changes from 2.50 volts to 2.52 volts.

Our digital computer, however, processes only signals equaling 1-degree changes in temperature. To do so, the computer sends the signal through analog-to-digital conversion circuits, where the analog sensor voltage is converted to a series of 0.020-volt changes for each complete degree. This is called ''digitizing'' an analog signal.

The analog-to-digital conversion process brings us back to binary numbers. **Transistors** can be designed to switch on and off at different voltage levels or with differing combinations of voltage signals. In the computer we are discussing, transistor groups must switch from off to on at 20-millivolt increments. The input signal is created by varying the transistor combinations that are on or off. In binary numbers, the 125-degree temperature is:

1111101

When the temperature increases to 126 degrees, the binary number also changes:

1111110

The computer reads the various voltage signal combinations as binary numbers, and then performs its calculations. It does so almost instantly because the current travels through the miniature circuits very rapidly.

Digital logic

Digital computers all handle data bits with three basic logic circuits called **logic gates**. This terminology describes the circuit switching functions only and has nothing to do with their physical construction. They are called ''gates'' because the circuits act as routes or ''gates'' for output voltage signals according to different input signal combinations. The circuit switching is done by the thousands of transistors in a microprocessor.

There are three basic logic gates: the NOT, AND, and the OR gates. Each of these has a different symbol and a **truth table**, showing the logical or truthful combination of input and output signals for that logic gate.

To help you understand what is happening in digital logic, compare the three gates to three simple electrical circuits. Suppose we connect two switches in series to a light bulb and a power source as shown in figure 9-12. The bulb will only light if both switches are closed; if either or both are open, the bulb cannot light. This is a circuit equal in function to an AND gate; two conditions must be met before a certain result can occur. Switch A and B are equal to the input (A and B) of the AND gate; the bulb is equal to the output (C) of the AND gate.

Now lets's connect two switches in parallel to the bulb and the power source, figure 9-13. The bulb will light if either switch is closed, or if both switches are closed. This is the basic OR gate, in which either or both conditions can give a certain result.

Notice what happens when we connect a normally-closed relay, a switch, and a bulb as shown in figure 9-14. When the switch is open, the relay is closed and the bulb lights.

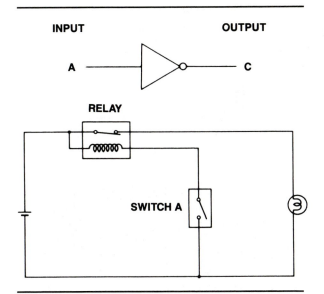

Figure 9-14. A NOT gate and a circuit to match it.

Figure 9-15. While this Delco microprocessor is about an inch and a half long, the actual chip inside the packaging is no bigger than a fingernail.

The bulb will not light if the switch is closed, since this opens the relay and shuts off current flow to the bulb. This is a basic NOT gate, in which the output is always opposite to the input, or inverted.

Computer Programs and Memory

Every computer needs instructions to do its job. These instructions are called the computer program, and consist of several elements. First are the mathematical instructions that tell the computer how to process, or "compute", the information it receives. Second is information that pertains to *fixed* vehicle values such as the engine type, transmission type, or compressor type. Finally, there is data that pertains to *variable* vehicle values, such as coolant temperature, car speed, and refrigerant pressure.

The fixed vehicle information is stored along with the mathematical instructions in a computer memory chip called a **programmable read-only memory (PROM)**, figure 9-15, which is installed in the vehicle's central computer. Since the PROM remembers the information programmed into it, the computer uses the PROM as its memory for comparison to input sensors and then adjusts the systems under its control accordingly.

Besides the PROMS, there are other types of memory in a computer. Permanent memory is called **read-only memory (ROM)** because the central computer can only "read" the contents of the memory, but cannot change anything in it. This permanent data is retained even if

the ignition is turned off and the battery is removed. Specific vehicle data is stored in ROM.

Temporary memory is called **random-access memory (RAM)** because the computer can both read the information and "write" new information into it as dictated by the computer program. This data is lost whenever the ignition is turned off. System trouble codes are usually stored in RAM.

Transistor: A three-terminal semiconductor device used for amplification, switching, and detection.

Logic Gates: Circuit switching functions within a computer that act as routes for output voltage signals according to differing combinations of input signals.

Truth Table: A table showing the logical, or truthful, combination of input and output signals for a logic gate.

Programmable Read-Only Memory (PROM): An integrated circuit chip installed in the on-board computer which has been programmed with operating instructions and database information for a particular vehicle.

Read-Only Memory (ROM): The permanent part of a computer's memory storage function. ROM can be read but not changed and is retained when power to the computer is shut off.

Random-Access Memory (RAM): Computer memory in which information can be written (stored) and read. Whatever is stored in RAM is lost whenever the ignition system is shut off.

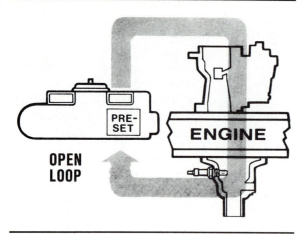

Figure 9-16. In open-loop control, the computer operates according to preset specifications.

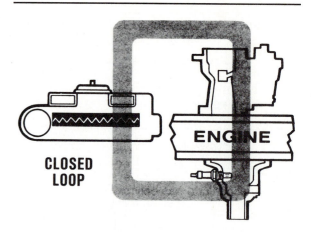

Figure 9-17. In closed-loop control, the computer monitors the sensor and sends corrections to the actuator.

Another type of memory is called **adaptive memory**. This allows the computer to compensate for the variables caused by engine wear, production variations, and other factors. Adaptive memory monitors the operation of the systems under computer control and makes a small modification to the program when a controlled value regularly falls outside the design limits.

Adaptive memory is stored in a chip which draws a small current from the battery to power its circuits, even when the ignition is turned off. If all power is removed, such as by removing the battery cables, this information is erased. When restarted, the engine may run poorly while the computer relearns vehicle-specific information and stores it again in the adaptive memory. This process usually takes several miles of driving.

Computerized Instrumentation and Control Systems

Automotive computer systems have two purposes, instrumentation and control. An instrumentation system is one which measures variables and displays the output in a form the driver can use. Speedometers, odometers, gauges, and warning lamps are examples of instrumentation devices. Many late-model cars use computerized instrumentation systems to display these on the instrument panel.

When a computer is used as a control system, it regulates the operation of another system or systems. The engine control computer or the BCM are examples of this. Computers can also perform dual functions by acting as both instrumentation and control systems. An automatic climate control system that regulates heating and air conditioning can also display

temperature information. The same basic microprocessor can receive and process an input signal in different systems for different purposes. The output signal it produces can be used for different instrumentation and control purposes.

Operating system control modes
A computer control system can be selective, with different operating modes. It does not have to respond to data from all of its sensors, nor does it have to respond in the same way each time. It may ignore sensor input under certain conditions, just as it might sometimes ignore the driver's control commands, as we saw in the previous chapter. Because of this, control systems are often designed with two operating modes: open-loop and closed-loop.

Open-loop control means that the computer functions according to pre-established conditions in its program. It gives orders and the output actuators carry them out. The computer ignores sensor input (feedback) as long as the pre-established conditions exist. For example, the ECM controlling an EATC system will ignore signals from the control head or refrigerant system sensors as long as there is a heavy demand on the engine, such as during parking maneuvers. Figure 9-16 is a simple diagram of open loop control.

When the system goes into **closed-loop**, the computer reads and responds to signals from all of its sensors, figure 9-17. Once the parking maneuver is done, for example, the computer will again accept input from other system sensors and will adjust the speed of the compressor and the output of the system accordingly. In this mode, we say that the computer is responding to a **feedback** signal, that is, a sensor

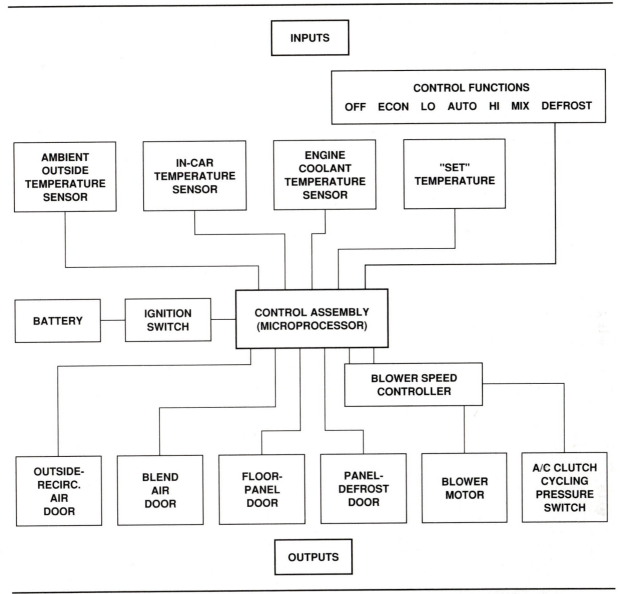

Figure 9-18. In a late-model EATC system, the microprocessor controls all elements of the HVAC system.

Adaptive Memory: A feature of computer memory that allows the microprocessor to adjust its memory for computing open-loop operation, based on changes in engine operation. Whatever is stored in adaptive memory is lost only when power to the computer is shut off, such as by disconnecting the battery.

Open-Loop: An operational mode in which the computer adjusts a system to function according to pre-determined instructions and does not always respond to feedback signals from its sensors.

Closed-Loop: An operational mode in which the computer reads and responds to feedback signals from its sensors, adjusting system operation accordingly.

Feedback: The return of a portion of the output (actuator) to the input (computer), used to maintain an output device within predetermined limits.

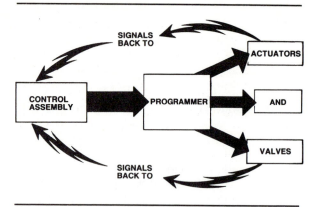

Figure 9-19. A fully automatic system provides feedback to the microprocessor (programmer) which adjusts operation accordingly.

is feeding information back to the computer that there is an error factor in its operation that must be corrected.

ELECTRONIC AUTOMATIC TEMPERATURE CONTROL SYSTEMS

As we stated earlier, the distinction between SATC systems and electronic automatic temperature control (EATC) systems often is blurred. However, in most EATC systems, input from several locations is sensed by automatic temperature control systems, figure 9-18. The system then moves control doors that direct circulation and adjusts the temperature and humidity of the vehicle interior. The input signals may include:

• Ambient air temperature
• Passenger compartment temperature
• Engine coolant temperature
• Driver operation of the controls
• Heat load from sunlight inside the vehicle
• Engine load demands from other systems.

This information is collected by the control module to operate the following control components:

• Blower speed controller operates the compressor clutch and blower motor
• Blend door actuator
• Panel/floor door actuator
• Panel/defrost door actuator
• Recirculation door actuator
• Compressor clutch controls
• Coolant control valve.

Control Modes

All EATC systems are full feedback systems, figure 9-19. Some are controlled by a single-

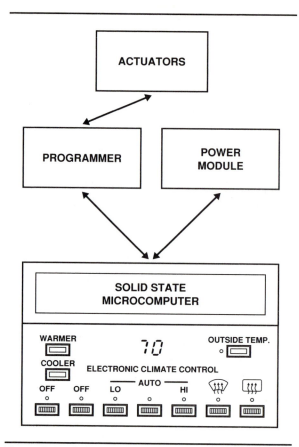

Figure 9-20. Some systems are controlled by a single-function ECM.

function electronic control module (ECM) microprocessor, figure 9-20, and some are controlled by a multifunction body computer module (BCM), figure 9-21.

In an EATC system, the driver selects a mode and a temperature. The necessary signals are automatically sent to the microprocessor to operate the system. In all late-model systems, the actuators are electric or vacuum servomotors that contain circuitry that allows them to send a signal back to the microprocessor to indicate their positions. This allows the ECM or BCM to continuously monitor the system and to make constant adjustments.

Because of this feedback, EATC systems store and can display fault codes indicating possible malfunctions anywhere in the system. Coupled with this is a self-diagnostic capability not found on SATC systems. For the technician, this may be the most important element of an EATC system.

In certain modes, when a fault is detected by the microprocessor, it signals the affected component to go into a default mode. For example, a shorted in-car temperature sensor would normally produce maximum cooling from the

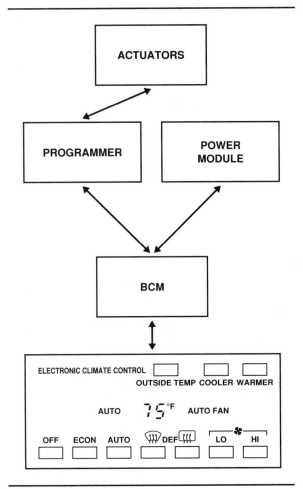

Figure 9-21. Other systems are controlled by a multifunction BCM.

air conditioning outlets. In default, however, it would produce blended air out the floor vents. This could be confusing, but it does provide reasonable car comfort.

Temperature Sensing

An EATC system uses three types of temperature sensors:

- Bimetallic vacuum modulators
- Thermistors
- Photovoltaic diodes.

Bimetallic and thermistor-type sensors have been widely used for years on SATC and even some manual systems. Photovoltaic sensors are unique to electronic systems.

The ambient air temperature sensor may be a bimetallic or thermistor-type sensor. It is located in the outside air duct of the plenum, figure 9-22. GM and others have used similar

devices mounted on the radiator frame support. The ambient air temperature sensor measures the temperature of the outside air entering the plenum or radiator air ducts. This information can be used to prevent operation of the air conditioning compressor when the outside temperature is too cold. The computer can also use it, along with the in-car sensor, to compute the ambient versus passenger compartment temperature differential.

Sunlight passing through the windows of the vehicle represents an energy or heat load on the system that must be compensated for. Sunload sensors can be of two types:

- Photovoltaic
- Thermistor.

■ Refrigerant Recyclers

The 1990s ushered in changes in air conditioning design and operation that will have profound effects on service technicians in the industry. Dichlorodifluoromethane — R-12 — the standard refrigerant of choice since 1955, will be phased out of use in Europe and North America. As R-12 becomes scarcer, recycling it from discharged systems will become a necessity.

Recycling equipment is available in several designs. The simplest systems contain a standard refrigerant drum into which the R-12 is discharged during normal air conditioning service. After discharge is completed, the unit is detached and air conditioning service is completed with a standard charging station. The R-12 in the recycler drum is then processed through an oil separator, a filter, and a drier, until it is ready to be re-used. When the drum is full, it is removed and used as an R-12 supply in the standard charging station.

More sophisticated designs integrate the recycler into the charging station. These systems permit the technician to discharge, clean, and recharge R-12 without disconnecting the service hoses. Some systems clean and filter the refrigerant while the technician services the system, and then recharge the air conditioner with the same R-12 that came out of it. Others have separate tanks — one for recovering and cleaning R-12, and a second one for recharging the system with previously cleaned refrigerant.

One of the most intriguing developments is a system that removes R-12 from the air inside the shop. This device uses a silicate molecular sieve to adsorb (trap) R-12, while allowing other gases to pass through it. The R-12 can be collected on the sieve, purified, and recycled into air conditioners. While not yet commercially available, this device or others like it may someday become a necessity.

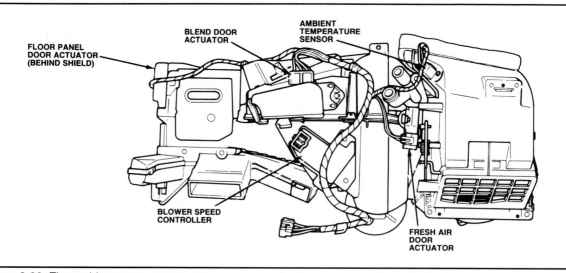

Figure 9-22. The ambient temperature sensor measures the temperature of the outside air.

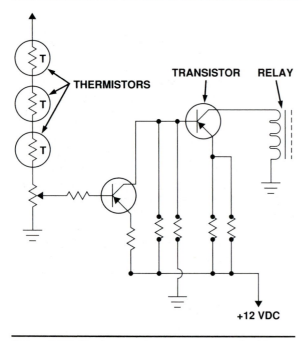

Figure 9-23. The temperature sensors are wired in series. This is called a sensor string.

Photovoltaic cells produce a voltage in direct relation to the amount of sunlight received. Placed at the top or at the base of the windshield these sensors directly measure the amount of sunlight falling on the vehicle. In this way, photovoltaic sensors indirectly measure the heat load on the air conditioning system.

Thermistor-type sun load sensors measure the temperature of the air or surfaces directly behind the windshield glass. The heated air represents sunlight energy that has entered the vehicle and been trapped behind the glass. Thermistors also directly measure the solar heat load on the air conditioning system.

The combined information of the heat sensors is used by the control element as input data that will be used to make the decisions of how much additional heating or cooling is needed to meet the driver adjusted control settings. The sunload sensor can alter the temperature setting by about 5 degrees Fahrenheit (3 degrees Celsius) between bright sunny conditions and dark cloudy conditions.

How temperature sensors work together
The sensors used to measure ambient, passenger compartment, and duct temperature are wired in series, figure 9-23. This is called a "sensor string." The value of each sensor depends upon the temperature of that particular device. The higher the temperature, the higher the resistance. The room-temperature resistance of the sensors does not have to be the same. By changing the value and the rate at which the value changes for each degree of temperature change, more weight can be given to one sensor than another.

For example, an ambient sensor measuring 90°F (32°C) may read 20 ohms. A passenger compartment sensor may read 100 ohms at 75°F (25°C). A duct sensor may measure 50 ohms when the air passing through the duct measures 60°F (16°C). The total resistance of the three sensors determines how much of the regulated voltage applied at one end will drop across the resistors. The remaining voltage is used as an input to the control amplifier. On

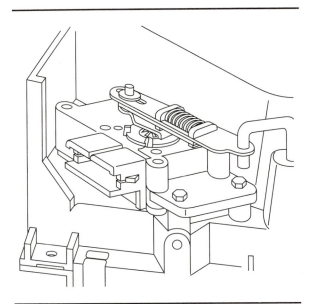

Figure 9-24. An electrically operated solenoid is a variable-position actuator on this floor-panel door.

the 1988 BMW 735i, for example, the blend door will move from 0 to 100 percent reheat in response to a 700-ohm change in the sensor string resistance.

Actuator Controls

Most of the actuators are the same as for earlier manual and SATC systems, except for the addition of the feedback circuitry. Especially in late-model systems, electrical actuators are used to alter system operating conditions. Solenoids are used to move air doors and vent controls. Motors are used to open and close water valves and to change blend door positions, figure 9-24, on systems such as Ford's Electronic Automatic Temperature Control (EATC) and GM's Electronic Touch Climate Control (ETCC). Chrysler's system uses an electronically controlled servomotor with the electronic controls built into the motor housing.

General Motors and others have used electrically operated vacuum valves to control vacuum switching. This eliminates the large, multiport vacuum switches in favor of directly wired vacuum control valves. As the motor rotates to position an air door, a potentiometer is also rotated. At any point in the 360-degree rotation of the motor, there is a resistance value associated with that position. By checking the resistance value of the potentiometer during and after the movement signal, the central computer can stop the movement at the exact

position desired and then make sure that it has been accomplished. Similar position feedback systems can also be used on linear-motion devices such as solenoids and solenoid or vacuum type servomotors.

One actuator not seen on earlier systems is the rotary electric motor used on some GM systems. Three reduction-gear motors are used to position the control doors based on input from the control element. The motors are the permanent-magnet type and use a feedback potentiometer to indicate exact door position, figure 9-25.

The direction of motor rotation is controlled by a series of four transistors called an H-gate. When the transistors marked A in figure 9-25 are **forward biased**, the motor will rotate in the forward direction. When the transistors marked B are forward biased, the polarity in the motor windings is reversed and the motor will rotate backward. The potentiometer is driven by the final drive gear. A 5-volt input signal, feedback circuit, and ground are used to signal door position.

In the feedback circuit, if the input voltage and the feedback voltage are balanced, there will be no current flowing in the motor circuit, figure 9-26. When input voltage is changed, a voltage imbalance occurs in the circuit. This causes one pair of transistors in the H-gate to be forward biased, driving the motor forward or backward as needed. As the motor runs, it moves the wiper in the feedback potentiometer until the control circuit voltage returns to a balanced condition. When the voltage balances, current flow in the motor circuit stops.

The most important aspect of the shift to electrically controlled actuators is that they replace vacuum lines and vacuum switches with electrical wires and switches, which are far more reliable. This system is easier to troubleshoot and more reliable in operation. Electrically operated systems also allow the use of computer-aided diagnostics for troubleshooting.

Photovoltaic: Capable of producing electricity when exposed to radiant energy, especially visible light.

Forward Bias: The application of a voltage to produce current flow in only one direction across the junction of a semiconductor.

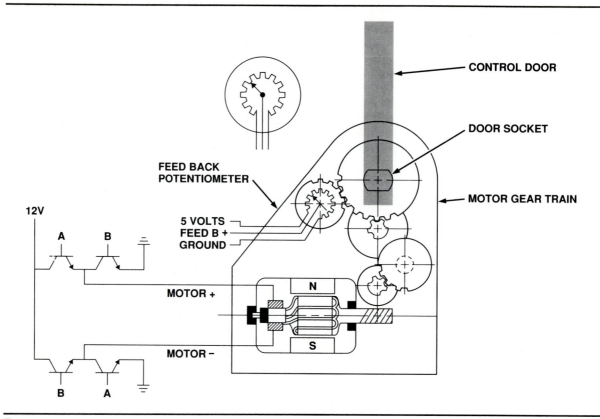

Figure 9-25. Reduction-gear motors can be used to change the mode doors.

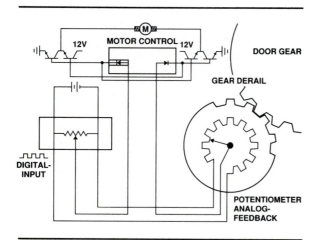

Figure 9-26. When the input voltage and the feedback voltage are balanced, no current flows to the actuator motor and the doors stop moving.

Blower and Air Conditioning Clutch Controls

The blower motor controls and the compressor clutch controls are contained in a single module. Typically they are controlled by relays that respond to output from the control panel relay driver. This converts the low-current voltage signals sent by the computer to the higher current needed to operate the 3-speed blower motor. The relay driver will energize one or more of the relays as needed to set the selected blower speed or engage the compressor clutch, figure 9-27. Power to the relays is supplied through a circuit that originates in the control head.

The latest blowers are infinitely variable. For these motors, the computer contains a delay timer that permits a gradual change in motor speed, rather than an abrupt change.

SUMMARY

Automatic temperature control systems are either semiautomatic or fully automatic. Most semiautomatic (SATC) systems are programmer-controlled, while all electronic automatic systems (EATC) are computer-controlled. The distinction between the two is whether the driver has to adjust the controls to maintain the interior temperature.

In most SATC systems, the programmer is the major addition over manual systems. This contains the electrical or vacuum control components for the actuators. Actuators include

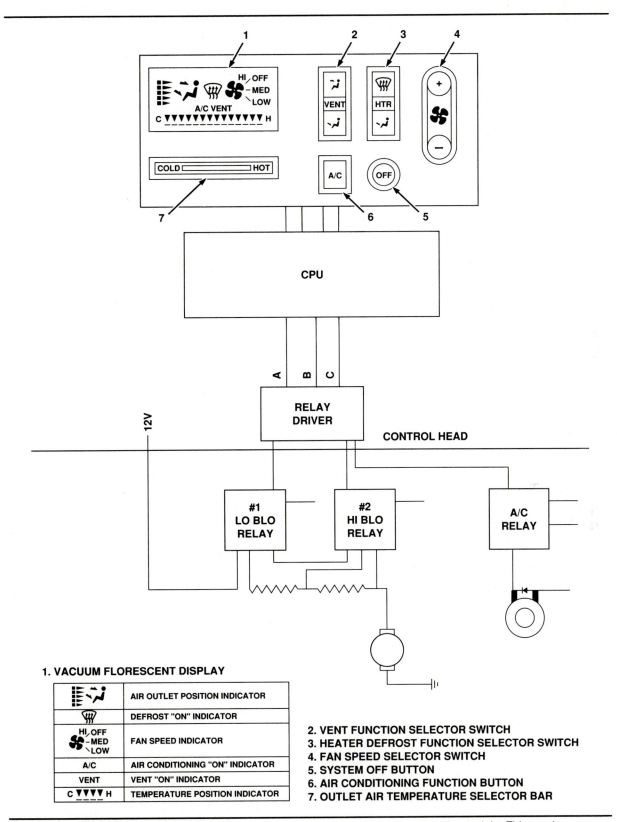

1. **VACUUM FLORESCENT DISPLAY**

	AIR OUTLET POSITION INDICATOR
	DEFROST "ON" INDICATOR
HI/OFF, MED, LOW	FAN SPEED INDICATOR
A/C	AIR CONDITIONING "ON" INDICATOR
VENT	VENT "ON" INDICATOR
C ▼▼▼▼ H	TEMPERATURE POSITION INDICATOR

2. VENT FUNCTION SELECTOR SWITCH
3. HEATER DEFROST FUNCTION SELECTOR SWITCH
4. FAN SPEED SELECTOR SWITCH
5. SYSTEM OFF BUTTON
6. AIR CONDITIONING FUNCTION BUTTON
7. OUTLET AIR TEMPERATURE SELECTOR BAR

Figure 9-27. The blower and air conditioning clutch controls are combined in a single module. This version uses two relays to control blower speed.

vacuum motors, electrical solenoids, or d.c. motors. The major actuator in any system is the blend-door motor.

Every computer works on four principle functions: input, processing, storage, and output. Computers can operate on analog and digital signals. An analog signal is infinitely variable. A digital signal is an on/off or yes/no signal. Most variable measurements on an automobile produce analog signals which must be changed to digital signals for computer processing.

Digital computers use the binary system in which on/off or high/low voltage signals are represented by combinations of 0's and 1's. These voltage signals are switching pulses for the thousands of transistors that make up a microprocessor.

Onboard computers are used in automotive instrumentation and control systems. A control system operates in open or closed loops. In open loop mode, the system does not re-spond to an output feedback signal. In closed loop mode, the computer responds to the feedback signal and adjusts the output value accordingly.

Electronic automatic temperature control (EATC) systems are computer-controlled, using inputs from various sensors to operate the air doors, compressor and blower, coolant control valve, and certain engine systems. All EATC systems are full feedback systems.

Bimetallic, thermistor, or photovoltaic sensors are used to measure temperature in various locations in and out of the car. Most of these convert the temperature reading to an electrical resistance value. Actuators generally are the same as for earlier SATC systems, with the addition of rotary electric motors used on blend doors.

Blower and clutch controls generally work together, and are usually controlled by a relay. Most blower motors have 3 or 4 speeds; some are variable.

Review Questions

Choose the single most correct answer.
Compare your answers with the correct answers on page 229.

1. A typical SATC system uses a
   _____ that is not found in
   manual systems.
   a. Control head
   b. Blower speed module
   c. Programmer
   d. Vacuum valve selector

2. The first programmers were:
   a. Vacuum-operated
   b. Electrically operated
   c. Cable-operated
   d. Mechanically actuated

3. Programmers typically include all
   of the following *except* a:
   a. Compensator
   b. Control head
   c. Vacuum checking relay
   d. Vacuum motor

4. Semiautomatic systems are
   controlled by:
   a. A microprocessor
   b. The body computer module
   c. The driver (manually)
   d. A programmer

5. An ATC system does *not* control
   which of the following?
   a. Recirculation air door
   b. Engine coolant fan
   c. Blend door actuator
   d. Panel/defroster door actuator

6. ATC systems will not operate the
   blower when the coolant
   temperature is below:
   a. 120°F (49°C)
   b. 100°F (38°C)
   c. 90°F (32°C)
   d. 70°F (21°C)

7. When a thermistor is heated, its
   resistance:
   a. Increases
   b. Decreases
   c. Rises to infinite
   d. Stays the same

8. The operational program for a
   specific engine and vehicle is
   stored in the computer's:
   a. Logic module
   b. Programmable read-only
      memory (PROM)
   c. Random access memory
      (RAM)
   d. I/O interface

9. The binary system used by a
   digital computer consists of:
   a. 5 digits
   b. 4 digits
   c. 3 digits
   d. 2 digits

10. The computer can read but not
    change information stored in:
    a. ROM
    b. RAM
    c. Adaptive memory
    d. All of these

11. Technician A says that analog
    input data must be digitized by an
    AD converter.
    Technician B says that output
    data must be changed to analog
    signals by a DA converter.
    Who is right?
    a. A only
    b. B only
    c. Both A and B
    d. Neither A nor B

12. A computer control system can
    do all of the following *except*:
    a. Ignore sensor input under
       certain conditions
    b. Respond in different ways to
       the same input signal
    c. Accept an input signal from
       another computer
    d. Ignore program instructions
       under certain conditions

13. The simplest digital sensor is a:
    a. Solenoid
    b. Switch
    c. Timer
    d. Generator

14. An engine coolant temperature
    sensor:
    a. Receives no voltage from the
       microprocessor
    b. Acts as a thermistor
    c. Is a potentiometer
    d. Provides the microprocessor
       with a variable frequency
       signal

15. An EATC system may use all of
    the following temperature sensors
    except:
    a. Piezoresistive sensors
    b. Photovoltaic sensors
    c. Bimetallic sensors
    d. Thermistor sensors

16. Sensors wired in series form:
    a. A parallel circuit
    b. A sensor string
    c. A sensor drop
    d. None of the above

17. A newer type of air conditioning
    system actuator is the:
    a. Vacuum-driven solenoid
    b. Solar-powered solenoid
    c. Rotary electric motor
    d. Air-driven motor

18. Variable blower motors achieve
    smooth speed changes with a:
    a. Delay timer
    b. Thermal resistor
    c. Smaller pulley
    d. Stepper motor

10

Representative Automatic Temperature Control Systems

In this chapter we will cover ten representative temperature control systems, using them as examples of how automotive HVAC systems operate. As you learned in Chapter 9, there are two types of automatic temperature control (ATC) systems: semiautomatic temperature control (SATC) and electronic automatic temperature control (EATC). The major difference is whether the system can operate the blower, air conditioning system, and air doors to maintain a constant temperature and humidity within the passenger compartment without continuing attention from the driver.

Within these two broad categories of automatic temperature control are numerous variations with considerable overlap. For example, many EATC systems use a programmer, but not all SATC systems do. Most of the two major systems fall into these subsystems:

- Vacuum-operated programmer SATC systems
- Electrically operated programmer SATC systems
- Microprocessor-controlled EATC systems
- BCM-controlled EATC systems.

VACUUM-OPERATED PROGRAMMER SATC SYSTEMS

Vacuum (sometimes called pneumatic) temperature control devices position the blend door based upon the relationship of the source vacuum to a second modulated vacuum. Typical systems use bimetallic elements or ambient temperature compensators to vary the amount of vacuum applied to the blend door servo.

General Motors Tempmatic Control System

The Tempmatic system is a typical reheat-type air conditioning system using a pneumatic programmer to automatically control passenger compartment temperature. This system uses a vacuum-controlled servomotor to govern blend door position. The Tempmatic system consists of two principle assemblies, the control head with vacuum mode switch, and the programmer.

The programmer, figure 10-1, contains a:

- Vacuum servomotor
- Ambient compensator assembly
- Vacuum checking relay.

These are mounted on a single chassis. Output linkages and control linkages connect the programmer to its mechanical inputs and outputs. The programmer is mounted on the air conditioning heater case and is connected to the

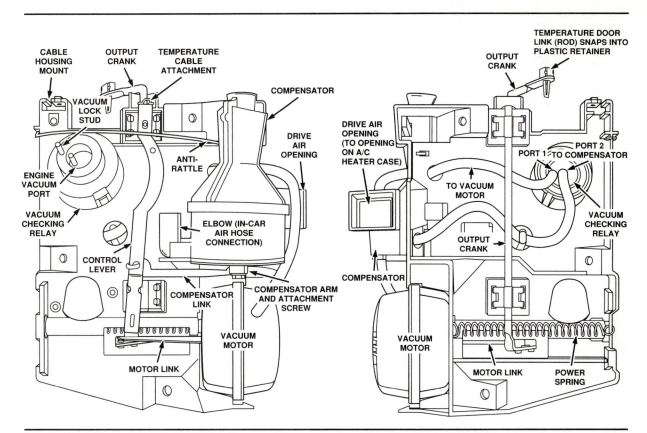

Figure 10-1. The front and back of the Tempmatic programmer, showing the vacuum motor, compensator, and vacuum checking relay.

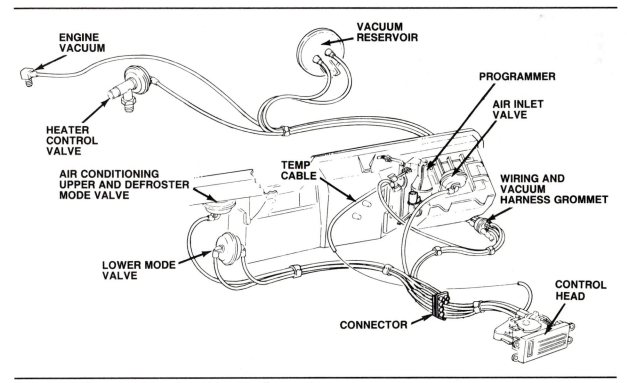

Figure 10-2. The vacuum lines to and from the Tempmatic programmer.

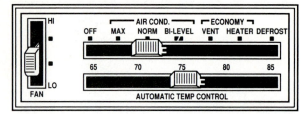

Figure 10-3. The control head of the Tempmatic system. The driver selects the fan speed, temperature range, and mode.

temperature door by a threaded rod. The programmer receives three inputs, figure 10-2:

• A vacuum connection that supplies engine vacuum to the vacuum relay.
• A temperature control cable from the control panel that positions the programmer for the desired comfort setting.
• An in-car source air hose that is connected to the compensator assembly. This provides a sample of in-car air to the programmer to allow regulation of air outlet temperature to compensate for temperature changes inside the car.

Operation of the Tempmatic
The control head settings, figure 10-3, are adjusted by the driver to determine system setpoints. The mode select lever operates both an electrical select switch and a vacuum select valve. Movement of the temperature selector lever on the control head is transmitted by a bowden cable to the programmer assembly. The blower speed is manually controlled by the fan switch. Several controls are used to prevent blower operation until the engine is warm or for other reasons.

The temperature slide switch positions the control lever and the compensator link. This changes the spring tension of the bimetallic coil, effectively changing the setpoint of the system.

Blend door position is determined by the compensator assembly. Engine vacuum is connected to the input of the compensator assembly. A bimetallic sensor, sensitive to the passenger compartment air temperature, regulates how much of the engine vacuum will be vented away from the servomotor. The remaining vacuum is applied to the servomotor to limit cooling. When no vacuum is applied to the servomotor, the system will produce maximum cooling. When vacuum is applied, the blend door moves toward the reheat position. Air door positions are controlled by vacuum motors located underneath the dash at appropriate locations, figure 10-4.

Chrysler's Early SATC System

Chrysler first used a system called SATC in 1979 as a replacement for the earlier automatic air conditioning control system called Auto-Temp II. This system is called semiautomatic because the driver must select the blower speed and the operating mode. For example, the driver must select heater operation even if the passenger compartment temperature is far below the thermostatic setpoint. Temperature regulation, though, is automatic.

In cold weather, the SATC system automatically positions the blend door to provide heat, and in warm weather the door moves to supply cooled, dehumidified air at a regulated temperature level. Temperature regulation is not active when the MAX air conditioning mode is selected. In this mode, the coolant control valve (Chrysler calls this the water valve) is closed, water flow through the heater core is stopped, and airflow is recirculated.

The control head is identical to earlier manual systems, figure 10-5. The vacuum portion of the switch controls the operation of the coolant control valve and positions all doors except the blend-air door. The electrical portion of the switch controls the compressor and blower motor, figure 10-6.

The controller on the early-model SATC is a programmer using a modulated-vacuum servo actuator. Even though the components are not grouped together into a single assembly, the SATC system works like a pneumatic programmer-type system. In this SATC system, a sample of passenger compartment air is drawn through a dashboard grille into an ambient compensator. The combination of inside and outside air temperature sensing is used to control the vacuum signal to the servo actuator controlling the blend door position. Temperature control of the early version was through a mechanical slide lever which was connected to the sensor assembly by a bowden control cable. The slide position controlled the amount of vacuum passing through the sensor assembly. The evaporator-heater assembly, vacuum harness, and instrument panel electrical harness are the same as used on the manual air conditioning system. Components are added to automatically regulate blend door position.

The Ford ATC System

The primary control element of the ATC system is the sensor assembly, figure 10-7. The sensor directly converts air temperature into corresponding levels of modulated vacuum.

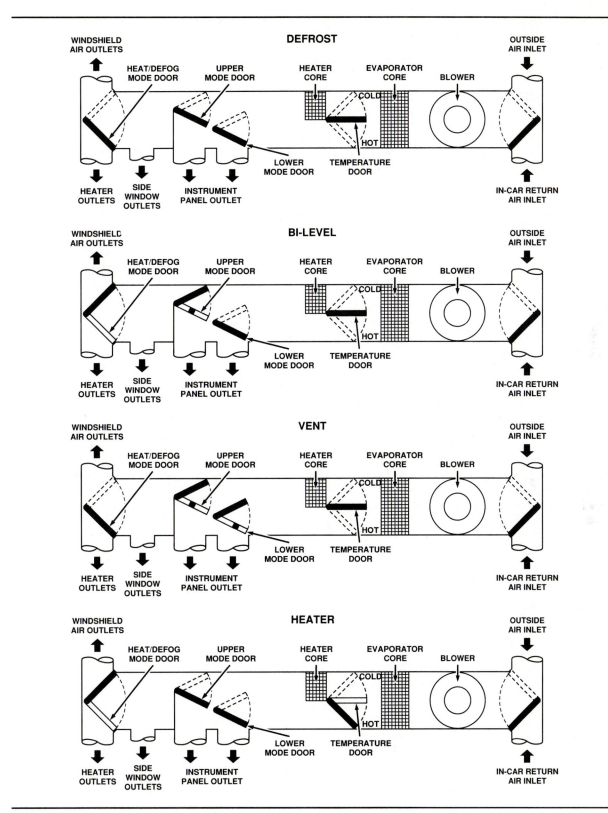

Figure 10-4. Air door locations for the four air delivery modes.

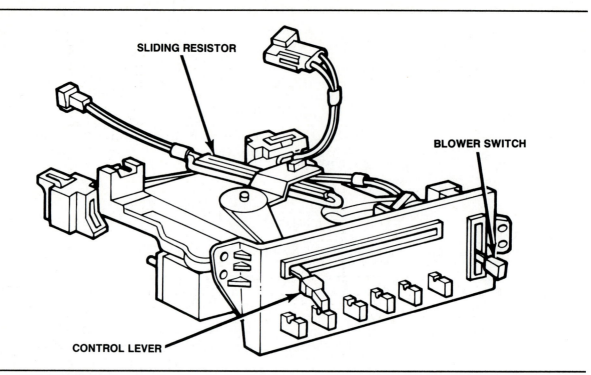

Figure 10-5. The control head on the Chrysler SATC system.

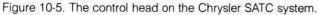

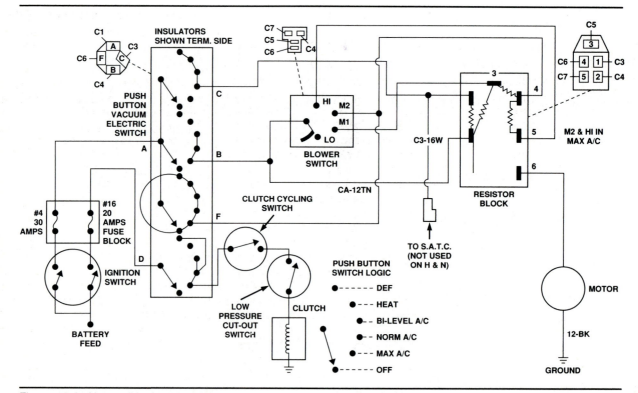

Figure 10-6. Air conditioning electrical control circuit on the Chrysler SATC system.

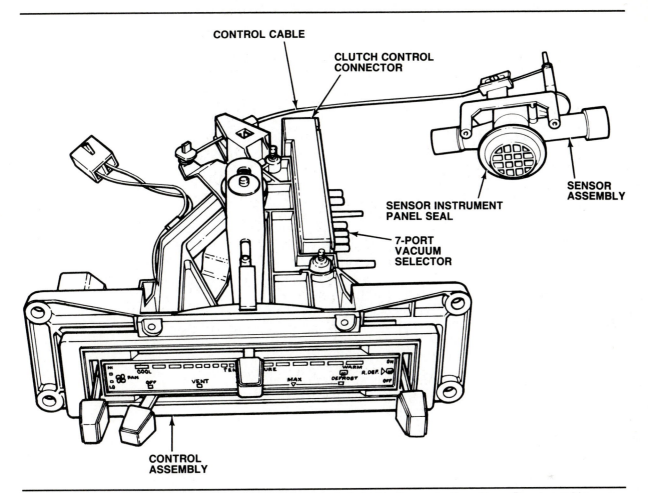

CONTROL CABLE

CLUTCH CONTROL
CONNECTOR

SENSOR
ASSEMBLY

SENSOR INSTRUMENT
PANEL SEAL

7-PORT
VACUUM
SELECTOR

CONTROL
ASSEMBLY

Figure 10-7. The Ford sensor assembly for the ATC system is linked to the control head by a Bowden cable.

The sensor uses two bimetallic discs: one disc responds to ambient air temperature while the other responds to the temperature of the passenger compartment air drawn into the aspirator portion of the sensor assembly. The sensor is linked to an internal vacuum modulator to directly control and regulate a vacuum that is proportional to temperature. The bimetallic disks and vacuum modulator are placed in a plastic aspirator assembly. The variable vacuum output of the sensor assembly is used to control the position of the blend door servomotor, figure 10-8.

A 7-port vacuum selector, figure 10-7, is a part of the ATC control head. The driver's mechanical movement of the mode selection levers is used to operate the switch. Each mode selection results in a different vacuum flow. Vent door and air door positions, as well as other system adjustments, are accomplished by changing the mode selection switch. For example, moving the mode selector to MAX air conditioning causes a vacuum signal to be sent to the coolant control valve to turn it off and a

second vacuum signal to be sent to the fresh air/recirculation air door motor.

Airflow through the earlier version of the Ford ATC system, figure 10-9, is controlled by the position of five air doors:

• Recirculation air door
• Outside air door
• Temperature blend door
• Air conditioning-heat door
• Heat-defrost door.

Because hot air rises and cold air sinks, different venting arrangements are made for heating and cooling. During the heating mode, warm air is discharged from vents located under the dashboard aimed at the passengers feet. During cooling, the air is discharged from vents in the dashboard directed at face level.

A later version of the ATC system combines the outside air door function with the recirculation door. The positions of all of the doors are determined by vacuum motors controlled from the rotary mode selector switch at the control head. The ATC system used a combi-

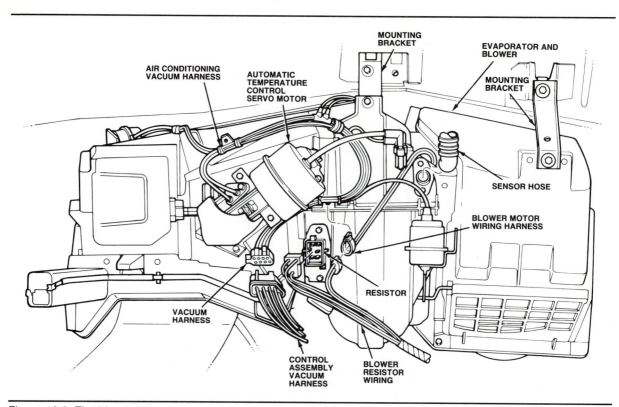

Figure 10-8. The blend door servomotor is driven by a variable vacuum signal from the ATC sensor.

nation electropneumatic (vacuum) valve to control blower operation, outside air door position, and recirculation door position under certain operating conditions. The electric vacuum relay (EVR) has three functions:

• Activate the recirculation door vacuum motor during MAX air conditioning mode
• Close the outside air door
• Prevent blower operation during warm-up when no heat is available.

The coolant control switch is wired in series with the electrical relay coil of the EVR, preventing its operation until the engine warms up. Operation in either the maximum cool or maximum heat mode causes the coil of the relay to be energized. Operation of the relay allows the passage of engine vacuum to the vacuum motors controlling the door positions.

ELECTROPNEUMATIC SATC SYSTEMS

Two types of electropneumatic control systems have been used: one with vacuum servomotors on the doors, and one with electric servomotors or solenoids. The first type uses analog amplifiers to receive and amplify signals from the sensor string. The output signal of the amplifier is used to control the position of a

vacuum transducer. The modulated vacuum signal is used to control the position of the blend door vacuum servomotor.

The second type uses a similar analog amplifier with a sensor string input. The output of the amplifier is related to the temperatures sensed outside of the vehicle, in the air ducts and inside the passenger compartment. The output voltage of the amplifier determines the position of the electric motor or solenoid that controls the position of the blend door.

General Motors Automatic Temperature Control

General Motors introduced the ATC system on its 1971 models. This system represented a standardization of the different automatic temperature control systems that had been used by various divisions since 1964.

The heart of the system is the programmer control assembly. The early GM programmer contained a vacuum servomotor, a vacuum transducer, and a rotary vacuum switch. The ATC system used an amplifier board that receives sensor signals related to inside and outside temperature and the position of the temperature setpoint selector. The output of the amplifier is used to control a vacuum

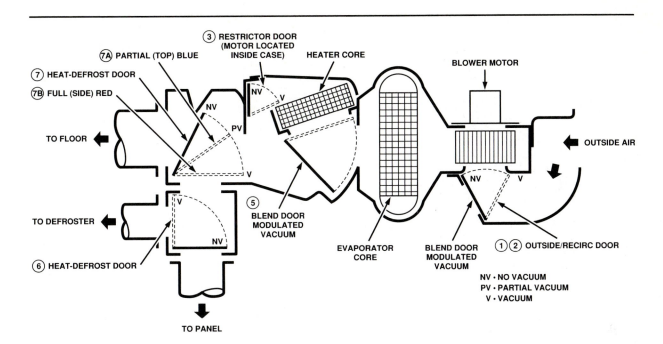

ATC VACUUM MOTOR TEST CHART

FUNCTION CONTROL LEVER POSITION		ATC REQUIREMENT	VACUUM MOTORS APPLIED WITH VACUUM					
			OUTSIDE RECIRC	RESTRICTOR DOOR	TEMP BLEND	HEAT-DEFROST		A/C DEFROST
						PARTIAL	FULL	
OFF			1-2	—		7A	7B	—
VENT		COOL	—	—	5	—	—	6
		MID	—	—	+	—	—	6
		WARM	—	—	—	—	—	6
A/C	PANEL*	COOL	1-2**	3	5	—	—	6
		MID	—	—	+	—	—	6
		WARM	—	—	—	—	—	6
	HI-LO*	COOL	—	—	5	7A	—	6
		MID	—	—	+	7A	—	6
HEAT		WARM	—	—	—	7A	—	6
	FLOOR	COOL	—	—	5	7A	7B	—
		MID	—	—	+	7A	7B	—
		WARM	1-2†	—	—	7A	7B	—
DEFROST*		COOL	—	—	5	—	—	—
		MID	—	—	+	—	—	—
		WARM	—	—	—	—	—	—
VACUUM LINE COLOR CODE			WHITE	GREEN	TAN	BLUE	RED	ORANGE

   * COMPRESSOR CLUTCH ENGAGED WHEN AMBIENT CUTOFF SWITCH IS CLOSED.
   † DELAYED BY ENGINE TEMP SENDER AND EV RELAY UNTIL 120°F ENGINE COOLANT TEMP.
 ** DEPENDENT ON HEATING COOLING REQUIREMENT OF SERVO DIVERTER VALVE.
  + MODULATED VACUUM.
  — NO VACUUM.

Figure 10-9. ATC system airflow schematic and vacuum motor test chart.

transducer. The transducer converts the electrical signals of the amplifier to vacuum signals which are used to control the vacuum motor and vacuum ported switch. Blend door, air door, and vent door positions are controlled.

Chrysler Electronic SATC

The electronic version of the SATC system was introduced in steps during the 1980-81 model years. By 1982 it was in widespread use

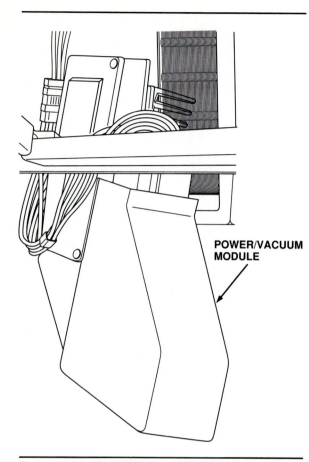

Figure 10-10. The power/vacuum module receives computer input and supplies vacuum to three door actuators.

throughout the Chrysler product line. It has been used throughout the 1980s especially on rear wheel drive models.

The electronic version has several significant differences compared to the earlier version:

• An electronic amplifier processes sensor data.
• The temperature control slide lever is a variable position resistor instead of a mechanical bowden cable link.
• An electronically controlled servomotor replaced the vacuum device on the blend door.
• An aspirator senses passenger compartment temperatures.
• An ambient air sensor is located on the evaporator housing to prevent compressor operation below 32°F (0°C).

Several control head versions are used with this system. The controls have temperature setpoints labeled in five-degree increments. These controls, and the E-SATC controller, are analog devices.

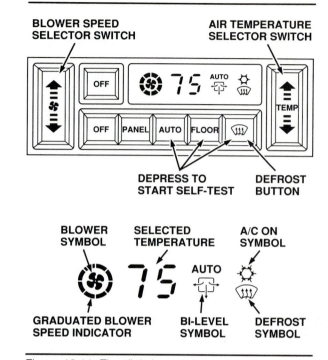

Figure 10-11. The digital control panel for the Chrysler EATC system.

MICROPROCESSOR-CONTROLLED EATC SYSTEMS

In all computerized ATC systems, the computer receives input from various sensors throughout the engine and passenger compartments, and sends signals to the actuators based on these inputs and the driver's wishes. There are two major types of computerized control:

• Microprocessor control, using a dedicated air conditioning electronic control module (ECM)
• Body control module (BCM) control, using the same main controller that controls all other systems.

Chrysler Electronic Automatic Temperature Control

The Chrysler version of electronic temperature control was introduced on some front-wheel-drive models in 1986. Chrysler EATC is a digital temperature control system that automatically regulates airflow direction, blower speed, fresh air or recirculated air, and the amount of cool or warm air allowed into the system to achieve the desired temperature. The system consists of an ATC computer, blower motor, control panel, power/vacuum module, in-car temperature sensor, and ambient temperature sensor.

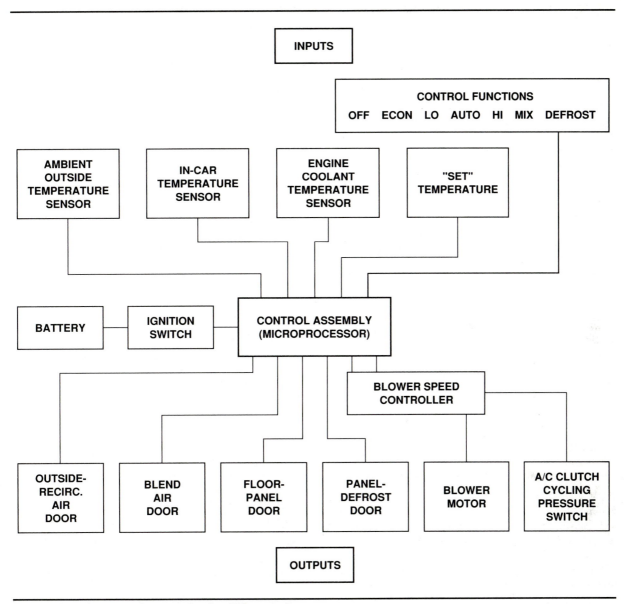

Figure 10-12. Inputs and outputs for the ATC controller.

There are several important features of this system:
- The blend door is controlled by an electric servomotor.
- Amplification and logic functions are handled by the computer.
- Blower speed is fully variable and automatically controlled.

A power/vacuum module (PVM), controlled by the computer, acts like a programmer, figure 10-10. It receives control signals from the air conditioning computer, and supplies vacuum to the coolant control valve and the actuators controlling the outside air, recirculated air, and airflow direction actuators.

The digital control head uses a numeric temperature and mode display, figure 10-11. It is the same control head as used on the SATC system. The system features an internally programmed self-test routine. Parts of the self-test program are run during the operating startup routine of the computer. Failures detected are indicated on the control panel. The full-scale diagnostic test can be started by the technician by pressing the correct combination of commands for the particular model.

Ford Electronic Automatic Temperature Control

Ford's Electronic Automatic Temperature Control system was introduced in 1984. A

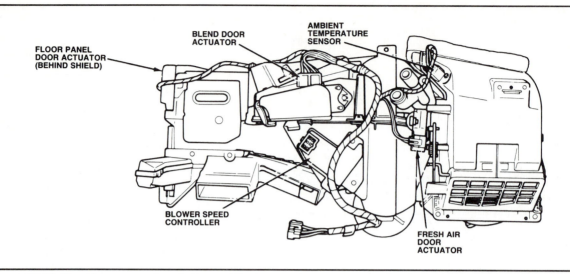

Figure 10-13. The blower speed controller and the temperature sensors are located on the evaporator assembly.

microprocessor-based controller works with five inputs to control the six outputs. Control actuators include motors and solenoids on some models and electrically controlled solenoid vacuum valves and vacuum motors on others. The controller, figure 10-12, is located in the instrument panel. It receives input from the:

- Ambient and in-car temperature sensor
- Engine coolant temperature
- Set temperature on the control panel
- Driver-selected control modes.

The controller sends actuating signals to four airflow doors and the blower speed controller, which activates the blower motor and the cycling clutch pressure switch.

The blower speed controller, figure 10-13, handles the high-power requirements of the blower and the magnetic clutch. This operates like an electronic relay by using the low-level control signals from the computer to control the high-power clutch and blower. The blower motor speed controller module is located in the cold-air inlet section of the plenum for air cooling of the control transistors.

The blower used on the EATC system is a variable-speed motor. The computer reduces the speed of the blower automatically as the passenger compartment temperature approaches the setpoint. A manual override of the blower speed is available. Power to the compressor clutch is regulated by the microprocessor-based controller wired in series with the pressure switch at the evaporator outlet. The switch will cycle the clutch to prevent evaporator freeze-up as long as power to the clutch is allowed by the controller.

A thermal blower lockout switch is used to prevent blower speed controller operation when the temperature of the coolant is too low. The switch is located on the heater hose in the engine compartment with its thermal sensor in contact with the coolant. When the coolant temperature reaches 120°F (48°C), the switch contacts close, allowing blower operation. At the same time, the recirculation door is allowed to move to the fresh air position. This control prevents needless operation of the blower while preventing fresh cold air from entering the passenger compartment during warm-up.

A thermal limiter fuse is a part of the blower motor resistor assembly. Four resistive elements provide three manual and one automatic speed setting. The thermal limiter fuse is of the link-type and opens current to the motor if the temperature of the resistor block exceeds 250°F (121°C). The thermal link is a one-time fuse that must be replaced if blown.

The four actuators used in the EATC system are small electric motors, figure 10-14. The actuators are mounted on the plenum assembly. The motors are not interchangeable. Included in the motor designs are resistive feedback networks that allow the computer to sense the actual position of the motor at any time. The computer can tell if the movement instructions sent to the actuator have been carried out. Later models, including Taurus/Sable, use vacuum motors for all but blend door control.

The digital control head of the EATC system, figure 10-15, uses pushbutton mode select controls. Pressing the cool or warm button changes the target temperature setting in one-degree increments. Seven function buttons are

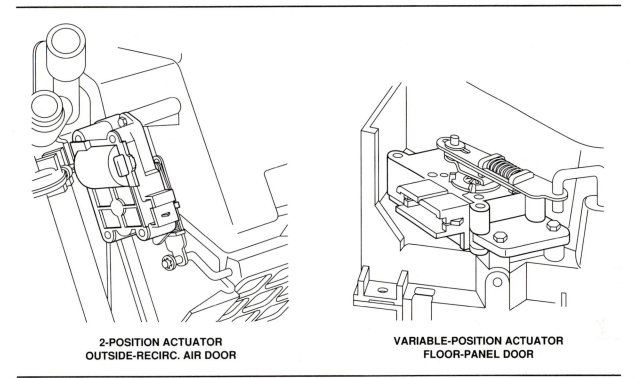

**2-POSITION ACTUATOR
OUTSIDE-RECIRC. AIR DOOR**

**VARIABLE-POSITION ACTUATOR
FLOOR-PANEL DOOR**

Figure 10-14. Two-position and variable-position motors are used to move the air doors.

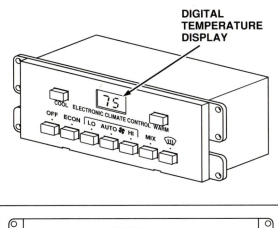

DIGITAL
TEMPERATURE
DISPLAY

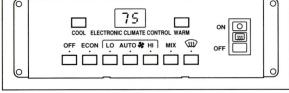

Figure 10-15. The control panel on the Ford EATC system.

used to select desired operation modes. LED lights above each switch indicate if the option has been selected. Also located in the control head is the switch for the rear window defroster if the vehicle is so equipped.

The Taurus/Sable and Lincoln Continental digital control heads are different than those used on other models. These control heads can

■ Sunny-Side Comfort Systems

One of the challenges facing designers of automatic temperature control systems is to keep the temperature of the air coming from the system as uniform as possible. Drivers can notice when the temperature changes by as little as two degrees Fahrenheit (one degree Celsius). Several solutions have been used to improve temperature stability:

● Vacuum storage canisters prevent changes in engine vacuum from affecting the blend door position.
● Electronic temperature controllers respond faster to changes in ambient or passenger car conditions.
● Variable-displacement compressors are used instead of cycling-clutch compressors because the smoother change in displacement prevents surges in refrigerant pressure that cause outlet temperature fluctuations.
● Compressors with as many as 12 cylinders have been used to provide smoother refrigeration pressures.

Future systems are being designed that will allow temperature monitoring for each seat location. This will allow the system to change vent flow levels to make sure that the passenger on the sunny side of the vehicle is just as comfortable as the passenger on the shady side.

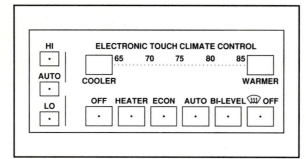

"B", "E", & "G" SERIES

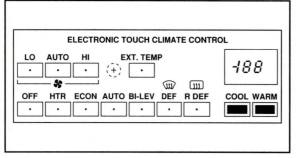

"C" SERIES

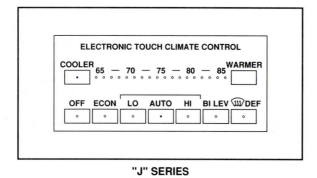

"J" SERIES

Figure 10-16. The GM ETCC systems uses at least three different control panels.

read out the outside air temperature, and give the driver control of the variable-speed blower and selection of individual vent door locations. These control heads also remember the control settings used when the vehicle was last operated. The system is returned to the same control settings upon start-up. Another feature of the system is its ability to register temperature settings in either the Fahrenheit or the Celsius scales.

GM Electronic Touch Climate Control

Electronic Touch Climate Control is one of at least four different computerized air conditioning control systems used by General Motors on late-model vehicles. It is a fully automatic

system capable of controlling passenger compartment temperature within the comfort range of 65° to 85°F (18° to 30°C). A microprocessor in the control panel controls the position of the blend door by use of a blend-door servo. The servo is a reversible, electrically driven motor with a resistor feedback system for position location. Unlike other motor- or servo-driven systems with spring-loaded blend doors, the ETCC system controls movement in both directions. Because of the feedback control, the controller always knows the exact position of the blend door.

Control heads
Three different control heads are used with the ETCC system depending upon the model in which it is installed, figure 10-16. The high-level system ("C" series) has a digital temperature readout and 14 controls to allow both manual and automatic operation. A diagnostic switch is located between the HI fan button and the external temperature switch. The diagnostic switch is not labeled or otherwise indicated to the driver. Controls for both the front and rear defroster are also mounted in this control head.

The middle-level version of the control head ("B", "E", and "G" series) uses an LED-type bar graph for temperature control indication. An LED lights up over the temperature that has been selected. Eleven switches located on the control head determine system operation. This control head does not have the rear defroster switch, the hidden diagnostic switch, or the external temperature readout control used on the higher level version.

The third control head ("J" series) uses a similar LED bar graph to indicate the temperature setpoint. The other controls used are somewhat simpler. Although the control heads are somewhat different, all the ETCC systems are essentially the same.

System inputs
There are two main sources of information inputs to the ETCC. Information from the control panel indicates the desired operating modes. Information from the sensors indicates the operating circumstances of the system.

An aspirator is mounted in the air conditioning heater module. The aspirator draws passenger compartment air in through a dashboard mounted grille past a thermistor type sensor. The resistance of the thermistor depends upon the passenger compartment temperature. The outside ambient temperature is measured by another thermistor located in the air intake cowl on the left side of the engine

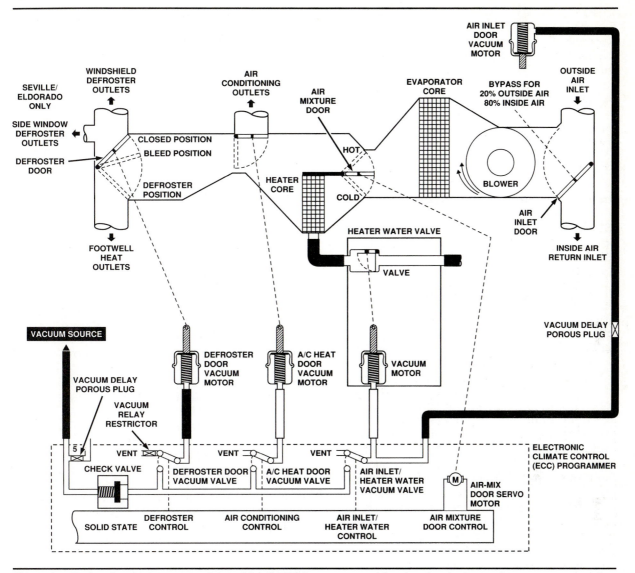

Figure 10-17. An electric servomotor is used in all ETCC systems to drive the air mix door; other actuators may be electric or vacuum-operated.

compartment. A sunload sensor of the thermistor type is used on some models to measure the heat load on the passenger compartment due to greenhouse effect.

ETCC system actuators
Control of the blend door on the ETCC is by a reversible electric servomotor using position feedback, figure 10-17. The multiple inputs and feedbacks to the control computer allow very precise and rapid modulation of the blend door position. This results in smooth, consistent passenger compartment temperatures. One-way electric motors are used as system actuators to control the position of devices such as the recirculation/fresh air door, defrost door and heater-AC select switch. These doors

return to position by spring action when the motors are turned off.

A variation of the ETCC system uses a programmer to control vacuum-operated actuators. The programmer determines which actuator needs to be operated. The programmer controls the electrical switching that completes the electrical circuit to the solenoid. When the solenoid pulse occurs, vacuum is released to the affected vacuum actuator. The vacuum is used to move the appropriate actuator to change system operation.

The blower motor and the compressor clutch are controlled indirectly through a blower and air conditioning clutch control assembly. The control is mounted between the blower motor and the HVAC plenum. The airstream of the blower motor cools the large heatsink to which the control transistors are mounted. The control assembly also serves as an electronic relay that uses the low-level instructions from the computer to control the high-power input to the blower and magnetic clutch.

BCM-CONTROLLED EATC SYSTEMS

The EATC systems just covered are controlled by a microprocessor dedicated specifically to the ATC system. The other type of computer control uses the main body control module (BCM) to control ATC functions along with other systems, such as engine management, ride levelling, cruise control, fuel and vehicle data collection, and emission control. As such, the BCM receives input from numerous sensors outside the normal ATC field, and thus has a wider range of information on which to base decisions. In this section we discuss two representative BCM-controlled systems.

General Motors Climate Control

The General Motors Climate Control system controls both heating and air conditioning functions automatically. All system switches, sensors and actuators are monitored by the BCM. The BCM uses the information from the sensors and from the control head to calculate the proper operating circumstances to achieve the control aims. A programmed memory segment in the computer contains the operating instructions for the system. The output decisions from the computer are carried out by electrically operated solenoids and motors.

On one Buick version of the system, a small television screen (cathode ray tube) is mounted in the center of the dash. The operating circumstances of the BCM are relayed to this screen. The driver selects system operation by touching the screen. The screen is covered with a clear overlay into which touch sensitive switches have been positioned. Like other computer screens, different pages of information can be brought onto the screen. The button selections made when the air conditioning page is brought up have a different effect than when the same button is pushed with another system screen on display.

The BCM decides what the operating circumstances will be. These decisions are relayed to the programmer module located behind the dash on the plenum assembly. The programmer controls blend door position and well as mode door positions and other system controls in response to instructions from the BCM.

System sensors

The sensor inputs include:

• In-car temperature sensor — An aspirator mounted on top of the HVAC plenum assembly is used to draw a sample of the passenger compartment air past a thermistor-type thermal sensor.

• Outside temperature sensor — A thermistor located ahead of the radiator and behind the grille prevents engine heat from influencing the ambient temperature reading, as can happen with cowl-mounted sensors.

• Air conditioning high-side temperature sensor — This sensor is mounted in the high-side line between the compressor and the condenser. High-side temperature is used as an indication of high-side system pressures.

• Air conditioning low-side temperature sensor — This sensor is located in the low-side of the system between the orifice tube and the evaporator inlet. It is used as an indication of the low-side pressure of the system. High- and low-side pressures can be indicated on the control screen.

• Sunload sensor — The sunload sensor measures the heat load being placed on the air conditioning system by greenhouse effect. The sensor is mounted in the defrost grille at the base of the windshield.

• Low refrigerant pressure switch — This switch is used to prevent operation of the air conditioning system when system pressure falls too low, usually as a result of refrigerant loss. The switch is located in the low-pressure side of the system at or near the evaporator outlet. The information from the switch is used by the diagnostics of the BCM.

• Power steering cutout switch — When power steering pressures exceed 300 psi (2070 kPa), the cutout switch opens to prevent operation of the air conditioning compressor clutch. This results in smoother low-speed idle and prevents engine stalls during parking maneuvers.

System actuators

The BCM uses the information from the input sensors to determine the needed system operation. This is accomplished by sending signals to the programmer assembly. This assembly contains a reversible d.c. motor that is used to position the blend door. Feedback is sent from the motor to the BCM to confirm that desired movements have been made. The programmer also contains four vacuum solenoids. When the electrical connections to the solenoids are completed, the solenoid energizes to move the diaphragm. This allows vacuum to be directed to the vacuum motor being controlled by a given solenoid.

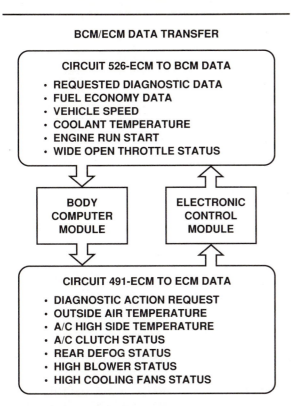

BCM/ECM DATA TRANSFER

CIRCUIT 526-ECM TO BCM DATA

- REQUESTED DIAGNOSTIC DATA
- FUEL ECONOMY DATA
- VEHICLE SPEED
- COOLANT TEMPERATURE
- ENGINE RUN START
- WIDE OPEN THROTTLE STATUS

BODY COMPUTER MODULE

ELECTRONIC CONTROL MODULE

CIRCUIT 491-ECM TO ECM DATA

- DIAGNOSTIC ACTION REQUEST
- OUTSIDE AIR TEMPERATURE
- A/C HIGH SIDE TEMPERATURE
- A/C CLUTCH STATUS
- REAR DEFOG STATUS
- HIGH BLOWER STATUS
- HIGH COOLING FANS STATUS

Figure 10-18. The data transfer between the BCM and the ECM in an Electronic Climate Control system.

The BCM also controls blower speed as a function of the programmer. The blower power module is located on top of the evaporator assembly where it can be cooled by the air from the blower motor. The transistorized control receives a signal from the programmer. The programmer receives a control signal from the BCM to govern blower performance.

The BCM controls actuation of the magnetic clutch by way of the electronic control module (ECM), which turns the clutch on and off depending upon a digital control signal received from the BCM computer. This system has a variable-door position between fresh and recirculated air. Proportional control of the air source allows options such as 70 percent fresh and 30 percent recirculated.

General Motors Electronic Climate Control

Various versions of the Electronic Climate Control (ECC) system have been used by General Motors divisions. In many respects it is similar to the Climate Control system just described. The control panel contains an ECM to allow continuous two-way communication with the

BCM, figure 10-18. Five system temperatures are monitored by the BCM:

- In-car — aspirator assembly draws air in from behind the instrument panel.
- Ambient — eliminates a falsely high outside temperature reading by using the computer's memory of the last stored ambient temperature.
- Coolant — located in the intake manifold and monitored by the ECM.
- Air conditioning high-side — located in the line between the condenser and the orifice tube.
- Air conditioning low-side — located in the line between the orifice tube and the evaporator.

The ECC system uses a programmer mounted on the heater assembly, figure 10-19. A circuit board contained in the programmer powers the d.c. motor driving the blend-air door. The programmer also contains four vacuum solenoids to control vacuum to the solenoids that operate the air doors. A power module controls the operation of the compressor clutch and blower motor. The motor receives the blower drive signal from the BCM and amplifies the signal to a strong output signal proportional to the input. The power module is transistorized to provide variable blower speeds. It receives its drive signal from the BCM via the programmer, which it amplifies to engage the compressor clutch.

On some versions of the ECC system, instead of cycling the power to the compressor clutch, the power module cycles the ground

■ System Pressure Readouts On The Dashboard

On many GM top-of-the-line models built after 1986, you can determine air conditioning high- and low-side pressures without having to hook up a manifold gauge set. Systems such as Buick's Climate Control and Cadillac's Electronic Climate Control have the capability to indirectly read system pressures on the dashboard.

In the Climate Control system, there are thermistors located on the high- and low-side fittings. The temperature information is used by the BCM to help determine system operation and to prevent system operation during times of overheating. Because of the standard pressure-temperature relationship of R-12, it is possible to determine the pressures by checking the R-12 chart. This information can help the technician separate system complaints into refrigeration and control system problems. The thermistor sensor readings follow the ECM and BCM trouble codes.

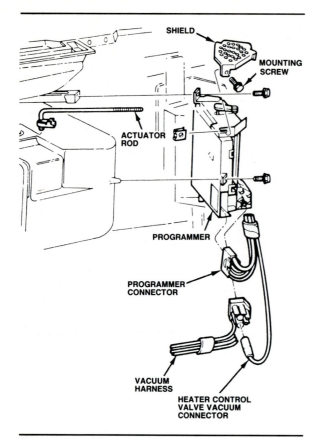

Figure 10-19. The programmer receives signals from the BCM to operate the blend-air door, four air doors, and the coolant control valve.

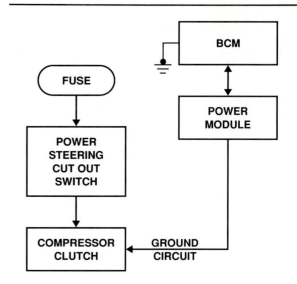

Figure 10-20. On some systems, the power module cycles the ground circuit to cycle the clutch.

circuit to the compressor. The compressor clutch receives power through a fuse and a power steering cutout switch or a diode, figure 10-20.

The blower speed is controlled by the BCM. For every given program number and control panel setting combination, the BCM has been programmed to control the motor to an appropriate speed.

SUMMARY

In this chapter, representative systems are presented in four broad categories of automatic temperature control: vacuum- and electrically operated programmer-type semiautomatic (SATC) systems, and microprocessor- and BCM-controlled electronic automatic (EATC) systems.

The GM Tempmatic system is a typical reheat system using vacuum actuators controlled by a programmer. The programmer contains a vacuum servo, ambient compensator, and vacuum checking relay. The programmer receives input from the control head, engine vacuum,

and an in-car aspirator. The driver controls the fan switch and the temperature setting.

The first Chrysler SATC system required the driver to select fan speed and temperature setting. The programmer is not contained in a single case but performs much of the same tasks as the Ford programmer. It uses a vacuum servomotor to control the blend door, an ambient compensator, and a mechanical linkage to the control head.

The Ford ATC system uses an air sensor that converts a temperature reading into modulated vacuum. This is fed to a 7-port vacuum selector switch to activate the doors when signaled by the lever from the control panel. Later systems use a rotary vacuum valve. A combination vacuum valve controls blower speed, outside air door, and recirculation air door under some conditions.

An early GM ATC system contains a programmer with a vacuum transducer, vacuum motor, and rotary vacuum switch. An amplifier board receives signals from two temperature sensors. This signal is amplified and used to control the vacuum motors on the air doors. The rotary vacuum switch is mechanically controlled by the levers from the control head.

The Chrysler electronic SATC system replaced the earlier vacuum servomotor with an electronic servomotor on the blend door. It uses an in-car temperature aspirator and an electronic amplifier to process signal data. The controls and the control head are analog devices.

Chrysler's electronic automatic temperature control (EATC) system uses digital temperature control. It is controlled by a dedicated electronic control module (ECM). The blend door uses an electronic servomotor, the amplification and logic is handled by the computer, and blower speed is fully variable. Like all EATC systems, it has a full self-diagnostic feature.

Ford's EATC system uses a blower speed controller to power a variable-speed blower and the compressor clutch. A thermal blower lockout prevents the blower from operating when the engine is cold. Electrical actuators control the air doors on most versions. Vacuum motors are used on all but the blend door assembly on other versions.

The GM Electronic Touch Climate Control (ETCC) is also a microprocessor-controlled system. It is fully automatic, with full feedback from all the actuators. The blend door is operated by a reversible electric motor for precise

control; the other doors are operated by one-way electric motors. The blower motor and compressor clutch are controlled indirectly by a control acting as a relay.

Among BCM-controlled systems is the General Motors Climate Control. This system uses electric motors for all actuators. Control signals are from the BCM to a programmer, which contains a reversible d.c. motor to drive the blend door. The BCM also controls blower speed and the compressor clutch, through the electronic control module.

The GM Electronic Climate Control is a similar, though more advanced, system. This also uses five temperature sensors and a programmer. The programmer contains a d.c. motor for the blend door and four vacuum solenoids to drive the air doors. Blower speed is controlled by the BCM through its programming for preset conditions.

Review Questions

Choose the single most correct answer.
Compare your answers with the correct answers on page 229.

1. Electronic automatic temperature control systems can be controlled by:
   a. A BCM
   b. An ECM
   c. Both a and b
   d. Neither a nor b

2. The GM Tempmatic system uses a _____ to regulate blend door position.
   a. Electric rotary motor
   b. Electric servomotor
   c. Electric solenoid
   d. Vacuum servomotor

3. Chrysler introduced its first SATC system in:
   a. 1969
   b. 1975
   c. 1979
   d. 1984

4. In the Chrysler SATC system, all air doors except the blend door are operated by:
   a. Vacuum motors
   b. Cables
   c. Electric servomotors
   d. None of the above

5. Ford's ATC system uses a:
   a. 5-port vacuum selector
   b. 7-port vacuum selector
   c. 9-port vacuum valve
   d. Vacuum-actuated compensator

6. The electric vacuum relay on Ford's ATC does the following *except*:
   a. Activates the recirculation door under certain conditions
   b. Prevents blower operation during warm-up
   c. Controls the compressor clutch through a separate relay
   d. Operates the outside air door

7. The early GM ATC programmer did *not* contain a:
   a. Vacuum servomotor
   b. Vacuum transducer
   c. Rotary vacuum switch
   d. Vacuum compensator

8. Technician A says the Chrysler E-SATC system uses an analog controller.
   Technician B says the Chrysler E-SATC system uses a bowden cable output from the temperature control slide lever. Who is right?
   a. A only
   b. B only
   c. Both A and B
   d. Neither A nor B

9. In the Chrysler EATC system, the power/vacuum module acts like a:
   a. Vacuum switch
   b. Vacuum valve
   c. Programmer
   d. Transducer

10. The blower in the Ford EATC system is the:
    a. 3-speed type
    b. 4-speed type
    c. 5-speed type
    d. Variable-speed type

11. The blend door in the GM ETCC system is controlled by a:
    a. Rotary electric motor
    b. Reversible electric motor
    c. Variable-position vacuum servomotor
    d. None of the above

12. The GM Climate Control system is controlled by a:
    a. Body control module
    b. Dedicated ECM
    c. Both a and b
    d. Neither a nor b

13. The GM Electronic Climate Control system receives input from _____ temperature sensors.
    a. 3
    b. 4
    c. 5
    d. 6

14. Some ECC systems cycle the compressor ground circuit through a:
    a. Fuse and a power brake diode
    b. Fuse and a power steering diode
    c. Relay and a power steering diode
    d. Relay and a power brake diode

ASE Technician Certification Sample Test

This sample test is similar in format to the series of eight tests given by the National Institute for Automotive Service Excellence (ASE). Each of these exams covers a specific area of automotive repair and service. The tests are given every fall and spring throughout the United States.

For a technician to earn certification in a particular field, he or she must successfully complete one of these tests, and have at least two years of "hands on" experience (or a combination of work experience and formal automobile technician training). Successfully finishing all eight tests earns the person certification as a Master Automobile Technician.

In the following sample test, the questions follow the form of the ASE exams. Learning to take this kind of test will help you if you plan to apply for certification later in your career. You can find the answers to the questions in this sample exam on page 229.

For test registration forms or additional information on the automobile technician certification program, write to:

National Institute for
  AUTOMOTIVE SERVICE EXCELLENCE
13505 Dulles Technology Drive
Herndon, Virginia 22071-3415

1. Separating molecules from a liquid by adding heat energy is called:
   a. Evaporation
   b. Condensation
   c. Transpiration
   d. Liquification

2. Which is true of heat when matter changes state?
   a. All heat is absorbed by the surrounding air
   b. Heat is absorbed or given off by the material making the change
   c. Heat is released as a vapor
   d. Heat is converted to thermal energy

3. Technician A says a hygrometer is used to measure absolute humidity.
   Technician B says relative humidity can be measured with a psychrometer.
   Who is right?
   a. A only
   b. B only
   c. Both A and B
   d. Neither A nor B

4. Which of the following hose and line connectors is used on air conditioning systems?
   a. Flare-type
   b. O-ring seals
   c. Spring lock connectors
   d. All of the above

5. Technician A says that stem-type valves are more common than Schrader valves on air conditioning systems.
   Technician B says Schrader valves may contain calibrated springs that release at specific levels.
   Who is right?
   a. A only
   b. B only
   c. Both A and B
   d. Neither A nor B

6. The air conditioning system accumulator is:
   a. Also called the filter-drier
   b. Only used with cycling clutch systems
   c. Attached to the inlet side of the compressor
   d. The same as a receiver-drier

7. Which of the following contains litmus paper in the sight glass that detects moisture in the system?
   a. Receiver-drier
   b. EEVIR
   c. VIR
   d. EPR II

8. Technician A says that an engine computer receives input information from the actuators, processes data, stores data, and sends output information to its sensors.
   Technician B says that most late-model computers are based on analog microprocessors.
   Who is right?
   a. A only
   b. B only
   c. Both A and B
   d. Neither A nor B

9. Digital computer switching circuits are known as:
   a. NOT gates
   b. AND gates
   c. OR gates
   d. All of the above

10. An onboard computer can act as:
    a. An instrumentation system
    b. A control system
    c. Both a and b
    d. Neither a nor b

11. The reference value sent to a sensor by the computer must:
    a. Be above battery voltage
    b. Be exactly the same as battery voltage
    c. Be less than minimum battery voltage
    d. None of the above

12. A variable resistance sensor is called a:
    a. Potentiometer
    b. Relay
    c. Transformer
    d. Diode

13. A stepper motor:
    a. Is either on or off
    b. Is one form of solenoid
    c. Is used to operate the coolant control valve
    d. Has discrete steps of movement

14. Constant operation of the compressor in automotive air conditioning systems is prevented by:
    a. A solenoid
    b. A servomagnet
    c. An electromagnetic clutch
    d. None of the above

15. The air conditioning compressor clutch can be controlled by:
    a. A power steering cutout switch
    b. A pressure cycling switch
    c. A power brake delay switch
    d. All of the above

16. Technician A says the user selects the mode in a semi-automatic temperature control system, and the actuators are electrically operated.
    Technician B says that a semiautomatic temperature control system uses in-car and ambient temperature sensors.
    Who is right?
    a. A only
    b. B only
    c. Both A and B
    d. Neither A nor B

17. Technician A says that Ford's heated windshield system will only work if the in-car temperature is below 40°F (4°C).
    Technician B says that the heated windshield module can control the EEC-IV module under certain circumstances.
    Who is right?
    a. A only
    b. B only
    c. Both A and B
    d. Neither A nor B

18. For 3 to 5 seconds, a power brake time delay relay will interrupt the:
    a. Throttle kicker circuit
    b. Cooling fan motor relay coil
    c. Air conditioning relay coil circuit
    d. Isolation relay coil circuit

19. The air conditioning compressor pulley and clutch hub are engaged by:
    a. Magnetic force
    b. Refrigerant pressure
    c. A rotating coil
    d. Centrifugal force

20. The power steering pressure switch typically opens when pressure in the steering system exceeds:
    a. 250 psi
    b. 300 psi
    c. 500 psi
    d. 600 psi

21. The Greenhouse Effect is a result of which type of heat energy?
    a. Convection
    b. Radiation
    c. Conduction
    d. Weather

22. How much of the engine's energy output is used to drive the car?
    a. Less than a quarter
    b. A quarter to a third
    c. A third to two-thirds
    d. More than two-thirds

23. Compressing a gas:
    a. Increases the pressure and decreases the temperature
    b. Decreases the pressure and increases the temperature
    c. Decreases the pressure and decreases the temperature
    d. Increases the pressure and increases the temperature

24. What is the *main* advantage of a pressurized cooling system in a vehicle?
    a. It lowers the boiling point of the coolant
    b. It raises the boiling point of the coolant
    c. It prevents evaporation of the coolant
    d. None of the above

25. A vacuum motor with two diaphragms and two vacuum ports is a:
    a. Single-action motor
    b. Double-action motor
    c. Three-position motor
    d. None of the above

26. Typical control system vacuum readings are:
    a. 0-10 in-Hg (0 to 7 kPa)
    b. 0-20 in-Hg (0 to 14 kPa)
    c. 0-30 in-Hg (0 to 200 kPa)
    d. 0-40 in-Hg (0 to 275 kPa)

27. Technician A says a cycling compressor clutch responds to the temperature of the evaporator.
    Technician B says a pressure control valve on the compressor responds to evaporator pressure, and therefore temperature.
    Who is right?
    a. A only
    b. B only
    c. Both A and B
    d. Neither A nor B

28. Which of the following is *not* a feature of refrigeration oil:
    a. Nonfoaming
    b. Sulphur-free
    c. Variable viscosity
    d. Wax-free

29. In a typical air conditioning system, the BILEVEL mode divides the airflow:
    a. 60% to the dash and 40% to the floor
    b. 40% to the dash and 60% to the floor
    c. 50% to the dash and 50% to the floor
    d. 80% to the dash and 20% to the floor

30. In MAX AC mode:
    a. The heater control valve is closed
    b. The defroster door is open
    c. The outside air door is open
    d. The blower is disabled

31. When the air conditioning is off, the compressor operates in the _____ mode to dehumidify the air.
    a. NORM
    b. DEFROST
    c. RECIRCULATE
    d. BILEVEL

32. Which of the following occurs at the fixed-orifice tube?
    a. The pressure on the refrigerant is relieved
    b. The refrigerant begins to evaporate quickly
    c. Latent heat is absorbed as the refrigerant changes state
    d. All of the above

33. Superheat is:
    a. The added heat absorbed by gaseous refrigerant at temperatures below its boiling point
    b. The heat released by cooling refrigerant in the condenser
    c. The added heat absorbed by gaseous refrigerant at temperatures above its boiling point
    d. The heat released by cooling refrigerant in the evaporator

34. Which of the following can result from evaporator freeze-up?
    a. The refrigerant may not properly evaporate
    b. Liquid refrigerant can be drawn into the compressor
    c. The air conditioning system produces little or no cooling
    d. All of the above

35. High air conditioning pressures can be caused by all of the following *except*:
    a. A leaking compressor front seal
    b. A jammed magnetic clutch
    c. A blocked condenser
    d. Faulty controls

36. An ATC system does *not* control which of the following?
    a. Recirculation air door
    b. Engine coolant fan
    c. Blend door actuator
    d. Panel/defroster door actuator

37. ATC systems will not operate the blower when the coolant temperature is below:
    a. 120°F (49°C)
    b. 100°F (38°C)
    c. 90°F (32°C)
    d. 70°F (21°C)

38. Air temperature regulation is accomplished by:
    a. Varying the ratio of heated air to unheated air
    b. Varying the flow of coolant through the radiator
    c. Changing the vent positions
    d. Combination of b and c

39. The major cause of compressor malfunctions is:
    a. Overpressure
    b. Underpressure
    c. Leaks in the compressor cylinder
    d. Loss of lubricant

40. A heater does not supply enough heat. The engine coolant level and blower motor check out okay.
    Technician A says a misadjusted heater control could be the cause.
    Technican B says a bad thermostat could be the cause.
    Who is right?
    a. A only
    b. B only
    c. Both A and B
    d. Neither A nor B

41. To charge an air conditioning system while it is operating, refrigerant must be added to the:
    a. High side only
    b. Low side only
    c. Both the high and the low sides
    d. Either the high or the low side

42. The air conditioning system high side pressure is too high. Which of these is the likely cause?
    a. Restricted airflow through the condenser
    b. Faulty thermostat
    c. Leaking thermal bulb
    d. Open bypass valve

43. There is a growling or rumbling noise from the compressor. When the clutch is engaged the noise stops.
    Technician A says that the compressor bearing is bad.
    Technician B says that the clutch bearing is bad.
    Who is right?
    a. A only
    b B only
    c. Both A and B
    d. Neither A nor B

44. On an air conditioning system with a thermostatic expansion valve, the compressor will not engage.
    Technician A says that a faulty capillary bulb is the cause.
    Technician B says that a blocked expansion valve is the cause.
    Who is right?
    a. A only
    b. B only
    c. Both A and B
    d. Neither A nor B

45. If a cycling-clutch type air conditioning unit freezes the evaporator no matter where the temperature control is set, which of these statements is probably true?
    a. The thermostatic switch is open
    b. The clutch bearing has seized
    c. The ambient air temperature is too low
    d. There is no moisture in the system

46. On a blend air heating system, there is no heat. All of these could cause this problem *except*:
    a. Faulty vacuum circuit to the control valve
    b. Incorrect cable adjustment
    c. Incorrect thermostat
    d. Low refrigerant

47. The manifold gauge set reads as follows:
    Low side: 5 in-Hg (125 mm-Hg; vacuum)
    High side: 190 psi (1300 kPa; pressure)
    Ambient temperature: 85°F (30°C)
    Technician A says the system is low on R-12.
    Technician B says the compressor gaskets are blown.
    Who is right?
    a. A only
    b. B only
    c. Both A and B
    d. Neither A nor B

48. The evaporator pressure control valve, found on some systems, is used to:
    a. Control the amount of refrigerant entering the evaporator
    b. Prevent evaporator core freeze-up
    c. Cycle the compressor
    d. Control the amount of refrigerant entering the condenser

49. A heater vacuum-operated control valve is installed backwards.
    Technician A says this will make the engine overheat.
    Technician B says this will cause cold air output.
    Who is right?
    a. A only
    b. B only
    c. Both A and B
    d. Neither A nor B

50. In pressure testing an air conditioning system, it is found that at normal speeds and temperatures the high and low side pressures are the same. Which of these statements is probably true?
    I. The clutch is not engaged
    II. There is a restriction in the expansion valve
    a. I only
    b. II only
    c. Both I and II
    d. Neither I nor II

51. Technician A says that evacuating (pumping down) an air conditioning system will remove air and moisture from the system.
    Technician B says that evacuating an air conditioning system will remove dirt particles from the system.
    Who is right?
    a. A only
    b. B only
    c. Both A and B
    d. Neither A nor B

52. The manifold gauge set reads as follows:
    Low side: 65 psi (450 kPa)
    High side: 90 psi (615 kPa)
    Ambient temperature: 85°F (30°C)
    Which of the following is *least likely* to cause these readings?
    a. Restricted screen in expansion valve
    b. Compressor head gasket blown
    c. Compressor not running
    d. Broken reed valve

Glossary of Technical Terms

Absolute Zero: The total absence of heat, when molecular motion ceases. Approximately –460°F (–273°C).

Absolute Humidity: A measurement of the actual weight of water in a given volume of air.

Accumulator: A component between the evaporator and the compressor inlet in which gaseous refrigerant may be stored, liquid refrigerant may change into vapor, and water can be removed from the refrigerant by means of a desiccant.

Actuator: Special component such as a vacuum motor or solenoid that translates a vacuum or electrical signal into the physical movement to operate an HVAC valve, door, or flap. Typically an actuator performs an on/off function.

Adaptive Memory: A feature of computer memory that allows the microprocessor to adjust its memory for computing open-loop operation, based on changes in engine operation. Whatever is stored in adaptive memory is lost only when power to the computer is shut off, such as by disconnecting the battery.

Aerodynamic Drag: The resistance to an object's forward motion caused by the obstruction of and friction with the surrounding air.

Ambient Temperature: The temperature of the air surrounding a component.

Analog: A voltage signal or processing action that varies continuously with the variable being measured or controlled.

Aneroid Bellows: A temperature sensor with accordion-shaped pleats in its surface, containing a small amount of volatile liquid. Temperature changes cause the bellows to expand or contract, as more or less of the liquid inside vaporizes.

Atmospheric Pressure: The pressure caused by the weight of the earth's atmosphere. At sea level, this pressure is 14.7 psi (101 kPa) at 32°F (0°C).

Atom: The smallest part of an element that still has all the characteristics of that element.

Barometric Pressure: Atmospheric pressure, as measured with a barometer.

Bimetallic Temperature Sensor: A device that uses two strips of different metals welded together. When heated, one side will expand more than the other, causing the strip to bend, which makes or breaks a pair of contact points.

Binary System: A mathematical system containing only two digits (0 and 1) which allows a digital computer to read and process input voltage signals.

Bit: A digital input or output signal. One bit roughly equals one computer keystroke, or one discrete piece of information. The word comes from *bi*nary dig*it*.

Blend Air: A type of HVAC system that controls air temperature using a door directing incoming air through or around the heater core.

Boiling: The very rapid change of state of a liquid to a gas (vapor) caused by rapidly adding heat or rapidly decreasing the pressure.

Bowden Cable: A wire cable inside a rubber or metal sheath, used to provide remote control of a valve or control actuator.

British Thermal Units (Btu): The amount of heat necessary to raise one pound of water one degree Fahrenheit. One Btu corresponds to 252 calories.

calorie (c): The amount of heat necessary to raise one gram of water one degree Celsius. One thousand calories are abbreviated ''C''.

Capillary Tube: A long, narrow tube used to transmit internal gas pressure from a remote sensing bulb to a thermostatic expansion valve diaphragm.

Centrifugal Force: The natural tendency of objects, when forced to move in a curved path, to move away from the center of rotation.

Check Valve: A valve that permits fluid or vacuum flow in one direction but prevents it in the opposite direction.

Chemical Compound: A chemically pure substance composed of molecules containing atoms of different elements.

Circuit: An electrical path composed of wiring, switches, and other electrical components that leads to and from a power source through the component operated by the electric current. A series of vacuum lines and vacuum-operated components is sometimes called a vacuum circuit; unlike electricity, vacuum does not require a complete loop leading back to the power source.

Closed-Loop: An operational mode in which the computer reads and responds to feedback signals from its sensors, adjusting system operation accordingly.

Coefficient of Expansion: The characteristic rate of expansion of a substance resulting from increased molecular vibration as the temperature increases, or of shrinkage from decreased vibration as the temperature falls.

Compressor: The air conditioning system pump, belt-driven, controlled by an electromagnetic clutch. The compressor applies pressure to the refrigerant and pumps it through the system.

Condenser: A radiator-like tube-and-fin heat exchanger exposed to outside airflow. As gaseous refrigerant flows through the tubes, it condenses to liquid and releases heat that the airstream carries away.

Conduction: The transfer of heat through a substance or between objects by direct molecular contact.

Control Head: The dashboard-mounted unit containing the controls for the heating, cooling, and ventilation system.

Convection: The transfer of heat from place to place by the circulation of a gas or a liquid.

Core Plug: Also called a freeze plug. A shallow metal cup inserted into the engine block to seal holes left by manufacturing. These cups are designed to pop out if the coolant in the block freezes, but do not offer complete protection.

Cowl Air Intake: The inlet vent at the base of the windshield that admits ram air into the HVAC system.

Cycling Clutch: A pressure-control system that maintains air conditioning refrigerant pressure by engaging and disengaging the compressor with its electromagnetic clutch.

Dehydrator: A device with a desiccant to remove moisture from the refrigerant, also called a receiver-drier.

Desiccant: A drying agent in the receiver-drier of an air conditioning system, used to remove moisture.

Dew Point: The temperature at which air becomes 100 percent saturated with moisture at a given absolute humidity.

Dichlorodifluoromethane: The chemical name for Refrigerant 12, (CCl_2F_2).

Dieseling: A condition in which extreme heat in an engine's combustion chamber continues to ignite fuel after the ignition has been turned off.

Digital: A voltage signal or processing function that has only two levels: on/off or high/low.

Diode: An electronic semiconductor device that acts as a switch. A diode allows current flow in one direction but not the other.

Electron: A negatively charged particle within an atom.

Element: One of 105 particular and unique chemical building blocks, that cannot be reduced to anything simpler by chemical means.

Ethylene Glycol: A chemical compound that forms a good engine coolant when mixed with water, increasing the coolant's resistance to both freezing and boilover.

Evaporation: The slow change of state of a liquid to a gas (vapor) caused by slowly adding heat or slowly decreasing the pressure.

Evaporator: A radiator-like tube-and-fin heat exchanger, exposed to airflow into the passenger compartment. As liquid refrigerant flows through the tubes, it vaporizes and absorbs heat from the air flowing between the fins.

Expansion Tube: Fixed-orifice tube; an expansion device that removes pressure from the refrigerant as it flows into the evaporator, but does not vary the flow rate.

Feedback: The return of a portion of the output (actuator) to the input (computer), used to maintain an output device within predetermined limits.

Field Coil: A magnetic coil fastened to the front of a compressor, used to engage and disengage the compressor clutch. Current applied to the coil produces a magnetic field that pulls in an armature to engage the clutch.

Flooding: An air conditioner malfunction, when too much liquid refrigerant leaves the evaporator without vaporizing.

Forward Bias: The application of a voltage to produce current flow in only one direction across the junction of a semiconductor.

Freeze-Up: Clogging of an evaporator core with frost, resulting from its temperature dropping below the freezing point of water. Freeze-up results in very poor cooling until the ice is melted off.

Gas: A state of matter of no definite shape or volume, easily compressed, with a high tendency to disperse.

Greenhouse Effect: In our usage, the warming of an enclosed space by trapped heat, resulting from sunlight entering through windows.

Heat Exchanger: A component in which heat is transferred from one medium (such as hot coolant) to another (such as the surrounding air) through conduction.

Heat: The disorganized energy in any substance caused by the rapid vibration of the atoms and molecules making it up.

Heater Core: A heat exchanger in the HVAC system through which hot coolant passes and releases its heat by conduction.

High Side: The portion of the air conditioning system in which the refrigerant is under high pressure and at high temperature. It includes the compressor outlet, condenser, receiver-drier (if used), and expansion device inlet.

Humidity: Water vapor in the air.

HVAC: An acronym for heating-ventilation-air conditioning systems.

Hygrometer: A device used to measure relative humidity containing a humidity-sensitive element.

Hysteresis: The failure of a device to return to its original value when the cause of the change has been removed.

Kinetic Energy: The energy associated with motion. The kinetic energy in vibrating atoms and molecules results in what we call heat.

Latent Heat: Heat that is absorbed or given off during a change of state of a material without changing its temperature.

Latent Heat of Vaporization: A characteristic amount of heat that is absorbed or given off while a standard amount of a material changes state between liquid and vapor, without changing the temperature.

Latent Heat of Fusion: A characteristic amount of heat that is absorbed or given off while a standard amount of a material changes state between solid and liquid, without changing the temperature.

Liquid: A state of matter of no definite shape, high incompressibility, and a tendency to flow and disperse.

Logic Gates: Circuit switching functions within a computer that act as routes for output voltage signals according to differing combinations of input signals.

Low Side: The portion of the air conditioning system in which the refrigerant is under low pressure and at low temperature. It includes the expansion device outlet, evaporator, accumulator (if used), and compressor inlet.

Manifold Vacuum: Low air pressure in the intake manifold of a running engine, caused by the descending pistons creating empty space in the cylinders faster than the entering air can fill it.

Molecule: Two or more atoms chemically bonded together.

Neutron: A particle in an atom that has no charge and is electrically neutral.

Nucleus: The center core of an atom that contains the protons and neutrons.

Open-Loop: An operational mode in which the computer adjusts a system to function according to pre-determined instructions and does not always respond to feedback signals from its sensors.

Orifice: A small hole, or opening, in a valve, tube, or pipe.

Photovoltaic: Capable of producing electricity when exposed to radiant energy, especially visible light.

Pilot-Operated: Referring to a smaller internal valve (the pilot valve) that regulates the movement of the larger valve into which it is placed.

Pintle Valve: A ball-and-seat valve inside a thermostatic expansion valve assembly. The ball-shaped pintle is attached to a normally closed diaphragm, which opens and closes the valve in response to pressure changes.

Plenum Chamber: The largest part of the air conditioning duct system. When operating it is filled with air at a slightly higher pressure than the surrounding air.

Pressure Release Grille: An air vent inside the passenger compartment that prevents pressure from building up inside the vehicle while the HVAC system is operating.

Pressure Control Valve: An evaporator control device located between the evaporator and compressor that controls refrigerant flow into the compressor in response to pressure in the evaporator.

Program: The instructions a computer needs to do its job. The program consists of mathematical instructions and may also include fixed data and require variable data from vehicle sensors.

Programmable Read-Only Memory (PROM): An integrated circuit chip installed in the onboard computer which has been programmed with operating instructions and database information for a particular vehicle.

Proton: A positively charged particle within an atom.

Psychrometer: A device used to measure relative humidity containing a wet and a dry thermometer.

Radial: Radiating from a common center.

Radiation: The transfer of heat as pure energy, without heating the medium through which it is transferred.

Ram Air Effect: Forced circulation of ventilating air by opening the HVAC system to a high-pressure area caused by the forward motion of the vehicle.

Random-Access Memory (RAM): Computer memory in which information can be written (stored) and read. Whatever is stored in RAM is lost whenever the ignition system is shut off.

Read-Only Memory (ROM): The permanent part of a computer's memory storage function. ROM can be read but not changed and is retained when power to the computer is shut off.

Receiver-Drier: The component between the condenser and expansion valve in which liquid refrigerant may be stored, gaseous refrigerant may change into liquid, and moisture is removed with a desiccant.

Reciprocating: Back and forth or up and down movement.

Refrigerant 12: Dichlorodifluoro-methane (CCl_2F_2), abbreviated R-12; the refrigerant used in all current automotive air conditioning systems. It has a high specific heat and low boiling point, but is environmentally hazardous.

Refrigerant: A chemical compound used as the medium of heat transfer in a refrigeration system. It picks up heat by evaporating and gives up heat by condensing.

Refrigeration Oil: A mineral oil especially formulated for use as a lubricant in automotive air conditioning systems.

Relative Humidity: The ratio of how much moisture the air actually holds at a particular temperature compared to how much it could hold.

Relay: An electromagnetic switch that uses a low amperage circuit to open and close separate contacts that control a high amperage circuit. Typically, a relay permits a light-duty dashboard switch to operate a component requiring much more current.

Resistor: An electric component that resists current flow, used to lower the voltage applied to another device such as a motor.

Rheostat: A continuously-variable resistor used to control current.

Saturated: A condition in which air holds as much water vapor as possible without forming water droplets, at a given temperature and pressure.

Sealing Beads: On a metal fitting, a ridge around the diameter of the fitting. This is inserted into flexible tubing to create a leak-tight connection.

Sensible Heat: Heat that causes a change in the temperature of a material when absorbed or given off, that is not involved in a change of state of the material.

Service Valves: Schrader or stem-type valves near the inlet and outlet of the compressor, provided for service access to the refrigeration system.

Servomotor: An electric motor used for automatic control of a mechanical device, such as a blend door.

Sling Psychrometer: A device used to measure relative humidity containing a wet and a dry thermometer.

Solenoid: An electromagnetic actuator consisting of a moveable iron core or shuttle that slides into a cylindrical coil when current is applied, and is forced back out by a spring when current is cut off. Typically, a solenoid is used to physically move a valve or door attached to the core.

Solid: A state of matter of definite shape and volume.

Solid-State: In electronics, consisting chiefly of semiconductor devices and related components.

Specific Heat: The number of calories needed to raise the temperature of one gram of a substance by one degree Celsius.

Starving: An air conditioner malfunction, when too little liquid refrigerant enters the evaporator through the expansion device.

Superheat: The sensible heat absorbed by the refrigerant after it has completely vaporized as it passes through the evaporator.

Swashplate: Axial plate; an offset plate attached to the drive shaft of a piston compressor to drive the pistons.

Temperature Gradient: A situation in which an area of high temperature is connected to an area of low temperature, causing heat to flow from the hot to the cold area.

Temperature: Heat intensity, measured by a thermometer.

Thermal Limiter: A special circuit breaker in the blower motor resistor block that opens the circuit if the resistor block fails and excessive current begins to flow through it.

Thermistor: An electronic component whose resistance to electric current changes rapidly and predictably as its temperature changes.

Thermostat: A device that automatically responds to temperature changes in order to activate a switch or regulate a valve.

Thermostatic Expansion Valve: An expansion device that removes pressure from the refrigerant as it flows into the evaporator and controls the flow rate in relation to evaporator temperature.

Transducer: A vacuum valve that converts (transduces) an electrical signal into a vacuum signal, which is then used to control another vacuum device such as a vacuum motor.

Transistor: A three-terminal semiconductor device used for amplification, switching, and detection.

Truth Table: A table showing the logical, or truthful, combination of input and output signals for a logic gate.

Vacuum Motor: An actuator that provides mechanical control of an HVAC component by using vacuum to create movement of a rod, lever, or crank.

Vacuum: A pressure less than atmospheric pressure.

Venturi Effect: The increase in speed and reduction in pressure of a gas as it passes through a restricted orifice, such as air through an aspirator.

Water Jacket: The passages in the engine cylinder head and block that allow coolant to circulate throughout the engine.

Wobble Plate: A variable-angle swashplate used in a variable-displacement compressor.

Index

Answers to Review and ASE Questions

Chapter 1: The Need for Heating, Cooling, and Air Conditioning
1-D 2-C 3-C 4-B 5-B 6-C
7-D

Chapter 2: Fundamentals of Heat and Temperature
1-D 2-B 3-C 4-B 5-A 6-D
7-A 8-C 9-D 10-A 11-A 12-D
13-C 14-A

Chapter 3: Ventilation, Heating, and Cooling Systems
1-B 2-A 3-D 4-B 5-A 6-D
7-C 8-A 9-D

Chapter 4: Ventilation and Heating Controls
1-B 2-C 3-B 4-A 5-B 6-C
7-C 8-A 9-A 10-B

Chapter 5: Basic Refrigeration Systems
1-A 2-D 3-B 4-C 5-D 6-B
7-C 8-D 9-A 10-A

Chapter 6: Compressors and Compressor Clutches
1-C 2-D 3-A 4-A 5-C 6-A
7-C 8-A 9-C 10-A 11-D 12-C
13-B 14-C 15-A

Chapter 7: System Component Description
1-D 2-A 3-B 4-A 5-D 6-C
7-D 8-C 9-B 10-A 11-B 12-A
13-C 14-D 15-D 16-A 17-B 18-C
19-D 20-C

Chapter 8: System Controls
1-C 2-B 3-C 4-D 5-D 6-B
7-C 8-C 9-A 10-D 11-B 12-A
13-C 14-B 15-D 16-B 17-C 18-C
19-A 20-B

Chapter 9: Automated Temperature Controls
1-C 2-A 3-B 4-D 5-B 6-A
7-B 8-B 9-D 10-A 11-C 12-D
13-B 14-B 15-A 16-B 17-C 18-A

Chapter 10: Fully Automatic Temperature Controls
1-C 2-D 3-C 4-A 5-B 6-C
7-D 8-A 9-C 10-D 11-B 12-A
13-C 14-B

ASE Technical Certification Sample Test
1-A 2-B 3-B 4-D 5-D 6-C
7-B 8-D 9-D 10-C 11-C 12-A
13-D 14-C 15-D 16-B 17-A 18-C
19-A 20-B 21-B 22-B 23-D 24-B
25-C 26-C 27-C 28-C 29-A
30-A 31-A 32-D 33-C 34-D
35-A 36-B 37-A 38-A 39-D
40-C 41-B 42-A 43-B 44-D
45-B 46-D 47-D 48-B 49-D
50-A 51-A 52-A